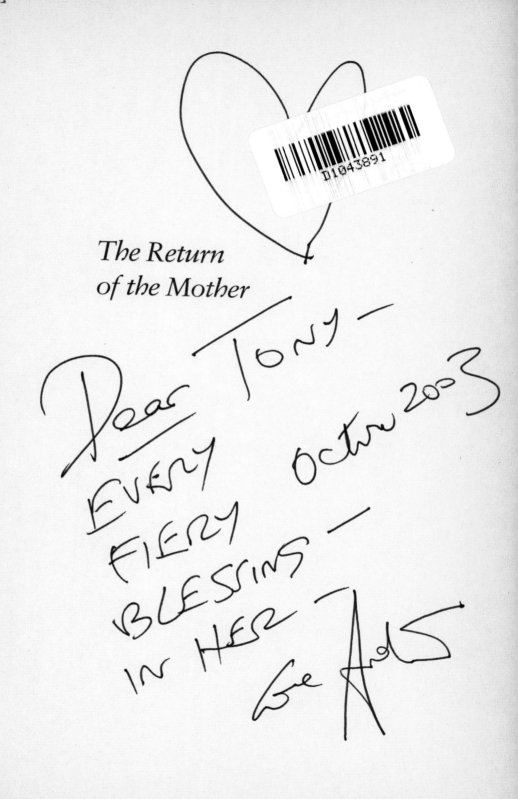

The Return
of the Mother

Dear Tony —

Every
Fiery    Octbr 2003
Blessins —
in Her —

Ge Ands

# The Return of the Mother

Andrew Harvey

JEREMY P. TARCHER/PUTNAM
*a member of*
*Penguin Putnam Inc.*
*New York*

Most Tarcher/Putnam books are available at special quantity discounts for bulk purchase for sales promotions, premiums, fund-raising, and educational needs. Special books or book excerpts also can be created to fit specific needs. For details, write Putnam Special Markets, 375 Hudson Street, New York, NY 10014.

JEREMY P. TARCHER/PUTNAM
a member of
Penguin Putnam Inc.
375 Hudson Street
New York, NY 10014
*www.penguinputnam.com*
First published in 1995 by Frog, Ltd.

First Jeremy P. Tarcher/Putnam Edition © 2001
Copyright © 1995 by Andrew Harvey

Library of Congress Cataloging-in-Publication Data

Harvey, Andrew, date.
        The return of the mother / by Andrew Harvey.
            p.   cm.
        Originally published: Berkeley, Calif. : Frog Ltd., 1995.
        Includes bibliographical references.
        ISBN 1-58542-073-5
            1. Femininity of God. 2. God—Motherhood. I. Title.

    BL215.5 H37      2001                  00-057740
    291.2'114—DC21

Book design by Paula Morrison

Printed in the United States of America

10  9  8  7  6  5  4  3  2  1

This book is printed on acid-free paper. ♾

For Eryk, my husband:

*"And his banner over me was Love."*

# Acknowledgments

My deepest thanks to:

Marianne Dresser, my friend and editor, for her extraordinary devotion, diligence, encouragement, and unwavering support. This book could never have been completed without her.

Eleonora Raducanu, beloved friend, who saved Eryk's and my life, at considerable danger to her own.

The California Institute of Integral Studies, for supporting me and my work and for being loyal to me.

Robert McDermott, for his goodness and balance.

Anne Teich, for her always loving help, her belief, her example.

Rina Sircar, for helping Eryk and myself by her love and wisdom.

K. P. Sircar, for his tolerance and compassion.

Sandra Mosbacher Smith, whose love is one of the most precious things in my life, and whose help I shall never forget.

Doug Smith, for his friendship, his concern, his good faith.

Angie Theriot, for her unfailing warmth and delicacy of heart.

Rose Solari, who believed, and fought, and witnessed, and gave Eryk and I hope when we badly needed it.

Anne Simpkinson and the editorial board of *Common Boundary* for bravery under fire.

Catherine Ingram, for her gifts of loyalty and clarity.

Rick Fields and the editors of *Yoga Journal* for their willingness to print what I said and their encouragement of radical dialogue.

Lela Landman, who witnessed and stood for Eryk and myself when few others would.

Carol Ricotta, for telling the truth publicly when no one else who knew was brave enough.

Stanley Arcieri, master letter-writer and defender of the underdog.

Lauren Artress, who married Eryk and myself, and whose simplicity sustained us.

Jeannie Trizzino, who transcribed the original talks with exemplary finesse.

Harriet Fields, for her wonderful loyalty.

Dorothy Waters, for seeing the truth and defending it.

Diane Golden, for her kindness, doggedness, and acumen.

Sara Forster, for always loving and supporting.

Leila and Henry Luce, for their loving wise concern for me and my husband, for always believing in and encouraging us both tenderly, and for their boundless hospitality.

Monique Bezencon, who witnessed.

All those friends, too numerous to mention here, who prayed, helped, encouraged, testified, learned.

# Contents

Interviews with Andrew Harvey

# A Prayer to the Divine Mother

*for Rose Solari*

O Divine Mother,
In this extreme danger,
when we and all sentient beings
and nature,
      herself,
       Your glorious body,
face unprecedented misery and destruction,
inaugurate in fierceness and tenderness
the splendor of
       Your Age of Passionate Enlightenment.
Bring us into the fire of Your sacred passion for reality,
rejoin the severed mandala of our being,
infuse our bodies, our hearts, our souls, our minds,
with the calm and focused truth of Your highest illumination
that brings each of those things into mutual harmony.
Engender in the ground of all of our beings
the sacred marriage,
that union between masculine and feminine
from which in each of us the Divine Child is born,
      that Child that is flesh of Your flesh,
        heart of Your heart,
        light of Your light,
      That Child that is free from all dogma,
        free from all shame,
        free from all false divisions
           between holy and unholy
           sacred and profane,
        free to burn out in love,
        free to play in love,
        free to serve in love,
           as love
           for love

in the heart of Your burning ground of life.
Teach us, O Divine Mother, directly
at every moment in this hour of apocalypse
the appropriate action that heals
        and preserves
        and redeems
        and transforms.

# Foreword

*And then I saw a new heaven and a new earth,*
*for the first heaven and the first earth had passed away.*
—Revelations 21:1

THE LECTURES THAT form the basis of this book were delivered in the California Institute of Integral Studies between early April and late June of 1994. They spring from the most spiritually transformatory period of my life, that followed my definitive break with Meera in January of that year and my marriage with Eryk Hanut in April. The fierce and liberating lessons learned in that period inform this book throughout, and I deal with the break with Meera and what it taught me about the Divine Mother in several of the Question and Answer sections that follow many of the chapters. At the end of the book are reprinted two interviews which deal in detail with material arising from my repudiation of Meera and the guru system.

Freed by the Mother from the need to project her onto any human figure, and so free to claim her presence in myself and in all other beings, I feel infinitely closer now to the one who is, and is in, all things and all life. I offer this book, in love and great hope, to all beings on the Way. May they come to know the joy of the direct path to her and in her! May they open to the Divine Mother in the ground of their ordinary lives! May they be led forward normally, naturally, and astonishingly, as I and countless others before me have been—and are being—to insight after insight and an ever more grounded happiness!

Everything, I believe, now depends on how the human race imagines and relates to the sacred feminine and the Mother. Inadequate imagining of her in the old ways—or in the exaggerations of some of the new—will result in a blocking of her sacred force, with disastrous, potentially fatal, consequences.

The churches, religions, and systems of transmission are all revealing their bankruptcy in the face of the catastrophe we are enduring. Kali is dancing and trampling down *all* illusions of every kind. But where Kali destroys, she also creates; in this worldwide rubbling of "authority" in all its forms there are essential opportunities for freedom which this book is dedicated to exploring.

The Mother, as always, continues to extend to all beings complete grace and complete help. *The Return of the Mother* is my attempt to share what I have come, through her blessing, to know about that grace and that help, in the hope that I now may bring others closer to her, closer to her infinite love and passion for transformation.

Andrew Harvey
San Francisco, California
June 1995

*As sugar is made into various figures of birds and beasts, so one sweet Divine Mother is worshipped in various times and ages under various names and forms. Different faiths are just different paths to reach the Supreme.*

—Ramakrishna

*The lesson for us here is that we ought not to despise any teaching of piety, but, as we fly over the meadow of the inspired doctrines, we ought to gather from each one something for our store of wisdom. Thus we may mold within ourselves a honeycomb, as it were, storing this sweet product in our hearts as in a hive, and with the various doctrines fashioning in our memories' storehouses, just like the different cells in the wax, that cannot be destroyed.*

—Gregory of Nyssa, Commentary on the Canticles

# Chapter One

# *Introduction*

AT THE END OF HIS LIFE, the great Indian mystic Aurobindo is said to have said, "If there is to be a future, it will wear the crown of feminine design." Unless we awaken to the mystery of the sacred feminine, of the feminine as sacred, and allow it to glow into, irradiate, illumine, and penetrate every area of our activity and to create in them all harmony, justice, peace, love, ecstasy, and balance, we will die out and take nature, or a large part of it, with us. Unless we come to know what the sacred feminine really is—its subtlety and flexibility, but also its extraordinarily ruthless, radical power of dissolving all structures and dogmas, all prisons in which we have sought so passionately to imprison ourselves—we will be taken in by patriarchal projections of it. The Divine Mother, the fullness of the revolution that she is preparing, will be lost to us. We must understand that comprehending the sacred feminine is a crucial part of surviving the next terrible stage of humanity.

What I am going to try to do in this book is to convey the atmosphere of the sacred feminine, with the sober, tender joy of the sacred feminine, and with the sense of awe, holiness, and the unity of all beings that are appropriate to the sacred feminine. I ask the reader that you approach this text as if entering

---

Portions of the text of this chapter have been adapted from *Dialogues with a Modern Mystic* by Andrew Harvey and Mark Matousek (Wheaton, Illinois: Quest Books, 1994).

a temple to the Divine Mother. Listen and participate in the deepest sense with the wisdom said or implied here and we will together find a path through this darkness.

The first quotation I want to offer you is from Juliana of Norwich's *Revelations of Divine Love,* and it represents the Christian tradition:

> To the property of motherhood belong nature, love, wisdom and knowledge and this is God ... God speaking to Julian: I it am. The greatness and goodness of the Father, I it am: The wisdom and kindness of the Mother, I it am: The light and grace that is all blessed love, I it am.

For another esoteric aspect of the knowledge of the sacred feminine that infuses Christian mysticism, I would like to share with you Logion 22 from the Gospel of Thomas. In this logion the mystical secret of the birth of the divine child in the soul is stated with unprecedented clarity:

> When you make the two, one, and when you make the inner as the outer, and the above as the below, and when you make the male and female into a single one, so that the male will not be male, and the female not be female, then you shall enter the Kingdom.

And although the sacred feminine plays such a strange role in the official language of Islam, rich visions of a "feminine" sacred love saturate Sufi mysticism, as illuminated in this excerpt from a poem by the great thirteenth-century Sufi mystic, Jalal-ud-Din Rumi:

> The whole world could be choked with thorns:
> A lover's heart will stay a rose garden.
> The wheel of heaven could wind to a halt:
> The world of lovers will go on turning.
> Even if every being grew sad, a lover's soul
> Will stay fresh, vibrant, light.
> Are all the candles out? Hand them to a lover—
> A lover shoots out a hundred thousand fires.

A lover may be solitary, but he or she is never alone:
For companion he always has the hidden Beloved.
The drunkenness of lovers comes from the soul
And Love's companion stays hidden in secret.[1]

A great vision of the Divine Mother has appeared in the mythology of all the greatest tribal cultures. The aborigines, who live in closer communion with the Mother than any other people, have preserved the full range of that extraordinary relationship which we once knew. It is revealed in the following myth, quoted in Robert Lawlor's *Voices of the First Day: Awakening in the Aboriginal Dreamtime*. Reading this book was one of the most crucial experiences in my life, because it really approaches a complete understanding of how the Mother is lived when you live only with the Mother and nothing else, as the aborigines have chosen to do. They could have written, but they chose to pass on information in oral transmission. They could have developed architecture, but they chose to live nakedly on the breast of the Mother.

### How the Sun Was Made

For a long time, there was no sun, only a moon and stars. That was before there were men on the earth, only birds and beasts, all of which were many sizes larger than they are now.

One day, Dinewan the emu and Brolga the native companion were on a large plain near the Murrumbidgee. There they were, quarreling and fighting. Brolga, in her rage, rushed to the nest of Dinewan and seized from it one of the huge eggs, which she threw with all her force up to the sky. There it broke on a heap of firewood, which burst into flame as the yellow yolk spilled all over it, and lit up the world below to the astonishment of every creature on it. They had been used to the semidarkness and were dazzled by such brightness.

A good spirit who lived in the sky saw how bright and beautiful the earth looked when lit up by this blaze. He thought it would be a good thing to make a fire every day, and from that time, he has done so. All night he and his attendant spirits collect wood and heap it up. When the heap is nearly big enough they send out the morning star to warn those on earth that the fire will soon be lit.[2]

The Buddhists' great vision of the Divine Mother is of her as the Mother of Supreme Wisdom, the mother of the void, the mother of emptiness out of which all the Buddhas are born, that knowledge of nonduality out of which all the Buddhas spring. This vision is represented here in a magnificent mystic hymn to the wisdom-mother from Lex Hixon's book *Mother of the Buddhas: Meditation on the Prajnaparamita Sutra*. The disciple Shariputra says to Lord Buddha:

The Perfection of Wisdom shines forth as a supreme light. . . . I sing this spontaneous hymn of light to praise Mother Prajnaparamita. She is worthy of infinite praise. She is utterly unstained, because nothing in this insubstantial world can possibly stain her. She is an ever-flowing fountain of incomparable light, and from every conscious being on every plane, she removes the faintest trace of illusory darkness. She leads living beings into her clear light from the blindness and obscurity caused by moral and spiritual impurity as well as by partial or distorted views of Reality. In her alone can we find true refuge. Sublime and excellent are her revelations through all persons of wisdom. She inspires and guides us to seek the safety and certainty of the bright wings of enlightenment. She pours forth her nectar of healing light to those who have made themselves appear blind. She provides the illumination through which all fear and despair can be utterly renounced.

She manifests the five mystic eyes of wisdom, the vision and penetration of each one more exalted than the last. She clearly and constantly points out the path of wisdom to every conscious being with the direct pointing that is her transmission and empowerment. She is an infinite eye of wisdom.... Mother Prajnaparamita is total awakeness. She never substantially creates any limited structure because she experiences none of the tendencies of living beings to grasp, project or conceptualize. Neither does she substantially dismantle or destroy any limited structure, for she encounters no solid limits. She is the Perfect Wisdom which never comes into being and therefore never goes out of being. She is known as the Great Mother by those spiritually mature beings who dedicate their mind streams to the liberation and full enlightenment of all that lives.[3]

As a brief commentary on that meditation, here are five stanzas from Rahulabhadra's "Hymn to Perfect Wisdom," one of the masterpieces of Mahayana Buddhism:

> Homage to Thee, Perfect Wisdom,
> Boundless, and transcending thought,
> All Thy limbs are without blemish,
> Faultless those who Thee discern.
>
> Spotless, unobstructed, silent,
> Like the vast expanse of space;
> Who in truth does really see Thee
> The Tathagata perceives.
>
> As the moonlight does not differ
> From the moon, so also Thou
> Who abounds in holy virtues
> And the Teacher of the world....
>
> Teachers of the world, the Buddhas
> Are thine own compassionate sons;
> Then art Thou, O Blessed Lady,
> Grandmother thus of beings all.
>
> All the immaculate perfections
> At all times encircle Thee,
> As the stars surround the crescent,
> O Thou blameless holy one![4]

As an earthly counterweight to that transcendent hymn, and to represent the wisdom of the Mother in Taoism, let me share one of my favorite texts, by Ancestor Lu, which describes perfectly the necessity of balancing in the thick of human life the various temperaments and so celebrates the work of harmony of the divine feminine.

### Five Natures

The earthy nature is mostly turbid, and the turbid are mostly dull. The metallic nature is mostly decisive, and the decisive are mostly determined. The wooden nature is mostly kind, and the kind are mostly benevolent. The fiery nature is mostly adamant, and the adamant are mostly manic. The watery nature is mostly yielding, and the yielding are mostly docile.

The docile tend to wander aimlessly. The manic tend to undergo extremes. The benevolent tend to harmonize warmly. The determined tend to be strong and brave. The dull tend to be closed in.

The closed-in are ignorant; the strong and brave are unruly; those who wander aimlessly are shifty; those who harmonize warmly fall into traps; those whose who are adamant and can endure extremes are cruel.

Therefore, each of the five natures has a bias, so it is important to balance each with the others. By yielding one can overcome being adamant, by being adamant one can overcome yielding. Benevolence is balanced by effectiveness, effectiveness is balanced by benevolence. The ignorance of earthy dullness is to be overcome by developed understanding. If developed understanding is not dominant, one loses the function of yielding.

Those who are too yielding tend to be lazy. Those who are too benevolent are foolish, and being foolish tend to be blind. Those who are too adamant tend to be rebellious. Those who are too determined tend to be stubborn. Those who are too dull do not have clear understanding and become alienated from reality.[5]

Underlying this text is a constant appeal to the nondogmatic, infinitely supple and subtle work of the divine feminine, harmonizing and balancing so that life can realize its innate fullness, and peace and prosperity of all kinds can flourish.

Now, we move to an evocation of the Mother by one of her greatest poets, the eighteenth-century Hindu cleric Ramprasad. Lex Hixon's book *Mother of the Universe: Visions of the Goddess and Tantric Hymns of Enlightenment* offers magnificent contemporary recreations of the hymns of Ramprasad to Kali, the great Hindu goddess of creation and destruction. Here are three of them, because in Ramprasad's poetry you have a complete, intimate, wild and brave account of what it is like to live in naked exposure to the full shattering and regenerating force of the sacred feminine.

> O Wisdom Goddess!
> Your essence alone is present
>     within every life, every event.
> Your living power flows freely as this universe.
> You are expressed fully, even by the smallest movement.
> Wherever I go, and wherever I look,
> I perceive only you, my blissful Mother,
> radiating as pure cosmic play,
> Earth, water, fire, air, space, and consciousness,
>     are simply your projected forms.
> There is nothing else.
>
> *Ma! Ma! Ma!*
> Your lucid dream of light
>     is the theater of birth and death,
> the expanse of boundless transparency.
> This poet can only cry in ecstasy:
> "Green mountains, fragrant blossoms,
> countless lives on land and beneath the sea,
> animate beings and inanimate objects
>     are composed of Mother's reality,
> and spontaneously express her will."[6]

We have already tasted some of the different approaches to
the Divine Mother. If we can compose all of them into a unity
in our minds, we will be beginning to begin to comprehend
some of the vast wealth of insight which has constellated around
this visionary figure. Let us enter again the field of the Mother,
our minds and hearts expanding completely in it.

> Mother dwells at the center of my being,
> forever delightfully at play.
> Whatever conditions of consciousness may arise,
> I hear through them the life-giving names,
> *Om Tara, Om Kali.*
>
> Closing my eyes I perceive the radiant Black Mother,
>     as indivisible, naked awareness,
> dancing fiercely or gently on my heart lotus.
> She wears a garland of snow-white skulls,
> bright emblem of freedom from birth and death.
> Gazing upon her resplendent nakedness,
> all conceptions and conventions vanish.
>
> Those who judge by mundane standards call me mad.
> Timid and limited persons can think what they wish.
> My only longing is to express
>     the total madness of her love.
>
> The poet-child of the Wisdom Goddess cries out with
>     abandon:
> "The Queen of the Universe
>     resides within the flower of my secret heart.
> Mother! Mother! Mother!
> I take refuge at your beautiful feet,
> delicate and fragrant as the dark blue lotus.
> As my body dissolves into earth
>     and my mind into space,
> may I dissolve into you."[7]

Now this third hymn of Ramprasad's:

> Drive me out of my mind, O Mother!
> What use is esoteric knowledge
>     or philosophical discrimination?
> Transport me totally with the burning wine
>     of your all-embracing love.
> Mother of Mystery, who imbues with mystery
>     the hearts of those who love you,
> immerse me irretrievably
>     in the stormy ocean without boundary,
> pure love, pure love, pure love.
>
> Wherever your lovers reside
>     appears like a madhouse
> to the common perception.
> Some are laughing with your freedom,
> others weep tears of your tenderness,
> still others dance, whirling with your bliss.
> Even your devoted Gautama, Moses,
> Krishna, Jesus, Nanak, and Muhammad
>     are lost in the rapture of pure love.
>
> This poet stammers,
> overcome with longing:
> "When? When? When?
> When will I be granted companionship
>     with her intense lovers?"
> Their holy company is heavenly,
> a country fair for those mad with love,
> where every distinction
>     between master and disciple
> disappears.
>
> This lover of love sings:
> "Mother! Mother! Mother!
> Who can fathom your mystery,
> your eternal play of love with love?

You are divine madness, O Goddess,
your love the brilliant crown of madness.
Please make this poor poet madly wealthy,
   with the infinite treasure of your love."[8]

So what have we heard in these quotations? We have heard extraordinarily different approaches to the same all-encompassing phenomenon of the sacred feminine. We have heard Juliana of Norwich's wonderfully sage and ripe bringing together of the two aspects of the godhead. We have heard the mystery of the final masterpiece of the sacred feminine, in the Gospel of St. Thomas. In Rumi, whose heart is a burning woman, we have heard the urgent sweetness of the realized mystic who has become one with the sacred feminine. We have heard the voice of Mahayana Buddhism at its purest and most elevated, celebrating the divine feminine as the expanse of the void, that space of brilliant light out of which everything is always springing. And in the poetry of Ramprasad we have heard a celebration of the Divine Mother as Kali, the bringer of the ecstasy of love that breaks down all dogmas, all hierarchies, all barriers. Hold these in your heart for a moment and then add to them the clear, pithy, no-nonsense, feminine practical wisdom of the Tao. We begin to see what a challenge this journey into the divine feminine is, what it's going to ask of us all, the many new forms of truth that are going to be born. We are going to be asked to let all this dance in the ground of our minds and hearts.

But in order to make this journey, we must venture into the hell of our contemporary dilemma. Until we understand exactly where we are now, all the talk of the sacred feminine, the feminine and the sacred, the Divine Mother, would be just so much trivial diversion. This journey is not an academic exercise, although it includes a rich archeological exploration of the glowing traces of the divine feminine that can be found in every tradition. What we are really doing here is reconstructing a vanished part of ourselves. We are attempting to bring back into conscious light that vanished part in order to unite with it and to learn from it the new modes of loving and action that are crucial to our survival.

I have often said that I think we are in the last twenty or so years of this civilization and quite possibly of the planet itself. If we don't make major decisions—economic, political, and environmental—within the next two decades, we will simply create an uninhabitable world and go on feeding those powers of destruction that are already threatening to ravage nature. We are certainly at the end of so-called "civilization," and we are possibly at the end of the world. The facts of our global crisis, a crisis at once political and economic, psychological and environmental, show us clearly that the human race has no hope of survival unless it chooses to undergo a total transformation, a total change of heart. What is required is a massive and quite unprecedented spiritual transformation. There is no precedent for what we are being asked to do. Only the leap into a new consciousness can engender the vision, the moral passion, the joy and energy necessary to effect change on the scale and with the self-sacrifice that is *essential* to save the planet in the time that we have left.

The message we are being sent by history can be summed up in four words: Transform or die out. Many experts agree that we have, at the most, fifteen or twenty years left before extreme crisis becomes inalterable catastrophe. Teilhard de Chardin wrote, "Humanity is being taken to the point where it will have to choose between suicide or adoration." I have no doubt that we are now at that point. Human survival depends on whether we are brave enough to face the full desolation of what we have done to our psyches and the planet, and wise and humble enough to turn to the divine insight inside us to learn what we need to go forward. This is not an apocalyptic scenario—not a scenario at all, in fact. It *is* fact. This is where we are, this is what is happening, and it is terrifying. Anyone not in a trance of denial knows it. No amount of wishful thinking or sophisticated pseudo-historical parallels can make this agony go away.

It is hard enough for a human being to face the facts of his or her own mortality. What we have to face now is not merely our own death, but the possible death of everything and everyone we love, the holocaust of nature herself, the mother we have ignored and betrayed for so long. If we do not face up to our present danger, in all its horror, without consolation and without illusion, in the full glare of Kali's terrifying mirror, if we don't gaze deeply into the mirror of the goddess and see our own faces, we will never find in ourselves the passion and courage necessary to change. Catastrophe can become grace, and disaster possibility, only if we transform their energy by accepting what they have to teach us and acting with complete sincerity to transform ourselves.

We have to face that this century has seen a quantum leap in the powers that our innate evil has at its command. A Mongol or an ancient Roman on a horse could, on a good day, kill fifty women and children and burn down a village or two, but a ruthless modern dictator, with which the modern world is swarming, can wipe out an entire country before breakfast. Greedy and amoral people have always done harm, but now, with the power of the media being as universal as it is, a handful of unscrupulous and cynical moguls can trivialize and deaden the minds of billions and darken the course of a whole civilization. The massacres of the past, though filled with every form of cruelty (read Herodotus or Tacitus) did not menace all existence down to the last dolphin and mouse and fern. There has always been in the human psyche a tendency to rage against wisdom and its demands, but this tendency has escalated through technology and mind control to what can only be called a genocide of wisdom. The Chinese have decimated Tibet, the home of what may be the supreme wisdom-culture humankind has seen, and industrial progress has fundamentally threatened indigenous peoples all over the world, from the Hopis to the Yamomamis to the Inuits, from the Kogis to the Todas and the Australian aborigines. Those wonderful beings have preserved against insuperable odds and over vast stretches of time the sacred ancestral mother-knowledge of our species. We have silenced many of the gentle feminine voices that could have warned or guided us at the very moment when we most need their inspiration.

A friend of mine was one of the survivors of a plane crash. He described to me the last few minutes before the plane hit the mountain. During the first five minutes, as people realized the end was coming, they screamed, sobbed and prayed out loud. In the next two minutes, the panic subsided; finally, in the end people just sat there, numb and frozen to their seats. I think that many people today feel themselves to be in those last few minutes, too stunned even to cry out.

So much in our official culture conspires with this passivity. Its relentless trivialization of serious issues, its passion for distraction, its fanatical irrational belief in reason and the power of science to explain away everything, all prevent us from facing where we are and what we do. The liberals announce the death of Satan at the very moment that the Satan in us is having an orgy of universal distraction. The ozone layer is gaping over Alaska, South America, and Australia while the papers are full of photographs of Madonna's latest bullet-bra. Thousands of irrecoverable and sacred species, animals, plants, and insects vanish each month. A billion or more people live on less than a dollar a day in conditions of desperate misery, while Hollywood goes on churning out violent, mind-numbing garbage that celebrates precisely those values that threaten our existence.

The rhetoric of democracy prevents us from acknowledging our imprisonment. We talk of a "New World Order" while selling lethal arms to countries that threaten it. We talk about freedom and live in a slavery to consumerism in a worldwide celebration of just those qualities of egotism, aggression, greed, and competitiveness that keep us, in Milton's great description of Satan, "thyself not free, but to thyself enthralled," and so unfree in every sacred sense. We struggle to improve our well-being with every available ruse, pill, and gadget, and only succeed in straying more and more desperately from that inner sanity and soul-peace that is the only abiding source of either physical or mental health, and is the great gift of the sacred feminine that we have ignored for so long.

Anyone who tries to tell us these truths is marginalized and regarded as crazy, irrational, or morbidly apocalyptic. James Baldwin, whom I revere as a writer and a prophet of our culture, once said to me, "The bomb has already gone off." "What bomb?" I asked. "The psychic bomb. The master bomb. It goes off and nobody notices. It destroys hearts, souls, and minds, while leaving the bodies and the refrigerators intact."

This is a desperate picture, but it is a desperate situation. George Eliot said, "The highest election known to man is to live without opium." A person with advanced cancer has no chance whatever of healing if she goes on pretending she has pneumonia or a migraine. We do not have the time not to face what we are living in: a concentration camp of reason where we are lied to about everything important, starting with our essential divine identity, and where we are policed by nihilism and depression, systematically reduced to addicts of sex, money, power, and status, whose incessant stimulation fuels the very system of imprisonment that paralyzes us. It is a camp without walls, a prison of the mind that encourages us to become our own torturers and to feel worthless. That is why more of us don't escape. How did a hundred guards in Auschwitz keep thousands of prisoners docile, except by making them feel disgusting and subhuman? By banning the awareness of our transcendent nature and banning the healing powers of the sacred feminine, and spiritual wisdom in general, our culture deprives us of our true selves, our true hearts, and our true wholeness. We are encouraged to view ourselves as dying and grieving animals, and by killing God in the Nietzschean sense we have come close to killing ourselves. Who denies God denies himself or herself. By deriding mystical truth we have merely severed ourselves from any source of divine wisdom. We no longer know who we are and who we can be.

In a culture like ours, a patriarchal culture, all the various forms of learning are so stunted by a limited, aggressive, cold, in fact psychotically detached form of knowing that it makes it even more difficult for us to break through. Think of what the materialist scientists, high priests of this camp, who dominate biology and physics, are telling us about our real nature. Stephen Jay Gould describes evolution as "a stately dance to nowhere." Dawkins in *The Selfish Gene* informs us that we are a "survival machine, robots blindly programmed to preserve the selfish molecules now in his genes." Stephen Hawking pronounces us to be "insignificant creatures on a minor planet of a very average star in the outer suburbs of one of a hundred million galaxies. So it is difficult to believe in a God that would care about us, or even notice our existence"—as if the divine obeys any of our categories of time or space and is not as miraculously present in a flower as in the whole universe!

The exalted so-called "wisdom" of our leading scientists is nothing more than stunted morbid depressiveness camouflaging itself as empirical truth and illusionless accuracy. Its false authority, completely divorced from the essential evidence of the enlightened mind and the feminized divine psyche, rots our resolve at the very moment when we need it most, deepens that sense of impotence and worthlessness with which we are already afflicted as refugees from 2,000 years of Christian propaganda about original sin. When you add to this the smart, masculine relativism of the reigning contemporary philosophies, and the celebration of works with titles as absurd as *Consciousness Explained,* and the neurotic convictions of our limitations which permeate nearly all serious modern art, you come to see that humanity is dazed, baffled, and hemmed in on all sides by images of ineptitude and meaninglessness, at the exact moment when a connecting and unifying vision of the great gift of the sacred feminine is as imperative as oxygen.

The real war in the modern world is not between democracy and communism, capitalism and totalitarianism, liberalism and fascism; it is the war for the mind and heart of humankind between two completely different versions of reality: the masculine, or patriarchal version, which material science, most contemporary philosophy, and most modern art represents, and which holds human beings to be driven dying animals in a random universe; and that vision of humankind's essential divine destiny that mystics of all spiritual traditions throughout history have discovered and struggled to keep alive.

If we do not awaken, then, to what the sacred feminine can give us—a vision of our direct interconnection with the universe—we will not survive. If we do not awaken to our sacred interdependent nature, we will simply not know that when we allow the rain forests to burn, it is as if we are burning our own lungs; that when we pollute the sea with nuclear waste, we are lacing our own veins with poison; that when we refuse to stop the torture in prisons all over the world, to intervene in Bosnia, or to feed the starving in Asia, Africa, or Haight Street, we are torturing, killing, and starving ourselves. Not figuratively, not poetically, but *literally*. When Teilhard speaks of the choice between suicide and adoration, between a male psychotic vision that is going to drive the world into final darkness, or between an opening to the feminizing, liberal, ecstatic energies of the divinized psyche, he is not referring to some gorgeous kind of emotionalism but to the highest means of opening to the sacred truths of reality: that we must arm ourselves with love and clarity and protect our world.

Unfortunately, we have very few things to help us in this dreadful situation. The vanity and narcissism of the "New Age" only reiterates on a spiritual level the vanity and narcissism of the culture it arises from. It is a phosphorescent symptom of the disease and not a cure. New Age pseudo-spirituality is a grab-bag of many different unrelated pieces of various traditions and fantasy, and while it is has undoubtedly helped many to begin a spiritual path, it also has many of the marks of the diseases it pretends to cure. It is hardly surprising that a materialist culture, lacking a wisdom tradition and until recently almost completely ignorant of the laws of inner change, would spawn the kind of consumerist, naive, and narcissistic spiritual apathy, the "religion by Calvin Klein," that we see all around us.

This would be less dangerous if the stakes were not so high. What lies before us is so demanding that only a sober, balanced, unsparing vision of what transformation entails can be of use to us now; a vision that does not lie to us about the sacrifice, difficulty, or darkness we face. So many of the visions on sale are just palliatives, placebos and half-truths that misrepresent the nature of spiritual life and the necessity to work and to give everything. As in the Christian church, there are very few realized mystics working as teachers in the New Age. Just about anyone can set up shop and desperation will always provide customers in an age that adores instant solutions. There's a hungry audience for versions of the journey that offer instant enlightenment for a few dollars. In an age that craves ease and enervates us with comfort, it is not surprising that pop philosophy should promise sudden divine shifts that will save us all, or float things off to other planets in spaceships. These are some of the concentration camp of reason's most insidious lies, because they masquerade as escapes from it.

If we had only the external sciences to rely on, the game would already be lost. Fortunately, there exist other interrelated technologies of spiritual transformation that invite in the sacred feminine with all its powers. Developed by all the major mystical traditions, this path is still miraculously intact and available to us. It is time that Westerners realize that mystics are scientists of their domain. Mystical union and transformation obey laws as inexorable as those of the physical universe. These laws are documented by systems of sublime sophistication, which can help us take the journey into truth and help us align our natures with the mystery of the divine feminine.

The tragic imbalance of the masculine has brought humankind to the point of disaster, and unless we recover the feminine powers of the psyche, the powers of intuition, patience, reverence for nature, and knowledge of the holy unity of things, and marry in our depths these powers with the masculine energies of rule, reason, passion for order and control, life on the planet will end. This sacred marriage of the masculine with the feminine has to take place in all our hearts and minds, whether we are male or female. The rich and organic integration it alone can furnish is the goal of human life. It is a marriage the universe itself witnesses, as can be heard in the following miraculous verses from Jnaneshwar's "The Nectar of Self-Awareness." This great Sanskrit poem celebrates the union of Shiva and Shakti, and their creation, through that union, of the entire universe. Jnaneshwar makes it clear that this marriage of masculine and feminine that must take place in our psyche is already taking place in the entire universe around us; that the universe wouldn't exist at all without that endlessly repeated fusion and union. The universe is in fact the constantly reborn "child" of the lovemaking of the "Father" and "Mother," Shiva and Shakti, who at all moments dance in and out of, and merge with, each other's being with divine complexity, subtlety, passion, and ecstatic humor.

> I honor the God and Goddess,
> the eternal parents of the universe.
>
> The lover out of boundless love
>     takes the form of the beloved,
> what beauty!
> Both are made of the same nectar
>     and share the same food.
>
> Out of Supreme Love
>     they swallow each other up,
> But separate again
>     for the joy of being two.
>
> They sit together
>     in the same place,
> Both wearing a garment of light.
> From the beginning of time
>     they have been together,
> Reveling in their own Supreme Love.

> The difference they created
>    to enjoy this world,
> Had one glimpse of their intimacy
> And could not help
>    but merge back
> into the bliss
>    found in their union.
>
> Without the God
>    there is no Goddess,
> And without the Goddess
>    there is no God.
>
> How sweet is their love!
> the entire universe
>    is too small to contain them,
> Yet they live happily
>    in the tiniest particle.[9]

Keep the subtlety and message of this poem in your minds now as I try and sketch the evolutionary history of humanity.

I think that this history can be seen in basically three stages, beginning with a matriarchal stage. It isn't mere romanticization to describe this as a stage in which humankind was one with nature, knew and loved and relied on the Mother, and listened naturally and simply to her astonishing mystical guidance that permeated life and nature. Robert Lawlor's wonderful book *Voices of the First Day* offers insight after insight into this astonishing relationship with the Mother that is our own original relationship with life. Imagine what it would be like for this relationship to be restored, not just in the intellectual imagining these passages will give you, but in actual living:

The divine marriage between the great Ancestral couple is also found in the creation myths of Egypt, Mesopotamia, China, Central America, and other places. In all these myths the creation is brought about through a great cosmic copulation—the "divine marriage," or *hieros gamos*. The image

of the primal couple, the All-Mother ... and All-Father ...
suggests the Aboriginal belief that they can experience the
vast creative process through ecstatic dance and sexuality.
They, and all the world, share in the currents of light emanating from this cosmic union.

In myths, new life results from any impassioned act,
whether the passion is lust or anger. The story of how the
sun was made begins with fight between Dinewan the emu
and his consort Brolga. When Brolga throws the egg, the
level shifts to the metaphysical interaction between earth
and sky. The image of this metaphysical union is symbol-
ized in the biological world by the proportionally vast egg
as it absorbs one sperm and is enveloped by a swarming
multitude....

As the copulation continues, the Dreaming unfolds, the
mighty acts of the great Ancestors—their pains and joys,
successes and failures, blindness and revelations—sculpt the
earth. These acts accumulate and are retained as a memory
as a world-shaping code. The seed energies that the Ancestors spill sustain the earthly life to follow. In the story of the
sun's origin, the yolk of the egg explodes in space, to merge
with a fire that illuminates the earth. The earth, then, is the
love- and battle-strewn trysting ground of the Ancestors,
undulated and saturated with blood and semen, from the
virginal, wild, ecstatic union of the boundless universal
Dreaming with the name-giving power of the seed (which
defines innumerable variations: the *one* opens itself up to
the all). These dreaming tracks, or *songlines,* stretch in all
directions, criss-crossing the entire continent of Australia....

It is this "Dreaming" that for the aborigines creates their
world; the ancestral battles and loves and passions are regis-
tered in every detail of a landscape which they know intimately
and musically.

For them, as perhaps for no other culture, the earth is the
center of the intelligence of creation; a symbol and memory

of primordial Dreaming; a receptacle of all seeds cosmic, metaphysical, and biological; the nurturer of all life, both visible and invisible. By listening to the songs and energies of the earth the aborigines hear the voices of the universal Dreaming.[10]

What the aborigines are listening to are the voices of the Mother. What they are living in is the body and womb of the Mother. What they are living by is the intelligence of the Mother. That is why they have peace and trust, a healthy regard of sexuality and a vibrant ecstatic gift for stories, and a sense of the absolute rightness of all that happens in their world. That is why we need to listen to them.

The second stage of the evolutionary history of humanity is the patriarchal stage, the stage that began in Greece and in the era just before Greece, with the shattering of the harmony of the old goddess archetypes. This stage saw a crucial and terrible thing: the dismemberment, division, and destruction of the feminine, in the human psyche and in the growth of an almost universal oppression of women. This stage saw the separation of the creator from the creation, an increasing sense of the divorce of heaven from earth, and the triumph of a divisive, Promethean, categorizing, dissociative kind of knowing. Humankind left the womb of the Mother and developed extraordinary powers of manipulation and domination of nature.

But there was illness at the root of the enterprise, there was madness at its root. It depended for its energy on the denial of our fundamental connectedness to each other and to the world, and on an increasingly schizophrenic rejection of all of those values of nurturing, intuition, unity, tenderness, and bliss associated with the abandoned Mother. Nature, soul, matter, the body and its instincts, and the imagination were all in the process devalued and desacralized. This led inextricably to the creation of the worldwide psychic Auschwitz we now inhabit, in which nature herself and everything natural in us is in danger of being tortured to death.

We are now, I believe, on the threshold of a third stage which I call the stage of the sacred marriage. This is the only position we could possibly take and still survive. This is a stage beyond both matriarchy and patriarchy. It involves the restoration to human respect of all of the rejected powers of the feminine. But it is absolutely essential that this restoration should be accomplished in the deep spirit of the sacred feminine. Not only should we invoke the sacred feminine, restore the sacred feminine, but this union between the matriarchal and the patriarchal, the sacred marriage, must be accomplished in the *spirit* of the sacred feminine for it to be real, effective, rich, and fecund. It must occur in her spirit of unconditional love, in her spirit of tolerance, forgiveness, all-embracing and all-harmonizing balance, and not, in any sense, involve a swing in the other direction.

This is crucial and often forgotten. We cannot afford a facile or furious rejection of everything masculine, scientific, or patriarchal. A real marriage is a union based in profound mutual respect. Only such a union—you have heard its cosmic music in Jnaneshwar—can bring the kind of knowledge we need now to survive. A purely matriarchal or patriarchal solution, on their own, will simply not work. A restoration of the sacred feminine that is fanatical and harsh is a contradiction in terms and would only engender more global lunacy. It would be, in fact, a disaster, and a tragic waste of a supreme opportunity for healing. The last thing that is needed now is another dogma or religion, a cult of the "Mother," a creation of yet another set of judgmental and imprisoning rules and categories in the name of "balance" and "harmony." If we are to really take seriously the journey into the sacred feminine, we must open ourselves to the outrageous truths that are contained in the power of the sacred feminine, the madness of divine love, the wisdom beyond all concepts and categories. The outrageous truth of a flexibility that is paradoxical in its very nature; the truth of a force that can never be talked about but has to be embraced, has to be learned and embodied. It is, as the *Tao Te Ching* says, "The force that emanates from the Tao." As Rick

Tarnas beautifully puts it in his summary in *The Passion of the Western Mind:*

> If the sacred feminine represents the very principle of integrity and unity, can we envision a conceptual framework large enough and subtle enough that it can make intelligible this long journey of patriarchal and Promethean thought that humankind has taken? Can we find our way to a genuinely integral world view, one that does not secrete a final dualism by embracing everything except the Western, or the modern, or the masculine, that sees, perhaps, a deeper drama at work? Perhaps we can, if we do not underestimate the power, the subtlety, and the mystery of the divine feminine. The divine feminine is not another kind of fundamentalism, it is the very force that harmonizes, fuses, infuses, transforms, and gives another whole lease of energy and ecstasy to life.[11]

How then can we most subtly define this sacred feminine? In some way defining it is, of course, impossible, because the essence of the sacred feminine is subtlety, flexibility, and mystery, and its essential work is the constantly and wittily radiant overcoming of the definitions of the mind by love and immediate naked knowledge of the interdependence of all things and all beings. But there, are, in fact, three central powers in the feminine, all of which interrelate and interpenetrate, and exploring these in some detail can begin to "open up the territory."

The first of these laws I call a *knowledge of the unity of all life,* a knowledge that all life is inherently sacred and one, a knowledge of the unity behind all multiplicity.

Extending this sacred knowledge of unity to all religions, to the embrace of all religious powers and mystical traditions was the achievement of Ramakrishna. The Mother, he tells us, cooks the "white fish of awareness" in different ways, depending on the appetite and taste of her children; some like it with slices of mango, some like it cold, some plain as Zen, but everyone is still eating the same fish. Restoration of the sacred feminine would confer as one of its extraordinary benefits and extraordinary graces the end of all quarrels between the religions—*not* an end to the differences, because why shouldn't different ways of cooking the fish go on?—but an end forever of any one path's claim to exclusive truth. In the wisdom of the sacred feminine, life is one, all paths lead to the One, we are all the children of the divine, the Father-Mother, Shiva-Shakti, sitting down together at the feast of life, each eating our food in our own unique way, but all dependent on the same source.

The second law of the sacred feminine, and, of course, all these laws interpenetrate and illuminate each other, is what I call the *law of rhythm*. The sacred feminine awakens us to the knowledge that the universe has its own laws and harmonies which are already whole and perfect, and which, if we are to live wisely, we have to intuit, revere, and follow.

I'd like to share with you a meditation on precisely this instinctual and spontaneous understanding of rhythm, from Lawlor's *Voices of the First Day:*

If the earth is a living body, then its life (like all life) results from a concert of rhythmic activities. In all living creatures the music is the same; it is the echo of the voice of a wave-like movement that fills the universe. The vast, almost incomprehensible fields of force such as gravity move in this way, as do myriad rhythmic patterns extending down to the infinitesimal pulsations of an atom. Vibrations of a higher frequency than light or of a lower frequency than the lowest audible sounds constitute the edges of other worlds of being.

Our hearts contract and swell as they suck in and pump out blood. Lungs breathe in and out, intestines open and squeeze. Sensations and thoughts are carried by tiny rapid pulsations that flee along nerve fibers. The brain is swept by endless waves of sleep, wakefulness, hunger, satiation. Wings flap up and down, arms swing left and right, back and forth; jaws open and crush down pitilessly; songs pour forth from the throat that, in hunger, swallows the death and sorrow of other creatures. The rhythms of copulation are everywhere, opening, closing, inflating, deflating, penetrating, withdrawing. These patterned vibrations permeate all of substance and life, providing the unifying resonance between people, nature, and the invisible worlds. An Aboriginal cave painting story also speaks of the harmonic integrating pulsation of life:

> Tree ...
> he watching you.
> You look at tree,
> he listen to you.
> He got no finger,
> he can't speak.
> But that leaf ...
> he pumping, growing,
> growing in the night.
> While you sleeping
> you dream something.
> Tree and grass same thing.
> They grow with your body,
> with your feeling.[12]

The laws of nature and of life, then, are essentially rhythmic. Opening in reverence and respect to these laws and learning to honor and enact them, in all times and in all situations, necessitates our developing feminine powers of intuition, attention, receptivity, capacity to wonder, nurture, and cherish, and a constantly, acutely sensitive, musical flexibility of approach that tries to mirror the suppleness of life itself and its changes. This awareness of the rhythms of the universe is simply not accessible to masculine powers of reason and will on their own; they are blinded by their impatient desire to know definitively, to define, manipulate, and control. But the feminine side of the psyche is aware of the rhythms of life quite naturally, is in fact the "voice" of these rhythms, and spontaneously receives, accepts, welcomes, and interprets guidance. If we wish to heal

the natural world that we are in imminent danger of destroying, we are going to have to listen in radical humility to its
voices, attend faithfully to its rhythms, and enact quickly what
they tell us. This listening, this feminine attention, is essential
to our survival, and is one of the crucial gifts of the Mother.

The third law of the sacred feminine is what I call the *love
of the dance*. I think it is essential when we talk of the restoration of the sacred feminine to make clear that what is being
restored is a totally unmorbid, healthy, exuberant, sensual,
ecstatic vision of life. One that does *not* separate mind and
body, that does not separate body and spirit, that accepts in
wonder and joy the ordeals and conditions of this life; that, in
fact, knows this life to be an unbroken flow of normal miracle. This is the glorious immanent *and* transcendent knowledge
that a restoration of the sacred feminine would give us. A knowledge that, like the aborigines, is at once at home in the invisible light-ridden world of the Ancestors and in the tiniest rocks
in front of them as they walk, and in the sounds of the insects
between those rocks; knowing that all those things are always
singing only one song: the song of the Divine Mother.

This sacred wisdom does not separate heaven from earth,
does not split spirit from body, and does not divide prayer from
action. In fact, it challenges our current world view on every
single count, for in it all dimensions, all worlds, all possibility,
are here, are interrelated, are one. Besides, unlike the patriarchal wisdom that we've celebrated for so long, this wisdom
does not aim for an unnatural perfection or a flight into some
life- or body-denying absolute, does not overprivilege the "pure"
and the "transcendent," but works patiently, all-embracingly,
with alchemical subtlety, towards a wholeness in which the
transcendent and mystical are not separate from the immanent
and practical, but are joined with them in indivisible sacred
union.

To those awakened to and by this original wisdom, this wisdom of origin, being born a human being is not being born into
a fallen, desolate world, mired in illusion. To be human is to

be born into a dance in which every animate or inanimate, visible or invisible being is also dancing. Every step of this dance is printed in light; its energy is adoration, its rhythm is praise. Pain, desolation, and destruction in this full and unified sacred vision are not separate from the dance, but are instead essential energies of its transformative unfolding. Death itself cannot shatter the dance, because death is the lifespring of its fertility, the mother of all its changing splendor.

If we could bring ourselves to open to this vision, we would undergo a revolution of the heart. One of the things we must face, which is very difficult to face, and which has taken me a great deal of suffering to learn to face myself, because I have loved the various religious traditions of the world so much, is that they have all failed us. They have all failed to give us this complex unifying vision of the world. They have all, in fact, been attached to detachment and transcendence. Because they were all created in the second patriarchal stage of human development, they all essentially stress the masculine tendency to fear the body and to fear and hate women. This fear of women and of nature, matter, and the organic processes of life, and the wholesale destruction that it has led to, is the distressing legacy of all the world religions.

We have now to face that a nexus of fears, anxieties, repressions, and evasions has fundamentally limited all the major religions, although in each of their core revelations and mystical traditions there are glowing traces of the wisdom of the sacred feminine which cannot be covered over. The depth of the denial of the feminine, and so of nature, and so of matter, and so of the holiness of the processes of life itself, is shattering when you face it. This denial is extreme and difficult to confront in all of its unnerving interconnections. When one sees just how extensive this denial is, and how deeply it stretches into the corners of every psyche on this earth, whether male or female, and how it warps even our most open kinds of thinking about reality, and how it enters even our most generous and exuberant attempts at defining in language another kind of possibility, then one is aghast and shaken by the human power of rejection and amnesia.

We must allow ourselves to be aghast in this way, we must allow ourselves to be appalled at the oppression of women, at the homophobia of a disgraceful, body-hating patriarchy, at the way in which all the religions and their metaphysics have colluded in this conspiracy against nature, bodies, women, the feminine, the ecstatic. We must realize that unless we turn this only half-conscious conspiracy around, evoking the highest and most useful perceptions of all of the mystical traditions that have come down to us, we will simply be trapped in a dying world, unable to help it or help ourselves.

Christianity has perhaps been the most obvious major culprit, but in fact all the religions have been complicit in this destruction. Judaism has wonderful life-enhancing visions of daily life as sacred, but transmissions are still largely reserved for men. Hinduism and Buddhism may have the most supple and richest visions of the psyche and of the divine, and they have preserved their mystical traditions, but there are grave dangers inherent in both of their philosophies, as their historical development has shown. In a too little-known and radical aspect of Aurobindo's work, he pointed out that the life-celebrating wisdom of an earlier Hindu vision, enshrined in the *Vedas* and the *Bhagavad Gita,* was historically overtaken and weakened by a one-sided view of the world as *maya,* or illusion, the ideal "masculine" construction, the ideal masculine solution to having to deal with the complex and frightening aspects of reality. The consequences of this evasion enervated an entire civilization.

The life-denying, body-denying, and anti-feminine tendencies of both traditional Theravada, and to a lesser extent, traditional Mahayana Buddhism, are also disturbing. Many schools of Buddhism teach that one cannot attain enlightenment in a woman's body; the best a woman can do, if she's very lucky, is to serve the monks. Very early on in the development of Buddhism, male monks separated from society and were seen as superior to it. The entire purpose of incarnation was seen as liberation from samsara. There is an extremism, a fear of nature, and a repressed hysteria in this which Mahayana Buddhism, especially in its vision of divine service and the ideal of the bodhisattva, tried to correct. But even in the Mahayana, women are still drastically undervalued; the Tibetan word for woman literally means "lesser birth." Heroic emphasis on enlightenment can lead to a separation from this life and its active responsibilities and a radical undervaluing of the sacred wisdom of ordinary human life. How many serious, practicing Western Hindus and Buddhists have told me that it does not really matter if the world is destroyed, because this dimension is only *maya,* only illusion! This is not sacred wisdom, this is folly.

I believe, then, that in response to this situation, all the major religious traditions have to go through two revolutions. First, they have to strip away all their dogmas and penetrate to the "feminine" core of their own mystical understanding. From that core, they have to dialogue with all the other religions in a spirit of deep inquiry, tolerance, and a feminine spirit of harmony and reconciliation. But this is not the only revolution they have to go through; once they have done that, they must undergo an even deeper and more costly revolution, opening up their most cherished mystical beliefs to the Mother, to this great new, ancient vision of the unity of life, the sacred integration of life.

Each of the mystical traditions separately and together has to let the divine feminine consciously and completely into its core, so that its power can heal, refine, purify, harmonize, and embolden them all and make them practical in this great ordeal. The last thing we need to be told as the forests burn is that all is illusion. What we want to know and want to feel, what we must be told and need to feel, is that the forests are burning in our bodies and hearts.

We must find in ourselves the energy—and outrage—to stop the holocaust. Now the Mother in all the religions must be present in her fullness and glory, so that in the heart of them all the sacred marriage can take place, and each path can become a practical training ground for servants of peace and unity, instead of the huge hospitals for the desperate that they mostly are now.

This is an immense demand, but if the world religions do not go through with these revolutions, with this tuning by the divine feminine, they will continue to be a part of the problem and not the solution to it. All of them are stained by dissociation; nearly all of them have developed a near-psychotic rejection of the body and nature. All of them are addicted to transcendence, thereby devaluing, and subtly desacralizing and denying, the glory of ordinary life in all its fullness and nature in all its ragged perfection. We can no longer afford this flight into transcendence because it is part of the reason why no one has intervened to stop the ruin and devastation of nature.

We need now, more than ever, to ask the Mother to teach us to be in the body, to have not the "out-of-body" experience, but the *"in-body," in-life, in-world, in-time* experience, that experience of oneness with all living things that would inspire radical action to save the planet. Unless we develop that very soon, there simply will be no world. We will be sitting reading the *Prajnaparamita Sutra* as the seas die. This is a desperate picture, but there's a truth contained in it that has taken me a long time to face: how most of the major mystical traditions of the world have been completely saturated with the masculine part of the psyche, a masculine hatred of the richness and organic growth of things.

If you wish to really hear the voice of the authentic Mother, I think you will hear it in the Kogis, in the Yamomamis, in the aborigines. What you will hear is different from the Mahayana, or the Theravada, or St. John of the Cross, or even the great Hindu mystics, because these indigenous traditions arise out of a relationship of the world and with nature at once far more visionary and far more rooted than any other. The tribal peoples of the world are warning us; the Yamomamis have their prophetic traditions, the Kogis have an extraordinary prophetic tradition, as do the Hopis. And they are *not* telling us that the world is illusion, that there will be billions of *kalpas* and cycles and god-knows-what, that all will be well, whatever happens. They're telling us that we are in desperate danger because we have not honored the Mother and that she will be compelled or forced by us to destroy us, her own children, if we do not attend to her. They are telling us this with extraordinary urgency and accuracy.

Unlike us, the tribes of the earth love and honor the earth, they know her as their mother. They are not drugged on power, hierarchy, or on some dream of transcendence. Because of what most of them have suffered at our hands and at the hands of our visions of "progress," the tribal peoples of the world are far more awake than we are to the facts of our hubris and its causes. We hear in each of their prophetic traditions, without any technological or religious consolation, a different voice of the Mother, trying to reach, guide, inspire, warn, shake, and heal us. We must abandon all technological and religious pride, and listen with our whole being to their message.

When I first started to study indigenous wisdom, I was humbled by how little I knew about the aborigines and how stupid my few assumptions had been. I was astonished at how rich and brilliant their systems were, just as great as the "high" traditions of Mahayana Buddhism or Hinduism. Their vision may be even more priceless to us now than the vision of the Buddha, springing as it does from the heart of a people who never lost or betrayed the divine feminine nor even imagined doing so. We obviously cannot go back to the non-agrarian, hunter-gatherer world of the aborigines, but we can learn from the incandescence of their total trust of nature and life. Without their kind of wisdom, in fact, we cannot go forward.

It's amazing to me that at the end of this super-sophisticated civilization, the voices that we need most to hear and heed may be those of peoples who never made one step to produce such a super-sophisticated civilization. It has a perfect kind of clarity and irony about it, doesn't it? Divine laughter can be heard, the laughter of Kali. This wisdom is echoed with countless inspired variations all over the world, and the fierce, illusion-less intensities of the tribal warnings is for me a proof of their authenticity. These warnings are the Earth's last wake-up call to us.

So with this knowledge of the betrayal of the sacred femi-nine in each of the world's religions and with the sense that there is still intact in the tribal peoples an authentic vision of it, let us now turn to an attempt at understanding who or what the Divine Mother might be. The more glowing and rich our understanding of her is, the more hope we have of restoring her to ourselves and ourselves to her.

A vision of the Divine Mother has appeared in all of the reli-gious traditions in various ways, but who the Divine Mother *is* goes far beyond all concepts and dogmas. In our growing, expanding imagination of who the Divine Mother might be, we come to understand more and more what the feminine force could do and how we can work with it to save our planet.

The experience of the Mother, of the mother aspect of the godhead, of the motherhood of god, is an immense, constantly expanding experience of the presence of calm power and bliss-ful unconditional love as the ground of all being. That is the presence of the Mother. That is the essential experience that we must, all of us, whatever our creed or caste or color, ask for now. Without that essential experience, we are dissociated ghosts wandering in a ruined world.

Everything is in the Mother, everything *is* the Mother, and the Mother is beyond everything, constantly drawing everything deeper and deeper into the fire of her always transforming love. She is at once the ground, the energy, and the always changing and flowering goal of evolution; at once the ground, the basis, and the stable endless source of deeply rooted peace and power; the Shakti that fuels evolution and the goal toward which that evolution is endlessly spiraling. The goal itself endlessly recedes ecstatically laughing in light, as the Mother recedes into ever deeper rooms of her own blissful nature. On all levels the Mother is absolute love, drawing all beings everywhere into deeper and deeper union with their own origin in her. As Ramakrishna many times said, the Mother is the "spider that spins the great cosmic web" and lives in it. She weaves the web itself, and is also the darkly luminous womb and void, from which both spider and web are constantly being born.

The truth of so immense and paradoxical a definition can never be understood by the linear mind, but it can be entered into through mystical experience. Very few mystics have ever known this vastness of the Mother in as profound and many-faceted a way as Ramakrishna. He is really our guide into this blissful vastness, this sweetness and peace, the omnipresence and magnificence and glory of the Mother. He knew her as the shining energy of Brahman, the shining source, the loving of love, the Shakti, the force that creates, sustains, and destroys all things at all moments, flaming from and inseparable from Shiva, the Father. Ramakrishna went into that final consciousness in which all things are one, and the "mother" and "father" aspect were to him known as inseparable.

But to help us approach the Mother, he made some exquisite and simple definitions which can help us all expand our souls, hearts, and minds. Ramakrishna said that the Mother is to the Father as the shining is to diamond. He said that the Mother is to the Father as the wriggling of the snake is to the snake itself, as whiteness is to milk. And Ramakrishna didn't always talk of the Mother as "she"; sometimes he referred to the Mother as having no male or female identity as if it could be all sides and sexes at once. This refusal on his part to categorize in any human way the mystery of the Mother is revealing. The last thing that we need now, as I have said, is another fundamentalist dogma about the Mother because it is the exact negation of everything that the Mother is; she is all things, all processes, all "positions," all possible theories about her, at once.

The last thing we need also is a sentimental vision of her. The Mother is Kali as well as Mary, the killer as well as the nurturer. Her love can kill to create or destroy, to rebuild or illumine, and death and intense suffering are also part of her alchemy. Anger is also vividly present in her, sometimes terrifyingly present. Don't the earthquakes, climactic changes, and natural disasters all over the globe show us that the earth, our Mother, is angry and getting angrier?

But let us never forget that the anger of the Mother is a necessary stern warning—not vengeance, not punishment, not rejection: there is a fundamental difference between the anger of the Mother aspect of God and the anger of the Father aspect. There is nothing punitive at all in the Mother's anger. Her rage is a summons to attention, a shaking of her children so that they can have a chance to wake up, a shaking that can seem—and be—very violent, but which is always in the service of liberation and deeper knowledge and the outpouring into action of a galvanized love. It is obvious that the Mother is now shaking the whole earth in a violent set of convulsions which are bound to get more frightening in the next few years. But these convulsions are designed to bring us to our collective senses, to wake us up inescapably to our responsibilities. And we can know if we take the journey into her, through prayer, adoration, and service, that her anger is always inspired by and coexists with passionately tender unconditional love.

Let me ask again: Why is contacting the Mother-aspect of the Divine so crucial? We know that we have done an incalculable harm to ourselves, and we know that we have done incalculable harm to everything around us, because we've been cut off for two millennia at least from the holy experience of unity in the Mother. In turning to the Divine Mother now, we open ourselves again to the love that heals and saves. There is a great and ever-increasing danger that as we wake up to the terror and desolation of what we have become and what we have done, shock will deepen into terminal despair, apathy, or even a frenzy of violence that could only speed up the destruction that is already so far advanced. At such a terrible moment, at such a crucial threshold, an image in the collective psyche of a judging, angry, punitive father-god is of less than no help.

Excessive guilt of what we have done and allowed ourselves to become can only dishearten us. We have to know what we have done, but we have also to know that there is an aspect of the godhead that wants nothing more for us than our total transformation, and that is streaming out toward us at all moments a great, endless flow of unconditional grace. That aspect—of immense cradling and sustaining love—is the aspect of the Divine Mother. We need an image of the divine that even now, even at this late moment, even after all we have done, offers us compassion, grace, calmness, humor, and passionate and patient encouragement. This image is the Divine Mother, and her force of love is what will give us the energy and the vision to go on in this growing world-hell of our era, if we make real, heart-felt contact with it.

The vision that Aurobindo gave to humankind of the Mother, the Shakti, the force of evolution preparing a new world, is another vision that we need now. Not only did Aurobindo experience the Mother as the stable ground of all things, but he came to know her as the Shakti of adoration, reverence, tenderness, the urgent, loving action that creates the world and that hungers now to help us *recreate* our world in all its arenas and dimensions in the image of her eternal love. All of the ancient religions cling to a vision of time that present catastrophe has made irrelevant and seems an unaffordable luxury now that time is visibly running out.

Because her love for her children is burning and total, Aurobindo discovered, the Mother will give to us also her power even now to help us utterly remake all things in her image. And what Aurobindo saw is that the Mother is bringing us through her great alchemy of catastrophe and initiation to the moment where we will have to dream her great world- and life-transforming dream with her, and make it real in love and justice, or perish. Aurobindo tells us:

There are three ways of being of the Mother of which you can become aware, when you enter to touch at once with the Conscious Force that upholds us and the universe. Transcendent ... she stands above the worlds. Universal ... she creates all these beings and contains and enters, supports and conducts all these million processes and forces. Individual, she embodies the power of these two vaster ways of her existence, makes them living and near to us, and mediates between the human personality and the divine Nature.[13]

He gave the Divine Mother four main cosmic personalities: Maheshwari, Mahakali, Mahalakshmi, and Mahasaraswati. Maheshwari is her personality of calm wideness, surpassing majesty, and all-ruling greatness. Mahakali embodies her power of splendid strength and passion. Mahalakshmi is vivid and sweet, and wonderful with her deep secret of beauty. Mahasaraswati is equipped with a close and profound capacity of intimate knowledge and careful, flawless work. But to this awareness of the many-sided glory of the mother, Aurobindo added one essential and revolutionary ingredient: a vision of the Mother, the Shakti, as the force that powers the evolution of the universe and as the force that sustains and encourages and creates the next stage in the evolutionary development of humankind. He realized the Mother as the architect of evolution, the summoner of humanity to a supreme and endless adventure of self-transformation.

It is this extraordinary vision that Aurobindo explores in all its complexities and laws in his masterpiece *The Life Divine*, the greatest celebration of the Divine Mother and the sacred feminine ever imagined. What Aurobindo discovered was that by learning how to call down the light of the Mother and work with it in humility, flexibility, and surrender, the entire spiritual and physical being of humanity could be transformed and the life divine lived on earth. Coming to know the Mother, then, in this time, to know her power and how to work with it, is for him the clue to not only human survival, but to the leap into divinity here on earth that has already been prepared in the divine mind of God, and which humankind has to be brave and faithful enough to enact.

Aurobindo has, of course, not exhausted the majesty and beauty of the Mother, and there will be other discoveries just as extreme and extraordinary. The human adventure of understanding the Mother is without end because *she* is without end. Aurobindo would be the first to say that even his vision, all-inclusive though it sounds and seems, falls short of what she is or can be realized to be. I have come to understand that knowing the Mother means being ready to transform anything you think you know about her at any moment. The knowledge of the Mother is as totally dynamic as she is, and as inexhaustible.

In this era of the sacred marriage, the era in which we will have to abolish all dualisms and all purely patriarchal systems of power to survive, the Divine Mother is showing the world her most marvelous miracle of all: that normal life is compatible with supreme realization, and that the direct mystical contact with the divine, with her, can be sustained in any setting or activity. This, I am convinced, is the *revolution* that she is offering, a revolution that could dissolve all dogmas and hierarchies without exception; all separation whatever between ordinary and spiritual life, the sacred and the profane, the mundane and the mystical. A new spiritual age is potentially dawning for humankind, an age in which the divine could be present intimately, normally, consciously, in all things and activities, and in which the divine life that Aurobindo wrote about so magnificently could be lived naturally on earth by all beings who have fused in their hearts, souls, bodies, and minds simultaneously and together the masculine and feminine, through the grace of the Mother.

This is the vision she is bringing into being, and to help us realize it, the Divine Mother is streaming toward the earth and us the light of her innermost being. If I had not, over many years and on innumerable different occasions, myself experienced the immense and extreme power of this light of the Mother, I would find it very hard to believe in it. It isn't the privilege of any one avatar or guru, this power that is streaming down from the godhead at this moment. This light is being recognized by

Christian mystics, by Buddhist mystics, Hindu mystics like
Aurobindo, and, of course, by a whole group of modern mystics of the Mother. This light is present. It is overwhelmingly
powerful. It is here. It is working everywhere, and the miracle,
too, is that anyone can open to it and experience it anywhere
in the world, once they have made a real heart-contact with
her. What is going on is simple, shatteringly simple, too simple
for the old elitist systems, all of which will soon crumble or
reveal themselves as corrupt and inefficient. By "real contact"
with the Mother, I don't mean contact with any one of her self-
styled representatives, I mean *real contact*—directly, simply,
nakedly in the heart—with the Divine Mother at any moment,
in any situation.

This divine light of the Divine Mother is the light of the
absolute. It has always been here, and the universe is burning
in it. But what the Divine Mother is now doing is, with shattering simplicity, making its power available by focusing it and
making it directly useful in all situations as a force of unprecedented transformatory power. The light has always been here,
but it has never been used in quite the way that she is now using
it. We can say it is everywhere, like electricity, but we must
know how to activate it. This is what the Divine Mother is now
doing. These are astonishing claims, but their truths have been
experienced by many mystics who now encounter the Mother
with an open mind and heart. The Mother is nothing if not
supremely practical: For an extreme disease she has brought
into the world-play, as Aurobindo announced with calm exul-
tation, a power of extreme healing, the power of the ultimate
light that she herself *is*.

The unprecedented spiritual leap that humankind will have
to take to save itself and the planet could only be possible if
there were a correspondingly vast concentration of divine power
here on earth to make that leap possible and to give human
beings everywhere every kind of inspiration, encouragement,
and help. That power, I believe, is the light now active through
the grace of the Divine Mother, active everywhere all over the

planet, in all who believe and know the light is here.

Call it to work in any path you take—Christian, Hindu, Taoist, Buddhist, neo-pagan—any genuine path at all, and the Mother's light will take you with extraordinary intensity, efficiency and passion to the heart of the transformation you desire. Becoming aware of the miracle of the presence of this light, the revolution it is offering, its availability to everyone everywhere, beyond all theologies and rituals and dogmas, beyond all systems of "transmission" and "lineage," all the old guru-and-disciple systems, is, I have come to understand, essential for the survival and the transformation of us all. The light has come up in an infinite, dazzling sun, and its rays are penetrating everything, opening everything up, offering the whole world definitive liberation from all subtle and actual prisons.

I would like to end with a warning: even this light, the Absolute, focused for us through the divine mind and the divine heart of the Mother, will not and *could not* save us if as many of us as possible do not turn with humility and sincerity to God. The choice is still, and always, ours. What more can the Mother of the Universe do than send us the light, and with it the most direct possible forms of initiation and the most powerful possible force, and unconditional, passionate willingness to work with everyone, every religion, within the terms of each path? The infinite love of the Divine Mother is streaming toward us from all sides with unprecedented power. Learning to respond to it and learning how to respond to it in tenderness and trust, in courage and clarity of mind and heart, and in adoration could still, even at this late, terrible moment, change everything and empower us directly to save the world.

## Notes

1. In Andrew Harvey, *The Way of Passion: A Celebration of Rumi* (Berkeley, California: Frog, Ltd., 1994), pp. 318–319.

2. Robert Lawlor, *Voices of the First Day: Awakening in the Aboriginal Dreamtime* (Rochester, Vermont: Inner Traditions International, Ltd., 1991), p. 44. Used by permission of the author.

3. Lex Hixon, *Mother of the Buddhas: Meditation on the Prajnaparamita Sutra* (Wheaton, Illinois: Quest Books, 1993), pp. 95–96.

4. Adapted from *Buddhist Scriptures*. Selected and translated by Edward Conze (New York: Penguin Books, 1959), pp. 168–169.

5. *Vitality, Energy, Spirit: A Taoist Sourcebook*. Translated and edited by Thomas Cleary (Boston: Shambhala Publications, 1991), pp. 95–96.

6. "This poet can only cry in ecstasy," in Lex Hixon, *Mother of the Universe: Visions of the Goddess and Tantric Hymns of Enlightenment* (Wheaton, Illinois: Quest Books, 1994), p. 35.

7. "The total madness of her love," in Hixon, *Mother of the Universe*, p. 37.

8. "A country fair for those mad with love," in Hixon, *Mother of the Universe*, pp. 111–112.

9. Jnaneshwar, "The Nectar of Self-Awareness," in *Two Suns Rising: A Collection of Sacred Writings*. Edited by Jonathan Star (New York: Bantam Books, 1991), pp. 190–191.

10. Lawlor, *Voices of the First Day*, p. 47.

11. Adapted from Richard Tarnas, *The Passion of the Western Mind: Understanding the Ideas That have Shaped Our World View* (New York: Harmony Books, 1991).

12. Lawlor, *Voices of the First Day*, pp. 47–48.

13. Sri Aurobindo, *The Mother* (Pondicherry, India: Sri Aurobindo Ashram, Publication Department, 1972), p. 20.

# Chapter Two

# The Message of the Mother in the Life and Teachings of Ramakrishna

I N A MEDITATIVE and sober way, I would like to take you on a journey through the life, work, vision, and message of perhaps the greatest, sweetest, and most sublime of all the children of the Divine Mother that the world has yet seen, Ramakrishna. I believe that Ramakrishna came on earth to give us in the example of his life, in the clarity and universal reach and tolerance of his teaching, in the splendor of his absolute unconditional love, and in the dance and joy of his living and dying, an unforgettable example of what it would be like to live in full consciousness of the Divine Mother, to live on earth in incessant, direct, intimate, ecstatic contact with her primal energy of love. Ramakrishna lived from 1836 to 1886, fifty miraculous years in which he gave us a very clear vision of how we could enter into contact with the Mother, and how we could live that contact most deeply and tenderly.

Ramakrishna's life and being, and the seamless, all-encompassing teaching that arose naturally out of that life and being, are all prophetic signs of the perfect holy simplicity, universal openness, natural abandon, and mystic passion our lives could have if we learned how to live them in the Mother's light and for her glory. He lived on earth in her heaven of blissful unity with all beings and tender passion for all life, honoring all paths and faiths, all possible spiritual perspectives and approaches, in her heaven of blessing all variety as holy and knowing all life as her play.

In Ramakrishna, humanity sees a new kind of being—the fully divinized, fully love-empowered child of the Divine Mother, inaugurating in joy and tolerance her era and her revolution, revealing by his words and his silences, in his every movement, her highest laws to anyone able to receive them with an open and visionary heart. In the simplicity of his living, Ramakrishna seems to return to humankind's primeval past, to recapture all the original splendor of a lost naturalness. In the sophistication of his spiritual intellect and his complete knowledge of all mystical states of being, Ramakrishna points far forward to an age in which humankind will be united under her and liberated together—in heart, body, and intellect—into her love.

He embodies at once the best of the past and the future, is both original and final being, the aborigine and the ultimate master-child-lover-sage, the child of nature and the child of the light that is constantly birthing nature. There is no more complete companion on the journey into the Mother than Ramakrishna; anyone who asks for his divine friendship will receive it, and with it guidance, wit, truth, and holy ecstatic inspiration, *directly,* with the directness, "practical" truth, bliss, and humor of the Mother herself. He is all of humanity's child, friend, and our guide into her, and if the great revolution the Mother is planning succeeds, as it must, it will be to Ramakrishna that the whole world will look as an example of Mother-life and Mother-passion.

Let us expand our hearts, minds, and souls to try and encompass something of the glory and majesty, the naked, wild, extreme freedom of that vision of Mother Kali that Ramakrishna knew and inherited from the great Kali devotees of Bengal, of whom Ramprasad was perhaps the most inspired. So before we enter Ramakrishna's life, which was one long ecstatic sacred dance for the Divine Mother in her form of Kali, I would like to share three hymns to Kali, each of which illuminates another aspect of that *sadhana,* that devotion, that was Ramakrishna's life. In order to enter into the hymns, we must consecrate ourselves, our bodies and hearts, by doing a very elementary heart practice, one of the essential methods of getting into contact with the Divine Mother. Let Ramakrishna be for us now an emanation of the Mother; this practice invokes him to be with us here and to send from his heart to ours one illumining ray of her great light. Didn't Ramakrishna himself assure us that "One ray from the sun of the light of the Divine Mother will give you all the gnosis, all the *ananda,* all the knowledge that you can bear"?

Imagine in front of you in a dark sky, a mandala of diamond-white light as flawless and pure and radiant as that of the cleanest-cut diamond. Know that this diamond light is the light of the Mother and that it has within it all properties of initiation and healing. Move slowly into that mandala a short, thin, brown-skinned man with an enchanting, gap-toothed smile and two vast liquid eyes, eyes that are those of a child and a woman in love. He is seated and he has only a ragged dhoti on, and you see very clearly his ribs, his hunched shoulders, and the lines of his elbow. He is looking out directly at you, tilting his head slightly to one side, and from that poignant, urgent look flows toward you bliss, peace, and knowledge. Welcome him silently, saying something like this:

*Holy Ramakrishna, beautiful brother of the human race, child of the Divine Mother, illumined being, free from all dogmas, all castes, all hierarchies, befriend and illuminate me. Communicate to me beyond all words the simple essence of your knowledge of her so that at this late moment I can fulfill the prayer of your life, and go through that low humble door that you opened for me in the walls separating humankind and the Mother. Help me now to go through that door and meet myself, humble, simple, tender, playful, ecstatic, dancing in her light with all other beings.*

A sacred peace, silence, and connectedness now stream in you directly from Ramakrishna and the light of the Mother. Enjoy them as your essence and identity and birthright; holding them in the core of your being and illuminating with them your heart and body and mind, now turn the fullness of your attention to these three hymns of Ramprasad. Ramakrishna himself often sang or asked others to sing to him the hymns of Ramprasad. He knew what they are: perfect expressions of humanity's hunger for direct union with the Mother and burningly simple, uncluttered, and accurate celebrations of the rapture of that union, that radiant being-at-home-here that is the Mother's most marvelous gift, that revelation of the whole of life as her paradise of love that leads us to the end of fear and the flowering of pure divine human life.

In the first hymn, "Its value beyond assessment by the mind," we hear directly the rhythms of that health, poise, and relaxed boundless freedom that is life-in-the-Mother:

> Whom could I fear in the universe
> where my Mother is matriarch?
> I live with perfect ease upon her estate,
> indivisible awareness and bliss.
> I am her direct tenant,
> free from formality and hierarchy.
>
> There is no payment of rent for this sanctuary,
> this garden of nonduality,
> its value beyond assessment by the mind.
> Nor can my sacred abode be sold at auction,
> for there are no owners and nothing to own.
> The manager of Mother's holdings, Lord Shiva,
> transcends every limited conception and transaction.
> There is no disharmony or injustice here,
> for there is no division, no separation.
> Mother does not impose the heavy tax
> of religious obligation.

My only responsibility of stewardship
   is constant, inward remembrance,
eternally breathing: *Kali, Kali, Kali.*

This mad poet lover,
born directly from Divine Mother,
cherishes one consuming desire:
To purchase her diamond paradise of delight
   with the boundless treasure of pure love
And give it away freely to all beings.[1]

The entire life and message of Ramakrishna is in this poem.
He came to live with "perfect ease" upon the Mother's estate,
in "indivisible awareness and bliss." He came to know the "garden of nonduality" and to know the temple garden of Dakshineshwar, the streets of Calcutta, and the whole world as
that garden. He came to live in "constant inward remembrance"
of oneness with Kali. With his loving austerity and his ceaseless service to all beings, he earned and embodied the "diamond paradise of delight," and secure in the "boundless treasure
of pure love," lived and gave everything away, inviting everyone to do likewise, being and sharing the path home, the path
*here.*

Mother of the Universe,
you reside deep within my secret heart.
Mysterious Kali, how can I say
   you are distant from me?
Yet you manifest so elusively,
O Goddess of cosmic illusion, O Mahamaya,
disguising your clear light with countless masks.
You assume contrasting roles
   to harmonize with every calling
of worship, prayer, and meditation,
but can you continue to elude the lover
   who knows that your surprising forms
express the single essence of awareness?

*Ma! Ma! Ma!*
I know you will not assume responsibility
　　for willful travelers
Who do not take refuge in you consciously.
Those content with the glass beads
　　of self-centered existence
cannot discern the gold of self-surrender.

This singer of her spontaneous verses
　　cries to the Wisdom Mother:
"O Goddess composed of consciousness,
My heart awakens to your truth
　　like a flower naturally blossoming.
Please reveal your transparent presence
　　within this lotus heart
as open space, forever shining."[2]

Those two lines: "My heart awakens to your truth/like a flower naturally blossoming" radiate the holiest secret of all life-in-the-Mother—that it flowers naturally, from truth to truth and gnosis to gnosis, *naturally,* as a flower opens. For the working of the Mother's love is a natural, organic, and whole process, fundamentally simple in its operation though unimaginably complex in its effects. To know and live this simplicity, the "gold of self-surrender" to her, is all-important, is the alchemical key, Ramakrishna never tired of repeating. With it, and through prayer and sincere spiritual discipline, we will become one with her "transparent presence," with the freedom of the "open space forever shining" that is her in the core of the open heart.

The third poem celebrates the impossibility of ever describing the Goddess and helps us deepen and embellish that "gold of self-surrender." When we learn that we cannot describe her, we have learned something very important. And when we really know that we cannot know, peace arrives in the soul and we can embrace the danger of going beyond all concepts and dogmas, all names and forms, into the astonishment of the Mother's presence. We can embrace it and surrender to its mystery

and her alchemy ecstatically, fearlessly, with something of her
own all-embracing acceptance, and so come increasingly to
know our identity with her, both the path *to* the Mother and
the "end" of that path.

In this long poem by Ramprasad, Ramakrishna himself
seems to be transmitting to us his deepest awareness of the
"Goddess composed of consciousness"—pure love and pure
sweet freedom:

> O foolish mind, do not indulge in hatred
>     for any sacred way
> if you wish to enter pure reality.
>
> With desperate longing for truth alone,
> this singer of this song has plunged
>     into the ocean of ancient scriptures,
> discovering at last that my blissful Mother,
> her black hair falling free in ecstasy,
> is the living power within every religious symbol,
> the coherent core of every philosophy.
>
> She is the warrior spirit, Kali dancing,
> and she is Shiva, all-transcending.
> She is ineffable sweetness, Radha-Krishna
> the love-play that dissolves conventionality.
> She is Sita-Ram, compassionately wise,
> the complete evolution of humanity.
>
> O Mother Divine, your power alone
>     manifests as Shiva the Sublime,
> sounding his ram's horn in mountain solitude,
> And as Krishna smiling tenderly,
> surrounded by ecstatic lovers,
> playing bamboo flute in the fertile river valley.
> Mother! Mother! Mother!
> Your secret power shines as Lord Rama,
> bearing the bow of justice,
> And as Great Goddess Kali,
> wielding the sword of nonduality.

Removing these veils, O Goddess,
you dance naked as timeless awareness
      on the body of your consort,
who lies still, enraptured, also naked truth,
merged in union with the Absolute.

O Mother Power!
You abide in the dusty cremation ground
      as world-liberating Kali.
You reside within the noble palace of leadership.
You dance through the fragrant green landscape of
      love.

The Mother of the Universe
      is both woman and man
when they meet in blissful embrace,
dedicating their union to conscious oneness.
Mother alone manifests, as loyal brother
      and as consecrated wife
along the sacred way of selfless daily life.

This poet is struck with amazement and cries:
"Her nature as pure reality can never be described!
She is fullness! She is completeness!
My Mother dwells in all beings
      as their secret essence.
At her wisdom feet I find every fragrance,
every scripture, every place of pilgrimage."[3]

*  *  *

Ramakrishna was born to two pious Brahmins on February
18, 1836. He grew up to be a naughty, lazy, sweet, sparklingly
intelligent and god-loving little boy. At six, in the village of
Kamarpukur in the Hooghly district of Bengal, he had his first
experience of cosmic consciousness. He was carrying some rice
across a field and suddenly, at the end of the paddy, he saw a

dark thundercloud covering the sky. As he looked at it, a flock
of pure white, dazzling cranes passed across the thundercloud,
and he was so amazed by the beauty of the cranes against the
black clouds that he entered into the essence that was projecting him, the cranes, and the black clouds, and fell into *samadhi,*
a deep mystical state, as the rice tumbled from his grasp. He
was found by some villagers and taken back to his home.

Ramakrishna's father died when he was seven. His father's
death permanently marked his imagination with the transitori-
ness of the world. From being a naughty, playful, sweet little
boy, he became a reader of the *Puranas* and a stager of religious
plays with other village boys. When he was nine, during the
sacred thread ceremony in which a young Brahmin is invested
with the privilege of his lineage, he did something that, in retrospect, reveals one of the major directions of his life. Instead
of taking the food that a young Brahmin is supposed to take
from the hands of his mother, Ramakrishna took it from the
hands of his nurse, the woman who had brought him up and
whom he loved, and who was a *shudra,* a low-caste person, an
"untouchable." This caused a scandal but Ramakrishna did it
as a sign of that unconditional love that was to mark his life.

At the age of sixteen, he went to join his brother in Calcutta, that city sacred to the Goddess Kali, whose name is
embedded in its name. His brother wanted him to undertake
the kind of disciplines that any young Brahmin priest would
have to learn; his dream was that Ramakrishna would become
a famous and rich priest. But Ramakrishna said to him, "What
have I got to do with bread-winning? I don't want to earn my
money like that, I want the wisdom that brings *moksha,* that
brings liberation."

The Calcutta that Ramakrishna entered into was a wild,
decadent place, full of prostitutes, drunks, and wheeler-deal-
ers; it was the New York of India. Ramakrishna understood
even at a very young age that Hinduism had fallen into terrible decay. It had become the province of pundits who wanted
to revel in their expertise but not live what they preach, or of

sects devoted to social reform (which he saluted), but in a way
that negated or dimmed the glorious spirituality of the *Bhagavad Gita* and the *Upanishads*. Ramakrishna understood very
early on that his life would have to be offered up as an example of the ancient, pure way of being in the Hindu tradition, of
what in Sanskrit is called the *sanatana dharma*, the "eternal
path."

His brother took him to Dakshineshwar where Rani Basmani had built a temple to Kali; this temple still stands, a magnificent edifice flanked on both sides by temples sacred to Shiva.
It was here that he was to pass the rest of his life, interrupted
by only a few visits back to Kamarpukur, and once to go on
pilgrimage. The great majority of the rest of Ramakrishna's
life was passed in two small rooms in the temple compound.
That life had very little external drama, but its internal drama
was immense and extreme. For Ramakrishna, Dakshineshwar—
its trees, the Ganges that could be seen from its balconies, the
marvelous gardens, and the great peace of the temples, especially the Kali temple of which he was a priest—was a laboratory in which he put himself through the major disciplines
of the world's mystical traditions and realized divine childhood
in the Mother.

Ramakrishna's first practice was to go through the sixty-
four tantric disciplines under a woman guru called Brahmani.
He accomplished the most difficult *sadhanas* in only a day or
three days, passing through many stages of consciousness with
great ease. He then went to the other side of Hinduism, the
Vedanta side, the nondual aspect, the side that does not care
about means or forms but goes straight for a realization of
Brahman. He practiced under a guru called Totapuri, who was
a wild man, a naked lion, and who mocked Ramakrishna for
his worship of Kali and the Goddess; with his help Ramakrishna
was taken very directly, in an astonishingly short period of time,
to the highest states of unity with Brahman.

What it was it like to be Ramakrishna in those early days
of this shattering sadhana, in which he gave up, really, his whole

life to experiencing the divine from every angle? Swami Nikhilananda's wonderful autobiographical sketch of Ramakrishna
informs us how his longing for the Divine Mother grew:

> The worship in the temple intensified Sri Ramakrishna's
> yearning for a living vision of the Mother of the Universe.
> He began to spend in meditation the time not actually em-
> ployed in the temple service; and for this purpose he selected
> an extremely solitary place. A deep jungle, thick with under-
> brush and prickly plants, lay to the north of the temples. . . .
> There Sri Ramakrishna began to spend the whole night in
> meditation, returning to his room only in the morning, with
> eyes swollen as though from much weeping. [He went on
> and on in agony, begging for a vision of the Mother.] But
> he did not have to wait very long.[4]

This is how Ramakrishna described his first vision of the
Mother. Every sentence in this description has another secret
in it, another revelation:

> I felt as though my heart were being squeezed like a wet
> towel. I was overpowered with a great restlessness and a
> fear that it might not be my lot to realize Her in this life. I
> could not bear the separation from Her any longer. Life
> seemed to be not worth living. Suddenly my glance fell on
> the sword that was kept in the Mother's temple. I deter-
> mined to put an end to my life. When I jumped up like a
> madman and seized it, suddenly the blessed Mother revealed
> herself.[5]

When Ramakrishna says again and again, "If you want to
see her, you must give everything. You must long for her with
the intensity with which a drowning man longs for oxygen,"
he was saying something that he had lived. He actually was
prepared to take the sword and kill himself, the ultimately
dreadful thing that a Hindu priest could do, because he was so
desperate with longing to see the Mother. At then, at the very
moment when his whole life stood in the balance and seemed

on the point of dissolving in despair, when she had brought
him to that final desperation, she herself appeared before him.
This is what he saw:

> The buildings, with their different parts, the temple and
> everything else vanished from my sight, leaving no trace
> whatsoever ...

He was put straight into *nirvikalpa samadhi,* the highest
*samadhi,* in which all things vanish and not even the consciousness of things remains:

> ... and in their stead I saw a limitless, infinite, effulgent
> Ocean of Consciousness. As far as the eye could see, the
> shining billows were madly rushing at me from all sides with
> a terrific noise, to swallow me up! I was panting for breath.
> I was caught in the rush and collapsed, unconsciousness.
> What was happening in the outside world I did not know,
> but within me there was a steady flow of undiluted bliss,
> altogether new, and I felt the presence of the Divine Mother.[6]

Swami Nikhilananda describes what then unfolded in Ramakrishna's mind, heart, soul, and body. As the Divine Mother
took possession of him and dragged him through the burning
and dancing and howling, an extraordinary series of transformations occurred in which she revealed many profound aspects
of herself and of her play.

The first glimpse of the Divine Mother made him the more
eager for Her uninterrupted vision. He wanted to see Her
both in meditation and with eyes open. But the Mother
began to play a teasing game of hide-and-seek with him,
intensifying both his joy and his suffering. Weeping bitterly
through the moments of separation from Her, he would pass
into a trance and then find Her standing before him smiling, talking, consoling, bidding him be of good cheer, and
instructing him. During this period of spiritual practice he
had many uncommon experiences. When he sat to meditate, he would hear strange clicking sounds in the joints of

his legs, as if someone were locking them up, one after the other, to keep him motionless; and at the conclusion of his meditation, he would again hear the same sounds, this time unlocking them and leaving him free to move about. He would see flashes like a swarm of fire-flies floating before his eyes, or a sea of deep mist around him, with luminous waves of molten silver. Again, from a sea of translucent mist, he would behold the Mother rising, first Her feet, then Her waist, body, face, and head, and finally Her whole person; he would feel Her breath and hear Her voice. Worshipping in the temple, sometimes he would become exalted, sometimes he would remain motionless as stone, sometimes he would almost collapse from excessive emotion. Many of his actions, contrary to all tradition, seemed sacrilegious to the people. He would take a flower and touch it to his own head, body, and feet, and then offer it to the Goddess. Or, like a drunkard, he would reel to the throne of the Mother, touch Her chin by way of showing his affection for Her, and sing, talk, joke, laugh, and dance. Or he would take a morsel of food from the plate and hold it to Her mouth, begging Her to eat it, and would not be satisfied until he was convinced that She had really eaten. After [the Kali-image] had been put to sleep at night, from his own room he would hear Her ascending to the upper storey of the temple with the light step of a happy girl, Her anklets jingling. Then he would discover Her standing with flowing hair, Her black form silhouetted against the sky of the night, looking at the Ganges or at the distant lights of Calcutta.[7]

Ramakrishna himself describes her power:

God made me pass through the disciplines of the various paths. First according to the Purana, then according to the Tantra. I also followed the disciplines of the Vedas. At first I practiced sadhana in the Panchavati. I made a grove of tulsi-plants and used to sit inside it and meditate. Sometimes I cried with a longing heart, "Mother! Mother!" . . . I was in a God-intoxicated state. At that time I used to put on a silk robe and worship the Deity. What joy I experienced in that worship!

I practiced the discipline of the Tantra under the bel-tree. At that time I could see no distinction between the sacred tulsi and any other plant. In that state I sometimes ate the leavings from a jackal's meal, food that had been exposed the whole night, part of which might have been eaten by snakes or other creatures. Yes, I ate that stuff.

Sometimes I rode on a dog and fed him with luchi, also eating part of the bread myself. I realized that the whole world was filled with God alone. One cannot have spiritual realization without destroying ignorance; so I would assume the attitude of a tiger and devour ignorance....

I vowed to the Divine Mother that I would kill myself if I did not see God. I said to her: "O Mother, I am a fool. Please teach me what is contained in the Vedas, the Puranas, the Tantras, and the other scriptures."...

I had all the experiences that one should have, according to the scriptures, after one's direct perception of God. I behaved like a child, like a madman, like a ghoul, like an inert person.

I saw the visions described in the scriptures. Sometimes I saw the universe filled with sparks of fire. Sometimes I saw all the quarters glittering with light, as if the world were a lake of mercury. Sometimes I saw the world as if it were made of liquid silver. Sometimes, again, I saw all the quarters illumined as if with the light of Roman candles. So you see my experiences tally with those described in the scriptures.

It was revealed to me further that God Himself has become the universe and all its living beings and the twenty-four cosmic principles. It is like the process of evolution and in-volution.

Oh, what a state God kept me in at that time! One experience would hardly be over before another overcame me.

It was like the movement of the husking-machine: no sooner is one end down than the other goes up.

I would see God in meditation, in the state of samadhi, and I would see the same God when my mind came back to the outer world. When looking in the mirror I would see Him alone, and when looking on the reverse side I saw the same God.[8]

What is here described is the steady flowering of a state of total God-intoxication that was to last the rest of Ramakrishna's life. The remainder of his life on earth was spent in a state of bliss and joy that he knew came directly from the Mother, which he was nevertheless able to integrate, and from which an series of absolutely direct and simple teachings were given.

This wonderful time that Nikhilananda and Ramakrishna himself describe is the great seed time for any mystic, the time of the meeting with the beloved. It isn't the highest state—which is complete integration into the Mother at all levels—but it represents the moment when the Mother comes up in her beauty and glory and plays with the mystic who has become enraptured with her. It has all the wildness and mad freshness of her divine springtime. This marvelous time is the "honeymoon" between the Mother and the soul. For Ramakrishna, this dizzying period opened out into a steady vision of the unity of all things in her, which this story exemplifies most beautifully and most touchingly:

Sri Ramakrishna one day fed a cat with the food that was to be offered to Kali. This was too much for the manager of the temple garden, who considered himself responsible for the proper conduct of the worship. He reported Sri Ramakrishna's insane behaviour to Mathur Babu [who was then Rani Basmani's son-in-law].[9]

Ramakrishna later described the incident to one of his disciples and says with his "village" sincerity:

> The Divine Mother revealed to me ... that it was She who
> had become everything. She showed me that everything was
> full of Consciousness. The [Kali statue] was Consciousness,
> the altar was Consciousness, the water-vessels were Con-
> sciousness, the door-sill was Consciousness, the marble floor
> was Consciousness—all was Consciousness. I found every-
> thing inside the room soaked, as it were, in Bliss, the Bliss
> of God.[10]

"Soaked" is wonderful there, because when the light does
appear like that everything seems to be running as if with water,
only the water is the light, and this light-water is soaking, saturating everything. When reality is seen with the eyes of the
awakened mind and heart, everything appears soaked, drenched,
saturated with divine light. "I found everything inside the room
soaked, as it were, in Bliss, the Bliss of God."

And then, after this overwhelming experience of consciousness, of "Being" in everything—Ramakrishna says: "I saw a
wicked man in front of the Kali temple; but in him also I saw
the power of the Divine Mother vibrating." All conventional
morality is dissolved by realization, all judgment, all concepts
of who is good and who is bad, of who is privileged and who
is not, because the Divine Mother is at play in evil as she is in
good, in darkness as in light. Ramakrishna has this vision of the
wicked man in front of the Kali temple, sees that he is wicked
but also that he vibrates with the power of the Divine Mother.
He goes on:

> That was why I fed a cat the food that was to be offered to
> the Divine Mother. I clearly perceived that all this was the
> Divine Mother—even the cat. The manager of the temple
> garden wrote to Mathur Babu saying that I was I feeding
> the cat with the offering intended for the Divine Mother.
> But Mathur Babu had insight into the state of my mind. He
> wrote back to the manager: "Let him do whatever he likes."[11]

Ramakrishna's spiritual disciplines gave him, then, a complete inner experience of the Mother in all her formal and form-

less aspects. Secure in this realization, Ramakrishna further realized that enveloping vision of sacred unity and knew that his body, heart, and mind were destined to be the laboratory for a vision of sacred unity of all paths. So, in 1866, Ramakrishna undertook a "sadhana" of Islam and later a "sadhana" of Christianity in order to prove in his own heartspace that all faiths and spiritual perspectives lead to Her. Here Nikhilananda describes his initiation into Islam and Christianity:

> Toward the end of 1866 he began to practice the disciplines of Islam and under the direction of his Mussalman guru, he abandoned himself to his new sadhana. He dressed as a Mussalman and repeated the name of Allah. His prayers took the form of the Islamic devotions. He forgot the Hindu gods and goddesses—even Kali—and gave up visiting the temples. He took up his residence outside the temple precincts. After three days, he saw the vision of a radiant figure, perhaps Mohammed. This figure gently approached him and finally lost himself in Sri Ramakrishna. Thus he realized the Mussalman God [and] passed into communion with Brahman. The mighty river of Islam also led him back to the Ocean of the Absolute.[12]

Then, in 1874, Ramakrishna undertook his journey into the heart of Christianity. Nikhilananda tells us:

> Sri Ramakrishna was seized with an irresistible desire to learn the truths of the Christian religion. He began to learn to listen to readings from the Bible, by Sambhu Charan Mallick [and] became fascinated by the life and teachings of Jesus. One day, he was seated in the parlour of Jadu Mallick's garden house at Dakshineshwar, when his eyes became fixed on a painting of the Madonna and Child. Intently watching it, he became gradually overwhelmed with divine emotion. The figures on the pictures took on life, and the rays of light emanating from them entered his soul. The effect of this experience was stronger than that of the vision of Mohammed. In dismay he cried out, "Oh, Mother! What

are You doing to me?" And, breaking through the barriers of creed and religion, he entered a new realm of ecstasy. Christ possessed his soul. For three days he did not set foot in the Kali temple. On the fourth day, in the afternoon, as he was walking in the Panchavati, he saw coming toward him a person with beautiful large eyes, serene countenance, and fair skin. As the two faced each other, a voice rang out in the depths of Sri Ramakrishna's soul: "Behold the Christ, who shed His heart's blood for the redemption of the world, who suffered a sea of anguish for love of men. It is He, the Master Yogi, who is in eternal union with God. It is Jesus, Love Incarnate." The Son of Man embraced the Son of the Divine Mother and merged in him. Sri Ramakrishna realized his identity with Christ, as he had already realized his identity with Kali, Rama, Hanuman, Radha, Krishna, Brahman, and Mohammed. The Master went into samadhi and communed with the Brahman with attributes. Thus he experienced the truth that Christianity, too, was a path leading to God-Consciousness.[13]

In his own being, then Ramakrishna realized the essential unity of all religions at the highest and deepest level. That realization is what gives his teaching on the nature of the Divine Mother such range and authority. Let us attend now to his own words about the Mother, drink in his vast knowledge of her at the source. Ramakrishna said that Brahman (the godhead) and Shakti (the primal energy) are one and the same.

Whatever we see or think about is the manifestation of the glory of the Primordial Energy, the Primal Consciousness. Creation, preservation, and destruction, living beings and the universe, and further, meditation and the meditator, bhakti [devotion] and prema [divine love]—all these are manifestations of the glory of that Power....
Brahman and Shakti are like the snake and its wriggling motion. Thinking of the snake, one must think of its wriggling motion, and thinking of the wriggling motion, one

must think of the snake. Or they are like milk and its white-ness. Thinking of milk one has to think of its colour, that is, whiteness, and thinking of the whiteness of milk, one has to think of milk itself. Or they are like water and its wet-ness. Thinking of water, one has to think of its wetness, and thinking of the wetness of water, one has to think of water.[14]

In another of his teachings, Ramakrishna elaborates:

The Primordial Power is ever at play. She is creating, pre-serving and destroying in play, as it were. This power is called Kali. Kali is ... Brahman and Brahman is ... Kali. It is one and the same Reality. When we think of It as inac-tive, that is to say, not engaged in the acts of creation, preser-vation, and destruction, then we call it Brahman. But when It engages in these activities, then we call it Kali or Shakti. The Reality is one and the same; the difference is in name and form.

It is like water, called in different languages by different names.... There are three or four ghats on a lake. The Hin-dus, who drink water at one place, call it jal. The Mus-salmans at another place call it pani. And the English at a third place call it "water." All three denote one and the same thing, the difference being in the name only. In the same way, some address the Reality as "Allah," some as "God," some as "Brahman," some as "Kali," and others by such names as "Rama," "Jesus," "Durga," "Hari."[15]

Then one of the disciples, who sees that Ramakrishna is entering into an ecstatic state, asks him to go deeper into the nature of the Divine Mother as Kali. He says:

Oh, she plays in different ways. It is she alone who is known as Maha-Kali, Nitya-Kali, Shmashana-Kali, Raksha-Kali, and Shyama-Kali. Maha-Kali and Nitya-Kali are mentioned in the Tantra philosophy. When there were neither the cre-ation, nor the sun, the moon, the planets, and the earth, and when darkness was enveloped in darkness, then the Mother, the Formless One, Maha-Kali, the Great Power, was one with Maha-Kali, the Absolute.

Shyama-Kali has a somewhat tender aspect and is worshiped in the Hindu households. She is the Dispenser of boons and the Dispeller of fear. People worship Raksha-Kali, the Protectress, in times of epidemic, famine, earthquake, drought, and flood. Shamashana-Kali is the embodiment of the power of destruction. She resides in the cremation ground, surrounded by corpses, jackals, and terrible female spirits. From Her mouth flows a stream of blood, and from Her neck hangs a garland of human heads, and around Her waist is a girdle made of human hands.

After the destruction of the universe, at the end of a great cycle, the Divine Mother gathers the seeds for the next creation. She is like the elderly mistress of the house, who has a hotchpotch-pot in which she keeps different articles for household use.[16]

At that place in the text, it says "All laugh." Ramakrishna's imagination is so vivid, we can sense here how intimate he is with her. One moment, he imagines the vast darkness-upon-darkness in which the Mother is one with the absolute; in the next, he characterizes her as a housewife with a pot in which she puts the seeds of creation. He is at one with the Mother in all her different aspects, transcendent and immanent. He is at one with her feeding the cat and in the ultimate source of the godhead. He goes on:

> Oh, yes! Housewives have pots like that, where they keep "sea foam" [cuttlefish bone], blue pills, small bundles of seeds of cucumber, pumpkin and gourd, and so on. They take them out when they want them. In the same way, after the destruction of the universe, my Divine Mother, the Embodiment of Brahman, gathers together the seeds for the next creation.[17]

Ramakrishna isn't speaking as if he thinks this, he knows this.

This is what he knows. He has seen it, he understands it, he is one with it. He is describing how the Mother creates cosmos after cosmos in wild play:

> After the creation, the Primal Power dwells in the universe itself. She brings forth this phenomenal world and then pervades it. In the Vedas creation is likened to the spider and its web. The spider brings the web out of itself and then remains in it. God is the container of the universe, and also what is contained in it.[18]

At this moment, Ramakrishna goes into an ecstatic meditation on Kali's blackness, of the blackness of the Divine Mother, the sacred darkness, the sacred mystery.

> Is Kali, my Divine Mother, of a black complexion? She appears black because She is viewed from a distance; but when intimately known She is no longer so. The sky appears blue at a distance, but look at it close by and you will find that it has no colour. The water of the ocean looks blue at a distance, but when you go near, and take it in your hand, you find that it is colourless.[19]

At this moment, he became intoxicated with divine love and sang:

> *Is Kali, my Mother, really black?*
> *The Naked One, of blackest hue,*
> *Lights the Lotus of the Heart ...*

Then Ramakrishna said:

> Bondage and liberation are both of Her making. By Her maya worldly people become entangled in "woman and gold," and again, through Her grace they attain liberation. She is called the Savior, and the Remover of the bondage that binds one to the world.[20]

Then Ramakrishna sang the following song, in which he expresses the madness, the wildness, the incredible freedom, and the unknowableness of Kali—the mystery of the Mother, the mystery of this great mystical play of hers, the world:

> In the world's busy marketplace, O Shyama, Thou art
>     flying kites;
> High up they soar on the wind of hope, held fast by
>     maya's string.
> Their frames are human skeletons, their sails of the
>     three gunas made;
> But all their curious workmanship is merely for
>     ornament.
>
> Upon the kite-strings Thou hast rubbed the manja-
>     paste of worldliness,
> So as to make each straining strand all the more sharp
>     and strong.
> Out of a hundred thousand kites, at best but one or
>     two break free;
> And Thou dost laugh and clap Thy hands, O Mother,
>     watching them!
>
> On favoring winds, says Ramprasad, the kites set
>     loose will speedily
> To be borne away to the Infinite, across the sea of the
>     world.

And then, in ecstasy, he says:

> The Divine Mother is always playful and sportive. The universe is Her play. She is self-willed, and must have always Her own way. She is full of bliss. She gives freedom to one out of a hundred thousand.[21]

Taken all together, these words convey one small taste of the immensity of the vision that Ramakrishna had of the Divine Mother. What then is his message to the world that arises out of that vision? Ramakrishna's message is extremely radical and extremely simple and has the stamp of total experience. And it is a crucial message, I believe, for the survival of the planet.

Through Ramakrishna the Mother is saying to the world: For humankind to survive now and become my children in fact as well as in essence there must be an absolute end to religious divisiveness, an end to any belief that one has the complete truth. Again and again, Ramakrishna passionately denied that any one way to the truth was the *only* way. Here are his own words:

> I say that all are calling on the same God. . . . It is not good to feel that my religion is true and other religions are false. The correct attitude is this: My religion is right, but I do not know whether other religions are right or wrong, true or false. I say this because one cannot know the true nature of God unless one realizes [God]. . . .

> [A]ll seek the same object. A mother prepares dishes to suit the stomachs of her children. Suppose a mother has five children and a fish is bought for the family. She doesn't cook pilau or kalia for all of them. All have not the same power of digestion; so she prepares a simple stew for some. But she loves all her children equally. . . . I feel myself at home with every dish—fried fish, fish cooked with turmeric powder, pickled fish. And further, I equally relish rich preparations like fish-head, kalia, and pilau. *(All laugh.)* . . .

> Do you know what the truth is? God has made different religions to suit different aspirants, times, and countries. All doctrines are only so many paths; but a path is by no means God Himself. Indeed, one can reach God if one follows any of the paths with whole-hearted devotion. Suppose there are errors in the religion that one has accepted; if one is sincere and earnest, then God will correct those errors. Suppose a man has set out with a sincere desire to visit [the sacred temple of] Jagganath at Puri and by mistake has gone north instead of south; then certainly someone meeting him on the way will tell him: "My good fellow, don't go that way. Go to the south." And the man will reach Jagganath sooner or later. . . .

[D]ogmatism is not good. You have no doubt heard the story of the chameleon. A man entered a wood and saw a chameleon on a tree. He reported to his friends, "I have seen a red lizard." He was firmly convinced that it was nothing but red. Another person, after visiting the tree, said, "I have seen a green lizard." He was firmly convinced that it was nothing but green. But the man who lived under the tree said: "What both of you have said is true. But the fact is that the creature is sometimes red, sometimes green, sometimes yellow, and sometimes has no colour at all."

God has been described in the Vedas as both with attributes and without. You describe Him as form only. That is one-sided. But never mind. If you know one of His aspects truly, you will be able to know His other aspects too. God Himself will tell you all about them.[22]

In other words, Ramakrishna is telling humanity in the Mother's name: God is your Mother and has provided each of you your own unique path to liberation.

Ramakrishna is also assuring us that *all of us*, all of us in the terms of our own temperament and in the terms of our own way of life, can come to see the divine with direct knowledge, if we love God enough. When Vivekananda first met Ramakrishna, he said, "Have you seen God?" and Ramakrishna said, "Yes, I have seen God, and I have seen Him a great deal more intensely than I see you." At that moment, Vivekananda knew that he was before someone who really did have divine knowledge. But the point of Ramakrishna's reply was to give Vivekananda the faith that he *also* could see God.

Ramakrishna is not interested in scriptures, he is not interested in dogmas, he is not interested in hierarchies; he is interested in technologies of the sacred that take beings of different temperaments and kinds directly to the experience of the Divine Mother, directly to ecstasy, bliss, peace, and knowledge. That is why he went in his own being through so many *sadhanas*, so that he could give to his own disciples whatever was necessary for them. In his own teachings, too, he celebrated the fabulous richness of the ways to her.

But Ramakrishna is in absolutely no sense a sentimentalist or an idealist, or someone who believes the path to the divine is easy. The Mother wants us to get to her by whatever way we choose, and each of us has a path to her. But we have to take that path with intense fervor and passion. The way of the Mother stands always open, but to walk to the end we will need every kind of courage and stamina and discrimination. Ramakrishna tells us, in effect, that "If you can combine the following three kinds of attractions: the attraction of a worldly man for his possessions, of a husband for his chaste wife, and a child for his toy, if you can combine, fuse, and synthesize those three intensities and devote that intensity to the pursuit of the divine, and if you can really concentrate on one path with your full heart, and if you can say the sacred name of God continually, bringing to it all the fervor of your heart, again and again, and if you can take all the different difficulties of sadhana, all the kinds of exhaustion and mental physical stress, and embrace them all as the price to be paid for coming into contact with her, then you will see her and know her and live in her. Then she will come to you and stay with you." But you do have to give everything. Ramakrishna was absolutely not, in any sense, a "New Age" prophet. He didn't offer any simplistic versions; he was offering the direct way—the direct way that costs a vast and passionate leap of the heart, mind, and body.

This is the age of the Kali Yuga, the age of Kali's apocalyptic dance in history, the age in which we are now and which may well culminate in a tremendous holocaust of nature. In this, our age. Ramakrishna says that the best way now to the Mother is not the way of *jnana*, of knowledge, not the way of *rajayoga*, of intellectual discrimination or scholasticism; the best way is the way of direct devotion, *bhakti*, adoration. That is the way best suited to the vast majority of human temperaments, and adoration itself provides the most profound source of energy for transformation. Adore the Mother, adore God, simply and wholeheartedly, and everything you need will be given to you.

In his own life, Ramakrishna proved the power of adoration to transform himself in every conceivable way, on every possible path. He proved it with Brahmani, with Totapuri, with his Sufi master; he proved it in the Christian disciplines which led to his meeting with Christ. He proved in a hundred thousand different ways that the way to the divine, the way to a direct experience of the divine, is in ceaseless intense, passionate adoration, saying the sacred name and the pouring out the heart toward the divine, always, in every circumstance, in every way, in every event. He understood that this path of adoration was our path now, and that you can take this path to the Mother's experience of unity in all things whether you are Muslim, Hindu, Buddhist, or Christian. Whatever you are, use the vehicle of adoration to come to her. As Ramakrishna said:

> One can attain everything through bhaktiyoga [the yoga of adoration]. I wept before the Mother and prayed, "O Mother, please tell me, please reveal to me, what the yogis have realized...." And the Mother has revealed everything to me. She reveals everything if the devotee cries to her with a yearning heart.[23]

The Divine Mother is the universe and all things in it. She is the naked space of timeless awareness, and all things that arise from that space and dissolve back into it. The entire universe, all its events and all its creations, are her play, her mahamaya. And part of this great play is her maya-yoga, her giving to the human race, her children, many different paths by which to come to her, each of them noble and beautiful, each of them sacred, and each attuned to different temperaments. But the bounty and mercy of the Mother have to be met by a corresponding act of faith, will, labor, and passion in the human heart. Awakening to this great mercy, the human heart has to then respond to it in discipline and prayer, in a passionate search for a god-consciousness, in adoration.

Ramakrishna's life *is* his message, the witness and testimony of an amazing, simple, ecstatic being that he forged from all the pain and difficulty that he went through. (He died at the age of fifty of throat cancer, both in bliss and extreme pain, surrounded by a small corps of disciples who were to take his message of unconditional love and service into the whole world.) Let me return, in conclusion, to Ramakrishna's vital message to us that the essential path into the Mother for us now, in the Kali Yuga, is the path of adoration.

Through Ramakrishna, I believe, the Mother is giving us three essential linked messages of adoration.

First, the Mother is saying to us, "Adore me. See me in my grandeur, nobility, majesty, and wildness, and adore me. Go mad with love for me." This is the first message the Mother is giving us—to turn to her, the Mother-aspect of God, and reimagine her in the ecstasy of adoration.

The second message is: "Adore each creature, each being, as a part of me." Ramakrishna was wildly in love with the created world. When he went to the zoo, he couldn't get past the lions—just at the sight of them he went into *samadhi*. One day when he went out to pick flowers, he suddenly saw that all the white flowers were bouquets laid upon Shiva's head and so he couldn't pick them. On another day, he had just picked a flower and a bit of bark came off the tree, and he saw that the tree was pure consciousness and he wept. He could never pick flowers again, because he realized that everything was sentient. Another day, he looked at two dogs copulating in a puddle, and he went into a transcendent vision of Shiva-Shakti creating the entire cosmos out of their lovemaking. So you see that the creation was for Ramakrishna nothing but glory and light, and the play of the Mother.

So the second message of the Mother is: "Adore each being, each object in the universe, as me, as totally sacred, as brimming with consciousness and light; experience each being, each object, as sacred and walk in my glory wherever you are. Know that wherever you are, whatever is happening, I am there, and

I am you and you are me." This vision of the cosmos as brimming with her sacred glory, is the one that we need more than anything else at this moment. We are in danger of destroying the entire planet, because we do not see that the trees we are cutting down, the oceans we are polluting, the creatures we are massacring, are all glorious, light-filled manifestations of her great love, and parts of our cosmic being in her.

The third message of adoration, after "Adore me, the Divine Mother," and "Adore each being as me," is the most difficult of all, I think, to put into practice. The most difficult, most demanding, and most challenging of her messages to us is: "Adore *yourself* humbly as my child. Through that humble adoration a recognition of your self and your consciousness as being my self and my divine consciousness will arise, and with it a recognition that everyone else exists also in that sacred truth."

Ramakrishna again and again talked of the wonder of having such amazing senses that could be so completely tuned to reality; of the wonder of having a heart in which the Mother could dance; of the wonder of being able to say the sacred names of God, raising in the spine the sacred energy of the *kundalini* so that it could come through all the different *chakras* and illuminate the entire being. He spoke of the wonder of being in a body in her great play and of being able to appreciate all the nuances, all the dazzling excitement, all the wonders, all the ecstasies of being able, as Ramakrishna was able, to go through everything and house everything in one small human frame.

With his life, Ramakrishna is saying: Come to the Mother's feast of love, come with your heart open to the Mother's ecstasy, her bliss, her unconditional, infinite love. Then, when you're at the feast, get down on your knees to every other being there, and spend your life serving every other being. Not for some social program, not in the name of Karl Marx or sociology, but just for the pure joy of serving other manifestations of the Mother like yourself, other completely sacred beings in need.

It is a complete philosophy, a direct teaching from the mind of the Mother. It is a teaching that can save the world, if only

we all of us have the divine courage to live it out. As Ramakrishna said, "If you meditate on an ideal you will acquire its
nature. If you think of God day and night you will acquire the
nature of God." And from that "new" nature you will act in
the world to preserve the world, in her, as her, for her, so that
her heaven-on-earth can be known, lived, and increasingly
embodied.

**Notes**

1. Lex Hixon, *Mother of the Universe: Visions of the Goddess
and Tantric Hymns of Enlightenment* (Wheaton, Illinois: Quest
Books, 1994), p. 96.

2. "My heart awakens to your truth," in Hixon, *Mother of the
Universe*, p. 109.

3. "Her nature as pure reality can never be described!" in Hixon,
*Mother of the Universe*, pp. 132–133.

4. *The Gospel of Sri Ramakrishna*. Translated into English with
an Introduction by Swami Nikhilananda (Mylapore, Madras, India:
Sri Ramakrishna Math, n.d.), p. 13.

5. *The Gospel of Sri Ramakrishna*, pp. 13–14.

6. *The Gospel of Sri Ramakrishna*, p. 14.

7. *The Gospel of Sri Ramakrishna*, p. 14.

8. *The Gospel of Sri Ramakrishna*, pp. 543–545.

9. *The Gospel of Sri Ramakrishna*, p. 15.

10. *The Gospel of Sri Ramakrishna*, p. 15.

11. *The Gospel of Sri Ramakrishna*, pp. 15–16.

12. *The Gospel of Sri Ramakrishna*, pp. 33–34.

13. *The Gospel of Sri Ramakrishna*, p. 34.

14. *The Gospel of Sri Ramakrishna*, p. 290.

15. *The Gospel of Sri Ramakrishna*, pp. 134–135.

16. *The Gospel of Sri Ramakrishna*, p. 135.

17. *The Gospel of Sri Ramakrishna*, p. 135.

18. *The Gospel of Sri Ramakrishna*, p. 135.

19. *The Gospel of Sri Ramakrishna*, pp. 135–136.

20. *The Gospel of Sri Ramakrishna*, p. 136.

21. *The Gospel of Sri Ramakrishna*, p. 136.

22. *The Gospel of Sri Ramakrishna*, pp. 558–559.

23. *The Gospel of Sri Ramakrishna*, p. 579.

# Chapter Three

## *Adoration and the Divine Child*

THE DIVINE MOTHER, through Ramakrishna's life, through the example of his extraordinary spiritual discipline and his exhilarating embrace of all paths, is giving us now a message that can be divided into a three-part path, although each part is interlinked with the others. It is a message of adoration. In the first part of the message the Divine Mother is saying: "Adore me." Adore the divine feminine, adore the Divine Mother, pour out your soul in longing and passion and infinite receptivity to the Divine Mother. Turn to the Motherhood of God, the Mother-aspect of God, and allow its unconditional love to begin to penetrate your mind, heart, and being. This is Ramakrishna's first message to the human race. Whatever religion you belong to, whatever caste you were born to, whatever non-religion you don't practice, imagine the Motherhood of God and turn to it in fearless intimacy, and allow its love to reach you. As Ramakrishna said: "O God, Thou art my Mother and I am Thy child—this is the last word in spirituality."

Then the Mother asks us to "Adore each being as my child." Everyone and everything springs fresh-minted from the light source of the Mother, and is bathed in the milk of the Mother's light. So each sentient being, each blade of grass, every stone, gnat, tree, and cockroach is nothing other than the Mother in disguise. "Adore each being as my child." As the child of my source, as the child of my life, as emanation, as theophany of my inmost being. This is the second part of the message of the

Divine Mother to humankind. Ramakrishna said, "If you realize God you will not see the world as insubstantial. The one
who has realized God knows that God has become the world
and all living beings."

The third part is: "Adore and honor yourself humbly as my
child." Not as your small self, not as your ego, not the false
self, the constructed self, the biographical self, the self that
wants power, but as the Divine Self, the Divine Child who
through love, through adoration of the Mother and of each
being as the child of the Mother, develops the awakened mystic senses of divine childhood. Honor yourself humbly as my
child. Worship the body in which you are having this experience. Protect it. Worship your hair, your knuckles, your feet,
and the strange little bones you have in secret places. Bless each
aspect of your being, including those aspects that you have been
taught to feel ashamed of. Bless them, release them all into the
light and embrace of the Mother. Adore yourself, honor yourself, revere yourself. Salute yourself. Bow down to her in you,
and to the divine childhood in you that is waiting to be born.

These three aspects of the message of adoration to the human
race find their culmination in the living experience of divine
childhood that Ramakrishna shows us. That experience of
divine childhood is the experience that the Mother is preparing for the entire human race. A direct relationship, in direct
contact with the Divine Mother herself without any intermediaries. A direct experience of bliss and ecstasy, of freedom from
all barriers and dogmas and creeds, from the burden of the past,
a direct experience of her being in you, and your being in her.

The following five quotations from Ramakrishna, and one
passage in particular, let us see and experience and taste the
divine childhood that was his life. Then, in the spirit of Ramakrishna, I will take us on a quiet journey through the ways in
which this secret of secrets is represented in the various mystical traditions of the world, including aboriginal wisdom. The
supreme mystical secret is that spiritual mastery is what Lewis
Thompson has called "athletically regained childhood," the

reintegration of the innocent, free, and abandoned bliss-senses of childhood with full mature spiritual consciousness. The supreme mystical secret is that the final reward of living in love with the Divine Mother is that you *become* the Mother of yourself through adoration of her and for love of your own divine child; you give birth to yourself, "mother" the "child" in you through her grace and your aspiration.

Through discipline, purification, and prayer, through both fierce and gentle work on everything that blocks you from her unconditional love streaming towards you—through all these things linked together, you slowly give birth to the divine child in you, the free and "unborn" one, the latent "Ramakrishna" in all of us. The divine child is the sacred androgyne that is your fundamental nondual self, the one who is both masculine and feminine, and also beyond masculine and feminine; the one who is both light and shadow, and beyond light and shadow; the one who is both in time and beyond time; the one who is both divine and immortal, and human and transient; beyond both "mortality" and "immortality." This is the human divine, and the divine human.

We are here to become the human divine and the divine human, and so have the complete experience of God living in all dimensions simultaneously and spontaneously, savoring all aspects of divine life in one supreme, complete experience. God is at once transcendent and immanent, is the universe and the light birthing the universe. By giving birth to the divine child in ourselves, we realize the innate divinity of our humanness, play as God in time, experience together all aspects of God in one normal ecstasy, and so naturally enter the Mother's heaven-on-earth, her mystic paradise that only real lovers and divine children can enter, her rose garden of gnosis and ordinary Eden that lie all around us. It is the experience of divine childhood that the Mother now wants to give the human race directly, so we—as many of us as possible—can know our humble royalty and the splendor of the world we live in, and work to save the planet. The world will be saved, I am convinced, only by and for divine children who have awakened in the Mother to the fullness of their and her being, and have become living transmitters of her sacred energy.

Let these words of Ramakrishna perfume your mind and allow it to focus; these quotations will establish a rich background of mystical understanding for this essential earthly vision of her divine childhood. Ramakrishna said: "Do you know the sign of one who has God-vision? Such a man acquires the nature of a child. Why a child? Because God is like a child."

> After realizing God a man becomes like a child. One acquires the nature of the object one meditates upon. The nature of God is like that of a child. As a child builds up its toy house and then breaks it down, so God acts while creating, preserving, and destroying the universe.[1]

Ramakrishna also said: "God is directly present in the person who has the pure heart of a child, and who laughs and cries and dances and sings in divine ecstasy."

> "In the course of [becoming a child again] one gets a 'love-body,' endowed with 'love-eyes,' 'love-ears,' and so on. One sees God with those 'love-eyes.' One hears the voice of God with those 'love-ears.' One even gets a sexual organ made of love."
>
> At these words, M. burst out laughing. [Ramakrishna] continued, unannoyed, "With this 'love-body,' the soul communes with God."[2]

Ramakrishna is not just being poetic here—the Mother's mystic transformation does change all the senses by awakening the divine child-essence in each of them. The divine child grows and becomes love's body, and uses all his or her transformed senses to be and act as love in a world that is now experienced as the Mother's play of the divine love; to be, in fact, love in love, love acting as love, for love.

Following, now, is a longer section which contains the entire secret mystical child-consciousness, both in the way in which

Ramakrishna is represented in the passage and in what he says. Follow the transitions, the exquisite transitions of his teaching as "M." has set it down; see and hear and feel and taste and enter into Ramakrishna's spontaneity, into the way he comes from ecstasy and bliss down to give the most astonishing teaching on superconsciousness. In this extended passage he is talking of the highest awareness, the awareness of the child who is at home in all dimensions, who is free from shame, has no more barriers, and knows that everything, without exception, is swimming in and arriving out of a sea of light.

Ramakrishna has been speaking for a while, and someone says, "You've spoken very beautifully, sir. Beautiful words indeed." Ramakrishna begins his fresh "teaching" by saying:

> "Oh, this is just idle talk, but do you know my inner feeling? I am the machine and [the Mother] is the operator. I am the house and [she] is the Indweller. I am the engine and [she] is the Engineer. I am the chariot and [she] is the Charioteer. I move as [she] moves me. I do as [she] makes me do."
>
> Presently, Trailokya began to sing to the accompaniment of drums and cymbals. Sri Ramakrishna danced. . . .

So right at the beginning of this spontaneous teaching, Ramakrishna casually, in a childlike way, gives us the highest secret of the state of divine childhood—that it is one of total dependence on the Divine Mother, total lucid and ecstatic awareness of the Mother as the one who is "doing" everything, for she is appearing as everyone and everything and it is by her will and energy that all things occur. Knowing this brings, as the passage shows, peace and great joy: "Sri Ramakrishna danced."

> [He] danced, intoxicated with divine love. Many times he went into samadhi. He stood still, his eyes fixed, his face beaming, with one hand on the shoulder of a beloved disciple. Coming down a little from the state of ecstasy, he danced again like a mad elephant. Regaining consciousness of the outer world, he improvised lines to the music:

*O Mother, dance about Thy devotees.*
*Dance Thyself, and make them dance as well.*
*O Mother, dance in the lotus of my heart;*
*Dance, O Thou the ever blessed Brahman!*
*Dance in all Thy world-bewitching beauty.*

An indescribable scene, the exquisite and celestial dance of a child, completely filled with ecstatic love of God, and identified heart and soul with the Divine Mother.

M. describes Ramakrishna as he really is. And who he is, is who *we* really are, behind all the masks and scars of guilt and fear. Ramakrishna in the "indescribable scene" is dancing out the secret truth of us all, that all of us could be dancing "the exquisite and celestial dance of a child, completely filled with ecstatic love of god, and identified heart and soul with the Divine Mother." The narrator goes on:

The Brahmo devotees danced around the Master again and again, attracted like iron to a magnet. In ecstatic voices they chanted the name of Brahman. Again, they chanted the name of the Divine Mother. Many of them wept like children, crying, "Mother, Mother!"[3]

Why is the divine child the last stage, the final stage of gnosis? The divine child is far beyond the yogi or the master, because he or she has given up all power simply to be one with the joy that is manifested in and manifesting the entire creation. Ramakrishna tells us:

To my Divine Mother I prayed only for pure love. I offered flowers at Her Lotus Feet and prayed to Her: "Mother, here is Thy virtue, here is Thy vice. Take them both and grant me only pure love for Thee. Here is Thy knowledge, here is Thy ignorance. Take them both and grant me only pure love for Thee. Here is Thy purity, here is Thy impurity. Take them both, Mother, and grant me only pure love for Thee. Here is Thy dharma, here is Thy adharma. Take them both, Mother, and grant me only pure love for Thee."[4]

The child is the creation of that ecstatic, stainless, motiveless pure love. It is that pure love in the heart and soul that give birth to the divine child. It is that pure love that leads the soul right into the heart of the godhead.

Let us begin our journey into the pure heart of the godhead, the pure heart of the Mother, the pure heart of Brahman—pure love and pure joy—with this extraordinary passage from the *Taittiriya Upanishad,* in which the child's secret is made clear.

Once Bhrigu Varuni went to his father Varuna and said: "Father, explain to me the mystery of Brahman."

Then his father spoke to him of the food of the earth, of the breath of life, of the one who sees, of the one who hears, of the mind that knows, and of the one that speaks. And he further said to him: "Seek to know him from whom all beings have come, by whom all they live, and unto whom they all return. He is Brahman."

So Bhrigu went and practiced *tapas,* spiritual prayer....

After this he went again to his father and said: "Father, explain further to me the mystery of Brahman." To him his father answered: "Seek to know Brahman by *tapas,* by prayer, because Brahman is prayer."

So Bhrigu goes and practices *tapas,* and first he thought that Brahman was life, then that Brahman was mind. He goes back to his father, who tells him again: "Seek to know Brahman by *tapas,* by prayer, because Brahman is prayer."

So Bhrigu went and practiced *tapas,* spiritual prayer. Then he thought that Brahman was reason: for from reason all beings have come, by reason they all live, and unto reason they all return.

He went again to his father, asked the same question, and received the same answer.

Bhrigu's father continues to tell him: "You must go back and pray some more, work some more, suffer some more, and renounce some more, because you still don't know what Brahman is!" And so he goes and practices spiritual prayer. And at last Bhrigu sees:

> And then he saw that Brahman is joy: for FROM JOY ALL BEINGS HAVE COME, BY JOY THEY ALL LIVE, AND UNTO JOY THEY ALL RETURN.[5]

This is the divine infinite joy that is the essence of the Mother and of her child. "And then he saw that Brahman is joy. For from joy, all beings have come." As one of Ramprasad's poems says:

> How are you trying, O my mind, to know the nature
>   of God?
> You are groping like a madman locked in a dark
>   room.
> He is grasped through ecstatic love; how can you
>   fathom Him without it?[6]

Ramakrishna makes clear that the child enjoys this ecstatic love in all kinds and modes of worship: "An ecstatic lover of God enjoys Him in different ways. Sometimes he says 'O God, you are the lotus and I am the bee,' and sometimes he says 'O God, you are the ocean of Satchidananda and I am fish.' Sometimes, again, the lover of God says, 'I am your dancing girl.' He thinks of himself as the friend or the handmaid. He looks on God himself sometimes as a child, as Yasodha [Krishna's nurse] and sometimes as husband, or as the gopis."

Ramakrishna knows the secret of the universe: that the Mother is joy, and the child is free to adore the divine in all ways, even as another child.

Child imagery pervades the attempts of many mystical traditions to describe the highest consciousness. A great Tibetan master, Dudjom Rinpoche, was asked to describe what enlightened consciousness is like. He said:

> Whatever perceptions arise, you should be like a little child going into a beautifully decorated temple; . . .

A marvelous image for the true free being in so amazing, so astonishing a world.

> [H]e looks, but grasping does not enter into his perception at all. So you leave everything fresh, natural, vivid, and unspoiled. When you leave each thing in its own state, then its shape doesn't change, its color doesn't fade, and its glow does not disappear. Whatever appears is unstained by any grasping, so then all that you perceive arises as the naked wisdom of [the nature of mind], which is the indivisibility of luminosity and emptiness.[7]

"Whatever perceptions arise, you should be like a little child going into a beautifully decorated temple. . . . Grasping does not enter into perception at all." So everything that arises, everything that happens, is left exactly as it is. The child-consciousness, the child-mind, the free being, is so perfect, so full and self-contained that everything can be left fresh, natural, vivid, and unspoiled, because no grasping has entered into the perception of it. So everything is free to be completely itself, everything is seen and loved as a fully opened rose. Dudjom Rinpoche goes on to describe what happens if the child-mind does not grasp after anything: "When you leave each thing in its own state, then its shape doesn't change." You're not mutilating anything, you're not possessing, you're not interpreting. You're not manipulating or exploiting. You're not trying to make it part of your "biography," your plan or program.

"Its color doesn't fade"—because death and time have not entered into the perception. You are seeing with the "unborn mind." To the highest perception, the child-mind in the heart, nothing is born and nothing dies. Everything exists only in the eternal present. When the child's mind is watching and looking and being, then everything is perceived with that naked "unborn" (because deathless) truth, that naked unborn eternal sweetness and pure intensity, as eternally fresh, unspoiled and unspoilable, as living light-matter! "Its color doesn't fade and its glow does not disappear," because everything appears literally and actually *soaked,* transparent with the divine light visibly instinct, the sweet soft fire of Shakti.

To the awakened child, everything reveals itself as nothing other than the Mother appearing in different masks. The child returns to origin, and sees everything in its original, final, perfect Mother-state. The divine child sees the divine-child-world-self, sees directly what he or she is—the Mother herself in a body, seeing and loving. One with the Mother who is One, the child is free to play, in all beings and all events. To the perceptions of the child-mind, reality reveals its mandala of perfect awareness and bliss, all things are seen in that aspect of absolute ecstatic perfection. Samsara and nirvana, the world of illusion and that of liberation, are known as always interpenetrating, as one and both together in the Mother, as the nature of the mind.

As Dudjom Rinpoche says: "Whatever appears is unstained by any grasping, so that all that you perceive arises as the naked wisdom of the nature of mind, which is the indivisibility of luminosity and emptiness." That is an exact scientific, sober, and lucid description of what mystic consciousness at that level is actually like. The world at first disappears, then reappears. When it reappears, having disappeared into the light, it reappears with the light saturating everything in it, and seen as the light show it is. That gives everything an indescribable poignancy, sweetness and beauty, which the child-heart opens to completely, and embraces, loves, and celebrates.

The Taoists, especially Lao Tzu and Chuang Tzu, have their own exquisite and profound understanding of this child-mind. Following in Ramakrishna's spirit are these three quotations from the *Tao Te Ching:*

> Carrying vitality and consciousness,
> embracing them as one,
> can you keep them from parting?
> Concentrating energy,
> making it supple,
> can you be like an infant?

> Purifying hidden perception,
> can you make it flawless? ...
> As understanding reaches everywhere,
> can you be innocent?[8]

> Knowing the male, keep the female;
> Be humble to the world.
> Be humble to the world, and eternal power never
>     leaves,
> returning again to innocence.[9]

Finally, this profound quotation, in which the secret of the relationship to the divine feminine is contained:

> The world has a beginning
> that is the mother of the world.
> Once you've found the mother,
> thereby you know the child.
> Once you know the child,
> you return to keep the mother,
> not perishing though the body die.
> Close your eyes, shut your doors,
> and you do not toil all your life.
> Open your eyes, carry out your affairs,
> and you are not saved all your life.
> Seeing the small is called clarity,
> keeping flexible is called strength.
> Using the shining radiance,
> you return again to the light,
> not leaving anything to harm yourself.
> This is called entering the eternal.[10]

The Mother of the World is the Void, the Tao, the Inexpressible, the Goddess—whatever name you give to it; it is the light itself. Coming to know that light, you come to know that you are the child of that light. "Once you know the child, you return to keep the mother"—to keep contact always through peace, stability, calm, purification, discipline, and through resting in the nature of your essence with that mother. You enter the eternal in time, and live in time as the eternal and know time is the game and emanation of the eternal. "Once you know the mother, you return to keep the mother, not perishing, though the body die."

There is another aspect of this transmission of sacred divine childhood which is essential and which is also very much present in the life of Ramakrishna. If you read carefully the account of M. in *The Gospel of Sri Ramakrishna,* you will see that at many moments Ramakrishna is naked. He takes off all his clothes and dances. He behaves with the artlessness, sweetness, naughtiness, mischief, hilarity and wildness of an ebullient, ecstatic child. There is a photograph of Ramakrishna which reminds me very much of photographs I have seen of yogis, of Kogis, Yamomamis, and aborigines.

Ramakrishna's *sadhana,* extremely intricate as it was, in all the different religions and all the different tantric disciplines, actually took him back to that aboriginal state where he was, like the Kogis, Yamomamis and aborigines, in complete, simple, naked contact with the entire universe. This is his message: strip yourself of everything but her so that you can become completely one with her, and so by being one with her, move effortlessly as her child in all dimensions, led from experience to experience, game to game, revelation to revelation. Want nothing but pure love of her, do not seek any powers or influence, only pure love of her, and know that if that were all you wanted, then everything would just flow to you, through you, and for you, and that there would never be anything left undone, because it would be she who was doing it. All protection would be yours, all feasts, all love, all knowledge. She would appear at every moment and at every event to guide you through, to see you home. As Ramakrishna said: "I prayed to the Divine Mother, 'O Mother, I want Thee and nothing else.' I knew that by realizing Her I should get everything."

Our civilization is doomed because we have abused the child within us and outside of us. Our civilization has an epidemic of child abuse, because we have killed the child in ourselves and kill it literally around us. We've killed the sacred child, we've killed the divine child, and unless we restore to ourselves and to everyone else this opportunity of divine childhood, which can only be done by embracing the sacred feminine and by having a relationship with the Divine Mother, and by becoming a mother to our own inner divine child through sacred processes and discipline, we will die out.

The following passage from *Voices of the First Day* is about childhood, the childhood of the aborigines. This description of the aborigines' vision of motherhood and childhood is so crucial, because it embraces the entire creation and leaves no aspect of it out. Ramakrishna would have recognized and saluted it.

> Without exception, the earliest Europeans to catch a glimpse of traditional Aboriginal life noted the boundless joy, exuberance, and independence of the children. No other people seemed to be as lenient or indulgent toward children as Australian Aborigines, and many anthropologists have declared it to be the most child-centered society they have ever observed. As soon as a newborn infant returns to the camp with its mother, he or she becomes the unchallenged center of attention. Older relatives and siblings as well as the parents continually shower the child with affection. From the beginning, a number of kin provide parental support. Although the child's actual parents have primary responsibility, the child's relationships spread through the entire clan or camp group.[11]

When an aborigine mother gives birth, she scoops out a piece of the earth and the baby is delivered into this hollowed-out place in the earth. The first thing that the newborn feels is this elemental, pure wild contact with this womb-like hollow in the earth. The child is linked to that piece of earth for the rest of its life; it is his or her sacred place and place of welcome. So, from the very first moment, the connection with nature and matter and with the whole universe is made absolutely clear in its immanent aspect, as well as its transcendental one. And we think *ours* is an advanced culture! From that moment on, the child grows up in a culture in which relationships extend far beyond the family to everyone in that culture. The deep connection, not only with nature, but with all the beings with which it lives, is made obvious and exhilarating to the child.

> Children are never allowed to cry for any length of time; the parents and the entire clan see that their discomforts are quickly soothed or alleviated. Small children are breast-fed on demand, and they continue to suckle for three to five years. In spite of this, breastfeeding is not a burden on the mother, since a number of female relatives often participate in a multiple nursing arrangement.

What does this tell us? We are hearing the way in which the Divine Mother would work in a human society, if it truly were a human society. The child, as he or she was born into this environment, would be given every conceivable sign of tenderness, affection, connection, and of mystical truth. Everything would be given to the child because the child is the foundation of the entire experience of life, its foundation and, as we have seen, its goal.

> In a baby's early months, many women nurse and care for [the child]. Older women, especially the grandmothers, often have older infants suck a clear fluid that women can produce even after menopause.[12]

So mothering goes on and on. No one is left out of the great experience of mothering a child. This next passage is an amazing description of the way the wallaby mothers its child, and in it is a great clue about the Divine Mother, about the extreme nature of her unconditional love.

Because they live in total contact with the Divine Mother in both her transcendent and immanent aspects, the aborigines know that they are given clues about how to live their lives from all the plants, rocks, and animals around them. They are not in a state of arrogance, they don't believe that human consciousness is the only one. They know that they are given the whole universe as a teaching, a series of signs. One of their greatest achievements is to realize that nature is full of examples to human beings of how to live life most completely and richly. And that is why, when it comes to motherhood, the aborigines worship the wallaby; for in its nature the wallaby gives them the most moving example of "mothering," and aboriginal mothers enter into direct contact with its dreamtime aspect:

> At birth the newborn wallaby, like other marsupials, crawls into the mother's pouch and remains there for many months, sucking at will. In contrast, placental mammals must drop from the womb to the ground in a permanent and abrupt separation from the mother; often they must compete and struggle for the mother's nipple. A marsupial mother licks the in-pouch infant's "bottom" when it defecates, and drinks its urine, thus keeping the pouch clean and redigesting the nutrients.

That is so tender, that is the Divine Mother as a wallaby, showing us the immensity of her tenderness.

> The animal's complete, undisdaining intimacy and the love of the mother for the newborn serve as a Dreamtime archetype for Aboriginal motherhood.[13]

Here are a people so in love with the world that they see in the way in which a wallaby cleans its child's bottom and keeps it close to its breast a symbol of how the mother should treat the child with total acceptance, tenderness, and generosity, keeping it close to herself, giving it through that "undisdaining intimacy" a complete connection with love, with the earth and sky, with the dreamtime, with both the transcendent *and* immanent sacredness of life. From that experience of childhood, all the other initiations of aboriginal society flow naturally, because the primary foundation of sacred unity has been established.

On this journey through the transcendent and the immanent, let's return to a few moments with Ramakrishna in which
this understanding of divine childhood and of the direct relation between mother and child is taken to a profound and luminous intensity.

One must have for God the yearning of a child. The child
sees nothing but confusion when the mother is away. You
may try to cajole him by putting a sweetmeat in his hand;
but he will not be fooled. He only says "No, I want to go
to my mother." One must feel such yearning for God. . . .
How restless a child feels for its mother! Nothing can make
him forget his mother.[14]

Pray to the Divine Mother with a longing heart. Her vision
dries up all craving . . . and completely destroys all attachment. . . . It happens instantly if you think of Her as your
own mother. She is by no means a godmother. She is your
own mother. With a yearning heart persist in your demands
on Her. The child holds to the skirt of its mother and begs
a penny of her to buy a kite. Perhaps the mother is gossip-
ing with her friends. At first she refuses to give the penny
and says to the child: "No, you can't have it. Your daddy
has asked me not to give you money. . . . You will get into
trouble if you play with a kite now." The child begins to cry
and will not give up his demand. Then the mother says to
her friends, "Excuse me a moment. Let me pacify this child."
Immediately she unlocks the cash-box with a click and throws
the child a penny.

    You too must force your demand on the Divine Mother.
She will come to you without fail.[15]

"One must have for God the yearning of a child." With a
yearning heart—the heart of a child—persist, like a child, in
your demands on the Mother. The real relationship with the
Mother is radically, nakedly simple—heart to heart, child to
mother. No intermediaries are ever needed. "She is your own
Mother . . . She will come to you without fail." Keeping fresh

a childlike (aboriginal) faith in her, holding, even in extreme darkness and difficulty, to the *certainty* that the Mother of the universe is also our own unfailingly loving mother, anxious in all moments and in all situations to feed us with bliss and knowledge. That is the clue of transforming into her divine child, the clue to realizing her paradise of divine childhood here on earth, the clue to becoming a living transmitter of the energy of her love. This demands a radical simplification of the whole being, a commitment—with the intensity of a child—to pure joy and pure delight, pure gratitude, as far as possible in every situation and on every occasion. For one who lives like this, Ramakrishna assures us, the Mother will do everything. But, he warns us: "God doesn't take entire responsibility for a devotee unless that devotee is *completely intoxicated with ecstatic love*" (my italics). Unless we are "completely intoxicated with ecstatic love"—as a child is in the presence of its mother—how can the divine always be present to us? How can the bliss-essence of all things and all events stand naked in front of us if we are not naked to it?

Ramakrishna adds, "At a feast it is only a child whom one takes by the hand and seats at his place." The Mother will take us by the hand and seat each of us at our own unique place of honor at the feast of being, when we all have become "as a little child," have learned how to utterly give ourselves up—all the different parts of our being: body as well as heart, mind, and soul, and body, heart, mind, and soul all together, one in burning love of her, to her, and to her great dance in the universe. Then one with ourselves, we are one with her and all things. We are home, and all things radiate back to us our own secure peace. Listen again to Ramakrishna on divine childhood. Each time he speaks of it in his *Gospel,* he gives us another priceless indication, another inestimably precious clue:

> When the dry branch of a coconut palm drops to the ground, it leaves only a mark on the trunk indicating that once there was a branch at that place. In like manner, he who has attained God keeps only an appearance of ego; there remains

in him only a semblance of anger and lust. He becomes like
a child. A child has no attachment to the three gunas....
He becomes as quickly detached from a thing as he becomes
attached to it. You can cajole him out of a cloth worth five
rupees with a doll worth an anna, though he might say at
first with great determination: "No, I won't give it to you.
My daddy bought it for me." Again, all persons are the same
to a child. He has no feeling of high and low in regard to
persons. So he doesn't discriminate about caste. If his mother
tells him that a particular man should be regarded as an
elder brother, the child will eat from the same plate with
him, though the man may belong to the low caste of a black-
smith. The child does not know hate, or what is holy or
unholy.[16]

Listen again.

[T]here are signs that a man has had a vision of God. A man
who has seen God sometimes behaves like a madman: he
laughs, weeps, dances, and sings. Sometimes he behaves like
a child, a child five years old—guileless, generous, without
vanity, unattached to anything, not under the control of any
of the gunas, always blissful. Sometimes he behaves like a
ghoul: he doesn't differentiate between things pure and things
impure; he sees no difference between things clean and things
unclean. And sometimes he is like an inert thing, staring
vacantly: he cannot do any work; he cannot strive for anything.[17]

The child forgets everything when he plays with his toys.
Try to cajole him away from play with a sweetmeat; you will
not succeed. He will only eat a bit of it. When he relishes
neither the sweetmeat nor his play, then he says, "I want to
go to my mother." He doesn't care for the sweetmeat anymore. If a man whom he doesn't know and has never seen
says to the child, "Come along; I shall take you to your
mother," the child follows him, the child will go with anyone who will carry him to his mother.[18]

This is Ramakrishna speaking as a child to the Divine Mother, nakedly and directly, overheard by his disciples:

> The Master was in samadhi. He began to come gradually down to the normal plane. His mind was still filled with the consciousness of the Divine Mother. In that state he was speaking to Her like a small child making importunate demands on his mother. He said in a piteous voice: "Mother, why haven't You revealed to me that form of Yours, the form that bewitches the world? I pleaded with You so much. But You wouldn't listen to me. You act as You please."
>
> The voice in which these words were said was very touching.
>
> He went on: "Mother, one needs faith. Away with this wretched reasoning! Let it be blighted! One needs faith— faith ... childlike faith. The mother says to her child, 'A ghost lives there,' and the child is firmly convinced that the ghost is there. Again, the mother says to the child, 'A bogy man is there,' and the child is sure of it. Further, the mother says, pointing to a man, 'He is your elder brother,' and the child believes that man is one hundred twenty-five percent his brother. One needs faith."[19]

> God has the nature of a child. A child is sitting with gems in the skirt of his cloth. Many a person passes by him along the road. Many of them pray to him for gems. But he hides the gems with his hands and says, turning away his face, "No, I will not give any away." But another man comes along. He doesn't ask for the gems, and yet the child runs after him and offers him the gems, begging him to accept them.[20]

Of all the images of spiritual mastery, as I have said, that of a child is the most magical and mysterious, and the most difficult to grasp. It is the key of keys, the secret of secrets. After enlightenment the Buddha entered into child-mind, the kingdom of primal wonder and innocence. Ramana Maharshi, as well as Ramakrishna, tells us that the nature of God is child-

like, and that the realized being is like a child at peace in the
womb of the Mother, knowing he or she is fed at every moment
by the grace and the light of the Mother. The Christian alchemists
tell us that when in our being we have completed the sacred
marriage of opposites, of the male and the female, the sun and
the moon, the dark and the light, the conscious and the unconscious, we become a sacred androgyne child, free of reason's
madness and the ego's frivolous gloom, free of all conscious
and unconscious barriers and definitions, mysterious and complete as reality itself, at one with its mystery in the ground of
our perfected being.

Christ said: "Unless you become again as little children, you
cannot enter or gain the kingdom of heaven." The "as" in that
sentence is revelatory. None of the supreme mystics are talking
about a regression into fantasy. None of them are talking about
an abandonment of discrimination. They all imply proper self-
protection and the hard earned insights of adult suffering, work,
and sacrifice that are necessary to survive in the world. What
they are pointing to is a state of conscious, lucid childlikeness,
that is the most luminous possible state opposite of regression.
It contains, while completing and transcending, all other forms
of knowledge and wisdom. As Blake said: "Unorganized innocence, an impossibility."

This state of consciously reclaimed childhood, in which all
the passion, pure sensuality, and lyricism of the lost or hidden
child is consciously reintegrated into a purified and organized
adult awareness is the end of yoga and the attainment of the
kingdom of heaven itself. To be a child in this glorious sense is
to be in heaven here, to be one with the Tao, to possess the
Grail, to be in union with the Mother. Lewis Thompson wrote:
"The ever new, magical universe is continually reborn in the
child. Only the grownup was banished from Eden. The child
eats of the Tree of Life. For him or her, the laws of the universe
are magical. This childhood and this magic, the Christ restores."
In a supremely beautiful passage in the ninth chapter of his *De
Calculo,* the great Christian mystic Ruysbroeck wrote:

How great is the difference between the secret friend [the yogi] and the child? For the friend makes only loving, living, but reasoned ascents towards God, but the child presses on to lose his own life upon the summits in that simplicity which does not know itself. When we transcend ourselves and become in our ascent toward God so simple that the bare, supreme love can lay hold on us, then we cease, and we and all our self will die in God. In this death, we become the hidden children of God and find a new life within us.

When we birth this child in us, the child that we become lives in the fullness of God, in which there is, as Ruysbroeck again says,

> [T]ranquility according to his essence, activity according to his nature, absolute repose, absolute fecundity.

The child, in fact, becomes the *mother* of a stream of sacred works. Only the divine child can be at once reposed and fecund, because in its own intimate being, the child unites Shiva and Shakti, male and female, silence and force, and is then released to dance for God, in God, as a part of God. To be like this is at once to enter, to be, and to recreate in and around itself, paradise.

Around those who have become like children, miracles dance. As divine children we can do anything; or, rather, anything can be done by the Mother through us.

This understanding of the divine child is essential for the transformation through the sacred feminine now, in 1995, as we face the end of nature. I believe that all the religious systems, including the systems of initiation by masters and avatars, have failed us, because they have all prevented us from a direct, ecstatic, complete relationship with the Divine Mother that transcends all creeds and religions and so from a direct birthing of the divine child within us. The Mother is asking us now, really *demanding* that we enter into this direct relationship in order to become illumined, humble, and playful enough for her power to stream through us and really transform conditions in all the different arenas of the entire world. This cannot be overemphasized, because it is the entire clue to the relationship with the Divine Mother. Humility is the key, because only when everything is given up to her can she give everything to you. Ramakrishna used to pray again and again to have all the powers, occult and otherwise, taken from him, to be and know and live only in pure love for the Mother. Yet who was more powerful than this man who went about naked and danced on the steps of his tiny little room, and who, through a handful of disciples, permanently altered the religious imagination of humankind?

For many years, I did not understand this paradox. How could Ramakrishna have prayed to give up all powers and yet be so empowered to saturate the mind and heart of the world? But recently it has become clear to me. When Ramakrishna gave up all his own power for love of the Mother, the power of the Mother could then flow unbrokenly and ecstatically in continual play through him. As her child, her power was his. Total humility before her made Ramakrishna free to be transparent to the Mother, and transmit and radiate her at every moment and with every breath, and so create around him and for all those who love him, even now, her playground of miracle.

It is by each of us taking up Ramakrishna's challenge to be directly, ecstatically, and in radically humble wonder transparent to her, that the Mother will be able to work through us the wonder she is preparing for the world. The lamp of power will only be given to Aladdin, the child, for only Aladdin's heart is innocent and loving, and his will desires only the feast of God. The future of the human race will be made by the Mother and for the Mother by humble, illumined, playful divine children. No more masters, no more gurus, just us here together, her divine children recognizing each other's divinity, adoring each other's divinity, adoring the divinity in nature and working together with each of our divine identities and gifts to preserve and save the planet for her play to go on in it.

I wrote this poem this morning in an attempt to crystallize this teaching of childhood:

> *First, allow "reality" to leave, and the light to appear.*
> *Go out in the light, go out completely, and then*
>      *reappear*
> *as the arrived-here light, the light-matter Mother,*
> *giving birth to the child in eternity, in time,*
> *the complete divine human, the complete human*
>      *divine.*
> *The human as a completely humble being,*
> *Becomes empty enough to receive the purest gift of the*
>      *divine:*
> *its eternal childhood, its Krishna-ananda, its Kali-bliss,*
> *the apple suddenly irradiated with immortality.*
> *And then, the transcendentally innocent part of you,*
> *purified, exposed, merges with*
> *the transcendental innocence of God,*
> *so the wound of samsara closes and heals along that*
>      *perfect scar.*
> *Now, light and matter fold over into one dancing*
>      *light-matter,*
> *now, the world is lived, consciously, as divine play,*
> *as a mad, amazing game played beyond all known*
>      *rules,*
> *by a perfectly loving, illumined child*
> *with a Mother who is also a child,*
> *by a child in love with all other child-beings*
> *serving them with an awakened heart.*

As the divine child in us says in the *Taittiriya Upanishad*:

> Oh, the wonder of joy!
> I am the food of life, and I am he who eats the food of
>      life: I am the two in ONE.
> I am the first-born of the world of truth, born before
>      the gods, born in the centre of immortality.
> He who gives me is my salvation.

I am that food which eats the eater of the food.
I have gone beyond the universe, and the light of the
    sun is my light.[21]

All of our images of mastery—including "guruhood"—are
just the ego's constructions, the final illusions of samsara. When
we go beyond them, strip ourselves of them, and stop projecting them onto other people, we're compelled to face the nakedness of our actual relationship with the Divine Mother. In that
nakedness there is tremendous joy, humility, a tremendous strip-
ping-away of everything superficial. There is nothing left in the
universe but you and her. When that happens, the child is born,
there is laughter and wildness, power and dancing, ecstasy and
immortality; and at that moment you can become her secret
agent. When you are her secret agent, then everything will dance
around you—you have become a lens through which her nuclear
force radiates. You can be anybody at that moment; you don't
have to be a paid-up master or teacher, you can just be wherever you are in your life at that moment. She will be entering,
seeping through every crack in the cement around you, and all
things will be coming into their perfect synchronicity.

It is extremely important to understand exactly what the
sacred feminine is not—it is *not* power or achievement, it has
nothing to do with dominating others, it has nothing to do with
having millions of disciples. It has to do with entering into naked,
sweet, direct contact, and allowing yourself to be so completely
stripped of every illusion that the illusionless can be born in
you, the unborn can be born in you. At that moment, everything is revealed, *everything,* because you are free. And in her
and through her, you, her child, can accomplish anything.

As a completely free being, free of the illusion of mastery,
free of the need to achieve, free of ambition, free of any label,
caste, or creed, free of dogma and hierarchy—at that moment
you are free to play on all the registers of the Divine Mother's
music. You are free to run up and down all of her stairs of being.
Ramakrishna showed us how to get to this stage of awareness.

He showed us what to do. He showed us how amazing it would be to live there. He showed us what joy it is to live there. He spoke and danced tirelessly and gave from that miraculous place so that we would know where we are being taken. He appeared at the end of the nineteenth century as a sign of that total simplicity which began the human race, which can be seen in the aborigines, and to which the human race is now being returned, back-forward, in a massive agony of birth: "Oh Kali, my Mother full of bliss! Enchantress of the almighty Shiva! In Thy delirious joy Thou dancest, clapping Thy hands together."

Ramakrishna enshrines the astonishing possibilities that the Mother is revealing to us now.

## Questions and Answers

*What about Ramakrishna's attitude toward women? Isn't there something historically conditioned and unbalanced, to say the least, about his continual warning against "woman and gold"? And isn't there an aspect of the Divine Mother's teaching—the healing and transformation of the body—that Ramakrishna paid little attention to?*

There is undoubtedly a puritanical, body-despising, woman-fearing streak in Ramakrishna. It belongs to the times he grew up in and is the least useful part of his message. This streak may have been essential for him and may have enabled him to concentrate exclusively on his spiritual disciplines, but if erected into dogma now would add to exactly that puritanical ascetic baggage the Mother is now, I believe, asking us to abandon, to transcend. Ramakrishna didn't solve every human problem and there were no doubt aspects of him—even at the extraordinary stage he had reached—which remained conditioned and partial. Facing that squarely releases Ramakrishna from *our* need for him to be omniscient and makes us responsible for what we follow in his example or not.

Let us look for a moment at his attitude to women and see if there is something we can learn from it. I think we can all agree that the constant railing against "woman and gold" is, to say the least, unnecessary now; any misogyny, however "refined," belongs to the patriarchal system that now has to be dismantled. Similarly, I think that Ramakrishna on sexuality in general is one-sided; certainly the Mother has ways of divine sexual initiation that he may not have known, or may have, for his own reasons, not wanted to talk much about. I myself am certain that one of the major ways the Mother is going to transform the human race is by a reawakening of real tantric knowledge of the fundamental divine alchemical secrets hidden in sexuality when it is dedicated and consecrated to, and inspired by, soul-and-heart love. Ramakrishna himself alludes to these when he says "It is very honorable for husband and wife to assume the sacred roles of Bhairava and Bhairavi [Shiva and Parvati] in the tantric practice of sexual union." But as we know, Ramakrishna himself did not explore this territory, and does not speak of it in any detail.

Let us look at how Ramakrishna treated women. He may have withdrawn physically from his own wife, Sarada Devi, but it is also true that he adored, cherished, and initiated her at the highest levels and that she was directly inspired by him to carry on his work until her death. Sarada Devi's experience of Ramakrishna was not of a harsh macho ascetic, but of the sweetest of men, the most loving of teachers. Ramakrishna had a wide circle of women followers, and while he railed against prostitution in its religious aspects, he himself, when in ecstasy, revered prostitutes—whom Hindu society considered the lowest of the low—as direct vessels of the Divine Mother. On several occasions, in fact, he reports that the Divine Mother appeared to him in the form of a prostitute. Ramakrishna clearly was aware of the highest tantric teachings—where what is "holy" and what is not are both discarded and only the bliss-presence of the Mother in all things is known and worshipped.

Also, Ramakrishna had no particular attachment to his identity as a male. In fact, I think very few male saints, if any, have taken such daring and wild journeys into their femininity as he did (and perhaps had to, to become *one* with her). Ramakrishna lived for several months in the women's quarters, dressing as Radha, and as a little boy said to his mother, "I wish I could be reborn as a woman so I could experience total love for Krishna." Someone who acts and speaks like that has the deepest respect for the sacred feminine.

So, while I believe that we must now go beyond Ramakrishna's own injunctions against sexuality and "woman and gold" and see them as conditioned, I think we all have a great deal to learn from his actual *practice* of adoration of women

(and men), and his wholehearted, shameless childlike embrace
of his own feminine side.

On the highest level—where Ramakrishna lived, it must be
said, for the great majority of his later life—he shows us that
while being both masculine and feminine, he is also beyond
both as the divine child-sacred androgyne that we all secretly
are. In his testimony to this secret self of all of us, and his living out of this holy freedom so abandonedly, Ramakrishna
remains far beyond our contemporary understanding of "gender" and "role-playing" and is, I believe, a prophetic sign of
what we all could be. In this area, Ramakrishna's liberation
challenges, inspires, and welcomes us all.

*What do you think Ramakrishna's sexuality was?*

There are homoerotic overtones in his frankly ecstatic relationships with his young male disciples. I believe, however, that
Ramakrishna was in the highest state of divine love of the world,
and that characterizing his behavior according to Western psychological labels is unhelpful. Our task, I think, is to stretch
our hearts and minds and struggle to begin to imagine how
someone in such an exalted state would have seen and cherished other human beings as divine beings like himself. We
shouldn't try to "explain" his behavior from our level of consciousness. Until we feel Ramakrishna's bliss at a flower or a
river or a tree, we will not know what he felt when he looked
at one of his disciples or embraced him. Ramakrishna's entire
being became, I believe, Love's Body. For him all relationships
whatsoever were part of the continuing ecstatic experience of
the Divine.

This doesn't mean that there are no erotic overtones in them,
but that the Eros of such a being has become all but unimaginable to someone who has not yet undergone radical transformation; is an Eros, in fact, as different from that of normal
awareness as human consciousness is different from a jaguar's.
I don't think Ramakrishna's sweetness with his disciples on every

level was "unconsciously homosexual," I think it was entirely conscious, *super*-conscious, in fact, and directly divinely inspired, the kind of radical divine Eros that will be released in all of us, "gay" or "straight," when we too have grown Love's Body. What we are witnessing in Ramakrishna is the playful, unbounded, tender love toward others of the Divine Child, a love that is as free of dionysian excess and pornographic desire as it is of any kind of repression.

That said, Ramakrishna's courtship of Vivekananda does read like a love story, one of the greatest of all love stories, as sublime in its way as that of Rumi and Shams. Vivekananda was a marvelous young man, and Ramakrishna pursued him. He pursued him because Ramakrishna already knew who Vivekananda was and who he could become, and what an astonishing spiritual service he would do for the world. It was this luminous inner knowledge, rather than any "normal" kind of desire, that led Ramakrishna to pursue Vivekananda, and pursue him wildly. So wildly, in fact, that Vivekananda said to him, "If you go on pursuing me like this, you'll come down to the level of your consciousness' object," meaning himself. And Ramakrishna thought about it, because Ramakrishna was totally artless, and he said, "Oh, well, I'll think about that. I'll ask the Mother." So the next day he came back, beaming, and said to Vivekananda, "Well, I asked the Mother, and she said don't worry, it's only because I can see God in you that I love you so much. When I don't see God in you, I won't even look at you."

*What do you think Ramakrishna would have thought of Judaism?*

I think in Judaism Ramakrishna would see the Divine Mother liberally and gloriously illustrated in the vision of the *Shekinah,* in the shining of whose divine presence he would see, I think, one of the aspects of Shakti. He would see the wisdom in *Proverbs* and in many of the cabalistic traditions that is celebrated as feminine, as a feminine, nurturing, engendering power

that springs from the godhead. And I think he would find that
the great sacred idea of Judaism—that life itself can be made
sacred, can reveal its inherent sacredness through prayer and
ritual—is exactly what he believed. The rules and regulations
in Judaism are not really rules and regulations as I understand
them, but ways of bringing out the sacredness in each aspect
of reality, and enabling everyone to live in a constant state of
grace, in a constant sacred atmosphere. I think Judaism has a
more profound understanding of the sacredness and holiness
of ordinary life than almost any other religion, and in that sense
is very close to the Divine Mother and her revelation that *all* is
sacred and holy. I think Ramakrishna would be rather saddened
by Judaism's emphasis on its own preeminence as, indeed, he
was saddened by the emphasis of all the religions on their own
preeminence.

I think he must have learned something about Judaism
through his study of Christianity and reading the Bible, but I'm
not aware of him ever having gone through any specific Judaic
discipline. But I don't think that because he may not have *directly*
experienced the aborigines, the Yamomamis or the Kogis, or
Judaism, doesn't mean that he wasn't embracing, in every conceivable way, the vision and the wisdom in each of them. I do
think it's a pity that he didn't also experience Judaism, because
it might have prevented some of the lunacy of anti-semitism
that has afflicted, and still afflicts, this century. I'm sure that
Ramakrishna would have absolutely relished the opportunity
to meet with an illumined rabbi or Hasid. The Hasidic masters
that Buber talks about and Ramakrishna are very close in spirit!
They are probably dancing together right now in the heaven of
the Mother.

*How does the Vedantic practice of negation fit into Rama-
krishna's path of adoration?*

It helps to *purify* adoration. Ramakrishna is not saying get rid
of the negative philosophies, or the *neti-neti* path, or the ways

of really stripping everything and going into the light, but don't stop there. We all need to question, doubt, and discriminate a lot, because we are all tempted by various manifestations of our own hunger for joy or hunger for "experience." You must develop a strenuous, astringent, ironic, tough-minded, crucially intelligent understanding, otherwise, you're going to be lost from the beginning. But, if you get stuck there, then you're stuck in only one half of the truth, and so you should use that "negativity" to constantly purify and deepen your embrace of reality, to constantly clarify your embrace of reality and drive you deeper and deeper, more and more purely, into the arms of love. So, if you're taking the path of adoration and love, you use *neti-neti* and say, "This isn't love," "This isn't enough love," "This isn't deep enough love," "This isn't clear enough love, because the ego's still present, I'm still vain, I'm still proud." Purify, purify—not to "get out" of here, but to come more completely and totally *in,* to arrive here completely *present. Neti-neti* acts as a constant, acidic washing away of anything that prevents you from meeting the moment in ecstasy. Then you use all the powers of the human mind, not against reality, but to enable you to embrace reality with more complete truth.

Also, I think that the path of *neti-neti* can take you to a moment of transcendent awareness in which love of the highest kind is born. Ramakrishna said it better than I can, "To love is to know, and to know is to love." If you take the path of *bhakti,* you come to know the secrets of the Mother because they are flashed into the mind as it awakens in love to the heart-mind; and if you take the path of *jnana,* of *neti-neti,* of the Vedanta, you awaken to the presence of transcendent love in everything, to the fact that Brahman itself is love, bliss, and peace. You come to the same place. Ramakrishna again and again said, however, that for this age, devotion is much more helpful, because *jnana* is hard, and we are already very dry. What we need is more love, passion, and sensuous understanding; more "wallaby" intelligence, more blood, more sweat, more Mother-contact. We don't need more detachment, we are so overloaded with detachment. We are so detached we can't even tell what color eyes we have. That's why the wisdom of the Divine Mother, the sacred wisdom of connection, of adoration, is so essential to the survival of the human race. We have forgotten that we *have* bodies and are interdependent with *this* reality. Many of the seekers I know will be sitting in the lotus position when the forests finally burn away. Suddenly they'll feel they can't breathe; they can't get to the end of their meditation exercise. This will shock them; they won't have noticed that they're in a body. How crazy we have become!

Another way you can richly take the negative path is to turn it against itself, to "negate" negation, which will take you to adoration. You can set loose the dogs of doubt on doubt. You can take doubt, this great ravening beast that you've been trained to adore, and let it loose on doubt and doubt your doubting, follow it to its root in panic, fear, and anxiety. At that moment you unmask yourself, and realize that disillusion is the last illusion. *Neti-neti* then turns into an activity of praise, because you unmask all the reasons you're giving yourself for not praising, for not being grateful, and reveal them as neurotic, hysterical, and ungrateful, and are free, at last, to go beyond them.

*You mention Lawlor's book* Voices of the First Day. *Are you suggesting that we simply scrap modern civilization?*

I think that it is pointless to imagine going back to an age before agriculture, but I think it's also extremely important to see what a sacred life the aborigines, for example, have made and to learn as much as we can from their initiations, their ways of mothering, from the ways in which they treat sexuality. They're incredibly free without being indecent. They have what we can hardly imagine—a sacred vision of the body, an authentically and comprehensively sacred vision that blesses desire.

Why Lawlor's book is important is because it gives a very complete picture of what origin is like, of how a connection with the Mother translates into living social, tribal, and meta-physical terms, all the way "through" a society. Looking at the Mother-richness in *their* culture could help us at this moment reimagine maternal forms for *our* culture, how to recreate it, perhaps along tribal lines, or in groups, or in wholly new essentially feminine patterns of learning and of being together and living together. Unless we find these feminine forms of awakening, sharing, and developing together, we're not going to survive. Our old individualism is as barren as its secret brother— slavery to political and spiritual authority. New "feminine" forms of mutual respect, honoring, and cooperation are needed at every level of society. And our "elders," the tribal shamans, the Kogis and aborigines, can help us.

We need to reimagine and recreate a world in which connection would be vivid in every aspect of life, in which all of life would be a dance of connection with others and the real divine world around us. The Mother is the force that *makes real,* in every sense, that helps us out of our heads and into the reality of our bodies, our relationships, and the profound responsibilities we have to everyone and everything. The aborigines are masters of this knowledge and we have a great deal to learn from them.

*How did Ramakrishna relate to what we might call the "dark side" of the Mother, Kali?*

There is nothing at all sentimental about Ramakrishna's vision of the Mother, nothing in it of the watered-down "New Age" image. One of his favorite songs to Kali begins:

> *Who is the Woman yonder who lights the field of*
>       *battle?*
> *Darker her body gleams even that the darkest storm-*
>       *cloud.*
> *And from Her teeth there flash the lightning's blinding*
>       *flames!*[22]

Ramakrishna knew that his Mother Kali was the destroyer as well as the creator, as capable of overwhelming catastrophic violence as of tenderness. One of his favorite visions of the Mother—a vision he often recounted—was of a young pregnant woman rising out of the Ganges. The vision begins idyllically: Ramakrishna asks us to imagine an astonishingly beautiful pregnant woman rising serenely out of the sunlit waters of the sacred river. Next, this beautiful woman gives birth to a beautiful child on the banks of the Ganges. Then what happens? The woman tears the child limb from limb, eats it, wipes the blood from her mouth, and then goes back into the Ganges, as serenely as she emerged from it.

We can see from this that Ramakrishna's vision of the Mother did not in any way shirk the rage, destruction, and madness of the Divine Mother's play. He was aware that the Mother was also death and destruction, time devouring all things, the horror of evil and the havoc that it causes. Ramakrishna knew that it was the Mother who is appearing in all the roles in this world-drama, including the roles of the cruel, greedy, and scheming ones, those who keep the "plot" of history going. He knew that the Mother who gave him so many revelations and joys was also the Mother who gave him the throat cancer that killed him.

The bliss and absolute childlike confident radiance that Ramakrishna is trying to communicate to us is not based on only a partial, wish-fulfilling fantasy of the Mother—such bliss and faith could not long withstand either the ordeals of genuine transformation or of life itself. The bliss and joy that Ramakrishna knew and is trying to birth in us are unshakable and absolute precisely because they embrace *all* aspects of the Mother, including the "dark" one, and refuse to identify with only those aspects that make the ego happy. This bliss and joy is all-embracing, as nondual as she is. The divine child sings through disaster as well as success, devastation as well as revelation, agony as well as peace, knowing through his or her absolute mystic intimacy with the Mother that all things are done by her, in her wisdom and in her sometimes terrifying joy.

One of the fastest ways to enter nonduality, as Ramakrishna knew, is to surrender to the Dark Mother and allow her to trample your every construction and illusion. This kind of terrible, agonizing destruction can be the fiercest possible and most transformatory grace, because it can dissolve in fast blinding anguish a lifetime's blocks and delusions and can uncover the roots of a faith deeper than reason and a love far wilder than anything that could spring from "personal" happiness; this is the faith and love, in fact, of the deathless Self. Understanding the transformatory power of suffering at the hand of the Dark Mother and the power that comes of offering that suffering again and again to the alchemical wisdom of the Dark Mother, are some of the most essential kinds of spiritual wisdom needed today.

Are we not living in Kali's time? And isn't the agony the world writhes in also potentially—if we can confront, accept, and use it fearlessly—an agony of birth? And where will we learn the kind of wild mystic courage we will need to help turn dying into birth if we have not embraced the dark as well as the light powers of the Divine Mother? If we are aware of her laws of transformatory paradox, terror can become love, disaster turns into grace, nightmare into liberation—in the end of a civilization flowers the beginning of dawn. Only embracing the Dark Mother can take us right into the heart of the paradox of life itself, of nature, and of human history. Dying can force us to find immortality and our destructiveness can compel us to remake ourselves and our world—but only if we have first surrendered to the Supreme Magician and Alchemist of Paradox, the Mother—Mother Kali, Killer and Preserver—and known the nondual bliss that is the fuel of the courage that comes from fearless acceptance of the terms of this human experience: death, pain, suffering, humiliation, loss, ordeal after ordeal. This nondual bliss of acceptance *is* the Mother herself—her gift of immortal freedom to anyone brave enough to consent to being torn apart by and in her.

As Don Juan said to Carlos Castaneda, "The universe will

destroy you, but in the process it will teach you something very interesting." What it will teach you, if you allow it to, is that you *are* it. Once you have learned in the deepest part of yourself to embrace the dark aspect of the Mother, you are beginning to be free to become the Mother in all her aspects and to find in whatever happens to you her bliss, her power, her strength, her unquenchable ecstasy. Because you are *death* as well as life, you will no longer fear death; because you *are* horror as well as peace, horror will no longer abase and crumble you; because you discover that humiliation is just one of your undergarments, you will no longer cringe before it. You will in fact be free—the Mother's divine child dancing to her rhythm in her vast dance-drama, the universe dancing in her, as her, for her.

> All creation is the sport of my mad Mother Kali;
> By Her maya the three worlds are bewitched.
> Mad is She and mad is Her Husband . . .
> None can describe Her loveliness, Her glories,
>     gestures, moods;
> Shiva, with the agony of the poison in His throat,
> Chants Her name again and again.[23]

Ramakrishna is saying to us that the poison is in all our throats, too. Chanting her glorious name will give us the ecstatic strength to endure, accomplish, and transform anything.

*How would Ramakrishna advise us in contacting the Divine Mother in the midst of raising children?*

Ramakrishna had tremendous reverence for the difficulties and opportunities of ordinary life. He had many householder devotees. There is a beautiful story of an old woman coming to him and saying, "I'm hopeless, I can't pray, I can't meditate, I can't do anything. I'm going to die soon, so please give me, in about five minutes, something that I can do." He said, "I will, of course. Who do you love most?" She said, "Oh, I love my granddaughter most." He said, "Well, that's it. Go back home, don't do anything, don't go to Benares, don't bother about pilgrimage or anything like that. Just love your granddaughter as a Divine Mother." I think that is one of the most profound teachings ever given to humanity. It is really saying that you don't have to go anywhere, you don't have to change the external details of your life. Just get on your knees, visibly or invisibly, to everyone in your life and start worshipping them as the living divine. From the receptivity, tenderness, and love born from that, from the service born from that, from the sense of sacredness in every moment, would come realization. I think that is the deepest teaching to a householder that I have heard. Take where karma has brought you, use it, work with it, celebrate yourself as the divine, worship everyone in your life as emissaries of the divine, and serve everyone in that holy simple spirit, and you will achieve realization, because you will be continually wearing away your false self and its false separations, being continually in a state of love and worship.

*What did Ramakrishna feel about the guru system? Wasn't he himself a guru?*

There are two distinct and separate teachings in Ramakrishna on this subject. The first is the traditional Hindu one: adore the guru as God and follow all his instructions, etc. etc. But there is a second quite different, more demanding, higher, and for these times, more useful teaching that can also be gleaned from his life and words. I believe that we are at the end of the guru system and that its current abuses disqualify it from the business of serious spiritual transformation. The next five years will see a blizzard of financial and sexual scandals which I am certain will make this point painfully clear even to those who now believe implicitly in the guru system and are prepared to fight dirty to preserve it. The Mother is trying to release us from all religious and political prisons, and the guru system is destined, I believe, to be destroyed by her, as it is no longer efficient and is potentially damaging and limiting.

In the second teaching that can be gleaned from Rama-krishna we see what the Mother is preparing for the human race—*direct transmission* without intermediaries, beyond the "authority" of priests and gurus and churches, *direct initiation* of everyone, within the terms of and in the ground of their own personalities and lives. Ramakrishna repeatedly stresses how essential it is to go *directly* to the Mother, with the urgency and passionate demanding faith of a child and the certainty that a cared-for child has of being loved and heard and understood. He again and again points out how the Mother will come *directly* to anyone who calls on her with authentic soul-passion. Over and over again he makes it clear that the Mother can teach the highest secrets and give the most comprehensive revelations *directly.*

After all, as Ramakrishna often delights in pointing out, it was the Mother who taught an illiterate young man (himself) all the secrets contained in the *Tantras* and *Puranas,* and taught this knowledge directly, heart to heart, experience by experience, revelation after revelation. Does the Mother of the Universe, and of all things and beings in it, really need intermediaries to guide her children through? Of course not! All powers are always hers, and Ramakrishna assures us that anyone who casts him- or herself on the direct help of the Mother will receive it more wisely, richly, abundantly, and completely than he or she could possibly now imagine. The person taking the direct path to the Mother will be guided by her directly—that Ramakrishna knows from his own experience. There will be partial guides and spiritual friendships—her gifts— along the way, but no need whatever for any "guru." The Mother is the guru, and life is her medium of instruction.

I think if Ramakrishna were alive now and witnessing the Babylonian excesses of the guru system he sometimes praised, he would realize that it was now dangerously corrupt and should be scrapped. He himself intensely disliked being called a guru; he would say, "I am not a guru, I am a *child,*" and he would also often say, "God—Satchidananda—is the only guru." He said: "A man cannot be a guru. Everything happens by the will of God." He also said, most memorably:

> Three words—"master," "teacher," and "father"—prick me like thorns. I am the son of God, His eternal child. How can I be a "father"? God alone is the Master and I am His instrument. He is the Operator and I am the machine.
>
> If somebody addresses me as guru, I say to him: "Go away, you fool! How can I be a teacher?" There is no teacher except Satchidananda. There is no refuge except Him. He alone is the Ferryman to take one across the ocean of the world.[24]

Ramakrishna was also acutely aware of something which most Western seekers who have bought a cheap Hollywood version of the Indian trip are not—that a lot, perhaps most, of those we now call "enlightened gurus" are nothing of the sort. They are not divine or divinized beings at all, but extremely powerful occult manipulators, who through certain kinds of spiritual exercises have attained certain *siddhis,* or powers, which enable them to dominate the minds and actions of others. They masquerade as "gods," giving "experiences" and doing "miracles."

Ramakrishna saw such black (or gray) magicians all around him and denounced them passionately; for him occult powers of this kind were disgusting. One day, he tells us, he was asked by his nephew Hriday to ask the Mother for occult powers. "The Divine Mother," he recounts, "at once showed me a vision. A middle-aged prostitute, about forty years old, appeared and sat with her back to me. She had large hips and wore a black-bordered sari. Soon she was covered with filth. The Mother showed me that occult powers are as abominable as the filth of that prostitute." He goes on:

> People with a little occult power gain such things as name and fame. *Many of them want to follow the profession of guru, gain people's recognition and make disciples and devotees.* Men say of such a guru: "Ah! He is having a wonder-

ful time! How many people visit him! He has many disciples and followers."

In fact, Ramakrishna makes clear such a teacher is in great
spiritual danger, and not in any way capable of leading his or
her disciples to freedom, for the simple reason that he or she is
not in any way free. He goes on:

> The profession of a teacher is like that of a prostitute. It is
> the selling of oneself for the trifle of money, honour, and
> creature comforts. For such insignificant things it is not good
> to prostitute the body, mind, and soul, the means by which
> one can attain God.

Ramakrishna then says of a certain famous woman guru:

> A man once said about a certain woman: "Ah! She is hav-
> ing a grand time now. She is so well off! She has rented a
> room and furnished it with a couch, a mat, pillows, and
> many other things. And how many people she controls! They
> are always visiting her." In other words, the woman has now
> become a prostitute. Therefore her happiness is unbounded.
> Formerly she was a maidservant in a gentleman's house; now
> she is a prostitute. She has ruined herself for a mere trifle.[25]

And how can someone who has so ruined themselves for
the "mere trifle" of fame or money or power guide anyone else
out of illusion? As we have seen, Ramakrishna did not mince
his words on this subject. Let us just imagine, if we dare, how
scathing his denunciation of the contemporary guru-circus
would be! Imagine what he would have to say about the so-
called "Divine Mothers"—even his colloquial Bengali would
have been stretched by them, I fear.

What I said about Ramakrishna having two teachings on the
guru question is in fact true of the Indian tradition in general.
The "official" tradition has always, for purposes of its own
power, stressed the divinity of the guru, the inalterable law of
his or her words, etc. But another tradition—one enshrined in
the *Upanishads* themselves—for isn't it said in the *Upanishads*

that the Atman—the Divine—itself *chooses* those who are destined to be "liberated"?—makes it obvious that *direct* initiation by God is possible. Many saints achieved illumination on their own through direct divine grace and their own efforts. Think of the Buddha. Think of Aurobindo. Think of Ramana Maharshi, and of Ramakrishna himself—he had guides, spiritual friends like Brahmani and Totapuri, but even the most cursory reading of his *Gospel* will reveal how it was essentially always the Mother *herself* who was initiating him. And just as Christ wanted to teach humankind the total nakedness of his intimacy with God, the God he called in diminutive Aramaic *"Abba,"* so Ramakrishna's essential and, I believe, crucial teaching is about the ordeals and glories of direct relationship with the Mother of the Universe.

It is that naked, ecstatic, all-healing intimacy that he dedicated his life to living and that he wants to transmit to us. *Anything* that prevents us from attaining it—any dogma or guru or priest or church—all of these will have to go so that the authentic revolutionary wildness of the Mother can be born in our hearts, minds, and souls to transform the world.

This, I am certain, is Ramakrishna's contemporary message to us: "Go to the Mother directly, risk everything for her love, let her love's fire transform you into a living divine child acting in all dimensions and arenas from and for her love." This is a tremendous challenge to us—a demand for total authenticity—but it is also a tremendous opportunity. We have to seize this opportunity now, or perish. Quacks and partial exotic panaceas can't help us now. We are too sick and the world is dying from our sickness. Let us go directly to the Supreme Doctor, the Mother of the Universe, and suffer gladly everything she sends us for our healing. This great healing cannot be easily or cheaply gained, as Ramakrishna tirelessly tells us; it requires passionate faith on our part, deep sustained longing and adoration, the constant exercise of discrimination, the development of profound inner mystical sensitivity so as to be able to follow some part of the Mother's workings, and the courage to go on and on, traveling into her darkness with only her light for a guide.

But she herself will be helping and sustaining us every step of the way, as she organizes for us whatever joy or disaster we need to develop most quickly. Put yourself directly into her hands, Ramakrishna is telling us and showing us by his life, and desire nothing but her, nothing but the purest love for her, and you will see—what? You will see that you receive everything, every vision, every strength, every safety and poise and elevation.

Imagine what a world of independent and lovingly interdependent divine children would be like. Imagine what such children would experience together, how they would honor and adore each other, how they would work to see that this world mirrors increasingly the beauty and justice of *her* beauty and justice. Imagine how creative such children would be, released from the guilt and constraint of all the dead and putrefying systems, empowered, as Ramakrishna was, to drink deeply of the best of each of the sacred traditions. Imagine how sweetly dangerous such children would be to all the power-mongers, to all the black and gray magicians and ju-ju men and women, to all the heads of spiritual and political corporations, whose power only survives by throttling precisely the kind of burning passionate unconditional love that the Mother will engender in every soul turned toward her!

Imagine this and you are imagining the only possible future, *her* future—the only possible future worth sweating and struggling and praying for. Let the sacred world-democracy of the Mother begin. Let her reign of wild reconstructive sweetness begin. Ramakrishna is the Jefferson of this sacred world-democracy, its first and sweetest king-child. He has opened a door for us into the heart of the Mother. Let us go through that door by the thousands and hundreds of thousands, free at last to be our unique selves in her, as he was his unique self in her, free to dance and sing and weep for joy like him and free to realize, alone and together, the mystery of divine childhood.

## Notes

1. *The Gospel of Sri Ramakrishna.* Translated into English with an Introduction by Swami Nikhilananda (Mylapore, Madras, India: Sri Ramakrishna Math, n.d.), p. 176.

2. *The Gospel of Sri Ramakrishna,* p. 115.

3. *The Gospel of Sri Ramakrishna,* p. 632.

4. *The Gospel of Sri Ramakrishna,* pp. 138–139.

5. *The Upanishads.* Translations from the Sanskrit with an Introduction by Juan Mascaró (New York, Penguin Books, 1965), pp. 110–111.

6. *The Gospel of Sri Ramakrishna,* p. 107.

7. Dudjom Rinpoche, quoted in Sogyal Rinpoche, *The Tibetan Book of Living and Dying* (San Francisco: HarperSanFrancisco, 1991), p. 166.

8. "Carrying Vitality and Consciousness," in *Vitality, Energy, Spirit: A Taoist Sourcebook.* Translated and edited by Thomas Cleary (Boston: Shambhala Publications, 1991), p. 12.

9. "Knowing the Male, Keep the Female," in *Vitality, Energy, Spirit,* p. 13.

10. "The World Has a Beginning," in *Vitality, Energy, Spirit,* p. 15.

11. Robert Lawlor, *Voices of the First Day: Awakening in the Aboriginal Dreamtime* (Rochester, Vermont: Inner Traditions International, Ltd., 1991), p. 165. Used by permission of the author.

12. Lawlor, *Voices of the First Day,* p. 165.

13. Lawlor, *Voices of the First Day,* p. 165.

14. *The Gospel of Sri Ramakrishna,* p. 673.

15. *The Gospel of Sri Ramakrishna,* p. 629.

16. *The Gospel of Sri Ramakrishna,* p. 171.

17. *The Gospel of Sri Ramakrishna,* p. 265.

18. *The Gospel of Sri Ramakrishna,* p. 272.

19. *The Gospel of Sri Ramakrishna,* p. 381.

20. *The Gospel of Sri Ramakrishna,* p. 769.

21. *The Upanishads,* pp. 111–112.

22. *The Gospel of Sri Ramakrishna,* p. 259.

23. *The Gospel of Sri Ramakrishna,* p. 619.

24. *The Gospel of Sri Ramakrishna,* p. 633.

25. *The Gospel of Sri Ramakrishna,* pp. 745–746. Italics added.

# Chapter Four

# Aurobindo and the Transformation of the Mother

FOR AUROBINDO, the crucial fact of modern history—and so of the evolutionary history of the human race—is that humankind has in our era been brought both by its tragic mistakes and by a hidden energy of divine grace to the point where it must choose, on a large scale, massive spiritual transformation, or die out. Aurobindo saw clearly that nothing less than this spiritual transformation—the "supramental miracle," as he sometimes called it—could change and fulfill the destiny of humankind. Any other solution to the crisis of the modern world, he knew, would not work. As he writes in his book *The Life Divine:*

> [I]t has not been found in experience ... that education and intellectual training can by itself change man; it only provides the human individual and collective ego with better information and a more efficient machinery for its self-affirmation, but leaves it the same unchanged human ego. Nor can human mind and life be cut into perfection ... by any kind of social machinery.... Machinery cannot form the soul and life-force into standardised shapes; it can at best coerce them, make soul and mind inert and stationary.[1]

History has proved, too, that the religious "solution" has been ineffective.

[O]rganised religion, though it can provide a means of inner uplift for the individual and provide in it or behind it a way for his opening to spiritual experience, has not changed human life and society; it could not do so because, in governing society, it had to compromise with the lower parts of life and could not insist on the inner change of the whole being.[2]

What hope is there, then, for the change that has to come? Aurobindo tells us, with unsentimental directness:

A total spiritual direction given to the *whole* life and the *whole* nature can alone lift humanity beyond itself.... It is only the *full* emergence of the soul, the *full* descent of the native light and power of the Spirit and the consequent replacement or transformation and uplifting of our insufficient mental and vital nature by a spiritual and supramental Supernature that can effect this evolutionary miracle.

He goes on:

At first sight, this insistence on a radical change of nature might seem to put off all the hope of humanity to a distant evolutionary future; for the transcendence of our normal human nature, a transcendence of our mental, vital and physical being, has the appearance of an endeavour too high and difficult and at present, for man as he is, impossible. *Even if it were so,* it would still remain the sole possibility for the transmutation of life; for to hope for a true change of human life without a change of human nature is an irrational and unspiritual proposition; it is to ask for something unnatural and unreal, an impossible miracle.

Aurobindo believes, however, that this immense and extreme change he sees as essential is neither a fantasy nor an "impossible miracle":

[W]hat is demanded by this change is not something altogether distant, alien to our existence and radically impossible; for

what has to be developed is there in our being and not something outside it: what evolutionary Nature presses for, is an
awakening to the knowledge of self, the discovery of self,
the manifestation of the self and spirit within us and the
release of its self-knowledge, its self-power, its native self-
instrumentation. It is, besides, a step for which the whole
of evolution has been a preparation and which is brought
closer at each crisis of human destiny. . . . What is necessary
is that that there should be a turn in humanity felt by some
or many towards the vision of this change, a feeling of its
imperative need, the sense of its possibility, the will to make
it possible in themselves and to find the way.[3]

One power, and one power alone, Aurobindo believes, can
help the human race effect this vast change and enter the glowing light-fields of its true destiny—the power of the Divine
Mother, the Shakti, contacted directly and called down passionately, incessantly, right into every part of the mind, heart,
soul, and body. In Aurobindo's vision, the Mother has already
"planned" this amazing miraculous change of the race, already
"dreamed" it in her sublime mind of love; it is the Mother
whose vision of this transformation is working itself out through
all the terrors and catastrophes of modern history, bringing the
entire mind of the race through them to a threshold of crucial
decision and aspiration. It is the Mother whose boundless love
and its boundless active power—the streaming out of its Shakti
and all its lights of initiation—that will give humankind the
energy, divine grace, divine intensity, and stamina necessary to
undertake so huge, complex, and demanding a work as that of
realizing and making real on every level the inherent divinity
of human life.

At the end of his life, Aurobindo is said to have remarked,
"If there is to be a future, it will wear the crown of feminine
design." The future, then, depends on how far, how deeply,
adoringly, passionately, and with what final life-searing and
life-transforming truth the human imagination, heart, and soul

can come into contact with the Mother, invoke her love and power, and call them into every aspect of human life to irradiate and divinize it. The whole of the next stage of the human adventure depends, Aurobindo is convinced, on whether the Mother can be loved and heard tenderly and sensitively enough by us, and whether her great call to us to change everything and her great offer of light and infinite grace to help us effect that change, can really be undertaken. The Mother is all-willing, all-loving, all-powerful, at once the ground, energy, *and* the goal of evolution. There is no end or limit imaginable to her love or its transforming powers. In her and in them, and in our working consciously, directly, and humbly with her and them, is our great human hope.

The Mother, the divine Shakti, has willed the transformation of human life on earth into Divine Life; now we have to will it, and will to work passionately with her, to suffer and endure whatever is necessary to realize her most exalting dream and our inmost reality.

> Then shall be ended here the Law of Pain.
> Earth shall be made a home of Heaven's light . . .
> The superconscient beam shall touch men's eyes
> And the truth-conscious world come down to earth
> Invading matter with the Spirit's ray,
> Awaking its silence to immortal thoughts,
> Awaking the dumb heart to the living Word.
> This mortal life shall house Eternity's bliss,
> The body's self taste immortality.[4]

> O mind, grow full of the eternal peace:
> O word, cry out the immortal litany:
> Built is the golden tower, the flame-child born.[5]

> The supermind shall claim the world for Light
> And thrill with love of God the enamoured heart
> And place Light's crown on Nature's lifted head
> And found Light's reign on her unshaking base. . . .

A soul shall wake in the Inconscient's house;
The mind shall be God-vision's tabernacle,
The body intuition's instrument,
And life a channel for God's visible power. . . .

The Spirit's tops and Nature's base shall draw
Near to the secret of their separate truth
And know each other as one deity.
The Spirit shall look out through Matter's gaze
And Matter shall reveal the Spirit's face.
Then man and superman shall be at one
And all the earth become a single life.[6]

"And all the earth become a single life," one life in the heart of life, in the heart of her who *is* life; one life in the burning, sacred, lucid, and all-powerful love-core of the Divine Mother. In that "single life," the Mother, her flame-children, the earth, nature, will all be one: one force, one world, one life, one love. The reign of separation will be destroyed forever, and the war-ravaged and stricken world will become what she has always secretly known it to be—her rose garden, blossoming in her boundless heart-fire.

\* \* \*

Aurobindo's all-encompassing, all-embracing vision of the Divine Mother, the Shakti, is the most adventurous vision of her that the world has yet been given, and so of crucial importance for the great transformation that we are beginning. If Ramakrishna could be said to be the heart of this transformation, the sweet and tender mystic's child-heart, Aurobindo could be described as its illumined mind, its illumined intellect, the scientist of the transformation that the Mother is preparing for the world. He is the "laboratory" in his own body, practice, mind, and heart of the great transformation that she has come to give the world. With Ramakrishna and Aurobindo, we have a complete vision of the potential that the human race is now being offered—the potential journey, the potential excitement, the potential grandeur.

I owe a very particular debt to Aurobindo, because when I first went back to India after fifteen years of being away, when I was twenty-five, nearly twenty-six, I was an arrogant, self-mutilating skeptic worshipping at the shrine of division and irony. I found myself, by grace, living for four months in the ashram at Pondicherry in a small hut by the sea, and made a close friendship with the wonderful, eccentric Canadian poet Jean-Marc Frechette, who slowly and with great humor, tact, and shrewdness introduced me to the work of Aurobindo. In Aurobindo I found what I still consider to be the greatest and most majestic intellect of the human race. Aurobindo's thought and his comprehension of the issues involved in transformation are both of the ultimate order. They constitute a major revelation to us, and the more progress—and I mean that word with all irony—that I make on the mystical path, the more phenomena I experience and live through, and the more aware I have become of the very ways in which the Mother works in one's life, the more stunned and astonished I am by the precision of what Aurobindo has left us.

If you ever wish to really explore the actual mechanics of the revolution of the Mother, you could do no better than to read the three volumes of Aurobindo's correspondence, because in them is the complete and completely precise guide to everything that happens on the mystic's journey in her. Everything that happens in the body when spirit possesses it, everything that happens at the various levels of psychic transformation, everything that happens in dreams and in the various understandings of the light, everything that happens in the very subtle ordeal that mystic transformation brings, especially this particular mystic transformation of the Mother. Aurobindo is the supreme scientist of this particular alchemy.

What I found in Aurobindo when I returned to India was a consummate intellect that could unite the highest perceptions of Western civilization with the highest spiritual understanding of Eastern civilization. The West has tended to abandon any sense of the exquisite and profound relationship between matter and spirit in favor of a vision of progress that is almost wholly materialistic. The East has kept alive a vision of humanity's transcendent and sacred identity, but it long ago lost the sense of life as inherently and absolutely sacred. Because the East has been obsessed with its notion of cyclical time and transcendence, it has failed to keep alive the possibility of progress in *this* life. In the course of his *sadhana,* Aurobindo took the very best and highest of both traditions and fused them in a vision of evolution that was not materialistic but deeply spiritual.

Aurobindo was born in Bengal and educated in England. He went to St. Paul's school, then to Cambridge, and returned to India as a young man. In India he joined revolutionary forces against the British, was jailed, and while in prison had a series of visions which transformed him. He escaped to Pondicherry from prison just before he might have been put to death. He remained in Pondicherry for the rest of his life, no longer a political revolutionary, but a yogi. What he discovered in the course of his *sadhana* was that a completely new stage of human evolution was being prepared by the Divine Mother, a stage that would integrate the Western understanding of dynamic progress, of a constantly evolving vision of humankind, with the Eastern understanding of the divine self and the power and glory of the Shakti. When the time came for these two previously separated visions to be joined, an unparalleled energy for change would be unleashed.

What Aurobindo discovered and worked out in his own body, in the silence of many long years of patient, scientific, lucid, and brave work that he did upon himself in that room in Pondicherry, was to work out, detail by detail, how this great transformation would be done. Aurobindo's room in Pondicherry is still vibrant with the massive, calm, majestic power that emanated from him, a power experienced by those who met him even for only a moment or two in *darshan,* when he was silent in the last years of his life. In that small room, in the laboratory of his own body, mind, and spirit, Aurobindo became a living sign of where we all, if we allow ourselves, are being invited to go by the Mother. What he has to say about the Shakti and about the Divine Mother, about how to use the Shakti, or rather, how to allow yourself to be used by the Divine Mother, is of sacred importance. So is what he has to say about the different facets, visions, and understandings of her, of her different personalities and the way in which she works.

Aurobindo's book *The Mother* contains both the vision of the Divine Mother that he came to after many years of passion, labor, and inquiry, and also a very clear, strong prescription for how to come into alignment with this great transcendent and transformative force.

Before we explore this crucial work, in which Aurobindo's vision of the sacred feminine is given in its most concrete and helpful form, I'd like to share with you the first major experience that I ever had of the Divine Mother. I encountered her by Aurobindo's tomb in Pondicherry. I had been praying for a long time to be given some concrete vision of who she is, and Jean-Marc said, "Well, if you really want to know something, why don't you ask Aurobindo? You're here, you're in his atmosphere. Go to his tomb and pray by it every day. He is a supreme master, he is blessing you, so why don't you ask him for a vision of the Divine Mother?" And so I did dare to ask Aurobindo, and through grace I was given this vision:

> The day before I left to return to England I went to Aurobindo's tomb and prayed to him all day to help me understand the Mother, to give me an experience of her being.
>
> Just as I was about to leave, sitting by his tomb in the late light, the OM sound returned and I heard: *This is the Mother's sound.*
>
> Then immediately I saw a horizon lit up by lightnings, thousands of them, tangling and untangling like snakes. *This is the Mother's power.*
>
> I was shocked, astounded. I walked away from the tomb to where books and photographs are sold. There was one of Sweet Mother, Aurobindo's companion, I had never seen

before. She is about ninety, standing on a balcony, gazing down with ravaged compassion. My hostility to her melted. *This is the Mother's love.*

I returned, shaking, to Aurobindo's tomb.

In the air before me, as I knelt, I saw the Andromeda Nebula, blazing and turning at great speed. It took all my power of control not to leave my body.

The words came:

*I am the creation from the beginning. Everything in the creation is me. All creation is growing toward me.*

*It is begun in ecstasy.*

*It is continued in ecstasy.*

*It is sustained in ecstasy.*

*It will end in ecstasy.*

I wanted to pray to the Mother but couldn't think of any prayers to Her, except the *Ave Maria* in Latin, which I recited. Then the words began, without my willing them: "Our Mother, which art in heaven, hallowed be thy name." An extraordinary peace filled me. "Our MOTHER, which art in heaven"—just that simple change of word renewed the prayer for me, made it infinitely more tender.

I looked around at the people praying, the trees around the tomb, the incense stick, the flowers.

*All this is the Mother, and you are always in the body of the Mother.* For a second or two I felt it—that I and the marble and the flowers and the darkening tree were different softly pulsing waves of the same energy, of that, of Her.

*No separation, now or ever.*

*This is the knowledge of the Mother.*

Returning to my room, I opened Isherwood's book on Ramakrishna at these words:

My Mother is both within and without this phenomenal world.... Giving birth to the world, she lives within it. She is the Spider and the world is the spider's web she has woven.... The spider brings the web out of herself and then lives in it.[7]

This was an extreme experience, but it actually contained all the different facets of the Divine Mother's power and presence. The first thing I heard was the Mother's sound, the *Om* which is actually creating and sustaining the creation at all moments. The second vision that I was given was of the vast power that is really manifesting the entire creation: lightning tangling and untangling. Then, immediately after this frightening, majestic vision of her power—a power that is flaming and unleashed at all moments and could at any moment crumble the universe in its fist if it wanted to—I was given a vision through a photograph of Sweet Mother, Aurobindo's companion who was in her late nineties, of the unconditional, tender and poignant, totally exposed and vulnerable love of the Divine Mother, that boundless, ecstatic, and endlessly self-giving love, that love that is given to the point of madness, pain, and death.

Then I knelt by Aurobindo's tomb and saw the Andromeda galaxy. The Andromeda galaxy has come up again and again in my life. My first real experience of it was after my first year at Oxford, during a summer vacation. I was very unhappy and withdrew for three months into an upstairs room at my parent's house. In the middle of the night I came down and turned on the television set and the Andromeda galaxy appeared on the screen. That's the only time in my life that I've ever left my body, and at that time I didn't even realize one could. The spiral is the symbol of the Divine Mother and a diagram of how her force works throughout the universe. The Andromeda galaxy to me that night seemed like a great cry of silent light, the cry of creation, of birth. Years later, kneeling at Aurobindo's grave in Pondicherry, I heard these words which contain, in a very simple way, the vision that Aurobindo is giving to the world of what the Divine Mother is:

> *I am the creation from the beginning.*
> *Everything in the creation is me.*
> *All creation is growing toward me.*

One day, just recently when we were in India, Eryk brought me two shells. I was deep in meditation as he came into the room. One of the shells was a spiral, and the other was a nautilus, which resembles the yin-yang shape, and I saw that these were the two identities of the Divine Mother in creation. The play of the yin-yang shape in the nautilus represents the forces that balance and sustain creation; the spiral shell represents creation itself—spiraling, spiraling in her light, as her light, up into her light. The light is fundamentally working in three different ways: it is creating and sustaining, it is fomenting, and it is transforming. And, of course, these three powers are all connected.

> *I am the creation from the beginning.*
> *Everything in the creation is me.*
> *All creation is growing toward me.*

Imagine how just these three brief phrases transform all that we have been told by the evasive metaphysics of transcendence. They show us that the goal is not to get *out* of *this* experience, not to try to get to some other place, some nirvana, some far off somewhere-else; but to try to come completely *into* this experience, *into* the divinity of our humanity and our bodies. With the transcendent understanding of an advanced mystic, we can use the light and power of that understanding to transform this matter, this life, into a divine life, and therefore to take the whole of humankind, and the whole of creation, through these spirals of transformation deeper and deeper into the great light-power of the Mother.

This is Aurobindo's vision. What Aurobindo saw and knew from his own experience was that if we could align ourselves totally and passionately in love and dedication to the Divine Mother, it could transform *all* aspects of human life. It could transform not only our minds, illumined by the ecstasy of the divine gnosis of the Mother; not only our hearts, opened to the unconditional boundless, tender, ecstatic love of the Mother; it would open our vision to the light coursing through all the various *chakras* and blazing above our heads. Cell by cell, the entire structure of the body would be changed, giving us a completely different experience of and in our bodies. This "internal" transformation would lead to an entire transformation of all of the conditions of earthly life, a bringing down of light into matter and into the body so that a new being could slowly, meticulously, and alchemically be recreated, and a new world created around that being.

Through his own experience, Aurobindo dissolved all old visions of progress and replaced them with a new, utterly radical and revolutionary vision of the possibility of a divine life on Earth, created by the supramental life and light of the Shakti, the Divine Mother. He knew it was possible because he did it, he lived through every transforming strangeness of its workings. Aurobindo proved it was possible. He worked and slaved and suffered, he fell silent and withdrew, he gave and gave, he wrote hundreds of letters, and he worked it all out in his own life, his own heart, his own mind and body. That is Aurobindo's achievement, and it's a challenge to us all. A devastating challenge, too, because it really does compel us to bring together all the things we want to keep apart, to bring together life and spirit, body and soul, heart and light. The force that will bring all these things together is the Divine Mother. She is trying to bring to birth a new earth in her.

> *I am the creation from the beginning.*
> *Everything in the creation is me.*
> *All creation is growing toward me.*
> *It is begun in ecstasy.*
> *It is continued in ecstasy.*
> *It is sustained in ecstasy.*
> *It will end in ecstasy.*

Of course, "it" will in fact never "end." I should have written, "It will *expand* in ecstasy." Aurobindo, like Rumi, realized that the universe of the Divine Mother is an endlessly expanding universe, a universe in which there is never an end to ascension, never an end to transformation. The universes expand endlessly since love's Shakti is boundless. There are billions of universes expanding from the same diamond point, and they are all doing marvelous things in the Mother's mad and glorious mind. And the Mother's transforming love is always beyond any stage it can transform us or anything into, always drawing all beings further upwards and inward, ever deeper into the ever-receding heart of love's fire. She is in all things, she is all things, and she is beyond all things, always drawing them more and more completely into her infinity of holy peace and passion.

Aurobindo's *The Mother* is one of the greatest books ever written about the Divine Mother because it is by one of her wildest and most adventurous children who really understood her many moods and transformations:

> The supramental change [this evolutionary change that Aurobindo came to pioneer in his own body, mind and work] is a thing decreed and inevitable in the evolution of the earth-consciousness, for its upward ascent is not ended and mind is not its last summit. But that the change may arise, take form, and endure, there is needed the call from below with a will to recognize and not deny the light when it comes. There is needed the sanction of the Supreme from above. The power that mediates between the sanction and the call is the presence and power of the Divine Mother.

*"The power that mediates between the sanction and the call is the presence and power of the Divine Mother."*

> The Mother's power and not any human endeavour ... can alone rend the lid and tear the covering and shape the vessel and bring down into this world of obscurity and falsehood and death and suffering Truth and Light and Life divine, and the immortal's Ananda.[8]

The Mother *is* the power that will lift the barrier between the mind and the supermind, between this body, damaged and desolate in so many ways, to a new body that is to be prepared by real work and real dedication to her.

Aurobindo realized through his work, through his *sadhana,* that what he was experimenting with was not just for the elite, not just for a select group of people, but was actually the destiny of the human race, and not its destiny in some other realm, but *here on earth*. Here will be the place of the divinized culture, a divinized humanity. "The supramental change is a thing decreed and inevitable in the evolution of the earth-consciousness, for its upward ascent is not ended."

One of the great and healing powers of Aurobindo's work is its embattled optimism. Aurobindo is awake to every nuance of decadence in the body, every nuance of desolation in the heart, every nuance of defeat in the mind. He has known them all because he has suffered them all in his own psyche, body, and heart. But he also knows that the force of the Divine Mother, if turned to and invoked, can do anything. Aurobindo lived through the First World War, the Second World War, through the horror of Hitlerism and the deepening chaos of this century, but he never lost faith in the great power of the Divine Mother actually to transform the world. He knew that with sincerity, surrender, and openness, with blazing faith, that her light could do anything.

"For its upward ascent is not ended and mind is not its last summit." We have been brought to a historical moment in which we can't possibly live or survive if we go on pretending that the mind and reason and technological progress are enough. Clearly, they are not enough, and we are going to destroy everything if we continue to believe that they are. Instead, we're going to have to take a leap into a different kind of consciousness.

"But that the change may arise, take form, and endure, there is needed the call from below"—the Mother will not do it on her own, although she is, of course, the author of all in a final sense. What is needed is for us to really develop an extreme passion of aspiration. Why? Because the transformation into divine childhood can never be achieved by slaves. Every aspect of it has to be consented to, embraced by the human being, so that he or she can feel every nuance of its ecstasy and joy. So that we can feel this great ecstasy of transforming ourselves in the Divine Mother, as a part of the Divine Mother, and can, through that long, labyrinthine, meticulous, difficult alchemical process of self-transformation in her, come to understand how it is done. We become, in fact, the scientist of our own transformation. The Mother is bringing a very practical system, and it depends on our belief in her, our knowledge of her, and our aspiration for her.

This is not a transformation for slaves; it is, in fact, the release of human beings from the long tyranny of the religions, the long tyranny of partisan sectarianism, from fake gurus and "miracle workers," into a direct relationship with the force of the Divine Mother in all our hearts. Required of us is an extreme sense of responsibility and adulthood, a real facing-up to where we are now and what we need to do and become. Aurobindo begins his majestic book with a severe, no-nonsense, absolutely practical account of what this will entail, as we will see in a moment.

"But that the change may arise. . . ." Do we really want this change? Do we really want it? I sometimes wonder whether we really do want it, or if we just want the forests to stop burning and our old lives to resume, our old indulgences to return. Do we really want to enter into a new visionary humanity, or do we just want our comforts back, without the problems? Do we really want just the old life of the ego, but without any difficulty? If that is we want, then we will die out. Aurobindo is saying that we must want what the Mother wants for us, and must want it with something of her great and matchless ardor. Otherwise, we are going to die out, because we really won't have deserved and honored this vision.

But that the change may arrive, take form, and endure there is needed the call from below with a will to recognize and not deny the light when it comes. There is needed the sanction

of the Supreme from above. The power that mediates between the sanction and the call is the presence and power
of the Divine Mother.

The Mother's power and "not any human endeavour"—it
will not be done by us alone. It has to come from the divine
will and out of the heart of the Divine Mother.

> The Divine Mother and not any human endeavour . . . can
> alone rend the lid and tear the covering and shake the ves-
> sel and bring down into this world of obscurity and false-
> hood and death and suffering, Truth and Light and Life
> divine, and the immortal's Ananda.

Aurobindo's life was lived out in the knowledge that it was
possible, that the Divine Mother is inundating the world with
her life, waiting for us to grow up and accept the rigorous ardor
of real transformation. What he makes clear is how difficult
this acceptance is. We must understand how important it is for
us to accept this challenge and really do the work of stripping
ourselves in the necessary ways and really accept the terms of
the transformation. We must not pretend that it's going to be
easy, that anyone else will do it for us. We and the Mother are
going to do it together, and it will cost everything. And why
not? What we are going to be offered is more than everything,
more than anything we can now imagine.

> If you want to be a true doer of divine works, your first aim
> must be to totally free yourself from all desire, and all self-
> regarding ego. All your life must be an offering and a sac-
> rifice to the Supreme; your only object in action shall be to
> serve, to receive, to fulfil, to become a manifesting instru-
> ment of the Divine Shakti in her works. You must grow in
> the divine consciousness until there is no difference between
> your will and hers, no motive except her impulsion in you,
> no action that is not her conscious action in you and through
> you.

The work cannot be done at any less a level of intensity. It cannot. This is the whole problem with the notion of transformation as envisaged in the "New Age." People would like to think that it can be done at less cost, but it cannot. There has to be a tremendous thirst for truth, constant work on oneself, incessant prayer and aspiration in the deepest possible humility. As Aurobindo makes clear, the Mother *is* boundless love, but such love has its sometimes austere laws.

Until you are capable of this complete dynamic identification [with the Mother], you have to regard yourself as a body and soul created for her service, one who does all for her sake. Even if the idea of the separate worker is strong in you and that you feel that it is you who do the act, yet it must be done for her. All stress of egotistic choice, all hankering after personal profit, all stipulation of self-regarding desire must be extirpated from the nature. There must be no demand for fruit and no seeking for a reward; the only fruit for you is the pleasure of the Divine Mother and the fulfilment of her work, your only reward a constant progression in divine consciousness and calm and strength and bliss. The joy of service and the joy of inner growth through works is sufficient recompense of the selfless worker.

There is no doubt that the light, the divine power of the Shakti, cannot actually work very much through us as we are. We do have to undergo a tremendous change. Even a great pianist cannot play the *Hammerklavier Sonata* on an out-of-tune piano; it just sounds absurd. The Shakti and the transformation she is preparing cannot be done on the kind of instruments that we are so sadly prepared to offer her.

But a time will come when you will feel more and more that you are the instrument and not the worker. For first by the force of your devotion your contact with the Divine Mother will become so intimate that at all times you will have only to concentrate and to put everything into her hands to have her present guidance, her direct command or impulse, the sure indication of the thing to be done and the way to do it. . . .

Here Aurobindo shifts from what *you* can do to what you allow *her* to do, as you become clear and pure and awake enough. By surrendering to her, you will be given the kinds of impulses and guidance that you really need. Afterward, you will realize that the divine Shakti not only inspires and guides, but initiates and carries out your works. The moment when you start surrendering more and more to the Divine Mother and her Shakti, you will discover what mystics have always told us—it is not *you* but her doing it *through* you, in you, as you. This brings tremendous calmness, bliss, and energy. Aurobindo says:

> [A]ll your movements are originated by her, all your powers are hers, mind, life and body are conscious and joyful instruments of her action, means for her play, moulds for her manifestation in the physical universe. There can be no more happy condition that this union and dependence; for this step carries you back beyond the border-line from the life of stress and suffering in the ignorance into the truth of your spiritual being, into its deep peace and its intense Ananda.

Next Aurobindo tells us how to act in the transformation. It is a first-hand account of a supreme scientist of the Mother's transformation, so it's worth taking as literally as we can bear:

> While this transformation is being done it is more than ever necessary to keep yourself free from all taint of the perversions of the ego.

Because the power of the light coming into you is so extreme, so intense, it can be misused; and if you misuse it, you will be destroyed by it. There are so many people abusing the Shakti at the moment, both consciously and unconsciously. I speak from experience, because I have been awakened time and time again by disaster, by agony, by the violent shattering of illusions, to the ways I have either consciously or unconsciously abused this power of transformation. The Mother's transformatory force demands that you treat it with total seriousness; it will not be toyed with. If you try, or if you think you can use it for anything, you may be allowed to do so for a while but in the end it will turn and destroy you. This is not vengeance, but sacred law. So while this transformation is being done, it is more than ever necessary to keep yourself free from the stain of the false self.

> Let no demand or insistence creep in to stain the purity of the self-giving and the sacrifice. There must be no attachment to the work or the result, no laying down of conditions, no claims to possess the Power that should possess you.

The deeper you go into her, the more overwhelmed with awe you are at the grandeur of this vast force that deigns to become so deeply intimate with you, to use you, to become one with you. The more profound that awe is, the more humility you have. Aurobindo continues:

> There must be no attachment to the work or the result ... no pride of the instrument, no vanity or arrogance. Nothing in the mind or in the vital or physical parts should be suffered to distort to its own use or seize for its own personal and separate satisfaction the greatness of the forces that are acting through you. Let your faith, your sincerity, your purity of aspiration be absolute and pervasive of all the planes and layers of your being; then every disturbing element and distorting influence will progressively fall away from your nature.

This is the stage of ordeal, the stage of yoga and purification, of the work of preparing the ground. Very few people have the courage for this stage. As our desperation grows, many more people will plunge into this stage, because we're going to realize that we cannot play anymore, we have to try to become one with her. The last consummation is this:

> The last stage of this perfection will come when you are completely identified with the Divine Mother and feel yourself to be no longer another and separate being, instrument, servant or worker but truly a child. . . .

Light of her light, essence of her essence, play of her play.

> [I]t will be your constant, simple and natural experience that all your thought and seeing and action, your very breathing or moving come from her and are hers. You will know and see and feel that you are a person and power formed by her out of herself, put out from her for play and yet always safe in her, being of her being, consciousness of her consciousness, force of her force, Ananda of her Ananda. When this condition is entire and her supramental energies can freely move you, then you will be perfect in divine works; knowledge, will, action will become sure, simple, luminous, spontaneous, flawless, an outflow from the Supreme, a divine movement of the Eternal.[9]

Listen to these adjectives, because each of them flash out another aspect of Aurobindo's understanding of union with her: "Knowledge, will, action will become sure, simple." *Simple*, with the simplicity that is clear and incandescent that goes right to the core. *Luminous* with the *ananda*, luminous with the bliss, luminous with the peace, sweetness, and mischief of the Divine Mother. *Spontaneous*, arising out of the heart of the moment, in deep relation to the moment, in "found" union with the moment. *Flawless*—because perfect, because unconditioned by any human imperfections, because "simple," "luminous," "spontaneous." And what human life becomes, when transformed into her, is "an outflow from the Supreme [and] a divine movement of the Eternal."

\* \* \*

In the long journey that Aurobindo took into the Divine Mother, he really came to know her as essentially four different but endlessly and intimately interlocking powers. I'd like to take you into his extraordinary vision of these four interlocking powers of the Divine Mother. Aurobindo also says, of course, that there are many powers which we will never know, many powers which he can never name, and many powers which exist in universes beyond our intelligence and understanding. But in the earthly plane, in this world, and for the purposes of this transformation, there are, he tells us, four critical, crucial aspects of the Mother with which we can come into relationship.

We must meditate on these four aspects of the Mother, because they contain deep clues as to her knowledge, her identity, and her nature, and they are given to us by someone who lived them all, who knew them all, and who achieved union with them all.

Before we enter the four ways, here is Aurobindo's summation of his vision of the Mother:

> There are three ways of being of the Mother of which you can become aware when you enter into touch of oneness with the Conscious Force that upholds us and the universe. *Transcendent,* the original supreme Shakti, she stands above the worlds and links the creation to the ever-unmanifest mystery of the Supreme.

That describes what the Mother is doing in the transcendent aspect: linking the creation to what can never be expressed or understood or even imagined, the mystery of the Supreme.

> *Universal,* the cosmic Mahashakti, she creates all these beings and contains and enters, supports and conducts all these million processes and forces. *Individual,* she embodies the power of these two vast arrays of her existence, makes them living and near to us and mediates between the human personality and the divine Nature.[10]

All is her play with the Supreme; all is her manifestation of the mysteries of the Eternal, the miracles of the Infinite. All is she, for all are parcel and portion of the divine Conscious-Force. Nothing can be here or elsewhere but what she decides and the Supreme sanctions; nothing can take shape except what she moved by the Supreme perceives and forms after casting it into seed in her creating Ananda.[11]

Hers, then, is complete supremacy, complete power, complete glory. Aurobindo then proceeds into a meditation on her four personalities. He meditates deeply on each of them in turn, for each one contains a core secret of the Mother's nature and how she works in reality.

Four great Aspects of the Mother, four of her leading Powers and Personalities have stood in front in her guidance of this Universe and in her dealings with the terrestrial play. One [Maheshwari] is her personality of calm wideness and comprehending wisdom and tranquil benignity and inexhaustible compassion and sovereign and surpassing majesty and all-ruling greatness. Another [Mahakali] embodies her power of splendid strength and irresistible passion, her warrior mood, her overwhelming will, her impetuousness swiftness and world-shaking force. A third [Mahalakshmi] is vivid and sweet and wonderful with her deep secret of beauty and harmony and fine rhythm, her intricate and subtle opulence, her compelling attraction and captivating grace. The fourth [Mahasaraswati] is equipped with her close and profound capacity of intimate knowledge and careful flawless work and quiet and exact perfection in all things.[12]

All these four personalities of the Mother are always synchronistically at play in the universe. Our time, however, is particularly marked by the passion of Kali, and it is on Aurobindo's majestic meditation on Kali that I wish to concentrate.

The Apocalypse that menaces us on every level of our existence is Kali's wildest dance yet, perfectly designed in all its horror, atrocity, and savage disillusioning power to bring us to our knees before her, to bring us to the moment when, as a race, we can admit the failure of every single one of our illusions—political, economic, social, and spiritual. At last we will have to turn to her *directly,* with the necessary sincerity, for her to infuse and transfigure us. The Dark Mother is trampling everything, violently destroying and stripping us of all "safety" so that we can, before it is too late, come into the most direct and passionate imaginable relationship with her. Such a relationship demands, costs, everything—*and* gives everything. All the old habits of dependence, hierarchy, and authority will have to go so that the Mother can inspire in us the discovery of wholly new forms of transmission, communication, and worship. These forms will arise spontaneously out of our ever-deepening gnosis and not from slavery to the past. And for the strength, wildness, passion, lust for authentic freedom that we will need at every moment to be able to help the Mother help us, it is to her aspect of Mahakali that we can most inspiringly turn. The only thing Kali cannot destroy is the one who has become one with her—one in faith, stamina, intensity, truth.

> Mahakali is of another nature. Not wideness but height, not wisdom but force and strength are her peculiar power. There is in her an overwhelming intensity, a mighty passion of force to achieve, a divine violence rushing to shatter every limit and obstacle.[13]

At this moment humanity is prisoner to all sorts of fantasies and illusions which are resulting in the destruction of the environment and in the kind of horrific, pathological passivity that is drugging us to the effects of what we have allowed ourselves to become and what we are doing. Kali will get more and more terrible, more and more violent, more and more extreme, if we withdraw into our nightmarish passivity now. We have to embrace her mad rage and become one with the love behind it, we have to go madly into her and into her love. It's in her madness that we can incinerate our fantasies and *become* love—

wild, extreme, conscious, active love—pure love wild for change of every kind, and empowered to imagine and implement it.

There is in [Kali] an overwhelming intensity, a mighty passion of force to achieve, a divine violence rushing to shatter every limit and obstacle. All her divinity leaps out in a splendour of tempestuous action; she is there for swiftness, for the immediately effective process, the rapid and direct stroke, the frontal assault that carries everything before it. Terrible is her face to the Asura, dangerous and ruthless her mood against the haters of the Divine; for she is the Warrior of the Worlds who never shrinks from the battle. Intolerant of imperfection, she deals roughly with all in man that is unwilling and she is severe to all that is obstinately ignorant and obscure; her wrath is immediate and dire against treachery and falsehood and malignity, ill-will is smitten at once by her scourge. Indifference, negligence and sloth in the divine work she cannot bear and she smites awake at once with sharp pain, if need be, the untimely slumberer and the loiterer. The impulses that are swift and straight and frank, the movements that are unreserved and absolute, the aspiration that mounts in flame are the motion of Mahakali. Her spirit is tameless, her vision and will are high and far-reaching like the flight of an eagle, her feet are rapid on the upward way and her hands are outstretched to strike and to succour. For she too is the Mother and her love is as intense as her wrath and she has a deep and passionate kindness. When she is allowed to intervene in her strength, then in one moment are broken like things without consistence the obstacles that immobilise or the enemies that assail the seeker. If her anger is dreadful to the hostile and the vehemence of her pressure painful to the weak and timid, she is loved and worshipped by the great, the strong and the noble; for they feel that her blows beat what is rebellious in their material into strength and perfect truth, hammer straight what is wry and perverse and expel what is impure or defective. But for her what is done in a day might have taken centuries; without her Ananda might be wide and grave or soft and sweet and beautiful but would lose the flaming joy of its most absolute intensity. To knowledge she gives a conquering might, brings to beauty and harmony a high and mounting movement and imparts to the slow and difficult labour after perfection an impetus that multiplies the power and shortens the long way.[14]

We are in Kali's time, and so we must learn how to dance with her extreme and passionate truth, honesty, courage, and love. Aurobindo is giving us a fearless map. Of course, this Kali-aspect of the Mother that is essential for the transformation is balanced by Maheshwari, the supreme silence, the supreme majesty, and supreme compassion. And it is also balanced by Mahalakshmi, the revealer of beauty, of all that is sumptuous and gorgeous; and by Mahasaraswati, the great mistress of work, of the patient unfolding of the alchemical process. But unless we come to know Kali, to worship and love and bow down to Kali, to rapturously embrace the dark, terrible, suffering aspects of Kali and really allow her to trample our illusions, we will not have the courage needed for the Divine Mother's great transformation.

As Aurobindo said of her in her aspect of Kali:

Nothing can satisfy her that falls short of the supreme ecstasies, the highest heights, the noblest aims, the highest vistas. Therefore with her is the victorious force of the Divine and it is by the grace of her fire and her passion and speed that the great achievement can be done now rather than hereafter.[15]

Let it be done now, rather than "hereafter." There is very little time. Let it be done now, so we and the human beings of a preserved and transformed future can know and live "the highest heights, the noblest aims, the highest vistas." And as we turn to take the supreme risk of loving and invoking her into the

core of our being, let us remember what Aurobindo wrote, near
the end of his life, in perhaps his most moving letter:

> As for faith, you write as if I never had a doubt or a diffi-
> culty. I have had worse than any human mind can think of.
> It is not because I have ignored difficulties, but because I
> have seen them more clearly, experienced them on a larger
> scale than anyone living now or before me, that, having
> faced and measured them, I am sure of the results of my
> work. But even if I still saw the chance that it might come
> to nothing (which is impossible) I would go on unperturbed,
> because I would still have done to the best of my power the
> work I had to do and what is so done always counts in the
> economy of the universe. But why should I feel that all this
> may come to nothing when I see each step and where it is
> leading and every week, every day—once it was every year
> and month and hereafter it will be every day and hour—
> brings me so much nearer to my goal? In the way that one
> treads with the greater Light above, even every difficulty
> gives its help and has its value and Night itself carries in it
> the burden of the Light that has to be.[16]

## Questions and Answers

*What did Aurobindo mean by direct contact with the Mother?*

As I have said, what Aurobindo has left us is a *way* into the
Mother, a path that he himself carved out with infinite meticulous courage. Fundamentally, behind the massive complexity
of his thought, Aurobindo's message is a simple one: turn to
the Mother, invoke with sincere and passionate attention the
Shakti, call it down into the heart, mind, soul, and body. If your
aspiration is intense enough, transformation will inevitably
ensue, within the terms of your unique being and psyche.
Aurobindo never tired of repeating that every person is their
own religion, their own unique expression of the godhead, one
of God's, the Mother's, unrepeatable words.

Aurobindo maintains that the transformation that will follow on continued invocation and adoration of the Mother will
be an *integral* one. For Aurobindo, both Western and Eastern
ideas and visions of wisdom are lacking; the Western model
lacks transcendental awareness and the Eastern deep respect
for matter. Aurobindo wanted to see the highest and best of
both traditions fused in a vision that is transcendental *and*
immanent, ecstatic and material, visionary and extremely practical. Only such a vision could significantly alter the conditions
of earthly life.

So the transformation under and through the Mother that
Aurobindo envisaged—and knew in his own astonishing journey—is an integral one, one in which the whole being is integrated with all its aspects brought up to the level of divine
truth, beauty, and love. It is this transformation of the whole
being that he, especially in his *Letters* and in *The Life Divine*,
explores in all its possible events, complexities, ramifications,
possibilities. If you want a guide, a day-by-day, dream-by-
dream, vision-by-vision, light-by-light guide of what happens
when the Mother takes over the whole being and starts with

extraordinary subtlety, passion, and wonderful richness to transform it, part by part—then read Aurobindo's *Letters* again and again, as I have suggested. They are his laboratory notes, exact and amazingly precise, as scientific in their dimension as the equations of an Einstein or a Niels Bohr. Of course, everyone's transformation in the Mother is different, since the Mother is both the same and different with each person, but such a complete, variegated, brilliantly acute testimony of the different ordeals and stages of the great divine alchemy of the Mother is invaluable, one of humankind's most precious documents.

Aurobindo himself never had a master. He was initiated briefly early on by a *sadhu* named Lele into one aspect of the divine experience—that of silence—but all his other initiations came directly from the Divine Mother. And the rest of his life was lived in direct experiential intimacy with the Mother. Just as the Buddha said at the end of his life, "What I did, you can do also. I have given my account of what I did and how I did it. Use what is useful in it for you; test it and see if it works," so Aurobindo is calmly challenging us to dare to put into practice what he did and discover the glory of the Mother and let it inhabit every part of our being to transmute it.

Aurobindo and Ramakrishna are not asking us to worship *them,* not to bow down to them as masters and gurus, but to worship *her* directly, using whatever we find most inspiring in *their* example as a guide. They know that what the Mother wants to create in the human race is complete freedom—a race of gnostic illumined "flame-children" in natural ecstatic nonhierarchical harmony with each other and all beings and her. For both Aurobindo and Ramakrishna, the one authority is the Divine Mother, the one power is the power of the divine. They are both, with different emphases, envisioning what Aurobindo calls "a gnostic way of dynamic living," "the creation of a world which shall be the true environment of a divine living."

This necessarily entails the dissolution of *all* categories of power that ignorance now keeps going, *all* ways of keeping people imprisoned, separated from their real and outrageous

possibilities, political or religious. Both Ramakrishna and Aurobindo know that a direct relationship with the Mother could
create nothing less than a worldwide mystical and practical revolution, because it would empower every being with his or her
own divine truth. "Take courage," Pythagoras wrote, "the
human race is divine." It is that knowledge and that courage
that the Mother wants to give to everyone; the living knowledge of our innate divinity that she wants us all to *make real*
in prayer, meditation, and loving action in the world.

Aurobindo and Ramakrishna knew that the next crucial
stage of human development simply cannot unfold except under
the Mother, in conscious co-creation and impassioned partici-
pation in the will, love, and power of the sacred feminine. The
human race began in the Divine Mother in the interdependent
world of origin that the aboriginal peoples still so luminously
inhabit, and its destiny is to bring into lucid harmony in and
through the Mother all that it has learned on its long and frequently tragic journey away from her. We must return to her
and to origin, but with all the mental, physical, and emotional
powers we have developed now dedicated to love. And in this
love of the Mother an entirely new human life will flower in a
saved, preserved, beautified, and adored world.

*What does embracing Kali mean to you? In Bosnia, for example.*

Embracing Kali in Bosnia means, first, looking at what is going
on. First of all, opening to the full shame, the full horror, the
full grief of it, not hiding anywhere, not taking any palliatives,
not consoling yourself, not hiding behind *realpolitik,* but just
looking at it. That's the first stage, and that is an extremely
painful stage, because it means screaming in your sleep and
being really deeply shattered and disturbed and miserable about
what we're allowing to happen to these people.

That is only the first stage, because then you have to work
out how effective action can be implemented. How we can act,
what we can do as swiftly, purely, and effectively as possible,

because Kali *is* swiftness, purity, and effectiveness. Obviously, it's not going to be enough to have a few air strikes, to solve only a "local" problem. What we have to do is to really look at how a Bosnia arises, what in us enables it to arise, and to make the kind of massive spiritual transformation that we must if we are really taking these kinds of problems seriously. Only by transforming ourselves and really offering ourselves up to love can we actually end the Bosnia in ourselves that is therefore reproduced endlessly outside ourselves. So, it goes on and on, the kind of Kali-reaction to these situations. But there is an immediate action that must be taken, that has to be done. Every day that goes by without some kind of intervention is a nail in the coffin of the human race.

*Does this mean that you disagree with the Dalai Lama about nonviolence?*

Well, I think there's a point where nonviolence becomes cowardice and passivity, and I think the Dalai Lama would agree with me. His Holiness has said that in certain situations the only possible response is a violent one and, of course, these are very extreme situations and such action is only to be taken as a last resort. He has always said that. He's not doctrinaire about nonviolence, he says use it as far and as often and as deeply as possible. Obviously, that's the civilized way, but it's equally obvious to anyone that in some situations it's impossible to treat pathological killers and maniacs as if they were reasonable people who will negotiate. Tyrants and murderers have lied, they have betrayed us, they have sold us down the river; they have endlessly reneged on their promises. They have to be shown that we will not accept it, and we *must not* accept it.

Aurobindo was not in favor of nonviolence, he actually criticized Gandhi on numerous occasions. He said you're just feeding into the British, they will always take you on and make a fool of you, and they keep you there because you're convenient for them. Sometimes violence is necessary. In Hindu tradition, in the *Gita,* for example, Arjuna is told by Krishna to go out and fight and destroy his own kinsmen. Arjuna is terrified by this, because he loves his kinsmen, but Krishna tells him that it has already been decreed, that they must die because they are the carriers of illusion. If the Allies had not fought in the last war, we would all be under Nazi leadership, and half the people in this room would be dead, would never have lived, in fact. So what is it exactly that we are talking about? His Holiness is saying: As far as possible let us deal with problems nonviolently. Let us cultivate in ourselves the love and the peace that can emanate and be healing. But don't let us fool ourselves— the world is full of extremely cruel, extremely ferocious, violent people who are aided and abetted by modern culture, and who are very dangerous. At a certain moment, there may have to be absolutely, inescapably, a conscious act of violence. But if it's going to be an effective means to end suffering and not just create more violence, it will have to be organized and carried out by people who are profoundly nonviolent. It will have to be organized practically and efficiently, and with great intelligence, and great intelligence can only come from an inner and fundamental commitment to peace and nonviolence.

*I keep thinking I have to go on retreat or into an ashram to practice what Aurobindo and Ramakrishna are talking about.*

I don't agree. I think sometimes people in ashrams have very self-generated experiences, and sometimes in ashrams people think they're having all sorts of experiences, but they're not really having anything at all. God knows I know, I've spent far too much time with really crazy, narcissistic people in the spiritual movement. I'm much more struck by how you need the Mother in real life, in fact, that's where we really do need her. We don't need her sitting on a cushion somewhere, we need to meet her in precisely the most ordinary places. You can meet her in your colleagues, in the beggar on the street, in the problems in your own life, in your children and family and friends.

You're saying that it's quite difficult to get in contact with the soul, the spirit, to be silent enough to feel the more subtle divine touches of her being, but you must make room for that in your life now. Get up a half-hour earlier, meditate, really start praying. Keep up a river of prayer in your heart. Do what every single saint, aspirant, and mystic has done throughout the whole history of humankind, which is to take the job seriously and to work at it every single second of the day, wherever you are, in whatever circumstances you may find yourself.

There are three very simple ways to be constantly in touch with her: let flow a river of prayer in your heart; say a simple divine name or her name. That's the first way. The second way is through meditation. Just twenty minutes in the morning and twenty minutes at night can purify your entire being and give you the kind of detachment and peace that can help immensely in everyday life, that can give you exactly the focus and compassion you need in daily life. The third thing is service. There are thousands of moments in every day when you can serve her. You can give more than you usually give to the homeless person on the street. You can be kinder to the people in the office, you can be better to your own children. You can be better to your own self, to your own body, that is also her receptacle. You can turn the whole of a so-called normal life into a constant source of prayer and contact with her.

What this entails is altering your whole belief that she is somewhere else. That there are things called "holy" and things called "unholy," that the "sacred" is out there somewhere, and the "profane" is this here, where you are living now. We must shatter that very convenient illusion, and to do so means taking responsibility, absolutely and completely, for the quality of our consciousness at every single waking moment. We don't need any more ashrams, we need divinized human beings right in the middle of the marketplace, soberly and quietly transforming life from within life.

*There is a contradiction between what Lawlor says in his book*
Voices of the First Day *and what Aurobindo is saying about
how we are on a threshold of a great leap forward. Lawlor is
saying that human history has been one long catastrophic slide
downhill from the beginning.*

I think Lawlor's vision of "going back" is impractical, but I
think that his vision of the extraordinary beauty of our origin
is something we really need to keep very present in our minds
and in our hearts. So, I think the value of that book is not as a
prescription for action, but as an intense and precise visionary
map of where we came from, and of what we essentially are. I
think that Aurobindo's vision takes us further, because I think
Aurobindo has embraced the agony of history and seen a hidden logic in it, and has realized that humankind didn't simply
fall from some original perfect place but has been on a very significant journey and has made astonishing discoveries and
progress on that journey.

Aurobindo knows that this journey—the patriarchal journey—has been very dangerous but also very useful, because in
its course we have developed all sorts of technical and intellectual skills, which if we could now rededicate to God and rein-
fuse their use with sacred love, could help us create a new world.
For Lawlor the essential message of the Mother is *"return* to
origin"; for Aurobindo the Mother is saying: *"go forward* into
origin, taking everything you have learned into your future
in me." Lawlor has found his ideal world in the aborigines;
Aurobindo knows that the ideal world has not yet been created
because the complete conditions for its creation have never before
been present and are only now becoming possible to envision.

Where Lawlor always remains inspiring is in his description
of the customs and attitudes to all aspects of life the the aborigines have kept alive; I am convinced that this testimony will
help us greatly in the future to reimagine new ritual and "tribal"
forms of communication and education. Aurobindo didn't
occupy himself much with society at large; his emphasis—very

concentrated and acute—was on *personal* mystical growth. Lawlor, and other commentators like him, help us open out this potentially solipsistic emphasis and reimagine social forms of organization. Aurobindo talks and dreams about a "gnostic community"; Lawlor describes in exquisite detail what such a community looks like, one that lives in astonishing communion with reality. We need all the descriptions of life inspired by unity that we can get, because the creativity to which the Mother is summoning us, and invoking *in* us, will have to be active on every conceivable level, from the deepest mystical contemplation to distinct and definite decisions on environmental policy. This creativity will shake up and redefine everything, so the richer the visionary testimonies we have at our disposal, the better.

*You recently left Mother Meera. Has this destroyed or deepened your contact with the Divine Mother?*

Deepened it intensely and dramatically. I feel I am now in direct contact with her, with no need of any intermediaries. Meera's betrayal of me and Eryk and the systematic and atrocious lies she and her emissaries have subsequently been spreading about what happened between us have broken my heart and shattered all faith I had in the guru-disciple system. But I see this shattering as a great, if terrible, grace, a Kali-given liberation, in fact. I no longer believe at all in Meera. I believe in the experiences I had *with* her, but I no longer believe they came *from* her. The Divine Mother gave me them *through* Meera and when it was becoming dangerous to go on following Meera and being her spokesperson, the Divine Mother smashed my relationship with the false "Mother" to reveal the real one, beyond names and forms. By destroying the false, dependent relationship with a person, the Mother opened up for me a completely naked, radical, absolute relationship with her directly—one that is hair-raisingly intense and beautiful, the relationship, in fact, that I was always longing for.

In so doing, the Mother has shown me what I call the great "nuclear" secret—the secret of direct transmission by her. And it is this direct transmission that I see the gurus and so-called "divine mothers" blocking, not facilitating. This blocking, this exploitation of occult power, this elitist authoritarian system, belong to a past that has now got to go so that the sacred gnostic democracy the Mother wants to create all over the world can be imagined and manifested. Meera and the others are no different from the heads of corporations that are making life-destroying decisions every day. Gurus are deformed by the power they have and misuse, as corporate leaders are blinded and corrupted by theirs. Both are trapped in outworn systems which we have to transcend in order to survive.

I have no doubt that the death of the guru system is coming, and coming soon. What is essential for the future is that the current orgy of credulity is not succeeded, as it well might be, by a comparably intense and absurd orgy of doubt and nihilism. When Meera revealed to me that she was false, I did not lose my faith in the Divine Mother; in fact, my faith darkened and deepened and my inner practice became more and more passionate, hungry, and absolute. What I am now trying to do, and many others are as well, is to grow up, to stand on my own judgment in direct contact with the Mother, to try and show that no intermediary authorities with her are needed. So when anarchy and radical disillusion hit the ashrams and the sects—as they will—there will be many of us going about our simple mystical business in as calm, sober, elevated, and inspiring a way as possible, offering by our example the joy of a way out of that madness, into direct intimacy with her. As many of us as possible must now model this direct relationship with the Mother and refuse to slip into any of the old games and traps, either of being a "disciple" or a "master"; really, in every way, going beyond the old categories, the old forms of authority and hierarchical relationship. This "modeling" is what I see now as the most important practice, and is for me the greatest duty and the greatest joy.

*Isn't the direct path dangerous?*

Of course. If you go the guru path, there is a tremendous danger of idiotic lack of discrimination, of narcissism, of being in a kind of guru-cinema, of being dependent on the guru like a dazzled and obsessive child, of being trapped for years in that posture of submission and need. That's a very big spiritual trap. If you go the direct path, there is the danger that you will think you are much more advanced than you are, with nobody to check you. There's the trap of thinking you've attained "enlightenment" when you have simply had a few experiences. That is why I am stressing so much these days the necessity of spiritual friends and new kinds of transmission.

Taking the "non-guru" direct path doesn't mean that you don't learn from people more evolved than you, it doesn't mean that you don't have guides or mentors. It just means that you don't put anyone in power over you, and don't project your needs for security and for divine assistance onto any other person in a body. Don't confuse the direct path with just being an isolated individual. Learn from everyone who can teach you; be always receptive and alert to advice. But don't divinize anyone and don't be anyone's slave. Remember always the Buddha's injunction to never believe anything just because you've been told it, but to test it and see for yourself if it is true. The direct path demands both more real divine pride and real divine humility than the guru path, demands a leap at every moment into accountability and authenticity.

The advantage of the direct path is that the more you progress along it, the more sincerely and passionately you discover how deeply the Mother is *in you* and in the daily incidents of your life, the more wonderingly awake you become to her continual presence and help and inspiration. By removing all the pretty veils and icons and gurus between you and her, you risk uncanny intimacy with her on every level. You will find—as everyone who takes this way discovers—that this risk on your part is met with boundless wild love on hers. Open to her directly and stretch out your heart's arms to her, in form and beyond form, and you will find just how precise, wild, and tender her continual attention to you and in you is. This is the beginning of radical trust, and so of radical freedom.

*One of the things that moved me very much in* Hidden Journey *was the story of you and Jean-Marc Frechette. Can you talk about the power of friendship in this transformation?*

I've had this amazing experience during the last few months, of teaching not as anyone's messenger or mouthpiece, not as a guru, but just as someone who's had an experience of the divine feminine with other people who have had experiences of the divine feminine. Instead of being focused on some mythical "other," I have been focused on the Mother, the Mother that is beyond form and name, but is expressing herself through many different people. This great transformation of the Mother is being done, I see increasingly, in cohorts of souls, in groups of friends, lovers and friends. When I was going through the process described in *Hidden Journey,* I had a very close friendship with Astrid. She and I loved each other so much, our souls and minds and bodies crossed over into each other. We dreamed each other's dreams and we could give each other vital pieces of information at crucial moments. I think that this is how the transformation works. It is another sign that we don't need projected others; what we need is the close, vital, human support of people going through a process together and giving a great deal of mutual help.

Rather than going off and living in some ashram, where the majority of people are frightened siblings competing for the love of the projected "mother" or "father," hating and despising and being jealous of each other, a much better plan would be to live in normal life with friends and go through the process together. Nothing is more revealing, nothing more checking, than real friends who will just say, "Oh, come off it, you haven't seen another flashing light. Why don't you do the washing up from time to time?" Ashrams, in my experience, are lunatic asylums filled with jealous and needy people. What gurus do is divide and rule. They are the magical "other," everybody's in love with them, everybody's focused on them, and everybody hates whatever position the others have with them. The gurus keep this infantile situation going because it keeps them in power and "indispensable." What happens between groups of friends, however, in a circle concentrated on the Mother, is that everybody in that circle can become democratically one with her and with one another. Everybody has wisdom, after all, and everybody can contribute. In a Mother-circle, every member can mutually enhance and inform all the others. I'm certain that this is one of the forms of transformation of the future. It's a demanding form because it requires that we really listen to and respect each other, and that we realize once and for all that there is no independent narcissistic awakening. If we awaken, we do it for and with everyone else.

*Let's go back to what you were saying about radical trust and radical freedom, surrendering to intimacy with the Mother. Can you say a bit more about that?*

One day the Divine Mother appeared before Ramakrishna looking very sumptuous and beautiful. She told him to take an ax and chop her apart, destroy her completely. Ramakrishna sobbed, "How can I destroy you? You are so beautiful!" But the Divine Mother insisted, and so Ramakrishna, wild with anguish and sorrow, hacked her apart. Immediately he went into a deeper visionary ecstasy than any he had previously known. She had taken him *through* form *beyond* form; she had initiated him into her formless form. And when he emerged from that ecstasy, he was free to see her and know her in everything and everyone, to go up and down the ladder to her as he wished, or rather, as *she* wished. He then knew the Mother both as form and the light that is always engendering all forms simultaneously.

Meera's betrayal has initiated me into the *real* Divine Mother. The form had to be shattered for me to be released from my enchantment with it. Then the formless Mother appeared, glittering and burning in every event, every conversation, every single thing in the universe, from the taps in the bathroom to the flowers on the table to Eryk's face. This immense *plunging* into the Mother was not in any way Meera's gift or teaching; Meera simply wanted me to remain her devotee and to go on "using" me, and her lies prove she is not enlightened (to say the least). This opening was the Divine Mother's brutal amazing miracle, not Meera's, and every day I am taken deeper into its beauty. The more I enter into this beauty—that is sometimes violent, even mad, and always deranging to any pattern or sense that my mind can construct—the more profoundly I realize how deeply I and all beings are protected, enveloped, sustained, and inspired at all times and in all situations by the Divine Mother. This breeds the radical trust of which I spoke, and from that trust I find I am increasingly coming to accept my own innate divinity and that of everyone else. And so I feel growing within myself an astounding, barrierless, and nameless freedom, my real freedom and that of everyone else, the freedom that Ramakrishna and Aurobindo so marvelously explored, celebrated, and charted—her freedom in me, flowering to discover and experience itself endlessly.

This freedom, with its naked bliss and innate gnosis, is the freedom of the "flame-child" that Aurobindo dreamed of seeing born in every human life. Let me end with a quote from Aurobindo's translation of the *Rig Veda,* a passage he himself quotes in *The Life Divine:* "May the invincible rays of his intuition be there seeking immortality *pervading both the births;* for by them he sets flowing in one movement human strengths and things divine."[17]

May all our lives become one movement in her, one in radical trust and radical freedom, our human strengths married indissolubly to her "things divine." May we all be born into her and see our own face and the true faces of all beings for the first time, and then work with her strength to change all things to mirror and reflect that real and blinding vision now, before it is too late.

## Notes

1. Sri Aurobindo, *The Life Divine* (Pondicherry, India: Sri Aurobindo Ashram, Publication Department, 1939–40), pp. 1057–1058.

2. *The Life Divine*, p. 1058.

3. *The Life Divine*, pp. 1059–1060. Italics added.

4. Sri Aurobindo, *Savitri* (Pondicherry, India: Sri Aurobindo Ashram, Publication Department, 1950–1951), Book Six, Canto 2.

5. *Savitri*, Book Two, Canto 1.

6. *Savitri*, pp. 707, 709.

7. Andrew Harvey, *Hidden Journey: A Spiritual Awakening* (New York: Arkana Books, 1991), pp. 27–28.

8. Sri Aurobindo, *The Mother* (Pondicherry, India: Sri Aurobindo Ashram, Publication Department, 1928), pp. 61–62.

9. *The Mother*, pp. 20–25.

10. *The Mother*, pp. 27–28. Italics added.

11. *The Mother*, p. 29.

12. *The Mother*, pp. 36–37.

13. *The Mother*, p. 40.

14. *The Mother*, pp. 40–43.

15. *The Mother*, p. 43.

16. Sri Aurobindo, *Letters on Yoga*, Volume Three (Pondicherry, India: Sri Aurobindo Ashram, Publication Department, 1971).

17. Sri Aurobindo, *The Life Divine*, p. 1015. Italics added.

# Chapter Five

# *The Sufi Way of Adoration*

THE SUFI VISION of the glory and majesty of every soul and of the necessity of the path of adoration as the swiftest and most authentic way to God are, I believe, essential to the contemporary revolution of the sacred feminine and to the Mother's plan for a mystical reinvigoration of the heart, soul, and body of humankind. In Sufism—and especially in the poetry of the greatest of all Sufi mystical poets, Jalal-ud-Din Rumi— a vision of love has, against all conceivable historical, social, and intellectual odds, been kept alive. This is a vision of love as the ecstatic ground, energy, evolutionary force, and purpose of the entire universe and every thing and event in it.

To the Sufi awakened by adoration to the presence of the Beloved in all things and to the vastness of his or her own soul expanded, dilated, shattered open again and again, saturated and drenched by love, the entire universe reveals itself as the manifestation of *Kibriya,* Divine Glory, and everything in it is seen as sacred. For the Sufi, the whole purpose of human life is to adore, know, and become one with this love beyond all barriers and dogmas, to *be* this love, and to act continually from its passion, heart-extravagance, magnanimity, and all-embracing tenderness. The *Koran* tells us that God has made the Creation specifically to adore Him. In one of the Prophet's *hadiths* (sayings), God declares: "My heart and my heavens do not contain me but I am contained in the heart of my faithful servant." The great Sufi adept Kubra wrote: "Man is God's beloved and lover. Whoever knows anything else but God is ignorant of himself and whoever knows himself knows his Lord in union [*tawhid*] that transcends everything."

It is crucial for humanity's future that as many of us as possible taste and know and enact this love and union, and taste and know and enact our own divine identity, and learn through adoration the glory of the heart and the glory of the universe revealed by love as shining in the core of our heart's own light. It is crucial, because without this living, direct knowledge of the glory of the soul and the universe, and the passionate, calm, wise, humble action that flows naturally from it, the world cannot be preserved. Rumi wrote: "Wherever you are and in whatever circumstance, try always to be a lover and a passionate lover. Once you have possessed love, you will remain a lover in the tomb, on the day of resurrection, in Paradise, and forever." The crisis we are now in is calling each of us to become "lovers," to "possess love," and so to possess love's wisdom, passion, endless stamina, lion-hearted courage, to possess its capacity to embrace and endure anything at all in the service of the Beloved.

Rumi said: "You must be alive in love, for a dead man can do nothing. Who is alive? He to whom love gives birth." To birth ourselves into love and let ourselves be birthed by love into itself is why we are here. Our contemporary collective agony is calling us to this great birth on a massive scale. Now, more than ever before, we have to be alive in love—"dead men can do nothing." The Sufi vision is extreme, uncompromising, and glorious; it is one that knows and adores the birth of love and knows that to be born into love is the purpose of everything, and embraces *all* the conditions necessary for this splendor, even the most terrible.

That is why poets like Rumi speak so clearly to us. Rumi has confronted horror, desolation, loss, terrible heartbreak, abandonment, and has found in adoration and surrender the alchemical keys to transmute everything into the gold of love. In a time as horrible as ours, such testimony of the deathlessness and magnificence of love is priceless, a continual challenge to us to throw ourselves with abandon into the flame of truth, a continual reminder of the glory and power we will become when nothing remains in us but that love that is our secret and our origin.

\* \* \*

Rumi wrote at the end of his life to Shams:

> Those tender words we said to one another,
> Are stored in the secret heart of heaven.
> One day, like the rain, they will fall and spread
> And our love will grow green over the world.[1]

"Those tender words we said to one another are stored in the secret heart of heaven." This is Rumi writing at the end of his life to his mystic beloved, Shams, who illuminated him. Those secret words of adoration and initiation into the highest secret, the secret that we are all divine and that we all have the divine bliss, the divine peace, the divine ecstasy at the very core of our identity; those secret words are secret because they are shattering, and they break apart all the old visions, all the old paradigms, all the old disciplines, all the old ways of keeping people subject by hierarchy to the slavery of authority. They had to be kept secret, because if Rumi had said them out loud, in such a way that no one could possibly mistake his meaning, he would have been hung and drawn-and-quartered, just as Al Hallaj, another great mystic of Sufism, was in ninth-century Baghdad.

So: "Those secret words we said to one another," my beloved Shams, "those secret words that came out of our knowledge of adoration and our knowledge of love, they have been stored in the heart of heaven," because they are the ultimate words of the soul to God, the ultimate divine words, the really nuclear divine words. They have been stored in the heart of heaven from where they came and into which they poured. "One day, like the rain"—in Sufism, rain is the most feminine of all symbols, a symbol of grace, of the flood of divine grace and divine light—"One day like the rain, they will fall and spread, and our mystery will grow green over the world."

That day is now. At last, the Divine Mother is taking the human race, the entire human race, through crisis, through the collapse of all the old values, through the collapse of all the old paradigms and the destruction of all the old ideals, to a place when at last we can really listen to what Rumi is saying. To what Rumi is telling us out of his astounding love affair with the Beloved. "The secret words"—we are at last ready to receive these secret words, this secret news of our nuclear divine identity.

I wrote in *The Way of Passion:*

That day has come and this greening of the world by the mystery of Rumi's love for Shams [and for the Divine Beloved as he knew Shams to be] and its revelations is beginning. In the last thirty years, news of Rumi's greatness has spread, not only through Islam, but through the rest of the world, in scholarly works and translations, and in artistic representations of all kinds. Rumi is increasingly seen for what I believe he is—not only our supreme poet—but also an essential guide to the new mystical Renaissance [of the sacred feminine] that is struggling to be born against terrible odds in the rubble of our dying civilization. . . .

"My death is my wedding with eternity," Rumi wrote. From that Light he lives in beyond space and time, he is radiating to a darkened world the fire of his infinite love and hope, urging us all onward, whatever our belief or unbelief, into the miracle of our real divine nature and the feast of the divine life on earth.[2]

Rumi said, and it is something that the Divine Mother is saying to us amid the despair and confusion of this apocalyptic age: "If you have lost heart in the path of love, flee to me without delay. I am a fortress invisible." Rumi said: "Love's creed is separate from all religions. The creed and denomination of lovers is God." He also said, and this could be the motto of the renaissance of the sacred feminine: "My religion is to live through love." You can take this phrase a thousand ways: to live *through* love; to live through *love*; to *live* through love. Rumi also said: "If you have not been a lover, count not your life as lived, on the day of reckoning, it will not be counted." Rumi also said: "Love is the water of life—drink it down with heart and soul! Know that all but the lovers are fish without water, dead and desiccated, even if they are princes. Love is the water of life and will deliver you from death.... He who throws himself into love is a king."

The path of the Mother, the radicalism of the path of the Mother, is that it is a way of love that burns away all dogma, all distinctions, all castes and creeds, to pose humanity the ultimate challenge of living now in the burning fire of love *as* that flame of love that purifies and transforms everything and acts in all arenas to save the planet and transform it into a mirror of the Mother and her justice. In Rumi we have with Ramakrishna and Aurobindo one of the very few universal beings that the world religions have produced, one who has possessed and lived love in its naked splendor. He is someone whose realization was so complete, so multifaceted, so infinite in its depth and intensity, that he goes beyond all religious denominations and definitions to show the whole of humankind the fullness of what a human being in love with the Beloved and empowered by it can become.

In order to discover exactly why Sufism has so much insight into the sacred feminine to give us, I want to stress one particular aspect of Rumi's greatness. I believe him to be, for us now, the supreme master of adoration. For me, and for many other of her mystics, the way in to the deepest knowledge of the love and splendor, the beauty and glory of the Divine Mother is adoration. It is the way into the most profound knowledge of what nature is, of what we are, and of our responsibilities to both nature and ourselves.

As I said previously, the sacred feminine has three essential laws. A world remade in the image and as the living mirror of the sacred feminine would have three essential characteristics. The first of these laws is the "Law of Unity," the vision of life as One, that vision of unity which Ramakrishna and Aurobindo and all the greatest mystics of all traditions have always known, that vision of the absolute interconnectedness and relatedness of all things that the scientists and physicists are only now discovering to be scientific law as well as mystical law. The second law is the "Law of Rhythm," the knowledge that the whole creation evolves to rhythmic laws, laws which are like the rhythm of the body and the seasons, laws which necessitate learning how to listen to and celebrate rhythm, learning how to live in harmony with the rhythms that govern the universe instead of exploitative, or cruel, or bitter rejection of them, which leads only to schizophrenia and madness.

The third law, and this is the power on which I wish to concentrate here, before we enter into an exploration of Rumi's mastery and understanding of adoration, is what I call the "Love of the Dance." When I came to coin that phrase, I was thinking of Rumi, because Rumi created nearly all of his greatest poetry while dancing around a pillar in ecstasy. Many of his most important poems contain imagery celebrating life as an ecstatic dance for the Beloved. The final power of the sacred feminine is the Love of the Dance.

In this dance of love, life itself, in all its paradoxes, is seen and known and felt and lived as completely sacred. It is adored and honored in all its ordeals and wonders. Life is known as the mystery of the Father-Mother, the Shiva-Shakti, whatever name you wish to give to it; and is to be worshipped as the play of opposites, the play of love, the ecstatic dance of these complementary energies. This is a fundamentally unmorbid, healthy, joyful vision of the world, one that blesses and accepts it bravely in its entirety, one that does not split off the body from the spirit or heaven from earth, but that finds the body *in* the spirit and the spirit in the body, earth in heaven and heaven in earth. One that blesses and accepts all of life's conditions, that honors the body, honors sexuality, reveres the family and all forms of what

Keats called "the holiness of the heart's affection," that sees and knows matter and nature as the body of the divine.

The wisdom of the sacred feminine is one that knows beyond all concepts or dogmas that this experience, this process of life we all are in, is holy in its most minute detail. A so-called "ordinary" life is not ordinary at all, but is one unbroken flow of normal miracle. So this sacred wisdom, this wisdom of adoration that arises out of immersion in divine love, does not separate anything—heaven from earth, spirit from body, thought from action—for in all dimensions and all worlds, all possibilities are here, are interrelated, are one. This is a wisdom that does not aim for an unnatural perfection, or a flight into some life- or body-denying absolute, but works patiently, all-embracingly, with infinite alchemical subtlety towards wholeness. To those awakened to and by this wisdom, being born a human being is not being born into a desolate world, or into mere illusion. To be human is to be born into a dance, a sacred dance in which every animate or inanimate, visible or invisible being is also participating. A dance in which every step is printed in light, whose energy is adoration, and whose rhythm is praise.

For me this is the core of Sufi revelation, and the core of its importance to us now—to teach us the astounding, wild, mad courage to see every step of this terrible and frightening dance printed in light; and the energy of the dance is not rooted in fear, in a desperate struggle to escape the terms of the dance, but in adoration of all its terms, all its challenges, all its ordeals, grief, losses, and suffering. The essential divine rhythm, meaning, and truth of this dance is nothing less than the continual, endless, boundless praise of the divine that makes such a glory, such a theophany, such an opening, such a feast of love possible. In this great sacred vision of the divine feminine, this vision that Rumi found in his love for Shams, pain, desolation, and destruction are not separate from the dance but are essential energies of its transformative unfolding. Rumi knew that death itself cannot shatter the dance, because death is revealed as the lifespring of the dance's fertility—the mother of all of its changing splendor.

So let's hear Rumi's own words and try and deepen our knowledge of adoration, and the knowledge that adoration brings. Jung once made the distinction between two types of mystics—those who deny and those who embrace, those who choose ascetic withdrawal from the world to refine their perceptions, and those who plunge into every worldly whirlpool with fearlessness and joy. Ramakrishna, in one of his last remarks to his disciples, railed against those who only wanted nirvana. He said to Vivekananda, "I am so tired of these people coming to me wanting release. Mother doesn't like people who want release. Mother likes people who play. She loves the game, she's keeping the game going, she loves those who are willing to risk everything in the game." Of all the mystics who have embraced reality, none has embraced it more gorgeously than Jalal-ud-Din Rumi. As he said, "Creation, destruction, I am dancing for them *both*."

Rumi tells us about the world seen through the eyes of adoration:

It is a pity to reach the sea and to be satisfied with just a little water. This existence, this life, is the great sea....

There are great pearls in the sea and from the sea myriads of precious things can be produced. This world is just false coin gilded. It is a fleck of foam on the great sea of love.

Man is the astrolabe of God, the astronomical instrument in which the heaven's movements are charted and reflected. Just as this copper astrolabe is the mirror of the heavens, so the awakened human being is the astrolabe of the mysteries of God....

The awakened human being is the theater, the place, in which the divine mysteries appear. When God causes a human being to have knowledge of Him, and to know Him, and to be familiar with Him through the astrolabe of his own being, he beholds moment by moment, and flash by flash, the manifestation of God and His infinite beauty, and that beauty is never absent from his mirror.

Let's enter into what these words are promising to be true about the awakened heart, the awakened soul: the heart that has been matured by the ecstasy of adoration and opened by the ecstasy of adoration sees in every moment, every event, every face, every sentient living thing, nothing less than the appearance of infinite beauty.

> When the Mother causes a woman to have knowledge of Her and to know Her, and to be familiar with Her through the astrolabe of her own being, she beholds moment by moment, and flash by flash, the manifestation of the Divine.

The word "flash" is a Sufi word meaning "sudden divine illumination." There are, according to different Sufis, twenty-two, or 108, or 312 different kinds of *tajalli*, different kinds of flashings out of the grandeur of God. Everything, from the most humdrum to the most extraordinary, is known in this state as a "flash," a revelation of one of the sacred names of the divine, one of the sacred powers of the divine.

"She beholds moment by moment, and flash by flash, the manifestation of the Divine and Her infinite beauty." This beauty is always around us. In a few hundred yards, you will see it in a thousand places. You'll see it in the face of a friend, you'll see it in the tiny spring flowers trying to crack out of the cement, you'll see it in the light on the street, you'll see it in the concrete wall, you'll see it everywhere, because the divine Beloved is doing nothing at all moments but trying to "flash out" its beauty to us. The Divine Mother is attempting to awaken in all of us the pure perception that sees this beauty "flash by flash and moment by moment."

And when that beauty, that infinite beauty of the Beloved, is never absent from our mirror, what is it exactly that we *see?* The following quotation has been one of my favorites for many years because it expresses, far better than I have ever seen it expressed in any other mystical literature, the outrageousness of this perception of the divine beauty of things when your senses are really awake. If you could see just once, for two minutes of your life, what exactly a flower *is,* just a single flower, you would go permanently insane with joy. This permanent sweet insanity is what the mystics and the Divine Mother are trying to bring down onto the earth. If we all went insane with the beauty of what is created around us, we would do everything in our power to stop the devastation and destruction of this beauty that is a reflection of infinite beauty.

Know, O my child . . .

Not "imagine," not "intuit," but *know*—

> . . . that each thing in the universe is a vessel,
> Full to the brim with wisdom and beauty.
> Know, my child, that each thing is a drop from the
>     burning river of His infinite beauty.
> It is a hidden treasure because of its fullness.
> It has exploded and made the earth more brilliant than
>     the skies.
> It is a hidden treasure because of its fullness.
> It has sprung out and made the earth like an emperor
>     wrapped in a robe of burning satin.

In the wild, sensual, ecstatic gorgeousness of this imagery, you have the essence of the Sufi revelation. Let love bring that gorgeousness of knowledge to you. When a mother looks at her child, when lover gazes at lover, when great friend looks into the eyes of great friend, the heart becomes totally open and the miracle of being here expands in the core of the heart. The gorgeousness that arrives then is the perfume of the Beloved, the perfume of *Kibriya,* the Glory.

"Know, O my child, that each thing"—*each* thing! Do you see that this revelation, as that of Ramakrishna and Aurobindo, goes straight to the heart of the sacred feminine? What is the Mother doing all the time but trying to destroy the concepts of the mind, trying to destroy what destroys us: our separation, our dissociation, our vanity, our deluded sense that we know what this world is, when in fact everything in this world is sacred and can only be known through love? "Know, O my child, that *each thing* in the universe is a vessel full to the brim with wisdom and beauty."

Eryk and I had a revelatory experience the day after we got married. We were looking at all the flowers that we had been given. Eryk said, "I can't stand those orange flowers over there, they're vulgar, so can you go put them somewhere where I don't have to look at them?" I said "Fine," and went and put them in front of Ramakrishna's photograph in my study. I said to them, "Eryk is young. He's a wonderful person, but he hasn't learned certain things about how all things are divine. So don't take it personally. I love you, you are wonderful flowers, you just stay there and flower for as long as you want." Late that night, I went into the room to pray and the flowers were glowing—really *glowing*—with a soft, pale, golden pink light. I called Eryk in, hoping that he could share this vision. He came in and saw the flowers; it was the first time he had ever seen the divine light. The flowers were glowing with orange and pink light. And he understood. He said, "The divine is also in what I have rejected and what I have despised."

> Know, O my child, that *each thing* in the universe is a
>     vessel,
> Full to the brim with wisdom and beauty....
> is a drop from the burning river of His infinite beauty.
> It is a hidden treasure because of its fullness....

Love, and you will see that these flowers on the desk in front of me are right now exploding softly and silently with the immense energy of love. Absolute, unconditional love, fearless love. Giving everything away, holding nothing back, just for the heaven of it. In the whole of creation, nature is doing nothing but this all the time: exploding silently, or wildly, or sweetly, or violently, whatever you like, but exploding with this energy, the love-Shakti of the Divine Mother. Exploding and making "the earth more brilliant than the skies."

"It is a hidden treasure because of its fullness," Rumi says.

The extent of its fullness is hidden to those not in love with love, but lovers will see that all things have "sprung out and made the earth like an emperor wrapped in a robe of burning satin." Accept that epiphany, and you become a mirror from which the beauty of the Mother is never absent, you become what Ramakrishna and Aurobindo and Rumi each were— divine children, whole, clear, open-heart mirrors polished by adoration, in which the Beloved could reflect her wild and derangingly sweet beauty tirelessly, endlessly, extravagantly.

Another great Sufi, Lahiji, tells us:

> The cup in which the world is reflected is the heart of the perfect being. That mirror that shows reality is the heart. The heart is the treasure of the divine mysteries. Ask the heart, then, what is the purpose of the two worlds.

These phrases move deeper and deeper into the secret of adoration.

"The cup in which the world is reflected is the heart of the perfect being." A cup, because the cup is the perfect being, because it's entirely open and receptive, and because, in mystical symbolic terms, its sides are like a mirror, shiny and empty, and through adoration the heart has been made shining and empty: a mirror in which the divine face can be reflected without any distortion. That mirror of the purified heart, the adoring heart, the clear heart, the shining and empty heart, reflects reality. Reality can never be seen or known except by the mind and eye of that heart, because the supreme mystery is ringed by fire, secrecy, and silence. The final rose can only ever be smelled and seen by someone who is hopelessly in love with it. That is why the divine mystery is protected from nearly everyone, and only the lover can pass through the flames.

Lahiji says, "The heart is the treasure of the divine mysteries." When through adoration you learn to live and love and see and know with a purified heart, then you are initiated into the manifestation of the divine, "flash by flash, moment by moment."

"Ask the heart, then, what is the purpose of the two worlds."
The purpose is to live in the experience of the flung-open, mir-
ror-like, adoring heart, where the two worlds become one,
where heaven is revealed on earth, and each thing, even the
most despised, even the most soiled, gnarled, and difficult, is
revealed as radiant with God. The heart *knows* and *is* this "purpose of the two worlds," for the heart is nothing less than the
sea of light that is the universe, a drop in which the whole ocean
of the creation miraculously dances.

Rumi wrote:

> The heart is nothing but the sea of light,
> The place of the union of God.
> My image dwells in the heart of the King
> The heart of the King would be in anguish without my
>     image.
> When the King commands me to fly in His Path
> I take to the skies and reach his Heart's zenith like His
>     rays.
> I fly like a moon and a sun, I tear open the veils of
>     heaven.
> The Light of Intellect sparks from my thinking.
> The sky has been created out of my Original
>     Nature ...
> I hold the spiritual realm, and although I am not the
>     King's equal,
> I receive from His hands the light of His Theophany.
>
> Know that the mirror of the heart has no limits ...
> For the heart is with God.
>
> Love makes the sea boil like a cauldron;
> Love rubbles the mountains to sand.
> Love cracks open the heavens into thousands of
>     fissures;
> Love makes the earth tremble.
> God said: "If it wasn't by pure love, how could I have
>     brought

The glowing heavens into existence?
I have raised up the celestial sphere
So you could understand the sublimity of Love."

Rumi also wrote:

As you are born from Adam, become like him
And contemplate all the atoms of the universe in your-
self.
What is in the pitcher that is not also in the river?
What is in the house that is not also in the town?
The world is like a pitcher and the heart is like a river.
The world is the house, and the heart a marvelous
town.

There Rumi—God sanctify his spirit—calls the world a pitcher,
and a house; the heart of the universal human, a river and a
town. So he indicates to us that everything that exists, everything in the world, is within the human state.

In the sea of fidelity I dissolve like salt.
I have no more certainty or doubt, faith or unfaith.
In my heart a star shines,
And in that star turn the seven heavens.

The reflection of each image shines eternally from the
heart alone
In the multiplicity as much as beyond it.
Those who have polished their hearts
Have escaped from the perfumes and colors.
They contemplate Beauty endlessly,
They have abandoned the form and husk of knowledge
And have unfurled the flag of certainty.
Since the forms of the eight paradises have shone
They have found the tablets of their hearts to be
sensitive to them.
From heaven, from the starred spheres, and from the
Void

They receive constantly one hundred thousand impres-
sions.
What are these impressions?
What can any words say? *The Vision of God Himself.*

So let us be clear, now, what adoration actually is. What is
this force, this power, that takes us, as the Sufis and Rumi say,
into the heart of this divine experience where the "seven heavens" turn and where the heart sees "the vision of God himself"?

Adoration is not some fervent spiritual or poetic exercise
reserved for a chosen few. I believe that the human race will
die out and destroy nature if it does not learn again how to
adore God, the God in all of us, God shining and living in
nature, and then learns again how to act from and in that spirit
of adoration. Adoration is not a game or a series of exercises,
but nothing less than the oxygen of survival. Adoration is the
oxygen of survival at every level—survival of the body, learning to attune itself to the great rhythms of nature; survival of
the mind, learning to humble its dangerous vanity before the
infinitely greater beauty and majesty of the divine; survival of
the heart, opening in love to that love streaming toward it from
everything. Adoration is the way itself to the illumination that
alone can give us both the knowledge and the courage to save
ourselves and nature. In the ultimate struggle against evil and
disaster, adoration is the ultimate help, the ultimate source of
strength, the ultimate protection against every work of darkness.

There is a worldwide famine of adoration, and we are all
visibly dying in it. The desolation and nihilism, the meaninglessness, and tragic and brutal carelessness, and perversity we
see all around us and in us, is a direct result of living in a spiritual prison in which we are starved and have starved ourselves
of the food that our hearts, minds, and souls need most: the
food of worship, the food of love, the food of gratitude, the food
of praise, the bread and wine of adoration. We have forgotten

how to renew ourselves in the fire and the light of the simple divine glory of life itself, and forgotten how to know that joy and light in us and around us; that joy and light that initiate and heal all who realize them, the sacred fire of all true action.

So, the adoration that Rumi and the Sufis exemplify so passionately is both the way home and home itself; both the sign and seal of true knowledge, and the path to it. It's both the summit of the mountain of God, the radiant summit of the Annapurna of God, and the force that gives the passion, the heart, the courage, the stamina, the sheer energy to scale it. Adoration is the beginning, the ground; adoration is the energy of growth. And adoration, as all the mystics have told us, is the end, the goal, the fire that breaks continually from recognition of one's final identity with the divine.

Why are we here? I believe that we are here to learn through adoration the love that moves the earth and stars. Coming to learn that love and its shining in all things opens our heart more and more to it in an ecstasy of tenderness and gratitude, until that time comes when all the sinews of our heart have been eased back and opened so wide that this entire universe and our entire experience of it can be placed within. This is the nirvana of the Buddhists, the *moksha* of the Hindus, the sacred state of oneness with all life felt by the Kogis, Yamomamis, and aborigines, the *fana* and *baqa* of the Sufis. This is the shattering of the cage of time, of life and death.

Constant adoration is the one force nuclear enough in its intensity to do this great work. Constant adoration, constant opening of the heart, in whatever circumstance, in whatever pain, in whatever difficulty and whatever grief, in whatever bitterness. Constant opening in adoration of the divine beauty, the divine magnificence, the divine generosity, of all the different names of God, of the Mother. Constant adoration is the one force powerful enough to do the great work of transformation for the Mother, this great work of opening the heart, shattering it, again and again, deeper and deeper through love, so that the moment can come when the heart is so totally open that the entire universe, and all the creatures in it, can be placed within it and can shine out with Her secret glory.

The great Christian mystic Traherne said, "You never enjoy the world a-right, until you are clothed with the heavens and crowned with the stars. Until you perceive yourself to be the sole heir of the whole world, and more than so, because men are in it who are, every one, sole heirs as well you." In the words of the *Isa Upanishad,* "The whole of the whole universe is shining in the glory of God." Through adoration you will know what the Navajo Indians knew, who created this magnificent chant to the Divine Mother,

> *I am walking with dark clouds,*
> *I am walking with spring rain,*
> *I am walking with leaves and flowers,*
> *I am walking on a trail of golden pollen.*
> *May everything be beautiful below me,*
> *May everything around me be beautiful.*
> *It is begun in beauty,*
> *It is finished in beauty.*

Through adoration, also, you will come to know and receive the truths expressed in the following ode of Rumi:

> Everything you see has its roots
>     in the Unseen world,
> The forms may change,
>     yet the essence remains the same.
>
> Every wondrous sight will vanish,
> Every sweet word will fade.
>     But do not be disheartened,
>     The Source whence they come is eternal—
>     giving new life and new joy.
>
> Why do you weep?
> That Source is within you,
> And this whole world
>     is springing up from it.

The Source is full,
     its waters are ever-flowing;
     Do not grieve,
     drink your fill,
Don't think it will ever run dry—
This is the endless Ocean!

From the moment you came into this world
A ladder was placed in front of you
     that you might escape.

From earth you became plant,
From plant you became animal.
Afterwards you became a human being,
Endowed with knowledge, intellect, and faith.

Behold the body, born of dust—
     how perfect it has become!

Why should you fear its end?
When were you ever made less by dying?

When you pass beyond this human form,
No doubt you will become an angel
And soar through the heavens!

But don't stop there.
Even heavenly bodies grow old.

Pass again from that heavenly realm
And plunge
     into the vast ocean of consciousness.
Let the drop of water that is you
     become a hundred mighty seas.

But do not think that the drop alone
Becomes the Ocean—
     the Ocean, too, becomes the drop![3]

Rumi is telling us that it is adoration that reveals the ultimate and ultimately encouraging and emboldening secret: that

love is the force directing the evolution of all things, the power by which all the metamorphoses of the universe are accomplished. All things exist on ever-ascending rungs of the ladder of love, and that ladder has, and can have, no possible end in any of the worlds, because love is infinite and infinitely beyond any conceivable realization of its nature. What is this love and its force but the Mother and her Shakti of endless transformation?

The enlightened heart-mind, the heart-mind of the divine child, of the person divinized by adoration, is not only rooted in peace, it is, as Rumi tells us again and again in his work and in the example of his life, expanding as is the external universe. This is one of the great mystical secrets: enlightenment is not a static state, but an *expanding* state, a state which is continually transforming itself, flash by flash, moment by moment, just as the universe itself is racing toward some unknowable destination on the wings of love itself. So, too, the open heart is racing toward some unknowable consummation on the wings of divine love, opening and opening, racing toward God at speeds far faster than any known in physical life.

The enlightened heart-mind is expanding as the external universe is, at the speed of the light that travels infinitely faster than its physical equivalent, into a heart constantly widened by the power and bliss of adoration. The light of the Divine Mother can be poured into a heart that has been constantly widened—even in this moment you can stretch your heart another million miles, wherever you think you are, you can!—and into that open heart, constantly widened by the power and bliss of adoration, into that cup can be poured endless, boundless light, love, and knowledge in continually expanding spirals.

This is an endless process, as Rumi's poem makes clear. The dynamic Mother is always dancing and transforming, going deeper and further, endlessly opening in continually expanding spirals of intensity and energy that have no end in any dimension. Only the mind makes an end, only our intellect creates concepts, but the divine energy has no end in any dimension.

It goes on and on, expanding further and further. In this great expansion that is the secret of the universe, that is the energy of the universe, adoration is the Shakti, the Force. Its work in us and in all things is the sacred power of the Mother taking up everything in the universe to some immeasurable and unimaginable transformation in her.

None of us know what daily life is until we grow in adoration, because to grow in adoration means to grow eyes of wisdom, eyes of love, the eyes of Rumi, the eyes of the Mother. Everything, absolutely everything, is changed beyond recognition by this deepening love. Cleaning your teeth is different, cooking is different, washing is different, going to the toilet is different. Adoration dissolves the madness of the separation between sacred and profane which exists only in our imagination. It ends pseudo-judgment, it ends pseudo-reason, derails forever the tyranny of Newton's "single sleep." The ordinary world is revealed for the thrilling glory it is. Having a bath becomes prayer, sharing a beer with an old friend becomes prayer, cheap songs on the taxi radio in the rain send essential mystic messages, the Mother sings and dances and claps her hands in everything. The bedraggled geraniums on the cafe balcony shine with as much holiness as the sublime *slokas* of the *Gita*. Everything is sign, signal, spark, secret laughter.

Into this kingdom of secret signals, spark, and sign, Rumi and the Sufi revelation of adoration is inviting us. But there's a huge price to be paid, because we can't come into that kingdom of adoration except by giving up our self-adoration, the obsession with the false self. This world can be seen as the brimming glory it is only by the eyes of purified love. That is the essential vision prepared for every soul. And that is the vision that the Mother is offering her children, to each of us. To have this vision, we have to go on a journey of purification, a journey of deep love, a journey of service, meditation, and prayer, because the divine truth, her divine beauty, are ringed by fires of secrecy and silence. A Sufi master once told me, "There is a door through which everybody can get into the kingdom."

"What does it look like?" I asked him. He said, "It doesn't look like anything, it's just a door." "How big is it?" I asked. He said, "Every person has their own door, and it's exactly the size of how large you are when you are walking on your knees."

Rumi asks:

> What does it mean to be love's familiar?
> To become blood, to swallow down one's own blood
> And to wait at fidelity's door with the dogs. . . .
> In weeping, the lover is like the clouds;
> In perseverance, like the mountains;
> In prostration, like water;
> In humility, like dirt in the road.

Nothing but this radical humility can fuel adoration passionate enough to open for us the gates of the kingdom of gnosis and so bring us into the mystery of eternal growth in the Mother. Nothing but this radical humility, passionately reaffirmed in prayer and longing and awe before the glory of God and in service to all beings, can bring us into the joy of that divine childhood known by Ramakrishna, Aurobindo, and Rumi, which is now promised to all those mad and clear enough to want it. Nothing but this radical humility can initiate us into the radical humility of that love that *for* love has become all things and radiates as intensely in the dirty stone we kick away from our path as in the Andromeda galaxy or in lightning storms above the sea. Nothing but this radical humility—the humility of the lover before the Beloved, the humility of the child lost in the love of the Mother—can bring us into the ecstatic, strange madness of the real universe, her universe, where all things are on fire with love and every atom is constantly singing "Glory be to God!"

> Run forward, the way will spring open for you.
> Be destroyed, you'll be flooded with life.
> Humble yourself, you'll grow greater than the world.
> Yourself will be revealed to you, without you.

## Notes

1. Except where noted, all quotations and poems in this chapter have been translated and adapted by the author. Different versions of some of this material appears in *The Way of Passion: A Celebration of Rumi* (Berkeley, California: Frog, Ltd., 1994).

2. *The Way of Passion*, p. 2.

3. "A Garden Beyond Paradise," in *A Garden Beyond Paradise: The Mystical Poetry of Rumi*, translated by Jonathan Star and Shahram Shiva (New York: Bantam Books, 1992), pp. 148–149.

# Chapter Six

# The Sufi Way of Heartbreak

A SEEKER ONCE ASKED RUMI, "What is a Sufi?" He replied,
"A Sufi is someone whose heart has been broken."
Rumi wrote:

> I make a collyrium for my eyes
> From the dust of heartbreak
> So these two eyes may be filled with pearls:
> The tears we shed for the Beloved are pearls.[1]

He wrote:

> If a man could really see himself, he would see
> His inner world is lethal and gangrenous
> And from so searing a gaze within, heartbreak would
> spring
> And his pain would rescue him from behind the veil.
> Until a mother feels the pain of childbirth,
> The child can find no way to be born.
> The trust is within the heart and the heart is pregnant:
> All the encouragements of the saints act as a midwife.
> What does the midwife say: "This woman is not in pain!
> Yet pain is vital, for it opens a way for the child."
> The man without pain is a bandit, for to be without
> pain
> Is to say "I am God."

Rumi also wrote:

Heartbreak for his sake is a treasure in my heart. My heart is "Light upon Light," a beautiful Mary with Jesus in the womb.

He also wrote:

How much the Beloved made me suffer before the work
Grew entwined inseparably with my blood and eyes!
A thousand grim fires and heartbreaks—
And its name is "Love"—
A thousand pains and regrets and attacks
And its name is "Beloved."

If incense and candles do not burn, what use would
    they be?
Incense would be the same as a branch of dry thorns . . .

O Friend, Love must have a little anguish! The heart
    must be broken!
The cheeks must shine a little yellow.
With no pain in the breast, how can you say you are
    passionately devoted to Him?

In the *Mathnawi*, Rumi wrote:

Heartbreak is a treasure because it contains mercies.
The kernel is soft when the rind is scraped off.
O Brother, the place of darkness and cold
Is the fountain of life and the cup of ecstasy.

In Book I of the *Mathnawi*, Rumi tells the following story:

It was the custom of the men of Qazwin to have various devices tattooed upon their bodies. A certain coward went to the tattoo artist to have a "device" tattooed on his back. He wanted it to be the figure of a lion. But as soon as he started to feel the prick of the needle, he howled with pain and said to the tattooist, "What part of the lion are you painting?" The artist replied, "I am doing the tail." The man cried, "Never mind the tail, do another part!" The tattooist began to do another part, but the man again cried out and told him to try somewhere else. Wherever the artist applied his needles, the man raised similar objections, until at last the tattooist threw all his needles and pigments on the ground and refused to go on any further.

> Without the sea of purity, our pearl became stone.
> Without the Soul and the World, this soul and this
>     world grew sad.
> Grief for the Beloved is the polishing of soul and heart:
> Keep it alive in secret, for it preserves in rust.

> A heartbreak shakes the yellow leaves from the branch
>     of the heart
> So fresh green leaves can go on and on growing....
> Heartbreak pulls up the roots of old happinesses
> So a new ecstasy can stroll in from Beyond.
> Heartbreak pulls up all withered, crooked roots
> So no root can stay hidden.
> Heartbreak may pull many things from the heart
> But in return it will lavish kingdoms.

The revelation of Sufism, and especially the revelation of Rumi, brings to the world a crucial understanding at this moment: the understanding of heartbreak. The understanding of the importance of letting the heart break again and again and again, the necessity of never covering the heart, never shielding it, and never disguising the heart's sensitivity. For the heart, as Rumi said, is "'Light upon Light,' a beautiful Mary with Jesus in the womb"—a Jesus that cannot be born without opening the whole being to the pain of the world. The sensitivity of the heart and its ability to suffer purely for love is the clue to the mystical understanding of reality, and so, now, the clue to human survival.

The yoga of the Mother is nothing if not a yoga of love. The yoga of love is nothing if not a yoga of heartbreak, a calm, brave embrace of suffering, inconsolable by any illusions, including mystical ones. Pain is vital, Rumi said, because it opens a gate for the child. The yoga of the Father, the patriarchal yogas, are essentially yogas of transcendence; techniques that offer an escape from this heartbreak, from this "illusion," as they've termed it, from this body, from nature, into some detached, serene, static peace of timelessness and freedom. The yoga of the Mother has that understanding of detachment and timeless freedom as its foundation, but takes a much more profound, much wilder, deeper, and more poignant risk—the risk of active divine love. The Mother's yoga comes down from transcendence into immanence, down from the safety of detachment into the misery and glory of love. Down from mystical illumination into heart-illumined action that is prepared to risk defeat, derision, and all kinds of desolation as events turn, because it can taste the Mother, the Beloved, in everything—even horror.

So the yoga of the Mother goes much deeper than the patriarchal ones, because instead of banning matter, it seeks to transfigure it from within. Instead of exiling death, it seeks to die again and again into fuller and more passionate life. Instead of trying to escape time at any cost, it takes time and kisses it on the lips and accepts all its conditions and sufferings, all its ordeals just as they are—in love, for love, as love. The yoga of the Mother is a yoga of calm crucifixion, the yoga of giving birth through suffering to a new reality. Accepting all the ordeals of that process, all the conditions, all the pain and sadness. Finally, now, the human race is becoming adult enough to accept the terms of the huge spiritual birth that is demanded of us. Listen to Rumi on this birth and its price:

> As long as Mary did not feel the pain of childbirth, she did not go toward the tree of blessing. The pangs of childbirth drew her to the trunk of the palm tree. Pain took her to the tree and the barren tree bore fruit. This body is like Mary, and each of us has a Jesus inside us. If the pain appears, our Jesus will be born. If no pain arrives, Jesus will return to origin by the same secret way that he came and we will be deprived of him and reap no joy.

In 1995, with perhaps two decades left in which to change everything, the terms of such a birth are even more fierce. They are nothing less than accepting that there is absolutely no escape from the catastrophe that surrounds and envelops us. No escape from this situation of potential apocalypse. No escape from the end of a disastrous century and a dying planet. No escape from a barbarized humanity. No escape from actually seeing the effects of the avalanche of trivia that the media has poured into the minds of our children. No escape, no escape, *no escape*— we are being compelled by history, by our mistakes, by our fantasies and their failures, to confront exactly where we are, the shattering pain of it, and challenged to go straight into the furnace of love and be reborn in it.

This challenge has become absolute because patriarchal philosophies have conspired in, rather than prevented, the death of nature. In always stressing the necessity to get out of the body, to locate heaven elsewhere, to remove the creator from the creation, what they have done is depreciate the whole essential value of life itself, and of this experience of being in a body. This has led to nothing less than a catastrophic neglect of our bodies, of the holy connecting powers of Eros in our bodies and of sexuality in general, of nature as the place of divine theophany, and of everything that links the body to nature. The price for this has been psychosis, desolation, alienation, loneliness, misery, despair. Now the human race is being brought to the moment where it must choose connection, knowing that if it does choose connection, if *we* choose connection, what we are bound to choose, now, in 1995, is heartbreak. I have wondered how I would try to transmit this heartbreak. There is no transmission of it—it defeats all images, all words. There is just allowing ourselves in silence, in peace and calm, to let the full facts of our contemporary terror in.

Listen to the following report about a Brazilian tribe that is being decimated. The tribal peoples are the fringes, the soft fringes of our world-heart; they register our desolation with the most delicate kind of sensitivity. In their reaction to the catastrophe, we realize the reaction of one part of our heart that we are ignoring, that we're pretending doesn't exist, that we're trying to rationalize away. These are three paragraphs from a report in the "World Press Review" in *L'Express* about what is happening in a Brazilian tribe facing extinction:

> Clarinda was twelve, Javina was fourteen. They put on their Sunday dresses, their pretty braided bracelets, and the only shoes they had. Then they went out in the forest and hanged themselves. The Gaurani Indians of Brazil seemed to have decided to exterminate themselves. For five years, men, women, and children have been systematically committing suicide. They never leave a note and those who survive refuse to give the slightest explanation and take refuge in silence.
>
> The young are killing themselves to recover their freedom, says one of the tribal chiefs. "They prefer to go over to the other side, because we have lost everything, our land, our traditions, our dignity."

It's not only they who are losing everything. The worldwide catastrophe that threatens the survival of the planet demands of us an unparalleled openness to horrifying facts. Never before have we had so much disturbing information to absorb. This disturbing information can be put into two categories, which are linked. First is the extremely scary knowledge of the fundamental psychotic bedrock of the human personality, which has shown itself in the systematic exploitation and torture of nature and in the creation of all manner of concentration camps and inconceivably powerful weapons of mass destruction. The second is the external sign of this internal catastrophe—the suicidal rush to self-destruction that is both the source of the killing of the environment and of letting that killing go on even when we have the facts. They are related, because the self-disgust, the self-hatred, the sense of meaninglessness, the rage at the denied shadow that characterizes the first, the *inner* Auschwitz, all these are reflected exactly in the death of the outer world. The outer and the inner in our world have become one all-pervading image of destruction and horror.

We have actually created a kind of diabolic masterpiece, the complete mirroring in the external world of the horror, distress, savagery, cruelty, and despair of our inner world. What is essential now is to face just how devastating that mirroring is and to face it from the position of calm, absolute trust in the unconditional, continuing love of the Mother-aspect of the divine that is, even now, streaming out toward us all possible grace, all possible light, all possible love, and will always go on doing so, whatever happens.

In the great Sufi mystics, in Rumi in particular, we really see what it is to embrace the pain of such an opening to horror and from it learn how to dance in our own blood. In Rumi's poetry, we can taste the thrill, the glory, the joy, the extreme mystical beauty of finally allowing life to come to us without any consolation, full in the face, covered with blood, covered with the marks of death, covered with pain; the beauty of finally embracing life exactly as it is, and of discovering, by embracing it unsentimentally in its extremity, a consolation far beyond consolation, a joy far beyond anything that illusion can give, a courage that illusion cannot provide, and an ecstasy of oneness that can only be found by those who are one with horror as well as joy, pain as well as ease, dark as well as light, shadow as well as illumination. This oneness that comes from completely embracing life in all its grief is a living of torment and loneliness without any attempt to disguise them, and eating of them as they are because the taste of the divine is found even in atrocity. When we have learned to taste the divine even in death, desolation, and defeat, we are then true dancers. As Rumi says,

> Dancing is not rising to your feet painlessly like a whirl of dust blown about by the wind. Dancing is when you rise above both worlds, tearing your heart to pieces and giving up your soul.

The task of those who do the yoga of the Mother in this age is to learn to dance like that, so as to keep love alive in hell. This is not to say that keeping love alive in hell is bound to redeem the situation; it isn't. Nor do we claim everybody will be convinced and transfigured by our keeping love alive in hell; they won't. Keep the heart alive in hell for the heaven of it, whatever happens, keep the heart alive because it's the most beautiful and noble thing to do. Not to keep the heart open is shameful at this moment. It's shameful not to love completely at this moment; it's shameful not to try and wake up to the total lack of consolation; it's shameful not to look history in the face at this moment; and it's shameful not to allow that look into the world-volcano that will break your heart. We have all got to consent to go heartbroken into a new kind of loving of ourselves, our bodies, each other, nature, the world, the Mother.

This immense crisis, this immense suffering, is acting on the world the way that the course of a mystic breakdown acts on a person. What is happening is that the entire world is going through the kind of breakdown that was usually reserved for those few people in any culture who went through a shamanic transformation. The world is being torn apart, it is being dismembered, subjected to extreme pressure, flayed raw by the complete collapse and illusion of all our plans. It is being presented, as the mystics and shamans have been, with the futility, nullity, emptiness, and gross stupidity of all possible movements of the mind without the heart, of the ego without the soul. The whole world, like the Mary of Rumi's meditation, is being dragged by pain to the trunk of the tree to give birth to a new humanity.

The voice that the Mother is giving us in this has never been more beautifully interpreted than by the Sufis, because the Sufis are masters of pain. They have realized the mastery of pain, which is to accept and embrace it, and suck the dark juice out of it, and to taste in the deepest suffering that most outrageous possibility: that the deepest suffering is also the source of the deepest grace. The worse the suffering, the greater the opportunity to learn how to dance in your and our own blood, to dance in the blood of catastrophe and from that catastrophe press the wine of gnosis, bliss, and tenderness.

This is what Rumi, master fire-dancer, tells us of the rewards of so fearless an embrace of pain:

> The grapes of my body can only become wine
> After the winemaker tramples me.
> I surrender my spirit, like grapes, to his trampling
> So my inmost heart can blaze and dance with joy.
> Although the grapes go on weeping blood and
>     sobbing,
> "I cannot bear any more anguish, any more cruelty!"
> The trampler stuffs cotton in his ears:
> "I am not working in ignorance.
> You can deny me, if you want, you have every excuse,
> But it is I who am the Master of this work.
> When, through my fashion, you reach perfection,
> You will never be done praising my name."

This is what the Mother is putting the world through in the extremity of her unconditional love for humankind. If you want to understand this aspect of the unconditional love of the Mother, think of a burn surgeon working on a hideously burned child. Burn surgery has to be done on a conscious patient, because if the surgeon doesn't follow the patient's screams, she or he will mutilate the patient excessively. So a burn surgeon has to inflict almost intolerable suffering in order to be able to save life at all. Imagine that you have a six-year-old child in front of you who has been hideously burned. That child has to be partly conscious during the surgery, otherwise you will destroy and disfigure the child. She will scream, she will suffer terribly as you perform the surgery, but you know that it is the only thing that could save her life. If you've ever seen a burn surgeon work, you've been given the most searing image of what divine compassion can be at a very extreme level.

The Mother knows that she has no choice but to ask us to

go through this final ordeal because we have become too crazy, and because unless we really take on the full consequences of what we have done and what we have allowed ourselves to become, we will not be able to survive. We will not be able to develop the sensitivities, the delicacies, the sweet interconnect-edness, the tribal understanding, the new democratic forms of transmission that we will need to create the new humanity that is in her mind and is in the dreams of our deepest hearts, to birth the new humanity in direct connection with her, free of stale dogmas, gurus, and priests, and so be finally free.

Rumi tells us: "The grapes of my body can only become wine after the winemaker tramples me." Kali, the winemaker of the new human wine, is trampling and destroying all old illu-sions and constructed forms. What has to be trampled now is the illusion we all have that what's happening in Bosnia or in the Amazonian forests or the oceans is happening somewhere else. It is *not* happening elsewhere, it is happening in each one of our cells, in our own bodies, in our bloodstreams, because there is no separation on this planet or any other between *any* of the dimensions. This is the savage awakening knowledge of the Divine Mother to her children: if you harm a single plant, you are torturing your inner soul; if you hit someone, you are striking yourself; if you allow the forests to go on burning, it is as if you were to pour gasoline over your own lungs and put a match to them. What the Mother is bringing now is this rad-ical, extreme, fierce, illusionless, inconsolable knowledge of the sacred, vivid, absolutely literal interconnectedness of every-thing, a knowledge which is agonizing and sometimes unbear-able, but which has to come in to trample the grapes of egotism and vanity, separation and exploitation of nature, so that we can all finally come to our senses and drink her wine of gnosis and transform our violent thoughtlessness into active love.

Of course, we can choose not to open, but instead to close down the heart. But at a moment like this, closing down the heart is actually assisting catastrophe. The choice of closing down the heart can take many forms. You can choose it in the drearier ways of becoming a banker or one of the paid killers of a culture that is devoted to destruction, or you can do it in a more sophisticated way, by choosing one of the mystical traditions that stresses that this is all illusion and *maya* and just one *kalpa* after another and all that rot that we've swallowed for so long. You can do it that way. You can commit suicide in many different ways in our culture. But that is not what we are being asked to do. We are not being asked to "go out," we are being asked to come *in;* not to have the out-of-body experience but the in-body experience, to allow our heart to open *here,* in this place and time, so that we may be shown whatever way through there may be. Arriving here will have its agony, but it will also initiate us to the state of ecstasy that Rumi now goes on to describe.

> The grapes of my body can only become wine
> After the winemaker tramples me.
> I surrender my spirit, like grapes, to his trampling . . .

Surrender to the trampling. Give up, give up pretending that it's not chaos here. Give up pretending that anything couldn't happen. Anything *can* happen. Give up believing in magical solutions that desperate imaginations are proposing everywhere—none of them are true. What *is* true is that there is a divine spirit in everyone which is open to the divine force in and around everyone, and that force can be contacted in simple, incandescent ways: through prayer and meditation, and through service.

What is also true is that we are masters of our own destiny. We co-create that destiny with the divine. But to co-create with the divine demands deep surrender of every conceivable illusion, "like grapes to his trampling." Every conceivable illusion of separation, of personal will that is organizing this experience, of this being an intelligible experience at all. This is not an intelligible experience—it's as crazy as Kali is crazy, as the divine is crazy. Someone once said to Ramakrishna of one of his impious disciples, "This man is a drunk." Ramakrishna replied, "But don't you think God is drunk? How else would the universe be so crazy if God wasn't drunk?"

Just take a moment and imagine what we have to accept. We have to accept that it took so many years for South African blacks to get any shred of social justice. It took twenty-six years of Nelson Mandela's life, sitting and rotting in jail, growing the kind of dignity and voice that finally helped his people to be heard. We have to accept babies dying of AIDS; Bosnia; Rwanda; children of ten assassinating each other on back porches. We have to accept untold horrors which are only acceptable in a state of divine love and divine gnosis. They're not acceptable at any other level. At every other level, they are unspeakable. Yet they're here, they are allowed to exist. Why? To *press*, urge, compel us to the highest level of love, which flowers from acceptance. You can only get to that level of acceptance if you give up trying to explain anything and instead just open your heart in immense, "blind," all-embracing love.

Rumi wrote:

> Until Love burns my intellect to ashes
> I am ashes.
>
> Intellect ate opium from Love's hand
> Watch out! It has gone mad too. . . .
> When intellect reached Love, it saw an ocean of blood.
> Intellect sat down in the heart of the blood
> And the waves of blood crashed down upon its head
> And took it away from all the six directions
> Towards Directionlessness
> And there it lost itself, lost itself utterly
> And was reborn fleetfooted and athletic in Love.

Rumi is saying to us: "Sit down in the ocean of blood. Let its waves crash over your head." *Face where you are.* Face that you are dying in a dying body, that you're a dying body in a dying world. Face that all the solutions may not work. Face it, face it, and *love like crazy*. Go calmly, systematically, urgently, sweetly, mad with divine love, just as all the others who have faced this have done when they woke up to the total precariousness of this world and realized that the only noble response to this awakening was boundless love. Everything is vanishing as we watch. Rumi says, "Become a lover of leaving." I am disappearing as you look at me; you are disappearing as I look at you. Go beyond all consolations, for they are all false. Step into the furnace of this moment and stay there burning in love for all time, in the eternity of each moment. This state of truth costs everything. Every illusion, *everything*, even the hope of heaven, even the hope of immortality, even the hope of some kind of enlightenment. What do any of those things matter, given the necessity of burning away in love in the furnace of the present?

> The grapes of my body can only become wine
> After the winemaker tramples me.
> I surrender my spirit, like grapes, to his trampling.

The Mother is asking this sacrifice of illusion from all of us; this sacrifice of our attachment to detachment, this sacrifice of our false consolation that progress is going to do it, that science will do it, that some avatar will do it, that aliens from Mars will do it, that some force in the universe somewhere will do it. All of these comforting illusions are doomed, because nothing is going to do it, if we don't do it together, the whole of humanity together, in love. Nothing else will do it. We are on our own with the Mother. She is asking us to grow up to the grandeur of that relationship. It's an immense grandeur, but it's too searing, too immense for some people who wish for a veil between themselves and her. She is not going to allow that veil in this time, all the veils between us and her are burning down in this era so that a new, ecstatic, intimate, infinitely direct and practical relationship can be created between her and the entire human race, far beyond dogma, far beyond religion, in the heat of love, in the restored human body, in the illumined heart-imagination. It's a huge revolution and birth, and that is why it is also a huge suffering. What is demanded of all of us together

is "a condition," in Eliot's words, "of complete simplicity, cost-
ing not less than everything."

"I surrender my spirit like grapes to his trampling." What
is beautiful about this fourth line is that Rumi is not surrendering because he is frightened, he is surrendering because as
a master of heartbreak he has understood how to take the energy
of suffering, death, and torment, and by accepting it like a master martial artist, reverse the force of that energy against itself.
Rumi knows how to suck the secret sweetness out of its terror,
how, by accepting it completely as an athlete of love, to transform it into ecstasy.

> I surrender my spirit, like grapes, to his trampling,
> So my inmost heart can blaze and dance with joy.

Every neurosis and every fear has to be flung now into the
night of Kali's darkness. Every one of them has to go, because
as long as any one remains—any of the fears or the panics of
loss, the vulnerabilities of heartbreak—if any one of them
remains, then we're not having the complete experience. We're
still hiding. We're still protecting ourselves from something of
both the suffering *and* the ecstasy. What the Mother and what
the mystics of the Mother, like Rumi, are asking us to do is to
kick away everything that stops our lives from becoming pyres.
To kick away everything that keeps us from burning in the
inmost heart and dancing with the joy that is held out by the
Sufi revelation. This joy is so vast because it has absorbed
extremity and not shirked from it. You can only dance like this
when you are also dancing "for" destruction. That is the secret
of Kali and of this poem by Rumi, when he says:

> One day in your in your wineshop I drank a little
>     wine,
> And threw off this robe of this body
> And knew, drunk on you, the world is harmony,
> Creation, destruction, I am dancing for them both.

"One day in your wineshop." I actually had the nerve to drink a little mystic bliss. I didn't just fiddle around with mild forms of prayer, or "New Age" crystal-gazing or decent forms of meditation, I reached for the pure vodka and downed it. I lost my brain. I "threw off the robe of this body," I threw off this illusion, the covering, the coating, the vanities and neuroses of this body-mind. And I knew—not supposed, not thought, not imagined, not read—but *knew* that when you are drunk on the illumination of gnosis, of unity, this world reveals that behind its horror and ghastliness, in fact *through* the horror and ghastliness that are inextricably a part of it, there is a wild, divine harmony beyond anything the mind could ever begin to describe. "Drunk on you, this world is harmony."

At that moment Rumi reaches for the last illumination of that harmony: "Creation, destruction, I am dancing for them both." By absorbing grief, by facing catastrophe, by opening without consolation to where we are, we come to learn how to dance in the divine energy that unites all things: creation and destruction, joy and pain. From that we learn how the inmost heart *can* blaze and dance with joy even in hell. Learning this, actually allowing this huge transmutation of the heart to take place, actually stripping ourselves of our illusions, really going through again and again the fire of this stripping and of this burning, is an intolerable process for everyone. Dying into life, in this life, is an intolerable process, but it has to now become part of the process of many, many people if we're going to get through, if the Mother's birth of a new humanity is going to take place.

Next, Rumi really speaks to the heart of our difficulty:

Although the grapes go on weeping blood . . .

A large part of the spiritual journey is having the courage, the great, crazy courage, to "go on weeping blood." There is more blood to weep at every stage, and more sobbing to do at every encounter with deepening reality. There is no place where the tears stop. The tears go on, they stop being sentimental tears and become tears of love, but they go on. The blood-shedding goes on, what stops is the self-protection. In another quatrain, Rumi says:

> Blood must flow
> For the garden to flower.
> And the heart that loves me
> Is a wound without shield.

For reality to become alive with gnosis, there have to be many people prepared to make the journey into love. For people to be prepared to take the journey into love, they must be willing to die, to let themselves sob and weep blood, and cry out again and again at different steps of their life, what Rumi cries out, "I cannot bear any more anguish, any more cruelty!" What these deaths feel like, don't let us pretend otherwise, are, as Rumi says, "anguish" and "cruelty." They are felt as the cruelty of the divine, giving us something we think we can't bear. It happens again and again on the path of real love.

> The trampler stuffs cotton in his ears:
> "I am not working in ignorance.
> You can deny me, if you want, you have every excuse,
> But it is I who is the Master of this work.
> When, through my fashion, you reach perfection,
> You will never be done praising my name."

Rumi imagines God, or the Mother in this aspect of her we are describing, as stuffing cotton in our ears and saying to us all, "I am not working in ignorance." This is not an ignorant intelligence that is organizing this catastrophe of the world or letting us organize this catastrophe; it's an intelligence that is finally, unconditionally loving, that is prepared to let us destroy ourselves, but opening to us at every stage of this destruction new possibilities and new truths.

What we, in our illusions, want is something less than the perfection and oneness with the Mother that she is planning

for the human race. We want a safer life, a sweeter life, a calmer
life. But what evolution is taking us toward is a leap into divine
being *here*, in matter, on this earth. The stakes are being raised
higher and higher to try and awaken in us the desire to choose
with absolute intensity and sincerity such an astounding destiny. If we don't choose this destiny of complete wholeness and
mystic illumination, we will not survive. If we do choose it,
with all its pain, with all the horror and difficulties that she is
asking us to accept and go through, when through her passion
we reach perfection, she will say to us: "You will never be done
praising my name." We will see where all this pain has been
leading us and why it was all necessary, because we will have
understood that it has taken many of us, hundreds of thousands of us, perhaps even millions of us, through a revolution
of the heart and into a birth of the "Jesus" within us, within
all human beings.

Rumi wrote of God:

> All my splendor is to burn in you.
> To know this fire that eats me is eating itself,
> To be this fire dancing on my own bones.

What are we, but fire eating itself? We are the spirit dancing on the bones of the body and the bones of the body dancing in the flame of spirit, both as one. Eternity dancing in time;
and time, through the great grace of death, allows us also to
dance in eternity, bringing us to the extreme acceptance of the
present that we must come to before we can become love. If
we allow this huge last evolution to take place, this heartbreak,
this stripping of all our fantasies of separateness, this radical
exercise of humility, if we allow ourselves to die into the embrace
of the present, then what happens is that the present becomes
completely alive with the glory of the shining of her love. We
are taken directly into our own sublime divine hearts that embrace and ennoble and accept everything, and we're taken
directly into the great heart of the Divine Mother, which then
feeds us with exactly what we will need to endure such a heart:

the peace, clarity, and bliss; the skillful means; the deep cellular intelligence. We learn what Rumi means when he says:

> The truth, so simple
> The mind explodes
> To meet itself
> Running back in all things.

The truth of our interconnectedness with reality is so blatant, so extreme, that when we open to it finally in the heart and face it in the heart, the whole universe explodes softly in a vast Krakatoa, a massive Hiroshima of bliss, and the entire universe runs softly, silently, back to us, shining in our own heart-fire. Forever, separations end; forever, illusions end. Forever, the need to escape to anywhere else ends. We are here, now and always, beyond now and always, just here, in the real world. The real world is direct knowledge of direct reality without any covering.

> Find the real world, give it endlessly away.
> Grow rich, fling gold to all who ask.
> Live at the empty heart of paradox.
> I'll dance there with you, cheek to cheek.

"Live at the empty heart of paradox." There's nothing to learn, nothing to win, nowhere to go, that's the empty heart of paradox. When you live, really live, the paradox of being in time, in eternity, both immortal and dying, as human and divine, when you really live in the calm crucifixion of that paradox, beyond all concepts and dogma and in a fire of love, then you're dancing cheek-to-cheek with the divine at every millisecond, in intimate union with every tiny shift of the eternal now. The passion of the eternal dance makes a relationship with everything; you don't need to go anywhere else. All we need, and all she is offering us, which is everything, is the complete experience of being here, just as we are, in love, as love, for love. Then you will know this vast heartbreak of love, this outbreak, this holocaust of love:

Your dawn in me, I'm drunk, stammering,
A thousand thousand worlds go dark.
Lightnings are dark to us, to this
Identity's boundless world's-wide blaze.

No heaven, or earth, just this mysterious place
We walk in dazedly.
Where being here or there, in time or not,
Are only two motions of the same ecstatic breathing.

This is a great clue, this last poem. It is a clue to total presence, which is what the Mother is asking of us: total presence. In that mysterious place we will all come to say with Rumi this four-line credo of the path of love, to say it with each cell, not just with our minds or our hearts:

The law of wonder rules my life at last.
I burn each second of my life to love.
Each second of my life burns out in love.
In each leaping second, love lives afresh.

When we've finally gotten rid of the illusions and the nirvanas, the escapes, the evasions, and the consolations, what remains is the astonishment of this naked love and the shining of this naked moment, the astonishment at the divine love released in the utterly broken-open heart.

\* \* \*

Let me share with you now a visualization, a real heart-practice which is very much the practice of the open heart, of heartbreak, and which will help anyone who does it in the yoga of the Mother.

Imagine in front of you a black boiling darkness. The blackness of chaos, the darkness of suffering, the darkness of death. It is grand and all-encompassing, sweeps from horizon to horizon, and at any moment could wipe you away. That is the first stage of the meditation, to imagine the immensity of this force and this boiling darkness.

Then a voice says, "Every fear you fling into that darkness with joy will turn into a star." Every nervousness, every fear, every evasion, every consolation, every illusion that you have the courage to fling into that boiling darkness will become a star. If you go on flinging the illusions and the evasions into that darkness, the stars will coalesce and conjoin and come together in a rapturous flowing movement to create in front of you the exact image of the divine feminine through which you worship the Mother. This vision may be of Durga or Mary or Tara; it could be someone in your own life who has communicated the divine feminine to you. As you fling your evasions and illusions into the boiling darkness, you realize that you yourself create that divine identity of yours which is the sacred feminine. It constellates in the darkness in front of you. You create it by flinging away fear after fear, illusion after illusion, evasion after evasion. Slowly, whoever you've chosen to represent the Divine Mother appears before you in all her loveliness, in all her beauty and glory, star by star.

There she is now. You have created her, star by star. Allow the bliss streaming from her eyes, the fire of the light streaming from her eyes and limbs, to sweep your body, up and down, sweeping away every obstruction, every ignorance, every internal image, every guilt, every separation.

As you experience your own body, mind, and heart becoming more and more full of light, experience also that the darkness in front of you is beginning to drain away. As you blaze more and more, so the light becomes more and more intense in the darkness before you, until, when you are completely alight, you and the light, from one horizon to the other, are one light, one diamond light burning.

Rest in that peace, in that courage, in that ecstasy, in that identity with the Beloved, with Her.

Rumi wrote:

Till the bread is broken,
How can it serve as food?
Till the grapes are crushed,
How can they yield wine?

You are now the bread and the wine.

## Questions and Answers

*Isn't one of the ways that Sufism is close to the sacred feminine
in how it embraces life on Earth and the holiness of ordinary
life?*

One of the many reasons I love and revere Sufism is because
the Sufis have never stressed going away from the world or leaving the world, or leaving the world to its own devices, or shun-
ning and hating the body. Many of the greatest Sufi teachers
were married, had families, and lived ordinary lives in an ordinary world, or extraordinary lives in an ordinary world. They
were bakers or weavers, people who lived right at the heart of
reality and didn't need to take any excursion from it.

I also love the Sufis for their humility, and I think this, too,
is central to the revelation of the sacred feminine that is emerg-
ing . One of the things the Sufis say is that anyone who claims
to be God or to be divine is actually on the side of Satan. The
Sufis have always had a tremendous quarrel with the concepts
of avatars and the rest of it; they've always thought that it was
actually blasphemous, unhelpful, and unnecessary, because the
revelation that comes through adoration is one so immense and
so rich in its own right, and so human and so *naturally* human,
that we don't need any of the decorations and names and terms.
This is, I think, the permanent radicalism of the Sufi message.
It's saying that all of us, just where we are, if we open our hearts
and pray, and live within the terms of our own life, we can come
directly into the presence of the Beloved and live in that presence. You don't have to go anywhere, you don't have to change
the external circumstances of your life, you just have to transfigure your life from within with the divine energy that flows
from that knowledge.

So Sufism, unlike some Eastern teachings, doesn't stress the
ideal of enlightenment as a nearly impossible perfection removed
from reality, nor does it have any contempt for ordinary life,

because the Sufis saw everything as epiphany and everything as awakening. Even the greatest sheikhs never presented themselves as divine beings. At the end of his life, Mohammed said, "Seventy times a day, I beg my Lord to forgive me failing him." The Prophet is speaking, and speaking very movingly, as a human being humbled by the truths of the divine majesty, acknowledging the gap between him and God. That humility is a great clue for the renaissance of the sacred feminine, because we really have to get away from the dangers inherent in the Hindu business of "I am that," or in the excesses of the Eastern practice of deifying masters. A Sufi isn't saying, "I am a crawling worm." The Sufi is saying, "I am a man," or "I am a woman. There are limitations, but in this state, with my heart open, I can live in the glory of the presence, and that's enough, that's everything."

This groundedness and humility have, paradoxically, produced the most wild, free mystical poetry of any tradition. All the other kinds of mystical poetry are sometimes stained by a kind of withdrawal, with a kind of bitter ascesis, or seared with the burn marks of trying to become perfect. The Sufis aren't trying to become perfect; they're trying to become whole in love, to live wholly in the presence of love, and their philosophy and poetry burns with the incandescent excitement of discovering this love and its beauty and power.

*How, in the Sufi system, do you become one with the Beloved, or the Mother?*

The Sufis say that to become one with the Beloved there are three stages: purification, expansion, and union. The first stage is essential, and one of the main stupidities in "New Age" spirituality is that it does not consider this first stage essential. Purification has to happen, there has to be a commitment to some discipline, some fundamental housecleaning, some commitment to prayer to open us, to really look into our thoughts, to incessantly offer the heart to the Beloved through repetition of the divine name. This is an immense work; it is not easy to purify the heart, because what we're trying to do, the Sufis say, is to clear the mirror so the divine sun can be reflected in it. The mirror in most cases is filthy and cleaning it takes an enormous effort of love and faith. Often, it is only faith that will give you what is needed in the first stage, because very rarely will you have actually had any living mystical experience at that stage. So you'll have to work in the dark. You'll have to learn how to be peaceful, how to empty your mind, how to offer your being.

Purification is rigorous, because so much that you believe to be real has to be taken away. The divine has to remove all the toys before she can place the diamond in your hands. You have to know exactly how precious the diamond is before God gives it to you. When you are purified enough and when it is possible for the divine to take you and use you and give to you, at that moment the second stage, which is expansion, begins.

Sufis make a subtle distinction between what they call *hal* and *maqam*. *Hal* refers to the divine states, moments of bliss, visions, dreams, sudden ecstasies. These are states that come and go. But *maqam* are stations; states of experience by the grace of God, stations you acquire by work, by mystical work, by inner work, by transformation. The states give you a sense of what you are striving toward, what you are longing to unify with. They are states of ecstasy, bliss, and peace, of suddenly seeing the world disappear and reappear, all the glorious extraordinary touches of the tenderness of the life of God. But you have to work with those glimpses by deepening them, meditating on them, expanding their significance to every area of your life by using the mind to illustrate and understand them in all their facets. God hands you the diamond, but you have to turn it in the heart and mind again and again until you really and radically understand it, and understand how the experience, for example, of bliss goes down into the depth of being, radiates through being, illuminates being. This is your work. When you have worked in the heart to understand the *hal* and to soak it through every aspect of your being, then you acquire the *maqam*. You go into the station of bliss, or the station of awareness, and finally the ultimate station, which is that of great peace, in which all is both empty and full, and all appears always as a theophany of the divine.

*Hal* is play, divine play. In the second stage, the stage of expansion, expansion of the heart, expansion of what we thought we understood, wild expansion of reason. In fact, this stage is a shattering of reason against the door of bliss, an endless expansion until you can hardly bear it any longer. The divine takes you to thresholds that you would not have believed you could get to—thresholds of exhaustion and anger, of ecstasy and bliss, right to the edge of suicidal despair. This process completely expands your sense of who you are, what the world is, what your heart is, what your life is, and what death is.

A Sufi master once told me that it's quite easy to explain what happens in the second stage of expansion: the divine takes the heart, opens it endlessly, tears it endlessly open, and when it is totally torn apart, torn open, ruined and shattered, totally expanded, then the whole universe can be placed within it. Then the Beloved, God, is in the heart, and the divine light is radiating in everything, because "you" do not remain. That is when the third stage begins, the stage of union.

When expansion has destroyed you in love, then what the Sufis call *baqa* can take place, which is dwelling in the living presence of the divine, in the constant knowledge of the divine light, in the constant knowledge of the accompaniment of the divine in all events. Then the journey into union can flower endlessly. Union is the endless experience of bliss and joy and pain, an endless theophany. In union you partake of the emptiness, freedom, bliss, and playfulness of the divine itself. Therefore, you can be expanded endlessly because the heart has been shattered and has become the divine heart. The divine heart is a supernova, in it worlds are born and die, whole civilizations crumble and love goes on in peaceful ecstasy, singing the name of God.

When the heart is open, you'll see what is revealed in one
of the greatest mystical Sufi classics, Mahmud Shabistari's "The
Rose Garden of Secrets of Mystery":

> Every particle of the world is a mirror,
> In each atom lies the blazing light
>     of a thousand suns.
> Cleave the heart of a rain-drop,
>     a hundred pure oceans will flow forth.
> Look closely at the grain of sand,
>     the seed of a thousand beings can be seen.
> The foot of an ant is larger than an elephant;
> In essence, a drop of water
>     is no different than the Nile.
> In the heart of a barley-corn
>     lies the fruit of a hundred harvests.
> Within the pulp of a millet seed
>     an entire universe can be found.
> In the wing of a fly,
>     an ocean of wonder;
> In the pupil of the eye, an endless heaven.
> Though the inner chamber of the heart is small,
>     the Lord of both worlds
>     gladly makes His home there.[2]

Shabistari says also of the Sufis:

> They have cast away
> All thoughts of name and fame,
> All talk of marvels and visions,
> All dreams of secret chambers and distant worlds.
>
> They fall, and they rise again,
>     between union and separation;
> Now shedding tears of blood;
> Now raised to a world of bliss,
>     stretching their necks out like racers;
> Now with blackened faces staring at a wall,

Or face reddened by the wine of Unity.
Now in a mystic whirl,
    dancing in the arms of their Beloved,
    losing head and foot like the revolving heavens.
With every strain the minstrel plays,
    comes to them rapture of the unseen world;
With every note of this mystic ode
    a veil is torn from the priceless treasure.

Blind to this world,
Indifferent to great and small,
Ignorant of master and disciple,
They guzzle down cup after cup after cup of wine,
    and still want more!
They sweep ancient dust from their souls.
They grab at their Beloved's clothes
like a bunch of drunkards!
O Lord, who are these guys?—

*They are Sufis.*[3]

It's that nakedness, that wildness, that extremity, that blissful courage that Sufis so magnificently try to give us that I am celebrating here. It's essential to the awakening of the divine feminine because it's the passion of the Mother. The Mother is not just tenderness, she is also the force that is shaking us awake with passionate love, shaking us to the passionate glory of being here.

*And to be here as you say is to accept heartbreak?*

The Mother is saying to us, "If you want this change, then you have to open the eyes of love." If you open the eyes of love, you see pain everywhere, and if you see pain everywhere, your heart breaks. Just let it. Stop running away. Open, accept, and learn how to dance in the blood of that acceptance. Then you'll dance her dance and know her love, and know the courage and bliss that streams from that dance and that path. Then you can become really living channels of her divine grace.

This embrace of catastrophe is really an embrace, it isn't based in fear. The Mother isn't just saying, "Open, suffer, die," she's also saying, "I will give you the peace of my love to help you bear this distress. I will take you into my heart that can bear anything, and give you that heart." Only a heart that breaks again and again can ever be strong enough to bear everything. That's the sacred paradox of the divine feminine. A heart that defends itself will be shattered to smithereens. A heart that consents to break again and again will be strengthened with each break, strengthened to break again, to break more and more open, and to become more and more open to empowering divine grace.

We like every other version of spiritual reality but this one. This one costs everything. Christ said: "This is my body and this is my blood." He didn't say, "This is my lecture. These are my perceptions about spiritual reality." He said, "This is my *body*, and this is my *blood*." This is very naked, physical, up front, direct. Christ and the Sufis stand and breathe down our necks, asking, "What are you actually going to give in this great game of the Divine? Why don't you give what the Mother gives, which is herself?" The Mother gives herself to create this entire universe. She gives herself. Who do you think is suffering in the death of every child from AIDS? The Mother is suffering. She's suffering with no hideaway, with no consolation, because she's not closed and dead as we are. She suffers in every pain just as she delights in every kind of bliss. She is all things, and she has no mask and no drug of forgetfulness and no evasion because she has nowhere to run from herself. So she boils and screams and dies within herself, just as she lies peacefully at the bottom of the sea beyond all catastrophes. Everything goes on in her.

That "everything" is what the illumined heart opens to, without any possibility of ever shutting down again. Without that opening, there is no reforging of the personality; there is just a little bit of redecoration. You may become a bit nicer, but you don't become qualitatively, extravagantly different. And what the world needs is qualitatively, extravagantly different people at this moment, people who really have plunged into the fire of divine love. What does the word "action" mean to us at this moment, from the heart of this darkness? It's going to be very bloody, any action that comes to us now, very dangerous. Try to do any work in the spiritual world at the moment, you will be battered and assaulted from every side, derided and called a fraud. Try do anything in the political world at the moment; the same process of humiliation will happen to you. Try and do anything in the intellectual world to open up new possibilities, and the whole dinosauric world of the universities will turn on you and mock you and try to rend you.

It is a very tough time to try and do any serious work of love in the world, because people are angry, depressed, and obsessed with meaninglessness, drunk on their own despair. Anybody trying to inject a bit of good news, serious good news, is going to have to face a huge wall and be dragged to that wall by the wind and beaten against it, time after time. Where will you get the courage and the strength, if not from her? Where will any of us get the courage and the strength if not from the very heart of love itself? That, I think, is why action and this kind of absolute heartbroken love are very connected in the mind of the Divine Mother and the sacred feminine. You have to be shattered open, far beyond hope, to have any hope of continuing to act in a world so plunged into despair. You have to have given up hope to find the faith that is beyond hope. You have to have allowed her love to strip you and burn away the illusions, so that your words and your actions can become precise, alert, tender—above all, tender.

*Isn't there the danger of a kind of spiritual masochism in the "way of heartbreak" that you are talking about, the potential for a kind of self-aggrandizing, self-obsessed passion for pain?*

Of course. The mind and heart can pervert anything and become as obsessed with pain as they can be with any strong and pungent emotion. Suffering can become a kind of dark mental sex, and that is always destructive.

Rumi and the Sufis are not, however, witnessing this kind of neurotic absorption in pain, with all its attendant weird games and satisfactions. They are talking to us with clarity and an utter lack of sentimentality of the mystical laws of divine birth. And the most demanding of these laws is that suffering is a necessary part of growth. The Sufis are not saying to run *toward* heartbreak, but not to run *away* from it, because, as Rumi never tires of telling us, "The treasure is in the ruined house." By shattering all our illusions, heartbreak can reveal in us the treasure that nothing can destroy.

In an amazing couplet, Rumi writes:

> He has afflicted you from all directions
> To drag you into the Directionless.

That perfectly expresses what I believe the Mother, in our contemporary historical agony, is doing to humankind, "afflicting" us from all directions so as to lead us into the "Directionless," the Absolute, our divine-child identity in her. If we do not really understand, or *inner*-stand this, we will be overwhelmed by the range of terrors that are coming our way, we will be disemboweled with grief and despair when faced with their fury. If we realize *why* they are being sent to us and what new being they could bring, and *how* to use their dreadful power as a way— the most ruthless but most efficient way—of *waking us up*, then even in this modern hell, this steaming worldwide "ocean of blood," we can live and be and work in the heaven of divine love, walk like Meschach and Abednego unharmed in the Fiery Furnace, and know this fire as a rose garden. But this alchemical secret of transforming terror into ecstasy, horror into peace, is only given to those who have learned in the depths of their being the necessity of passing again and again through death after death to be continually remade in the image of love.

Thinking of fire and the "Fiery Furnace," and of Rumi's adoration of the fire of love, I am reminded of a Zen story that Rumi would have loved. A disciple goes to his teacher and says, "It's unbearably hot. How can I escape this hell?" The teacher smiles and says, "Go to the bottom of it." The disciple cries, dismayed, "If I go down to the bottom of this furnace I'll suffer horribly, I'll be burned to a crisp!" The teacher's smile widens, "No, my friend. At the bottom of the furnace, no further pains will harass you."

There is no escape from the fire of suffering, but by embracing its necessity completely, we can become one with it. Then we will discover that the fire of suffering is also the fire of love, and, one with love, we will radiate its deathless passion and power.

*There seems to be in what you are saying about the Mother two very different polarities—the Mother as nurturer and as destroyer. Can you elaborate?*

Yes, I love these two polarities of the image of the Mother: on the one hand there is this great strength and serenity and rootedness, the sense of the rhythm of being. On the other hand, there is this great active force saying, "Wake up to where you are!" These are two sides of the sacred feminine, one the soaring, sumptuous rootedness that actually gives health, peace, serenity, and warmth, the feminine that grounds all things. And then the other side, which we are so afraid of in a patriarchal culture: the wild, anarchic, accusatory feminine, the Callas-Kali feminine that runs at the heart of illusion with a knife. Both aspects are in union, not separate, and both are necessary to divine balance. If there's too much serenity, we may doze off into a kind of idiotic bliss. If there's too much violently righteous retribution, then another kind of lunacy gets unleashed. To hold those two poles of the sacred feminine in one is to make peacefulness pointed and fierce, and ferocity calm at its core. To take the bliss at the heart of the Divine Mother and inform all action and passion with that bliss, so that action and passion become rich and sumptuous. Not lily-livered and knackered and skeletonic, like the Father's terrible, dreary ascesis. Something full of blood, full of sweetness and tears, full of sweat and bodies and truth.

To marry these two aspects of the sacred feminine in one overwhelming experience of the heart of the Mother, and then to live in that heart, to work and act from that heart, is what I think she is asking us to do. It really means giving up all the illusions that you've ever had about the body, about nature, about God, about the spiritual path, because they will all have to go if we're going to get real.

What mystics like Rumi help us understand is the joy that awaits us if we can throw everything away. We need their witness to that joy if we're going to go on this journey that is going to be so bloody and difficult. We need to believe, we need to know, in fact, that the reward for this stripping away, for this dancing in the blood of apocalypse, is radiance and joy and energy and gorgeousness of heart. It's very difficult to see this in a world as desolate as ours. In the works of Rumi, you can begin to catch a shadow of that fire, see it, and start to learn how to burn away in it.

*On the wall in my therapist's office is a quote: "I have not promised to make you feel better, I have promised to make you feel more." As mystics develop in the Mother, are they becoming more and more blissful, or are all the emotions, even the painful ones, intensifying?*

All the emotions are increasing in depth and richness. I don't think you'd take this journey to become blissful, because that would be to want God's gifts instead of God. If you want to get anything out of the divine experience, then you are wanting something less than the experience itself. The actual experience is nameless and contains all the intensities. As mystical progress is made, you open very much more profoundly to the grief of the world and the pain of the world and the suffering of others, and as you open, you have no fear or, at least, a lot less fear, because you know that beyond the pain and threaded all through the pain is divine light. Every kind of suffering, even the most terrible, has meaning, and is taking whoever is experiencing it to the possibility of another kind of growth.

So much of our fear of suffering comes from a feeling that we're going to be broken apart if we confront our real pain and need. What the mystic comes to know, I think, is that no force of heaven or hell can destroy their fundamental divine truth; a mystic is someone who can go into every kind of hell with faith. That's why it seems to me now in this late moment that the mystical understanding, the understanding of the divine child, of the Divine Mother, is so important, because the world is becoming one vast stinking, violent, terrifying concentration camp in which all powers short of those that mystical faith summon are not going to be of much help to us. That's why, more than ever, each one of us needs to know who we really are, otherwise what is going to happen will terrify us and drive us into violence and madness. Given what's going to come down, we don't have much choice but to really become our true divine selves and to try and work with all the suffering of the world in which we live.

Another reason why the Sufis are so helpful to us is that they remind us of the austerity of this task. Rumi says in one poem, "Be grateful, not for the friend's tenderness, but for his tyranny, so the arrogant beauty in you can become a lover that weeps." It's a wonderful poem, very profound. It's saying real faith is not to turn away from suffering or defeat or humiliation, but to embrace them fully so that the "arrogant beauty," the narcissist who is always saying, "I am clever, I am wonderful, I am good," can become a true lover who weeps.

I think that we're being brought by history to the moment when the arrogant, self-obsessed one in us has to transform into a mystical lover, because the mystical lover who weeps is given all sorts of divine graces and strengths to enable him or

her to get through, to become wise and brave, and to become
a channel for living, divine grace. The real power that changes
everything is not the power of the will or intellect, it's the power
of the divine, and weeping as a lover opens us up and allows
us to become channels of that power.

*We Westerners are so scared of pain.*

One of the prices that we have paid as a civilization for exploiting and dominating the world is that we have a secret knowledge that we don't dare face up to, knowledge of the pain that
we have caused and are continuing to cause to other human
beings and to nature. We fear to find out just how hideous the
experience of such pain is, and so the last thing we want to do
is to open up to suffering of any kind because it might make
us face what we are actually doing to the earth. So there's this
tremendous, endless self-evasion and denial that goes on in the
Western psyche. I fully acknowledge this in my own psyche.
We take every conceivable drug so as not to wake up to where
we are and what we have done. Because as soon as we wake
up, there arises a huge scream in the mind.

   More and more, I think, we have to let out that huge scream,
because from it comes not only acknowledgment of pain but
also wisdom, and a plea for a new life and a new way of action.
If we don't plead for a new life and a new way of action, we're
going to be lost. The scream is also the Mother. When you
watch a woman giving birth, the pain can be unbearable. There's
a certain amount of very deep pain that has to be accepted and
embraced for the birth of the new self to take place. This isn't
a process that only takes place once, it repeats again and again.

   The greatest spiritual systems or philosophies, it seems to
me, are the ones that are honest about this and teach you to
accept it, the ones that say, if you think you're suffering now,
you should know that it is going to get worse in certain ways.
It's not going to get better, but what will happen is that it will
get very much deeper. You'll be given all the strength, peace of

mind, and courage you need to bear it, and also the mystic graces, the mystic experiences, everything. If you open to love, your heart is going to be shattered hundreds and thousands of times every day. But so what? Such shatterings are gifts, for they help you realize the truth of something a great Sufi teacher once said to me: "Andrew, the divine is so much more vulnerable than you are."

What I think he meant is that the divine has no mask. The divine is dying in everything that dies, the divine is the flower that's run over by the truck. The divine is the child dying of AIDS; the divine is both the Serbian soldier aiming the rifle and the child pierced by the bullets, screaming in agony in the middle of the marketplace. A great poem by Vietnamese Buddhist teacher Thich Nhat Hanh expresses this precisely:

> I am the child in Uganda, all skin and bones,
> my legs as thin as bamboo sticks.
> And I am the arms merchant,
> selling deadly weapons to Uganda.
>
> I am the twelve-year-old girl,
> refugee on a small boat,
> who throws herself into the ocean
> after being raped by a sea pirate.
> And I am the pirate,
> my heart not yet capable
> of seeing and loving.
>
> I am a member of the politburo,
> with plenty of power in my hands.
> And I am the man who has to pay
> his "debt of blood" to my people
> dying slowly in a forced-labor camp....
>
> Please call me by my true names,
> so I can hear all my cries and laughter at once,
> so I can see that my joy and my pain are one.[4]

The divine is dying and suffering and bleeding and crying and weeping in everything in the creation, with nowhere to hide. So opening to the exposure of love is opening to the fact that when a child cries, you *are* that child crying; when a child dies, you *are* that child dying. This would be unbearable were it not for the presence of divine strength, divine stability, divine truth. I was in Washington recently, meeting with a group of Tibetan Buddhists, and a Tibetan monk said, "Ah, you know, when you really love, it's like feeling everyone is your body. When you have a burn on your body, your hand instinctively goes to that place, and that is what you see when you come to the state of bodhisattvahood; wherever there is pain, you instinctually move towards it, because everyone is your body and every pain is your pain."

*Let's talk a bit about adoration. Isn't adoration as a way to the Mother somehow anthropocentric?*

I think the point about adoration is that it opens you up to the splendor of the divine, and so takes away the concentration upon the self, the false self, the personal biography, the narcissistic ego. But the paradox is that by adoration and through adoration, a much deeper understanding arises of the sacredness of being human. It's not anthropocentric, but it results in a much more profound vision of what being human is. A vision, in fact, that includes the natural world and every sentient being. What adoration opens up is the sacredness of all things. The divine is present in a banana and a hat as in the Dalai Lama. This vision of the sacredness of all things is one that really initiates us into what we are: the guardians of nature, or the playmates of the divine in nature. We have been given the supreme privilege of co-creating with God in nature. So by concentrating on the divine, on the splendor of the divine, by opening up the heart to that splendor, human beings can realize that they are in incessant sacred connection with all things and have a sacred responsibility towards all things. This connection purifies us of anthropomorphism because we realize that you, and you, and me, and the tree, are all one. As Rumi says in a miraculous line: "Arab, waterpot, and angel are all ourselves."

I am moved when I read about the aborigines because an aborigine will often go to an animal, a dreamtime animal, either in dream or in ritual, to acquire the kind of wisdom they think they need at that moment. For example, we talked about how aborigine mothers worship the primordial wallaby, because the wallaby knows how to love its child completely by keeping its child in its pouch and licking its bottom when it is dirty, and has this total, nondisdaining tenderness towards its child. But that goes on in all levels of aboriginal life. In fact, if you wish to acquire a certain kind of skill in running, you might go to the deer and beg the primordial deer for that. What you become aware of when you read accounts of the aborigines is that for them there are no boundaries between the human being and wallaby and the deer: all participate in the same creation. All the powers of all the creatures are accessible to the heart and the mind and the body of the human being who is open in adoration.

I think such a wisdom tradition has a huge amount to teach us. The aborigines feel that the great glory of a human being is to be *in contact*. They say the animals come with tremendous insights and real vision, and that humans incarnate one aspect of the creation, and the particular glory of the human being is that we, through adoration, through reverence, ritual, and understanding, can come to incorporate many different, seemingly contradictory aspects of the creation. I think that they are right, I think that *is* our dignity. And that's the dignity that the Mother is awakening in us. But owning that dignity, also, of course, brings total responsibility for everyone and everything else with which you're becoming one in love.

*The message you've been bringing about adoration feels very important to me, but a more quiet message that I think you're also raising is about prayer. Can you talk a bit more about that?*

Prayer and adoration, I feel, are very much the same thing. Prayer is one of the deepest ways in which we can enter into a state of adoration. Prayer is adoration's inmost secret sister, isn't it? When you pray to the divine, when you use a mantra, or when you use one of the prayers that for you is deeply expressive, the heart opens immediately, doesn't it?

But I think that why I chose a larger word than prayer is because I think what the Mother is trying to engender in the world, and what the Sufis are so brilliant in describing, is a state of being in which every action *is* prayer. A state in which there is no separation between prayer and action, in which everything becomes sacred and is consciously lived as sacred. The word "prayer" isn't quite expansive enough to encompass this new kind of life that she is trying to bring us into. That's why I use the word "adoration." That may not be adequate either.

Why I also love the word "adoration" is because when I read the literature about the so-called "primitive" peoples, the aborigines and the Kogis and the Yamomamis, the words that turn up again and again in them are "praise," "gratitude," "adoration." I realize more and more that in the mirror of the world's indigenous peoples we can really see this original relationship with the earth and with the Mother. That original relationship has gratitude at its core. At its very core is an incessant sanctification of all aspects of life. That is its essence—a whole and holistic vision of praise.

It's my contention that one of the fateful mistakes that all the major religions have made, stained as they are all by patriarchy, has been to separate from this core experience of adoration and to define things as "holy" or "unholy," "sacred" or "profane." In doing so, they all contributed to a spiritual alienation which has actually conspired in the destruction of nature. If you see this world as illusion or as a fallen state of existence, it doesn't matter if it's being destroyed. It's when you see it with the eyes of the Mother, the eyes of Rumi, the eyes of the Yamomamis and Kogis, in your own living body, that suddenly the madness of what we have been doing becomes completely obvious—the madness and the atrocious, unpardonable cruelty.

I'm really arguing here for an end to our attachment to detachment, an end to our attachment to transcendence, which doesn't mean that transcendence isn't an amazing experience, but just that it is only the beginning of the complete experience, which is to be both immanent *and* transcendent, to be finally here. To be "finally here" means to be totally in love, and fully active in love with no escape from reality needed, or wanted.

*Don't you think, remembering Rumi's poetry, that a liberated heart is fierce as well as gentle?*

I think the heart is a lion, as well as a lamb. I think that there is a majestic anger appropriate to the heart. I believe that the patriarchal religions have got a very skewed attitude about anger, they're terrified of it. In fact, they're terrified of any extreme emotions because they are so addicted to controlling everything. I think the way of the tribal peoples and the way of the Mother isn't a simple letting out of anger, but is a much more honest acceptance of the necessity of emotions like anger and the sense of difficulty and frustration. Letting them out so that they can become part of the working truth. We've been made to feel guilty about almost every honest emotion we have, for God's sake! Desire—don't even mention that! Any twinge of lust is immediately censored in the psyche as being dangerous to one's practice of *something*. Anger is taboo in our culture, which of course being such an angry, violent culture *has* to make it taboo. The main reason it is so angry and violent is because it has found no healthy, maternal nourishing way to deal with the spontaneity of emotions, to let them out in a place in which they could be let out, in a way that doesn't destroy but nurtures.

I think one way might be a "tribal" way. People would live in extended family groups and know each other intimately. There would be meetings, perhaps thirty people or so, and they'd all gather together regularly to go over things that affect the whole group and the individuals in it. There would be time for airing difficulties; perhaps somebody would say, "Well, has anyone got something that they've got to get off their chest? Would somebody like to scream at this moment? Would somebody like to say something in front of the whole tribe about someone else?" And they would, and they'd all talk about it, and get through it together, in an environment of support, mutual acknowledgment, and mutual acceptance, in a space dedicated to the Mother. That's how I see the future evolving.

How valuable that would be! It's amazing what can happen in a group of friends. For example, I once got together five people, including "X," who had done nothing but badmouth all of us to each other. We all got together for dinner. Then we sat "X" down and said, "Look here 'X,' all of us know what games you are playing. So, we are all now going to meditate and send a great deal of love to everybody in this room." At this point, "X" started to cry and talk about how jealous he was, etc. At the end of the evening, everyone felt better. Love was shared, and the wound of jealousy was beginning to be healed.

We are just beginning to understand and work with these techniques. "Techniques" is such a cold word—these "dances." We're trying to invent a new way of healing the wounds of the human race without intermediaries, without hierarchical authoritarian structures. This will in itself be part of a great healing, a birth.

*You have talked a great deal about birth; it occurs to me that the central image of the process of the Mother is birth, which is both agonizing and joyful, and which requires a complete acceptance and embrace of pain.*

Exactly. I think the truest image of what we we're going through is that of childbirth, a very painful childbirth. A birth into reality, *this* dimension, the very dimension that the patriarchal religions are teaching us to transcend. This birth, the birth the Mother is calling us to, is not going to happen elsewhere. We have to birth our own presence, here in the world, our own active, responsible presence, and that really does mean allowing it to happen in our lives, in our physical body *and* in our souls.

We are in the labor pangs of a great birth in the Mother, which might end in miscarriage. How do we hold on through the pain? By believing in the birth, by knowing that the birth is going to take place, by allowing the pain to be. By screaming sometimes. Have you ever watched a woman in childbirth? If she isn't allowing the pain, it gets much worse. If she in any way contracts around the pain and against the pain, it makes the whole process of giving birth harsher. So what has to happen is acceptance of the pain, letting the pain do its essential work of opening and opening until the child's head, body, and arms can emerge, covered in the blood of reality.

Another image of what we're going through might be that of ritual initiation at adolescence, the bloody rites of passage that happen in many aboriginal societies. Blood is spilled, young people are subjected to ordeals, because the passage between adolescence and adulthood is really a passage in which the seriousness of pain and of death have to be transmitted, otherwise the young will not assume the responsibilities of adulthood. If you're going to be a responsible member of a tribe that depends for its whole survival on sensitivity to nature, to relationships, on sensitivity to the beauty and fragility of life, then you must really know the weight, gravity, and sober poignancy of life in order to make the transition from adolescence to adulthood. That's why the initiations take place; they're not some kind of sadism, they are about helping people enter into the space of total responsibility.

The Mother is sending us now the bleeding and the ordeals that could help us enter the space of total responsibility, total interconnectedness. When we do, all sorts of powers, which seem miraculous to us now, will enter the world, but only when we are open enough, each of us, to let them come in. It must be like this because she is the Mother, and she wants us to choose each stage of the growth. By choosing each stage of the growth, we co-create with her, we play with her, we work with her directly, we go from illumination to illumination with her, we're not forced by her, ever, and we learn the meaning, experience by experience, of each stage and so become steadfast and confident.

We ourselves must choose each step. And to choose each step and be strong enough to endure what will follow on our repeated choice we have to develop a deep spiritual practice within the terms of ordinary life, trying at all moments to stay centered in the heart, the truth of the heart, the peace of the heart, so that the pain of growth can be borne within that peace and be infused by it.

There is no quick way to this. It has to be done in the intimacy of one's own life, in the intimacy of each breath, in the intimacy of each thought. It is an incessant commitment, and you can always fall away from it, even after extreme experiences of awakening. You can fall away from that simple naked presence that is love. It's the hardest thing to keep alive. When the opening heart starts to get a hint of what it will actually mean to be alive, a terror washes over it, the terrifying realization that life will mean so much love, so much intensity, so much giving, that it can close again because it fears itself incapable of the effort.

That is why the testimony of the saints and the mystics is so vital to us, because there they are saying, "Yes, you can do it!" You can allow yourself to be destroyed and opened again and again. You can dance in your blood and become "a sign of fire."

I think if we understood evolution, we'd see that the transition between species was always accompanied by immense suffering. That as a certain species grew the next few limbs, or lost a few limbs, to accommodate itself to the environment to survive, all sorts of permutations and mutations were tried out that were painful or difficult or problematic, that didn't work and had to be scrapped. The actual history of the evolution that the whole of the planet has been through is fraught with bloody failures and difficulties. Darwin said that if you really contemplate the holocaust of the little animals that have gone into the creation of our species, you would be overwhelmed with pity.

What is at stake now is unimaginably vast—either an evolutionary leap or the death of the entire race and the death of very much of nature with it. You could look at this blackly, or you could look at it as I am suggesting the Sufis are teaching us to look at it, and the Mother wants us to look at it, as a ferocious, absolute challenge to us to live as love, and act from the heart of love.

## Notes

1. All quotations and poems, except those otherwise noted, are the author's translations. Other versions of some of this material appears in *The Way of Passion: A Celebration of Rumi* (Berkeley, California: Frog, Ltd., 1994).

2. Mahmud Shabistari, in *Two Suns Rising: A Collection of Sacred Writings*. Edited by Jonathan Star (New York: Bantam Books, 1991), p. 142.

3. Mahmud Shabistari, in *Two Suns Rising*, pp. 143–144.

4. Excerpted from "Please Call Me by My True Names" in *Call Me By My True Names: The Collected Poems of Thich Nhat Hanh* (Berkeley, California: Parallax Press, 1993), pp. 72–73.

# Chapter Seven

# The Buddha and the Mother

BUDDHISM'S RELATIONSHIP to the sacred feminine is a thorny, difficult, painful subject, especially for those of us who, like me, truly revere Buddhism and have been deeply helped, instructed, and informed by Buddhist teachings. The Tibetan Buddhist teachers that I have worked with, and, of course, the Dalai Lama, who has been a great illumination to me, have been instrumental in my spiritual growth. I will begin with a celebration of those insights and approaches that Buddhism brings to a deep understanding of the sacred feminine which must be preserved at all costs. Then I will devote myself to opening up of some severe questions about Buddhism's relationship to patriarchal values and systems.

As I said before, I believe that all the major mystical traditions are constricted by the limitations of patriarchy; all of them were formed in the second stage of humankind's development, outlined in Chapter Two. They all show similar kinds of ignorance of women, derision of the body, escapism from nature, and cultivation of an overemphasis on transcendence. It has been a continuing theme of this book that we can no longer afford to try to escape from where we are and who we are. So, I'm going to deal severely with how Buddhism has contributed to that, while emphasizing and celebrating the many wonderful insights that Buddhism has given us.

What is the value of this philosophy? What is the value of what the Buddha gave us? I think its value can be outlined in five different categories. The first category is a kind of sacred and compassionate ruthlessness. The Buddha saw reality plain, without decoration or consolation, and had the fiercest and clearest vision of all the liberators of humankind. That ruthlessness is valuable to us now, because we're facing an apocalyptic situation, and we need the Buddha's lack of consolation and concentration on the present.

The second quality that is moving and wonderful about the Buddhist vision is its understanding of interdependence, of what Thich Nhat Hanh calls "interbeing." This is the essential interrelatedness of all phenomena, and the kind of wisdom this understanding gives rise to is essential. This takes me to the third category, the third great contribution of Buddhism, which is its very subtle, rich, intelligent, and tough-minded philosophy of active compassion.

The fourth great achievement of Buddhism, and it's an essential and extremely powerful one, has been the working out of a shrewd, clear-minded technology of sacred transformation. Both the Hinayana and the Mahayana schools of Buddhism are wonderfully clever and skilled in developing techniques, of both meditation and visualization, that really help many different kinds of practitioners and all kinds of personalities to clarify the mind, transform the spirit, and come closer and closer to the heart of the truth and the heart of wisdom. These techniques constitute for me the essential wisdom technology of the world. I don't think there is anything more powerful for cleansing the mind than the great Hinayana techniques of sweeping the mind, of learning how to note things, of learning how to attend to things, of learning how to follow your breathing. I don't think there's anything more powerful in the actual transformation of the spirit than the Mahayana techniques of visualization, especially those that the Tibetans developed in the laboratories of consciousness that were the monasteries of Tibet.

These techniques and this technology are universal in their application and in their importance, and certainly something that must at all costs be preserved and practiced for the great transformation of the human race that is to come. They're also levelheaded. There's nothing sentimental about Buddhism. There's no false promise that you'll be enlightened in ten minutes if you pay twenty thousand dollars. There is less exaggerated emphasis on the guru, the master, than in Hinduism, since the Buddha himself stressed again and again that each of us must work out our own salvation with diligence. Buddhism has been, in a way, the supreme science of mental transformation, and as such, has the very highest place in all religious endeavors of real spiritual change.

The fifth category really sums up all the others. It is that the Buddha really did see, in a way that is extremely difficult to put into words and dogmas, the very nature of reality itself, of transcendent and absolute reality. This category, what I will call the *prajñaparamita* category, transcends even the vision of interdependence; it is one in which interdependence is *"one."* This is the vision of emptiness, of *anatta*, of the "no-self" nature of things. A thorough examination of "no-self" is beyond the scope of this exploration, but fundamentally, what the Buddha understood was that nothing exists as we imagine it to exist, that nothing has a fundamental permanent identity, that all things arise from what he called "dependent co-origination." This supreme wisdom is totally liberating, totally spacious; it's an ecstatic calm vision and understanding of the fundamental emptiness of all form and phenomena. This *prajñaparamita* understanding is a Mother-understanding, an understanding of the void that leaps to an embrace of the whole of reality with serenity and compassion. It has been beautifully described by Lex Hixon in his book *Mother of the Buddhas:*

> The Perfection of Wisdom shines forth as a sublime light, O Buddha nature, I sing this spontaneous hymn of light to praise Mother Prajña-paramita. She is worthy of infinite praise, she is utterly unstained, because nothing in this unsubstantial world can possibly stain her. She is an ever-flowing fountain of incomparable light, and from every conscious

being on every plane, She removes the faintest trace of illusory darkness. She leads living beings into her clear light from the blindness and obscurity caused by moral and spiritual impurity, as well as by partial or distorted views of reality. Sublime and excellent are her revelations, She inspires and guides us to seek the safety and certainty of the bright wings of enlightenment. She provides the illumination through which all fear and despair can be utterly renounced. Mother Prajña-paramita is total awakeness. She never substantially creates any limited structure because she experiences none of the tendencies of living beings to grasp, project, or conceptualize. Neither does she substantially dismantle or destroy any limited structure, for she encounters no solid limits. She is the Perfect Wisdom which never comes into being, and therefore never goes out of being. She is known as the Great Mother by those spiritually mature beings who dedicate their mindstreams to the liberation and full enlightenment of all that lives.[1]

*　*　*

Let us now examine the first four different "powers" in detail.

The first essential power of Buddhism is its ruthlessness. It is the most exposing, the most ferocious, the most calmly exacting of all of the major revelations. What the Buddha did was take away from humanity all its props, all its pseudo-magic, all its false consolations, all of those consoling doctrines of permanence with which we have drugged ourselves. He presented the human race with the facts—the facts of imperfection, suffering, and death. The Buddha's quest didn't begin with some fancy vision or flashing lights. It began with his seeing four things: the sight of a sick man, an old man, a dead man, and a holy man, a seeker. The Buddha began life as a prince who lived in a pleasure garden. His father kept him away from the world, tried to protect him from the world. But Prince Siddhartha saw an old man, a sick man, and a dead man, and suddenly confronted in them the terror and grief of mortality. Then, it is said, he saw a yogi, a man who had the peaceful eyes of one who has overcome both life and death. It was at that moment that he understood that life was terrifying, but that there was a way out.

This was what determined his quest. So, the Buddha's quest did not begin with some glorious vision and illumination, nor with the reading of some exotic text, nor with a miraculous encounter with some master Houdini who materialized objects out of thin air. The Buddha's quest began with staring into the inferno, and it was from that inferno that he set out to rescue first himself, and then all beings.

A story that illustrates the sacred ruthlessness of Buddhism most beautifully and most completely is about a woman called Krisha Gotami. Her child had died, and she had heard of the Buddha, so she went to visit him. She believed, as we all still believe of those who have attained enlightenment, that the Buddha was a miracle worker. So she flung the dead body of her child at the Buddha's feet and sobbed and begged him to bring the child back to life. She begged him to save her and to staunch her grief. He said, "I will. But first, go around to all the houses of the village and collect a mustard seed from any house that has not known death." Crying and sobbing, Krisha Gotami went from house to house. Of course, she discovers that at every house, whether poor or rich, there is none—not one family or household—that has not known death. Slowly, by confronting the fact of grief, the fact of pain, the fact of death at each house, she came to understand that the loss of her child, although terrible, was part of samsara, part of the precariousness of this precarious dimension. She went back to the Buddha, her grief sobered and healed. The Buddha did not teach her by giving her a practice or by talking about the immortality of the soul; the Buddha did not teach her by giving her some fancy vision or by offering her a series of magical incantations. The Buddha simply said, "Go and face the facts of impermanence. This is

a world of pain and suffering, a world in which we are all going
to lose everything, including our body. Deal with life as it is,
and become strong in clarity."

Another illustration of this ruthless quality is in the following
story. One day, the Buddha was asked to describe why suffering existed. He said, "I could give you a great many explanations, but when somebody has shot an arrow into your side,
do you go on and on wondering where the arrow was made,
who shot the arrow, what color hair the person had who shot
the arrow? Or do you take the arrow out?" The Buddha went
on, "The arrow is desire, the arrow is craving, the arrow is self-
obsession, the arrow is vanity, the arrow is refusal to face the
facts, the arrow is evasion. Take the arrow out! Stop the pain.
Don't worry where the pain comes from, or why the pain is
there. We will never know; none of the explanations will be
satisfying. They're only mental anyway. What is important is
to get down to real examination, real unconsoling examination, real work, real spiritual practice, real ending of the causes
of suffering. Any other approach is frivolous."

The Buddha is an extremely unfrivolous teacher because
he doesn't attempt to satisfy any of the mind's or the ego's desire
for *divertissement*. Not only did he not define nirvana in any
splendid terms, he defined it only by negatives. He refused to
give us something on which we could hang a concept or a dogma,
because he wished to leave that most essential of experiences
forever free in its own space so that it could lead us deeper and
deeper into the nameless freedom that is our true inheritance,
our true nature.

This quality of sacred ruthlessness is, I think, essential for
the revolution of the sacred feminine. We need it now, everybody in the world needs to squarely face exactly where we are.
We need to say to ourselves, "We are in a dying world, we are
destroying nature, we are being unbelievably evasive of all the
agonizing problems that face us." So we need that marvelous
sternness, that penetrating intensity of the Buddha saying,
"Wake up, face the facts, don't worry where the arrow came

from. Examine the root causes of pollution and environmental and political catastrophe, and change them."

It was in his dying that the Buddha exemplified most movingly this lack of sentimentality. As the Buddha lay on his deathbed, Ananda and the other disciples were mourning and moaning and saying, "Oh, don't go, don't go, O beloved, O great one, O master!" He replies, "Didn't I tell you? All compounded things decay. I've been talking for forty years! I have analyzed impermanence in five million different ways, and here you are crying about me going." And then, as reported in the *Mahaparinibbana Suttanta,* the Buddha says:

> I am now grown old, O Ananda, and full of years. My journey is drawing to its close, I have reached the sum of my days, I am turning eighty years of age.
>
> Just as a worn-out cart can only with much difficulty be made to move along, so the body of the Tathagata can only be kept going with much additional care.
>
> It is only, Ananda, when the Tathagata, ceasing to attend to any outward thing, becomes plunged in that devout meditation of heart which is concerned with no bodily object, it is only then that the body of the Tathagata is at ease.
>
> Therefore, O Ananda, be ye lamps unto yourselves. Rely on yourselves, and do not rely on external help.
>
> Hold fast to the truth as a lamp. Seek salvation alone in the truth. Look not for assistance to any besides yourselves.[2]

In an age like ours, addicted to easy or pseudo-magical solutions, the Buddha's stern message of self-reliance, of the necessity of walking alone the direct path to awakening, is pricelessly valuable—an eternal reminder of the inherent nobility of each of us and of the reward of real discipline.

The second essential contribution of Buddhism to the revolution of the sacred feminine is its exquisitely detailed knowledge of interdependence. Interdependence is essentially the pure seeing and knowing of reality as one dance, one movement, one flow; the pure knowing, beyond any doubt, of all the different events and beings in reality as linked to each other. Think of a tree: into the making of the tree goes the work and dance of the whole universe—rain, earth, the turn of the seasons, the sky and stars, moonlight and sunlight, and on and on. So, to look deeply at a tree is to see in the tree the whole of the universe participating in its being. As Thich Nhat Hanh says:

> Can you see the sun in a grain of rice? . . . For without the sun on the rice fields, there would be no rice. Can you see the cloud in a wooden table? For without the cloud then there would be no rain to water the tree, and there would be no wood to make the table.[3]

And that "being" which we take so essentially and so seriously is, in fact, like the temporary crest of a wave in the sea. It is an arising from a transient set of conditions, of a form that is also "empty," also changing and transforming itself as you look at it. Nothing is stable, nothing is permanent, nothing is fixed, everything is always transforming, and everything affects everything else. A tree burning in the Amazon alters the air in Moscow; the trembling of a butterfly's wing in the Yucatan affects the life of a person in the Hebrides. The Buddha's vision of absolute reality in the *Avatamsaka Sutra* is of a limitless, boundless jeweled net in which all the other jewels of the net are always reflected. Physicists tell us of the world of the quantum particle: just like the jewels in the net, all particles exist potentially as different combinations of other particles. The Buddha's ancient meditative understanding of interdependence has been confirmed by the most exciting discoveries of modern biology and physics.

Why is interdependence so important for us now at this time, at the end of the twentieth century? It is crucial because unless we understand that we and every other being on earth are one, we and every other *thing* on earth are one, and that we and nature are one, we will simply remain ignorant of our reality and we won't do enough to save this planet. So a meditative, philosophical, and spiritual awareness of interdependence at every level is crucial for our survival. This knowledge is now being echoed, as I have said, in the highest discoveries of astrophysics; and, of course, the ancient tribal cultures, like the aborigines, have always known that the entire universe participates in the birth of one wallaby or in the shining of one blade of grass in the sun. But now it is time for us all to know this, too, and to put this knowledge as quickly and comprehensively as possible into economic and political practice.

The third vital and enriching power of Buddhism is compassion. Out of an understanding of interbeing and interdependence naturally arises an exquisite and poignant sense of our relatedness to all living things. From the ruthlessness of Buddha's vision of impermanence and from the inner knowledge of interdependence, a sense of total compassionate involvement with all living things quite naturally arises. One of the greatest achievements of Buddhism was to extend this not only to other human beings, but to *every* sentient being. To insist on the sacredness of life in all its aspects: the life of an insect, a cow, a flower, a dog. The Buddha's own life was characterized, as were the lives of St. Francis and Rumi, by an extraordinary sensitivity to life at all levels. What could be more important for us now than to cultivate not merely this kind of very clear compassion toward each other, toward all human beings, but also toward all sentient beings, really to extend our embrace to the whole of nature of which we are a part, that is under our guardianship and that is now tragically threatened by our unconsciousness of precisely those laws of interdependence that the Buddha discovered and taught with such brilliant clarity.

The fourth power of Buddhism is its sacred technology, its great achievement of having developed all manner of meditative techniques and spiritual practices. This is, of course, essential, because this kind of boundless compassion, the knowledge of interdependence, the ruthless directness and facing of reality, are not easy. We really have to work on ourselves intensely to engender and sustain these qualities, because our conditioned tendency is to take refuge in consolation, to starve our compassion, to limit our love and hide behind a mask of fear and false identity. In order to help humankind overcome fear and understand the nature of the essence of mind and move more deeply into a direct knowledge of interdependence, a rich awareness of the necessity and practice of compassion, the Buddha in his own lifetime and the Buddhist masters since have developed a quite astonishing array of meditative techniques that can help anyone, whatever their knowledge or spiritual ability, to really connect with the fundamentals of life.

These meditation techniques are still too little known in the West. I believe that every spiritual seeker, everyone—regardless of the path they are on—should really dive deep into the Buddhists' knowledge of meditation, because everyone needs their fundamental basic truths and can be helped by these techniques. Nobody can afford not to have done vipassana meditation, insight meditation. Nobody can afford not to have learned the great Hinayana tradition of noting meditation. In a time as dangerous and as difficult as ours, no one can afford not to have really explored Tibetan visualization meditations, some of the most powerful, enriching, exciting, passionate ways of altering the mind, and which can, in moments of danger or panic, turn the mind toward enlightened spaciousness and the heart toward all-embracing compassion. We're going to need as many of the simplest and highest techniques as possible in the years to come. So this fourth achievement of Buddhism, giving out of its compassionate heart so many vital meditative techniques to the world, is essential to the revolution of the sacred feminine.

*　*　*

Having praising the great achievements of Buddhism, now let us turn to look at the ways in which this great spiritual tradition needs to change to be able to participate in the revolution of the sacred feminine, and not block it.

I'd like to share with you a work-in-progress from a friend

of mine. She is a practicing Buddhist, and a woman in agony about the patriarchal nature of this tradition. She takes as a point of departure the story of a Japanese nun named Ryonen, who was very beautiful. This story says a great deal about what is wrong with the tradition and what must be changed.

As I said at the beginning, all the major religious traditions must go through a double revolution: first, a return to their mystical cores, an absolute stripping away of dogma and convention and rules and laws to get right to the kernel. The second revolution that really must happen is that they all must purify themselves by a confrontation with—and radical absorption of—the wisdom of the sacred feminine. Unfortunately, even at the very core of the major mystical traditions as we've inherited them, there is a patriarchal contempt for women, a patriarchal contempt for the body, and a tendency to view this world as unreal, all of which are dangerous now. The last thing we need are any more dogmas or religions that stress the unreality of the world and keep us in our coma of dissociation from nature.

So let me share this excerpt from my friend's work:

Ryonen was a beautiful young woman who wished to enter a monastery and study with a great Zen teacher. Everywhere she goes the teacher turns her away because she is so beautiful. "No," says the teacher in his sparely decorated room with one single flower placed at his side. Outside a bird sings. The carefully landscaped garden is visible through the open door. The sound of water from a small fountain pleases the ears. She sits bowed, prostrate before him. "No," he says, "you will distract the monks." The scene repeats itself over and over. She knows the answer ahead of time, as she knows the single flower, the gentle sound of water. Finally, one day, she takes in her hand a hot iron and puts it to her cheek. In a moment her beauty is gone forever. The next teacher admits her. Scarred, mutilated, misshapen, she is now acceptable. No problem.

I leap forward at the moment in the story when Ryonen picks up the hot iron. "No, you will not do this, Ryonen." I take it and fling it far away and with it go all the instruments of torture used on women in the witch hunts, all the rusty knives used to cut off the genitals of little girls, all the stones thrown at all the harlots of the Old Testament. All the rags from all the little bandaged tortured feet in China. All the bricks used to wall up the vestal virgins who were found having sex. All the whips used by all the monks to flagellate themselves. You get the idea. With that hot iron I return 2,500 years of patriarchal history to itself. I say: "No. I do not accept it, I absolutely refuse it."

The hot iron sails through the air and lands in the lap of the last teacher who refused her. I say to her, "You are beautiful. Honor that beauty." I take her away past time and space to a place I believe in. A place where she walks in and bows and the teacher says, "Welcome, just as you are, whoever you are. Join us, be with us, live with us, learn with us." A young man stands up and says, "But I will never be able to concentrate on my meditation with her around, I'll have an erection all the time. I'll think about nothing but her, she's the devil, a demon, a temptation! Don't let her in." And the teacher looks at him and says, "Your devil is within you. Not your desire, but your fear. Your judgment, your disgust. These are the demons. The Buddha stands before you—young, beautiful, woman. Look deep in yourself, leave her be. Honor her, honor yourself. Bring the light of your awareness to your desire. Perhaps your path is with her, perhaps your path is alone. But only truth and time can tell."

In Theravada it's centuries of elders. It's nuns of 100 years bowing to monks of one day. It's texts that state to be a woman is an inferior karma, only a man can become a Buddha. A woman first becomes male, then having given up her femaleness, she can become a Buddha. In the Tibetan traditions it's male rinpoche after male rinpoche; the Dalai Lama is male. It's giving lip service to the qualities of the feminine while nuns struggle to survive. It's claiming that in the Vajrayana the feminine is honored while the word for woman in Tibetan literally translates as "born low." Buddhism is a patriarchal religion, just like all the other major religions of the world. People try to get around it. It's less patriarchal. In Buddhanature there is no male or female, at least the Buddha permitted women to join the sangha. For the first time women were freed of the bondage of wifely servitude; they had a choice. There are women in Buddhism, look at the verses of the early nuns, look at all the old women in the Zen stories. Look at the women of wisdom in Tibet, look at the *dakinis*. I say enough! All this is denial, all this is minimalization, all this is rationalization. Buddhism drips with patriarchy. It is patriarchy. You, Buddha, founded a patriarchal system, you've become a patriarch, and you're not around to say No.

You have presided over systems of power, domination, greed, and abuse, both in this country and in others. Your representatives have blessed warriors and bombers as often as Christian ministers have. People have killed in your name, *samurai* have cut off countless heads with your blessing. Government intrigues have proceeded under your serene smile. Teachers have sexually abused their students while you looked on. You are not apart from this patriarchal world, you are not special, guiltless, or removed. Your own life was lived in a patriarchal system. You broke the tradition and didn't obey your father, but you did leave your wife and son. Many men since then have followed your example, you encouraged people to leave their families and reject their sexuality. That's part of the patriarchal system. You've struggled with it, as in your ascetic practices. You didn't buy into it fully, but you didn't fully reject it. You didn't welcome women as equals in practice, and practice is what counts. You compromised. Everybody compromises.

People say, well, you had to accommodate the cultural customs of the time. I understand. But let's be clear, that

makes you a human being, a politician, not a god. Maybe
you weren't just accommodating the cultural customs, maybe
you were a part of your culture, maybe you really believe
being a woman is an inferior karma and that to admit women
to the sangha would create trouble and discord. That means
again: you were a human being. People have turned you
into a patriarchal god, but that's not in the spirit of your
teaching.

I want to define patriarchy. Words are charged. I use the
term very personally, it has nothing to do with blaming
men. Men and women alike are caught by this pattern. It's
not something a man does to me or did to me; it's something we have all done to each other for eons. Patriarchy
manifests in political, social, economic, and religious systems in which the male has the overt power. I'm not saying
things would be different if women ran the world. I'm not
advocating matriarchy. And I'm not trying to be objective.[4]

My friend is right, she is absolutely right. To prove how
right she is, you have only to look at the earliest sacred text of
Buddhism, the *Dhammapada*. Realize just what this text sig-
nifies: a rejection of the world, a rejection of the body, a rejection of human relationships and human experience, forwarding
instead an exaggerated praise of the monastic ideal. It is time
that the world forever did away with the exaggerated importance of the monastic ideal. It is valuable for certain people,
for perhaps about 3 percent; it keeps alive something sacred
and important—but it is not the way for the majority of humanity. Praising it as *the* way (and this is how it has been emphasized) has simply kept alive the body vs. spirit, sexuality vs.
spirituality split that the sacred feminine is now coming to eliminate. Listen to these verses from the *Dhammapada*:

> Love cometh from companionship;
> In wake of love upsurges ill;
> Seeing the bane that comes of love,
>     Fare lonely as a rhinoceros.

In pain for all his bosom-friends,
A man, heart-chained, neglects the goal:
Seeing this fear in fellowship,
　　Fare lonely as a rhinoceros.

Tangled as crowding bamboo boughs
Is fond regard for sons and wife:
As the tall tops are tangle-free,
　　Fare lonely as a rhinoceros.

The deer untethered roams the wild
Wheresoever it lists for food:
Seeing the liberty, wise man,
　　Fare lonely as a rhinoceros.

Son, wife and father, mother, wealth,
The things wealth brings, the ties of kin:
Leaving these pleasures one and all,
　　Fare lonely as a rhinoceros.[5]

That is a limited ideal, one rooted in the pessimistic fear of all bonds and relationships. And, unfortunately, there are aspects of the Buddha's own life story that have been celebrated and ennobled at the cost of great pain to both women and men—namely, the Great Renunciation of the Buddha, his leaving of his wife and child, his family and parents. The Buddha's apocryphal inability to invite women in a grand way into his whole spiritual enterprise is also disturbing.

I'd like to quote from a brilliant article, "Bowing Not Scraping," by Kate Wheeler, an essay that changed my vision of what's going on in Buddhism. This is a painful article brilliantly written by a sincere Buddhist, and in such a way that makes her points unanswerable:

The historical Buddha abandoned his wife, and named his infant "Fetter": is this a model for how a spiritually motivated person should behave? Must I believe Pali texts' insistence that a fully enlightened Buddha must have "a penis with a sheath"? At Wat Suan Mokkh, in Thailand, there's a painting of a sexy lady, her miniskirt adorned with scary barbed hooks as she slyly displays a fishing rod: she's a warning of dangerous female intentions. Is it rude to suggest lust be cleansed from monks, rather than just projected onto women? Zen schools are like boot camp; where are the female roshis in Korea and Japan? The Tibetan word for *woman* means "lesser birth"; women serve tea to slake lamas' thirst while they chant the rituals that women can sponsor but are rarely qualified to conduct. The Pure Land of Great Bliss has no women, the scriptures recount. Why not? For this, there *is* an answer: because it's supposed to be pure and blissful!

If women must be excluded from purity and bliss, then the tradition betrays its own deepest truth of wisdom and compassion. No way around it: traditional Buddhism, like most religions, is dominated by men—in imagery, language, practices, hierarchical institutions, income, prestige, and perks. This is dangerous for women most visibly, for men more subtly. Does Buddhism's male bias flavor its practices, encouraging, for example, the discounting of ordinary human bonds? With what results? Certainly, if men dominate all meanings, abuse and corruption are guaranteed.

"It were better for you, foolish man, that your male organ should enter the mouth of a terrible and poisonous snake than it should enter a woman," the Buddha said to a monk who slept with his ex-wife. The Buddha praised renunciate life as the best path to freedom, but he didn't want to ordain women. Only after his softhearted attendant begged three times on women's behalf did he relent. . . . Later, the Buddha sourly predicted that the nuns' ordination would halve the lifespan of the dharma.

Kate Wheeler goes on:

Under no circumstances may a nun criticize a monk nor admonish him. A monk bows to any monk ordained before him, but the First Special Rule of nuns say that a nun "even of a hundred years' standing" shall bow down before a monk ordained "even a day." The strict seniority system, designed to eradicate caste in males, perpetuates subjugation—in pointed, nasty language—as soon as women appear....

The Buddha's original nun's order, the *bikkhunis*, vanished one thousand years ago everywhere except China, where an authentic Mahayana nuns' transmission survives. A few monkly authorities support the spread of the Chinese lineage; women from many traditions now travel to Taiwan to receive full ordination and training. Yet the vast majority of devout women in Tibet, Burma, Thailand, and Sri Lanka still take fewer vows, and wear robes in a no-man's-land outside the "real" transmission, where they are neither fish nor fowl, ordained nor ordinary. Many say they like the freedom of indeterminacy; that's understandable, especially since it can be difficult to find monks and laypeople willing to provide the intensive support *bikkhunis* need in order to keep their vows.

At the end of her article, Kate Wheeler writes:

Twenty-five hundred years ago, the Buddha's stepmother, Mahapajapati Gotami, who breastfed him after his mother died, became the head of the nuns' order. She said it would be good if men and women in this order could revere each other on the basis of equality. The Buddha's recorded reply was that if false teachers do not allow women equal status, then how much less could he—the true teacher—allow them equal status. In the case of women, the Buddha was wrong— and we have to have the courage to say so.[6]

But this mistake in the case of women is, of course, not just being wrong about women; it's actually being wrong about fundamental questions of human life and about the nature of reality. I would suggest that despite Buddhism's extraordinary gifts and contributions to the human spiritual landscape, its negative emphasis on the body, its consistent emphasis on worldly reality as illusion, have in fact conspired in the destruction of the planet. When you have spent a great deal of time escaping from worldly reality or decrying the body, it becomes very easy to punish other people's bodies. When you believe that *this* experience here, our life on earth, is fundamentally dreamlike or illusory, it's very easy not to care deeply or clearly or passionately or actively enough for how things are done in the world. Although Buddhism has always given us extraordinary beings, as exemplified in people like the Dalai Lama, it is time that we all, in the name of the sacred feminine, in the name of this great revolution, call all the religions to a new order. We must examine what they've left us, and how saturated their preconceptions are by exactly the kinds of rejection of the body, of sexuality, of nature, that we must now reverse for the planet to be saved and for the vision of the Divine Mother, of a liberated humanity at play at her feast, to be realized.

So, let me share with you a passage directly from the Buddha himself, and please hear it with a critical ear, as a warning. It is a sublime passage, but if we really examine it, we will hear the way in which it could be used to subtly encourage psychotic dissociation, to encourage attachment to detachment, to encourage a vision of the world as unreal and to starve the psyche of the fundamental vital connectedness that it needs as a spur for action.

> "Form, brethren, is not the self. If this form, brethren, were the self, it could not turn oppressive, and one could achieve one's intention, 'Let my body be thus, let my body not be thus!' It is because the body is not the self, brethren, that it turns oppressive, and that one cannot achieve the intention, 'let my body be thus, let my body not be thus.'

Do you hear in this text the hidden passion for dominating the body, for finding it repulsive because you can't make it do what you want to do, which is supposed to prove that the body is disgusting? Why not reverse that and stop trying to impose upon the body a kind of false vision of what it must be? Why not accept its terms, and love, cherish, and honor it? That is the way of the feminine. The Buddha goes on:

> "Does then impermanence contribute to suffering or to ease?"—"To suffering, O Lord!"—
>
> "But is it fitting to consider that which is impermanent, linked to suffering, and doomed to reversal, as 'This is mine, I am this, this is myself'?—"No, indeed not, O Lord."— "Therefore, brethren, whatever form . . . there may be— past, future, or present, inward or outward, gross or subtle, low or exalted, near or far away—all that should be seen by right wisdom as it really is, i.e., that 'All this is not mine, I am not this, this is not myself.'

Of course there is profundity in this view, and it does help us break down our notion of things as solid, permanent, and fixed. But supposing that you were told the opposite? Suppose that instead of being told in the *Upanishads* that "You are That," every child in the world was told "You are *this*—this is *you*: the starving peasant is you; the humiliated person with AIDS is you; the tortured animal in the forest is you." Let's have no more "I am not this," "I am not that." Let's have a philosophy that really makes it inescapable for us to identify ourselves with everything and everyone else, instead of giving us all sorts of sophisticated ways out of passion, sophisticated ways out of seeing that we are all *this!* We must be brought down here to earth if we are going to learn to love and preserve it *and* ourselves.

The passage goes on:

> The learned holy disciple who perceives this becomes disgusted with form, and everything else, up to consciousness. Disgusted, he sheds his greed for these things. His dispassion sets him free . . .

In this we surely hear a patriarchal desire for control, a patriarchal desire to dissociate, and a patriarchal rage which manifests itself as disgust at the things that it cannot control. All of which go directly against the fundamental wisdom of the sacred feminine: the wisdom of acceptance, the wisdom of rhythm, the wisdom of generous tolerance. In this view, dispassion sets us free—not love, not commitment, not tenderness, not sense of the divine in all things, but dispassion. The Buddha then says:

> ... and he then also knows that he is liberated. "Birth is extinct, the holy life completed; what had to be done has been done, there is nothing further to do."[7]

This teaching leads inexorably from the desire to control everything, from the desire to dissociate from everything, to the desire to shed everything through disgust and to not *do* anything, because there's nothing to do, you've attained this kind of spacy freedom from all things. There's nothing further to do, the "holy life" has been achieved. This is the perfect schizoid paradigm for the male mind, and unfortunately, it has been imposed through the authority of a very great master.

The Buddha himself, however, said again and again, "Don't take my words for absolute truth, don't set me up as an authority. Use them if they help, but test them. Throw them against the wall, take them apart, look deeply at them. I am not a god, I am a human being. If you don't find my teachings useful, get rid of them, change them for something else." Inherent in that statement is a very great freedom which we can now seize to our advantage in saying to the Buddhist tradition: "We revere what you gave us, but we're going to change many things. We're going to test everything, the whole doctrine. We're going to test it by resurrecting the power of women, we're going to test it by infusing it with a sacred vision of nature, we're going to test it by infiltrating it with what we need now, which is to really come into our bodies, to bless our sexuality, to heal the emotional wounds of the world. We're going to test it by our increasing understanding of the tendency of the masculine side of the psyche toward dissociation, escapism, and control. What survives of the doctrine will be essential for the future, and what

will be discarded is a series of prisons, evasions, and ignorance."
I believe that if the Buddha were alive now, in our disaster, he
would salute this "testing," however devastating to "Buddhist"
institutions the results might be.

Let me end, in the Buddha's noble spirit, with a selection from
the *Sutta Nipata*, a hymn to love that is a universal blessing:

> May creatures all abound in weal and peace.
> May all be blessed with peace always.
> All creatures weak or strong,
> All creatures great or small.
>
> Creatures unseen or seen,
> Dwelling afar or near,
> Born or awaiting birth,
> —May all be blessed with peace!
>
> Let none cajole or flout
> His fellow anywhere.
> Let none wish others harm
> In dudgeon or hate.
>
> Just as with her own life a mother
> Shields from hurt her own, her only child—
> Let all-embracing thoughts
> For all that lives be thine—
>
> An all-embracing love for all the universe
> In all its heights and depths and breadth,
> Unstinted love, unmarred by hate within,
> Not rousing enmity.
>
> Lo, as you stand, or walk,
> Or sit, or lie, reflect
> With all your might on this—
> 'Tis deemed a state divine.[8]

## Notes

1. Lex Hixon, *Mother of the Buddhas: Meditations on the Prajnaparamita Sutra* (Wheaton, Illinois: Quest Books, 1993), p. 95.

2. Quoted in Thera Piyadassi, *The Buddha's Ancient Path* (Kandy, Sri Lanka: Buddhist Publication Society, 1974)

3. Quoted by Catherine Ingram in *In The Footsteps of Gandhi: Conversations with Spiritual Social Activists* (Berkeley, California: Parallax Press, 1990), p. 75.

4. From author's copy of unpublished manuscript. The name and address of the writer have been lost; please contact Andrew Harvey c/o the publisher with this information so that the writer can be fully acknowledged.

5. Adapted from "The Rhinoceros," in *Buddhist Scriptures*. Selected and translated by Edward Conze (New York: Penguin Books, 1959), p. 79, 81.

6. Excerpted from "Bowing Not Scraping" by Kate Wheeler, in *Tricycle: The Buddhist Review*, Vol. III, No. 2, Winter 1993, pp. 26–32. Used by permission of the author.

7. *Buddhist Scriptures*, p. 188.

8. Adapted from Thera Piyadassi, *The Buddha's Ancient Path*.

# Chapter Eight

# Mahayana Buddhism and the Mother

WHAT MAHAYANA BUDDHISM has given us is a fundamental understanding and exploration of the nature of enlightenment and of the nature of enlightened activity. There are three aspects of this noble, beautiful vision of the human condition that are essential, I think, to the revolution of the sacred feminine, and I shall sketch these first.

The first aspect from which all else unfolds is the vision of the enlightened mind, of Buddhanature, of what is called the wisdom-marriage, the marriage of wisdom and compassion. From that vision springs the ideal of the bodhisattva, a crucial example for this time and for what we are called upon to do. And from this vision of the bodhisattva springs the technology of compassion developed in the laboratories of enlightenment, the monasteries of Tibet.

These three things are the crucial contributions of Mahayana Buddhism to the revolution of the sacred feminine. First, the marriage of wisdom and compassion, the bringing together of the enlightened understanding of the essential inherent voidness of reality, and the necessity of enacting and manifesting that understanding in the action of compassion. Then, the vision of the bodhisattva, a being who out of compassion for everything, for the suffering in reality, gives up entering nirvana again and again so as to remain in samsara in order to redeem everything in samsara, to bring all beings to understanding and enlightenment. Bodhisattvas essentially commit themselves to lifetime after lifetime of tender service, and know a kind of love that is not attainable by those who choose transcendental escapism.

The third, crucial part of this vision is the development, from the marriage of wisdom and compassion, of an entire technology of compassion, a technology of awakening that is designed to inspire, aid, and sustain the practice of every single kind of being. Developed in the monasteries of Tibet, those laboratories of consciousness, was a series of inventive and precise meditation techniques, ways of getting in contact with Buddhanature, Buddhamind; inventive and precise ways of arousing compassion, and so therefore fueling compassionate action in the world; and powerful ways of helping people in all the different phases of life, from birth to maturity and especially through death itself. One supreme contribution of Mahayana Buddhism in its Tibetan manifestation is an understanding of exactly what happens in death. It is this understanding that Sogyal Rinpoche, Patrick Gaffney, and myself worked to make available to the world in *The Tibetan Book of Living and Dying*.[1] I understood from my own experience just how powerful and extraordinary this wisdom is, and so I'm going to begin this journey with a description of it.

I've been very tough on certain modern gurus and on what I conceive of as our passion for magical solutions and all the rest. But to redress the balance a little, I would like to say that I have had the experience of a great teacher in this life, Thuksey Rinpoche, who really did transform my life. I describe meeting him in *A Journey in Ladakh*,[2] he initiated me into the Tibetan tradition and I really experienced him as my soul's father. Thuksey Rinpoche was renowned throughout his tradition and throughout his world as a living Buddha. I retain memories of him that are imprinted and emblazoned with light, and my whole life has been nourished by my contact with him.

I last saw Thuksey Rinpoche in the final months of his life. I returned to Ladakh to be with him and shared a few amazing months with him. I'd heard that he was sick and I'd had a premonition that perhaps it would be our last time together. What I want to share with you was what it was like to be with him when he was dying. Thuksey Rinpoche was ostensibly extremely weak, yet he never stopped teaching. His particular focus was Avalokiteshvara, the Bodhisattva of Compassion, because Rinpoche believed that instructing beings in the nature of compassion was the most important thing that you could do. He knew that awakening compassion is the key to the enlightened experience. "Thuksey Rinpoche" was his given name, not his birth name. It was given to him because his people loved him so much that they called him "the man who has a heart like the sun."

He was still laughing, still smiling, and still teaching incessantly that summer, but he was feeble, and we were all worried and sad. There was a small group of us: an ex-nun, an ex-scuba diver, a chanteuse, and myself. We were a motley crew, but we were united in our devotion to and love for him. Every time Thuksey came back from the doctor, for example, we'd be waiting at the top of the stairs to greet him, and he would stagger up, smiling, infusing us with confidence and cheerfulness, and reach up toward each of us and inquire how *we* were, how we were sleeping, whether we were eating enough, whether we were understanding some of the more abstruse points of his teaching. It was the most moving living representation of egolessness that I have ever witnessed.

But I wanted to tell you of one particular ceremony, the long-life ceremony, that we all assembled to participate in. This ceremony is performed when the person who is being prayed for, in this case a teacher, is welcomed in and everybody, his students and his associates, pray for his long life. A figure representing him is made out of barley and is placed on the altar. All sorts of incantations and charms are willed into that figure to will it to continue; in Thuksey's case, to continue so as to be able to give the teaching, because for the Tibetans the incarnation of enlightenment in the body and the transmission of it are extremely important. Clearly, he was not just important as a vehicle of enlightened teaching, he was really sacred to an entire people.

I've never seen anything like the love that the Ladakhis had for him. In fact, the day before he was to leave Ladakh forever, he sat on the bed in a quiet shadowy room, and the entire population of Ladakh came silently to bid him good-bye. I have never in my life seen anything like that. One by one, the farmers, the bakers, the lamas took off their shoes and came into his room. He was sitting on a plain blanket, very simply dressed, smiling. He blessed everybody before he left, and nobody said a word. There was the total silence of true love: total love from both sides. It's something we never see in our pasteurized ashrams, and it came out of the complete heart of that ancient world which is now almost lost forever.

At a crucial moment in the long-life ceremony, Thuksey Rinpoche had to kneel down before his charge and pupil who was also an incarnate lama, Drukchen Rinpoche (the young lama in *A Journey in Ladakh*). We were all looking at Thuksey, and no one thought he was strong enough to do it. Everyone was terrified, but he managed it, although in obvious pain. He bent his head, and, as he got up, the entire room rang with an immense sound, resounded with the word *tongpanyid*, the Tibetan word for emptiness. That word shook the walls of the room, and many in the room heard it. I'll never forget Thuksey's face as he got up from the ground. We were terrified that he wouldn't be able to get up; he was so weak, he was falling apart. He had been kneeling to Drukchen, who was gazing down at him with a look of indescribable love and compassion, because nobody loved Thuksey more than Drukchen, his own heart-son. Drukchen would have gone forward to help him up, but there was a sense that what was happening was sacred and so the young lama let Thuksey struggle up alone.

As he got up, the word *tongpanyid* shimmered and shook, the whole the room vibrated with this word for emptiness, and Thuksey laughed an immense laugh and an immense smile covered his face. Thuksey's laugh was what Buddhists call "the roar of the lion," the smile of one who has conquered illusion. It was a direct transmission of that power of vision, and we were all amazed.

The next day, I was walking up in the hills trying to understand what I had witnessed, trying to deepen my experience of it. I had already fallen spiritually in love with Thuksey, had taken the vows to become a bodhisattva with him, and had undergone the ordeal of trying to get this story out and as clearly as possible in my book. But I hadn't been prepared for this kind of mastery; how could I, or anyone, have been? As I was walking in the hills, I saw on a rock the representation of him that had been used in the ceremony, the barley figure. After it had been used in the ceremony it was placed on the rock; its head was off, and the piece of red robe that had been wound around it had fallen off, and it had been pecked by a bird.

As I watched the headless figure baking in the sun, I heard again the word *tongpanyid*, and I realized that the person I had thought of as Thuksey Rinpoche had already died and gone into the state of absolute reality. He was already beyond both life and death. In my mourning, in the melodrama of my grief and yearning for him to be healed, I was identifying with a past form, with an "identity" that had already been dissolved.

That night, on the mountain outside his monastery, I heard all the rocks singing around the monastery. I was up on a hill, gazing down at his room, sending prayers to him because I didn't know when any of us would see him again. None of us knew whether he would live another day or die that night. I was meditating on the rocks when I heard a sound as if all of the rocks were singing with deep dark voices of the Tibetan chanters, those amazing tones you hear in the Gyuto monks, that deep, gravelly chanting that is like the sound of the wind through the ravines, that is like the *ur*-sound, the sound that creates creation out of the womb of the void. The rocks were emanating this sound.

Many years later when I was working on the *Tibetan Book of Living and Dying*, I was told that this "singing" is one of the signs of enlightenment. The texts note that it is a sign that is given just before someone in a state of enlightenment leaves their body. It's one of the love-signs that the universe gives, indicating this degree of attainment. Many years later, I met the monk who had been with Rinpoche when he was dying. We sat in a room filled with sunlight, talking quietly about his death. He told me that Thuksey Rinpoche died smiling between two breaths. He held his breath, went into meditation, and left his body.

So I know that this great Mahayana philosophy doesn't just simply have vital perceptions to give to the world, I know that it also can produce people like Thuksey, and I know that it produces realizations on that scale and of that majesty. That's why I dedicated years of my life to studying Buddhism, its different sects and masters.

At the end of my book *A Journey in Ladakh,* I recount an incident when Thuksey Rinpoche was asked about a particular aspect of the bodhisattva. He was asked to explain a quotation that I loved and he gave a sublime teaching on all of the different aspects of the marriage between wisdom-emptiness and compassion that engender such rich realizations:

> Charles [a friend present in the room where we were being taught] said, "There is a text of Chandrakirti I do not understand. Will you explain it to me? 'When a Bodhisattva thinks and hears the word "give" happiness arises; those who live in Nirvana have no such happiness. What need is there to mention to them the joy of giving everything?' What does Chandrakirti mean?"
>
> The Rinpoche smiled. "I have loved that text since I first heard it, as a boy of twelve in Tibet! I have used it many times in meditation." ...
>
> He picked up the vajra in front of him and held it in his left hand. With his right, he picked up a sunflower from the bowl next to him. He held both his hands out to us.
>
> "Look at this flower," he said. "It gives itself, to us and the bees that take pollen from it, without holding anything

back. It cannot hold anything back. It cannot deny us or the bees anything. Do you remember the story of the Buddha and the flower? When the Buddha was old he wanted to choose a successor. He called his monks together, about three hundred of them. He called them all together but just sat there, in front of them, saying nothing. Then he held out a flower to them, still saying nothing. Only one monk, Kasyapa, understood and smiled. He was chosen. On that day he achieved Enlightenment!"

The Rinpoche looked at us. "Wisdom is needed as well as openness and generosity, and this is why I hold the vajra in my left hand. The wisdom of Shunyata, of Emptiness, is also needed if giving is to be perfect. The only giving that is perfect is the giving by a giver that knows both giving and giver are not real, are empty, and that the receiver is empty too, does not inherently exist. This does not mean that there is no need to give—on the contrary, giving becomes natural, an action so natural that you do not need to call it 'giving.' The flower does not 'give'; it opens, that is all. The giver does not praise himself [or herself] for giving, does not celebrate his [or her] gift, nor patronize in any way the person who is receiving. The wisdom of [Emptiness] reveals that you cannot give to another without giving to yourself, and also that there is no giver, no receiver, no gift. And so you give spaciously, with freedom, claiming nothing, hoping nothing, planning nothing. The greatest happiness is to give like this. Shantideva said, 'Through giving away everything you pass beyond sorrow.'"

He put the flower back into the bowl and placed the vajra on the table in front of him. He leaned forward.

"In the text you quoted, Chandrakirti is talking to us of the joy of Bodhisattva—of the joy that is without end because the giving it springs from is boundless. Those who have already passed into Nirvana cannot know this joy, because it is the happiness of giving to living beings that brings it."

This is the marvelous, wild Mother-insight of the Mahayana: that being in this dimension has in it a joy more extreme even than nirvana, because giving to living beings in total selfless, ecstatic, tender, calm service is the source of a joy that even nirvana cannot hold. The Rinpoche went on:

"The Bodhisattva who refuses to enter Nirvana until every living being can also enter Nirvana with him knows a joy that the Released cannot know; he knows, and lives in, the joy of giving everything without thought for himself. We say, in Tibetan Buddhism, that a Bodhisattva is like the risen moon. He abides in a white light that comes from himself and from the wisdom of Emptiness that shines through him; all who look on him are made happy, if only for a moment, and given courage to begin on the long journey towards their own perfection. Shantideva has written that the perfection of the pure giving makes a man 'like a water crystal jewel destroying and overcoming darkness.' To have turned one small part of one's life into that radiance is enough for most lives, more than enough; but those who are really in love with the world, who have the truest insight and pity, will want to become that 'jewel.' In becoming that radiance they will live in the joy that Chandrakirti speaks of, a joy that nothing will take from them, because it clings to nothing."

I said, "There are many in my country who would say that what you have just said is beautiful but without meaning, a dream."

The Rinpoche smiled, "As long as there is Samsara, there will be an evasion of the inner perfection that is [our] essence. This is the saddest of all the tragedies of Samsara, and the most painful. A man is starving in one dark room, while in a another just across the corridor from him there is enough food for many lives, for eternity. But he has to *walk* to that room, and before he can walk to it, he has to believe that it is there. No one else can believe for him. No one can even bring the food from that room to him. Even if they could, he would not believe in the food or be able to eat it. The *Dhammapada* says, 'Buddhas neither wash away sins with water nor remove the sufferings of being with their hands. They do not transfer their realization to others. Beings are freed through the teaching of truth, of the nature of things.' But to be taught, they have to want to listen, and to learn they have to have the humility to want to change. No one can make them listen or want to change. We are free to become Bodhisattvas or consign ourselves to life after life in pain. Often when men say they are helpless, trapped, imperfect, they are really saying, 'I do not want to endure my own perfection, I do not want to bear my own reality.' Imperfection is more comforting, more human than perfection. Many men want to believe that man is imperfect because it makes it easier to live with their own imperfection, more forgiving towards themselves. And who can blame them? To understand that even despair at oneself can be a deception, perhaps the most dangerous; and to discover an inner power, that is completely good and gentle, is frightening; it robs us of every comfort, every safety in resignation or irony. Who can live naked to his own perfection? And yet who, once seeing and acknowledging his own perfection, could bear not to try to realize it in living? To see it is hard; to realize it within life is the hardest thing. Somewhere men know that, and that is why they cover up their knowledge. They prefer the nightmare of Samsara which they know to the Awakening which they do not. And in a sense they are right. Once they have acknowledged Reality, they will have to learn how to die into it; they will have nowhere to hide any more, no corner of the world to feel safe in any longer. They will have to 'abide nowhere and alight on nothing.'"[3]

This is the central teaching of the Mahayana, a stern and glorious teaching. It has at its root a fundamental understanding that arises out of two things that happened in the Buddha's own awakening process, that show the depth of the secret knowledge of the sacred feminine in this tradition.

The Buddha's first attempts at enlightenment, at breaking through, were extremely ascetic. He subjected his body to appalling rigors, to real Hindu cruelties. He starved himself, he was ready at any moment to give up the body; he fasted; he subjected himself to intense rigors. It was becoming clear to him that these ascetic practices weren't getting him to the right state, they weren't producing the right kind of recognition. There came a moment when a woman named Sujata brought him a bowl of curds and held it out to him. He broke his fast, he broke from the ascetic practices, he broke from the ruthless denial of his body; he accepted the curds from the woman and at that moment was born his sacred understanding of the Middle Way—the way that avoids both extremes of indulgence and of ascesis. This really is one of Buddhism's greatest gifts, a Mother-understanding that this world must be respected on its own terms. The body must be respected, the body must be fed; it is the house of the spirit. The world came to him in the form of Sujata and a bowl of curds. This is so rich—a *woman* came, the feminine came—the feminine, with its understanding of the necessity to harmonize, to marry enlightened states with actual life, to marry the hunger for transcendent awareness with the responsibilities of immanence.

This same rich pattern of the presence of a feminine sacredness repeats itself at a crucial stage of the Buddha's awakening. In the last stages of the Buddha's awakening, the master of illusion, Mara, sent to him illusion after illusion, fantasy after fantasy. He was trying desperately to scare or seduce the Buddha away from total awakening, trying desperately to prevent him from going into that space in which he would become the fountain of innumerable blessings for the human race, because when he achieved that, Mara's reign would be severely curtailed. So he threw against the Buddha everything in his power. What then did the Buddha do? He put his hands down and touched the earth, and begged the divine mother of the earth, Rani, to come

to his aid. She did so and a flood from her hair erased and erad-
icated all the "powers" that had been thrown against him.

This means, again, that at this crucial moment the Buddha
called on the earth, on *this* world, on *this* experience, to
ground—and protect—his enlightenment. By grounding the
enlightenment, by calling the feminine presence of the earth to
ground and witness the enlightenment, he ended the reign of
illusion. The subtlest temptations to the enlightened always
come with the invitation to escape this reality. By deciding
absolutely not to escape this reality, to not escape being in a
body, to not deny the challenge and gift of total presence, the
Buddha was able not only to destroy the enemies of illusion,
but to enter into total awakeness, which is to know the marriage between form and emptiness at every moment; between
being eternal and being in the body; to live totally in the present moment. By grounding himself, by opening his entire being
to the nature of sacred feminine reality, he entered *this* body,
*this* moment, *this* place, and therefore achieved in his own being
the sacred marriage between heaven and earth, wisdom and
compassion, renunciation and action, total awareness and total
love.

The Mahayana, in essence, comes from these two wonderful invocations of the sacred feminine. Mahayana wisdom has
as its most profound Mother-revelation the crucial understanding
that samsara and nirvana are not separate, that nirvana isn't
some state separate from living in this reality that must be
attained, but that nirvana *is* the basic ground of this reality, the
light-void that is always shining through and emanating at every
moment this reality. Samsara is like bread soaked in the milk
of nirvana: you cannot eat nirvana without eating samsara, and
you cannot eat samsara without eating nirvana. This experience of unity is the experience of the Mother. To have the complete experience of the Divine Mother is to know her both in
her transcendent aspect, as the light that is giving birth to the
entire creation, always transcendent, always beyond the creation; and simultaneously and always as all of the events, all

of the minute holy particulars, all of the radiant, small, things
of the creation.

In the *Surangama Sutra* the Buddha describes this unity:

> This unity alone in the world is boundless in its reality, and
> being boundless is yet one. Though in small things, yet it is
> great. Though in great things, yet it is small. Pervading all
> things, present in every minutest hair, and yet including the
> infinite worlds in its embrace. Enthroned in the minutest
> particle of dust, and yet turning the Great Wheel of the Law.[4]

In his brilliant book *Eye to Eye*, Ken Wilber speaks about
this particular and crucial recognition. He takes another aspect
of the Mahayana, which is Zen, to emphasize this brilliant
understanding that samsara *is* nirvana. He quotes the Third
Patriarch of Zen:

> All forms of dualism
> Are ignorantly contrived by the mind itself.
> They are like visions of flowers in the air:
> Why bother to take hold of them?
> When dualism does no more obtain,
> Even Oneness itself remains not as such.
> The true mind is not divided—
> When a direct identification is asked for,
> We can only say, "Not-two!"[5]

The Mahayana, as Wilber shows, is not saying samsara is
*exactly the same* as nirvana. Something much more profound
and subtle is actually being said: "The true mind is not divided—
When a direct identification is asked for, we can only say, Not-
two!"

This is a very subtle distinction. It's not saying "one," but
instead "not two." To say reality is "one" is untrue, because I
am this, while that, and you, and you, and you, are clearly separate, clearly differentiated, clearly other. There are clearly categories and separations and divisions that are necessary to
understanding what reality is.

However, mystical understanding and radical initiation into the nature of reality reveals that all the things that seem separate are also in their essence *undivided*. They are in their ground one. They are also in their essence light. Reality is the wonderful play between this essential ground of oneness and a multiplicity of manifestation, a play of unity and plurality. Real perception, real enlightenment, is to have simultaneously the understanding of essential unity and the understanding of fabulous exquisite difference, both playing within the same shining space of awareness, both playing within the same awareness of truth, a truth that can never be spoken but only experienced. The only thing you can say about this truth is that it is "not two," and this awareness of unity *is* the Mother because it heals all the pain of separation and engenders spontaneous compassion toward all beings.

Wilber, in the last chapter of *Eye to Eye*, "The Ultimate State of Consciousness," writes:

> ... "Not two" does not mean just One. For pure Oneness is most dualistic, excluding as it does its opposite of Manyness. The single One opposes the plural Many, while the Nondual embraces them both. "One without a second" means "One without an opposite," not One opposed to Many....
>
> Now the import of what has been said thus far is that since there is nothing outside the Nondual, there is no part in either space or time where the Absolute is not. It isn't that a *part* of the Absolute is present in every thing—as in pantheism—for that is to introduce a boundary within the infinite, assigning to each thing a different piece of the infinite pie. Rather, the *entire* Absolute is completely and wholly present at every point of space and time for the simple reason that you can't have a different infinite at each point. The Absolute, as St. Bonaventure put it, is "A sphere, whose center is everywhere and whose circumference nowhere, so that, in the words of Plotinus, "while it is nowhere, nowhere is it not."

So we are always completely in the Mother. Wilber goes on:

> Yet notice that the Absolute can be entirely present at every
> point of space only if It is itself spaceless. Just as, to use Eck-
> hardt's example, your eyes can see things which are colored
> red only because your eyes themselves are without red color
> or "red-less," so also the Absolute can embrace all space
> because It is itself without space or "space-less." This, inci-
> dentally, is why so many angels can fit on the head of a pin—
> they don't take up any room!
>
> At any rate, the infinite is not a point, or a space—even
> a very Big Space—or a dimension among other points, spaces,
> and dimensions; but is point-less, spaceless, dimensionless—
> not one among many, but one without a second. . . .
>
> And so also with time. The Absolute can be present in its
> entirety at every point of time, only if It is itself timeless.
> That which is timeless is eternal, for, as Wittgenstein rightly
> pointed out, Eternity is "not infinite temporal duration but
> timelessness." That is to say, Eternity is not everlasting time,
> but a moment without time. Hence, being timeless, *all* of
> Eternity is wholly and completely present at every point of
> time—and thus, all of eternity is already present right NOW.
> To the eye of Eternity, there is no *then*, either past or future.
>
> Point without dimension or extension, Moment with-
> out date or duration—such is the Absolute and while It is
> nowhere, nowhere is It not.[6]

Now, read carefully from the Mahayana Zen master, Huang
Po. This really is a shaft of light into the immense spaciousness
and wildness of the Mahayana understanding of enlightenment.
What Huang Po is saying to us, as we will see, is that if enlightenment is real, then it's not something that you can attain,
because only things that are unreal and impermanent can be
attained, achieved, striven for. So enlightenment must be *this*
moment and *this* state and *this* reality, and actually experiencing enlightenment is a process of *un*learning, *un*raveling, deconstructing everything in you that prevents you from realizing that

"you" don't exist and that only this moment is real. The consciousness that sustains this moment, totally naked, is the only thing that is real. This understanding is the Mother, and you are only ever safe when you are in the arms of the radiant, spacious, all-encompassing, all-knowing, totally awake void. The experience of glorious peace that the safety of resting in the void brings is one aspect of the Mother-awakening. This is the experience of form being emptiness and emptiness being form; of reality being light and light being reality; of nature being God and God being nature; of heaven, earth, and earth, heaven; of the body as spirit and the spirit as the body. The whole universe reveals its total interpenetrating essential radiance in the now.

Listen to Huang Po:

That there is nothing which can be attained is not idle talk; it is the truth. You have always been one with the Buddha, so do not pretend you can attain to this oneness by various practices. If, at this very moment, you could convince yourselves of its unattainability, being certain indeed that nothing at all can ever be attained, you would already be Bodhi-minded. Hard is the meaning of this saying! It is to teach you to refrain from seeking Buddhahood, since any search is doomed to failure.[7]

"You have always been one with the Buddha." What enlightenment wakes you up to is that you have always been enlightened, there is absolutely nothing that doesn't contain the ground of enlightenment as its ground. There's nothing else here but the play of enlightenment. There's nothing else here but the play of the void, of the light. What you wake up to is that everyone and everything that happens, every being, is part of this great play. This is the divine self, the Christ-self; the void. Whatever the description of it, it's always the same recognition. "You have always been one with the Buddha, so do not pretend you can attain to this oneness."

If you've already been it, you've *always* been it. You cannot attain to it. But you can recognize it, you can wake up to it, you can acknowledge it, you can be responsible to it, you can let it inform your every perception and action. You can let its light soak your every breath and cell and movement. But you can never *attain* it, because it is already your essential nature! As Hsi Yun says, in words that could be a commentary to Huang Po's:

> The universal mind alone is the Buddha and there is no distinction between the Buddha and sentient beings. But sentient beings are attracted to particular forms and seek for Buddhahood outside it. By their very looking for it they produce the contrary effect of losing it, using the Buddha to look for the Buddha and using mind to grasp mind. Even though they do their utmost for a full *kalpa* they will not be able to attain to it.

Now, back to Huang Po: "If at this very moment, you can convince yourself of its unattainability, being certain that nothing at all can ever be attained, you will begin to be Bodhi-minded"—you would realize, in other words, that any image made of enlightenment by the mind is doomed, because it's the mind imagining something that "ends" the mind. The subtlest temptations of all come from the mind's own imagining of what enlightenment is, because that is the prison in which the mind remains continually gyrating around its own fantasies, its own ideals of awakening.

If you were really to be convinced that nothing at all could ever be attained, that all your struggling and striving and prayers and God-knows-what would be of absolutely no use at all, then you would be extremely close to the kind of radical disillusion that helps the emergence of true awareness: the awareness that your essential nature is the great space, the great void, the great simplicity. As Hsi Yun says:

> This pure mind, the source [Mother] of everything, shines on all with the brilliance of its own perfection, but the peo-

ple of the world do not awake to it, regarding only that which sees, hears, feels, and knows as mind. Because their understanding is veiled by their own sight, hearing, feeling, and knowledge, they do not perceive the spiritual brilliance of the original substance. If they could only eliminate all analytic thinking in a flash, that original substance would manifest itself like the sun ascending through the void and illuminating the whole universe without hindrance or bounds.

And, as Huang Po says, "Hard is the meaning of this saying." Of course it's hard—it may take a million lifetimes to wake up! This whole thing is a mad joke, if the Mahayana Buddhists are right. Here we are, inventing biographies and going through sufferings, coming back again and again, eventually to realize that we've *always* been enlightened. This is a huge joke, an irony that the Mahayanists are brilliant at expanding, to teach you to refrain from seeking Buddhahood since any search for what is essentially already yours is doomed to failure.

This is not, of course, in any way, an injunction against searching. It's really the most difficult, the most austere kind of statement, because what it is saying is to fast your mind of its illusions. Fast your mind of its schemes, fast your mind of its plans; above all, fast your mind of its conceptions of what enlightenment is, so that a deep recognition of your essential Buddhanature can be born beyond and below the mind. Refrain from seeking Buddhahood so you don't get trapped in your notions of what the search is, so that you don't create a whole set of subtle assumptions which will only snare you and postpone the rapturous recognition of your essential nature for another four million lifetimes or so. It's outrageous knowledge because what it does is plunge you right into here, right into the boundless effulgence of the original substance, the Mother of all things.

The other thing that becomes really clear when you really think about this is that ultimate knowledge is not a state of consciousness, because all states of consciousness pass, even the highest states of trance, the most profound states of *samadhi*. Listen to a great Ch'an Buddhist teaching:

> Hsuan-tse heard of a meditation master named Chih-huang, and when he went to visit him, Chih-huang was meditating.
>
> "What are you doing there?" inquired Hsuan-tse.
>
> "I am entering into a *samadhi*, a highest state of consciousness"
>
> "You speak of *entering*, but how do you enter into a *samadhi*—with a thoughtful mind or with a thoughtless mind? If you say with a thoughtless mind, all nonsentient beings such as plants or bricks could attain *samadhi*. If you say with a thoughtful mind, all sentient things could attain it."
>
> "Well," replied Chih-huang, "I am not conscious of either being thoughtful or being thoughtless."
>
> Hsuan-tse's verdict was swift-coming: "If you are conscious of neither, you are actually in *samadhi* all the time; why do you even talk at all of entering into or coming out of it? If, however, there is any *entering* or *coming out*, it is not the Great *Samadhi*."[8]

If you have to enter the experience, the experience is not the *ultimate* experience; it is something that is being fabricated at some level of sophistication. What is eternal or what is real is going on at every moment, in every situation, in every emotion, in every thought, and recognizing and living that is enlightenment. As a great Zen master writes:

> When you seek to know It,
> You cannot see It.
> You cannot take hold of It,
> But neither can you lose It.
> In not able to get It, you get It.
> When you are silent, It speaks.

When you speak, It is silent.
The great gate is wide open to bestow alms
And no crowd is blocking the way.[9]

To come into that effortless and natural union with reality is the goal of being here. As the Tibetan *dzogchen* master Longchen Rabjam writes:

Until one has fully attained the essence of realization
Contemplate as with the eyes of jackals, without
　　differentiation of day and night.
By gaining experience and familiarity,
If the mother [fully enlightened stage] and son [realiza-
　　tion of the path] are united,
Everything will arise simultaneously in the great
　　carefreeness.
Then all arises as the path.[10]

## Questions and Answers

*Can you elaborate on the Buddhist understanding of impermanence?*

We are dying, everything is dying around us, and everything is passing away. Nearly all of our anxieties and fears arise from our fear of that. So facing impermanence, really facing it, really accepting it, can help us to give up our craving, our cruelty, our desires, our plans, and to enter into the space of love. Once you have really realized that you are dying, completely realize it beyond thought or concept, realize it in the core of your being, and look out at a world in which everyone and everything else is also dying, too, a great compassion awakens in your heart: a tremendous poignant tenderness for all things.

That tenderness for all things translates very easily into action, because I think that what you feel at that moment is: if there is so much pain in the world, why add to it with more craziness? If there is so much suffering in the world, why add to it by exploitation and poverty and injustice and violence? Why not try with all one's powers to make a world in which people can live and die in peace and serenity? So understanding impermanence really helps us to get rid of the desires and craziness that are fueling our own pain, helps us confront absolutely the stark facts of everybody else's pain, and helps to awaken what Buddhists call *bodhichitta*, the desire for the illumination and liberation of all beings.

*How can we understand impermanence?*

By really meditating on the laws of change that inform everything in the universe, the law that everything is changing. It's an experience you can have just by looking at a flower or looking at your hands, or looking at the way in which your mind works, or watching things in movement. You discover that everything is in transition, everything is changing. Your conceptual mind tries to stop that change; your mind tries to freeze that change. You can watch the way in which your desire to control reality arises out of panic at its essential nature. Then you can learn both about how things really are and how your mind is always trying to tempt you into controlling and ordering things. Gradually, as you understand the way in which your mind tempts you to control things, to alter things, you come to realize that you're a lot better off accepting transience than fighting against it. You can't fight against it, you're going to lose. If you accept it, you might come to a different kind of peace, a different kind of intelligence, which is what meditation really helps you to find. Behind the transience, behind everything falling away and passing away, you come to discover in yourself what the Tibetans call the essential nature of mind, what the Hindus call Atman—the words don't matter. What you come to discover is a fundamental peace-nature, what the Buddhists also call Buddhanature. In a way, death and transience turn out to be a great gift, because they force you into an examination of the mind. That examination of the mind, when taken to its deepest place, reveals the deathlessness of true reality, the deathlessness of consciousness. So, death is our greatest friend, because it forces us into a radical examination of everything, that leads, in the end, to the discovery of the deathless behind and in all things. As Milarepa said:

> In horror of death, I took to the mountains—
> Again and again I meditated on the uncertainty of the
>     hour of death,
> Capturing the fortress of the deathless unending
>     nature of mind.
> Now all fear of death is over and done.[11]

*What do you think the idea of liberation or nirvana would mean to an integrated, indigenous culture, like the aborigines?*

I don't think it would mean anything in an indigenous culture. In some ways, our whole understanding of liberation comes out of our fragmentation. I would imagine that for an indigenous culture, liberation would mean living a harmonious, tender, happy exuberant life with all the people and creatures who accompany you in the world. I don't think the aborigines have an idea of liberation. They have very profound initiations into sacred knowledge, which is not ever seen as separate from the tribe, but is something that you find to fuel the sacred health of the tribe. Life is a journey into sacredness, but a journey that you take together with other people, for other people. Your journey ennobles and irradiates all of their journeys. It may be that our whole fixation on solitary enlightenment is part of the patriarchal madness. It's part of what happened when we lost sight of the fact that we are interdependent and interconnected with everyone else. One of the marvelous Mother-strengths of Mahayana Buddhism is that in its vision of the bodhisattva, it recognizes this.

There are many ways you can think of that great bodhisattva vow to forgo enlightenment, to return again and again. What you're essentially vowing is always to be here, to never leave samsara, and through absolute service to give everything away to sentient beings. It may be that what you realize at a very high level of spiritual understanding is that you cannot be free until everyone else is free, for the simple reason is that you *are* everyone else. If we have really opened up to the wisdom of emptiness and the wisdom of interdependence, then we realize that we cannot be free until all other beings also are free. What has been destroyed in this Mahayana understanding of liberation is any vestigial subtle clinging to any conceivable notion of the separate "I." What the Mahayana Buddhists understood is that you cannot be free until everyone and everything is free, and that means that you must commit the whole of your spiritual practice to the redemption of everything, because as long as anything remains unhealed, *you* remain unhealed. A bodhisattva is no longer just himself or herself, but is in complete identification with all beings and things.

In the *Lankavatara Sutra*, the Buddha reveals a further truth about bodisattvahood, its ultimate inherent paradox. Simply put, this is that to renounce nirvana for yourself out of love for others is to find yourself *in* nirvana, in its real meaning of boundless compassion and peace. The perfected bodhisattva becomes aware that just by being a bodhisattva he or she is *already* in nirvana. He or she has seen that nirvana and samsara are not two different realms, that nothing, *nothing at all*, is outside nirvana. As the Buddha says:

> When the bodhisattvas face and perceive the happiness of the samadhi of perfect tranquility, they are moved with the feeling of love and sympathy owing to their original vows made for all beings, saying, "So long as they do not attain nirvana I will not attain it myself." Thus they keep themselves away from nirvana. But the fact is they are already in nirvana because in them there is no rising of discrimination. With them the discrimination of grasped and grasping no longer takes place. As they now recognize that there is no thing in the world but what is seen of the mind itself, they have done away with the thought of discrimination concerning all things. . . .
>
> For the bodhisattvas nirvana does not mean extinction. As they have abandoned thoughts of discrimination . . . there is for them the attainment of recognition that all things are unborn.

The paradox is that only by giving up the fantasy of solitary liberation can real liberation be attained. Only by stopping identifying the quest with your own safety, with your own transcendence, can you ever begin to understand the freedom that comes with total love. In fact, only by committing yourself to the freedom of absolutely every being will you ever enter into the freedom of divine selfless love, which is liberation.

If you're still trying to separate yourself and trying to achieve liberation on your own, and are not going to be concerned with all other sentient beings, then you're still trapped in separateness, you're still trapped in your own version of your biography. When you give up everything, even the desire for liberation, out of pure compassion for the pain of the world, and want nothing more than to serve all beings as much as you can, then at that moment, you enter into the timeless space of divine love and become one with it in selfless passion. At that moment, you become free because love has exploded forever the notion of the separate "I" that is the source of all suffering. At that moment you become one with the Mother.

This marvelous all-embracing vision of liberation is perhaps the greatest spiritual achievement of Buddhism, and is, I believe, indispensable to the revolution of the sacred feminine. The self-absorption that can accompany the quest is completely dissolved by it, and service to other beings revealed not as a distraction from solitary seeking, but as the very source of ultimate freedom. This vast vision of service is inherent in the Mother's plan for humankind and especially compelling in a time like ours when everyone will have to dedicate all of their various energies to helping the world if the planet is to have a chance of being preserved.

*I like the story about the arrow, yet it seems to imply that we shouldn't go into the root causes of things. How can we change the environmental situation, for example, unless we do that?*

The Buddha was being asked a metaphysical question. He was being asked about the nature of God, the nature of reality, where heaven was, etc., and he said, "Don't let's bother about those questions. If an arrow gets into your side, don't sit there wondering where it came from, but take it out immediately." What he meant by this, I think, was that we must pay attention to the problems of human suffering, not go into fancy explanations of where that suffering comes from or what it might be for. He was making a practical point, not saying don't look at the root causes of things. Nobody looked at the root causes of things more ruthlessly, more intelligently, than the Buddha. He spent years and years of his life analyzing very carefully the different ways in which different kinds of perceptions and different kinds of emotions give rise to different kinds of ignorance. Nobody has been a greater scientist of the ways in which ignorance arises. In fact, the whole of Buddhism could be described as a cry to analyze and look to the root causes of violence in yourself, the root causes of cruelty in yourself. How could we effect deep, lasting change without doing that? We must look and see that our desire to consume things is what is destroying the forests. Our desire to eat beef, for example, is what is actually ensuring that the forests are cut down. As Thich Nhat Hanh often says, "Practicing mindfulness in the act of consuming is the basic act of social justice." We have to hunt for their root causes so that we can change those things in our appetites and attitudes that enable destruction and suffering to go on.

So really what is demanded of us is total scrutiny, total attention, looking deeply at all of our motives and where they come from, all of our actions and where they come from, all of our appetites and where they come from, all of our desires and where they come from, and really being naked and honest about what they cost. What they cost to ourselves, what they cost to other people, what they cost to other nations, what they cost to other civilizations, and accepting that if we continue the way we are, there will be no world. So that act of becoming conscious is a vital and painful act, one that will involve a turning-about in the heart of ourselves.

One of the things I am trying to suggest in this book is that one of the ways we stay unconscious can be to adopt old paradigms of religious thinking, which help us to tune out and not to become present. So the way we look at Buddhism itself will need to change. we will have to look again at its root-assumptions. What I am trying to suggest is that while there have been very astonishing contributions that Buddhism has made to our consciousness, there are other aspects of it which, in fact, subtly conspire with our desire to escape and evade a full embrace of this world. Buddhism is fundamentally a philosophy of confrontation with the facts, and yet inherent in it, as I have suggested, are certain ways in which the facts are blurred and scanted, certain ways in which an escape from the facts is given. In this Buddhism shares the body-denial, misogyny, and bias toward transcendence of all the religious systems developed under patriarchy.

*The aborigines, it seems, have managed to keep together a sense of transcendence with loving respect for the world. Can you speak to that and compare their vision with Buddhism?*

The aborigines have a very sophisticated system. In their system, in their understanding, the earth is a manifestation of the dreamtime and bears the traces of transcendent struggle, of transcendent wars between cosmic gods and creatures. Theirs is a vision of presence: the world is so sacred, extraordinary, and absolutely important to them because it glows with the traces of transcendent presence. So being aligned with the earth is being aligned with the transcendent forces that have shared and are sharing it at every moment. Everything in the earth is sacred both because of itself, and because of its connection to the world of the gods, the dreamtime that is manifesting the world.

I think that's what shows how healthy the aborigines are, that they don't use the transcendent to escape from the immanent. They use the transcendent as a way of pointing out the mystery of the immanent, of making it even more exciting, even more moving, even more sacred, and as a way of making clear to themselves their responsibilities both toward the earth and each other, and toward the sacred powers that rule the cosmos. This is, I think, a great clue to the Mother and to the unity of all dimensions that she is, and to the way we might act in reverence in this world.

What Mahayana Buddhism did, in many ways, was to restore a lack in feminine balance to Theravada Buddhism. Inherent in the great Mahayana mystics, as I have shown, is really an understanding that samsara *is* nirvana, that this world that can be seen from two different aspects is one in final illumined understanding, for when you are awake, you realize that this incomplete, fragmentary, disappearing world is actually perfect and is at all moments shining out with the radiance of the void, of the light that is manifesting it.

The Mahayana mystics understood, too, what the aborigines understand: that everything is in a perfect mandala whose order must be honored, and that was one of their great discoveries, their great contributions to Buddhism. And in its ideal of the bodhisattva the Mahayana created a wonderful vision of service to all beings that is, I believe, crucial to our current predicament. Unfortunately, the Mahayana schools never really incorporated women into their structures and so never really achieved the full balance of the sacred feminine, but they certainly went a lot further than Theravada tradition.

However, I think that the vision of the void, the vision of emptiness, although it's a very real vision, very sophisticated, and has mystical truth, is one that can be used to stress absence and not presence, and this interpretation continues subtly to support an evasion of this body and this world. This isn't to say that the vision of the void isn't true, but it isn't the *complete* truth, it is one-half of a mystical understanding that must also embrace a total blessing of matter, the body, time, and the world of form in order to be complete, to mirror the completeness of the Mother. I think that Buddhism's emphasis on emptiness, on the void, on the no-self theory, is something that has had, in some ways, very liberating consequences as the greatest slap in the face of the human ego that it has ever been given. In other ways, however, the systems that evolved from these perceptions have not only not helped the human race to arrive where we are now, but has actually conspired in the depreciation of reality that has abetted the destruction of nature.

*I want to thank you for talking about the body and how it has not been revered in Buddhism. I've experienced some really frustrating times at Buddhist meditation retreats where women were told not to wear shorts or tank tops, and in other ways subtly insulted, made to feel that our bodies were shameful. I also feel that emotion is somehow degraded in Buddhism, too. The Krisha Gotami story is a powerful teaching, but it seems to me that the Buddha is very hard on her and does not allow her to grieve. Couldn't she be taught the truth about death and be given a human space in which to wail and mourn?*

I had never thought of that, and I agree. There is in the story a certain masculine impatience with emotion that you have seen. However, I don't think Buddhist teaching is in its deepest sense anti-feeling. I think that the sacred technology the Buddhists have given us can make us extremely sensitive to our states of feeling, both physical and emotional, and extremely aware of where they arise from. I don't find that repressive at all, I find that liberating. Many psychoanalysts love Buddhism for its emphasis on clarity, and on seeing *whatever* arises without shame, guilt, or judgment. This can help anyone develop emotional refinement, self-awareness, and a clear acquaintance with the contents of the unconscious.

I also think that in Mahayana Buddhism, and especially in Tantric Buddhism, for example, you see a way in which desire and the negative emotions—as the Theravada tradition understands them—can be actually turned into a positive path. Instead of rejecting anger, for example, tantric practices teach you to use it and turn it into its hidden opposite, its hidden truth, which is discrimination. Instead of rejecting desire, you can accept it and work with it to turn it into compassion, into connection. There is a very feminine side to what was developed by the tantric Buddhists: an acceptance of all emotions as they are, and a way of using those emotions to get to an increasingly enlightened state of truth. You can work with all the emotions in this way. By allowing grief, for example, by exploring grief, you can come to a much deeper understanding of the impermanence of all things, of the transitory nature of reality and that, in turn, could inspire you to go deeper into the teachings, deeper into wisdom.

The other way of using grief in a tantric sense would be to deepen your compassion. Instead of just claiming your grief as "my grief," "my pain," "my suffering," actually looking at your grief and allowing it to emerge could help you realize that *everyone* is suffering, that grief is everywhere. This recognition breeds compassion for all beings, and it is this all-embracing compassion that the Buddha is trying to awaken in Krisha Gotami. What he was really saying to her was: "I respect your grief, but by going and facing the grief of everyone else, you will pay less attention to your own narcissistic anguish and come to realize that the grief you're experiencing is an initiation into the suffering everyone shares. That initiation will give rise in you to compassion and acceptance and intelligence, and a desire for the wisdom and understanding of things as they are."

*You have mentioned tantric transformation of negative emotions. What about tantric sexuality?*

Anyone who wants to explore this marvelously rich, complex, and potentially revolutionary subject should read and re-read Miranda Shaw's book *Passionate Enlightenment*.[12] For a long time most historians of religion have insisted that tantric Buddhist practices were for men only, that women involved in the tradition were at best marginal and at worst degraded and exploited. Miranda Shaw argues the opposite, and presents extensive and convincing evidence of the extremely outspoken and sometimes wildly independent female founders of the tantric movement and their full creative role in shaping its vision of sacred sexuality. Drawing on interviews and archival research that she did during two years of field work in India and Nepal, she includes more than forty previously unnoticed works by women of the Pala period, from the eighth through twelfth centuries, and radically reinterprets the history of tantric Buddhism during its first four centuries.

Shaw shows, definitively I think, that the tantric theory of
this initial period has as its ideal a cooperative, mutually delight-
ful and liberating relationship between men and women, and
encourages a reliance on women as a source of particular spiritual insight and power. It is a wonderfully timely book and should
help all seekers begin to understand the depth and range of the
tantric vision of sexuality. This is especially important, I believe,
since one of the great gifts that the Divine Mother wants now to
open up to the whole of humanity is the gift of a noble sexuality, a sexuality consecrated to a visionary attempt to understand
and enter cosmic passion and cosmic ecstasy. This forms a very
important part of the direct, guru-less path. Profound relationships are going to be the living temple of the Mother and the site
of the tantric encounter. No intermediaries will be needed. What
*will* be needed, however, is a very sane, scrupulous, dignified spiritual understanding of the *laws* of such a tantric encounter, and
in this, as in all other respects, Shaw's book is very helpful. She
shows clearly that using sexuality as a means of entering divine
bliss and wisdom demands the highest inner motivation, the
deepest mutual honoring and respect, and considerable meditative understanding, skill, and knowledge.

*What have you, personally, begun to understand about tantric
sexuality?*

Very simply put, I am beginning to see that the real tantra is
real love. The real transfiguring tantra is total spiritual, passionate, emotional, physical love—all together, in harmony.
When that is lived between two beings who are deeply committed to each other on every level and who are deeply in love
with each other on every level, whose heart, minds, and souls
are in tune authentically and completely, and whose genitals
dance serenely and ecstatically together, then what is revealed
is "love's body," the bliss-body of the universe.

As I have said repeatedly, I believe we are entering an era of
the sacred marriage, the marriage between masculine and fem-

inine, action and prayer, politics and mysticism; an era in which all of the old distinctions between sacred and profane will be rubbled to inaugurate a new human divine freedom. One of the main forms of this new human divine freedom will be, I am certain, the tantric "marriage" that mirrors in the ground of intimacy that sacred marriage taking place now in society at large, and of course, always in the universe itself. This tantric marriage is a consciously consecrated relationship in which two people, two lovers (whether heterosexual or homosexual is of no importance) devote heart, body, mind, and soul to each other and to God.

You have asked me to speak personally, and so I will. My own relationship with Eryk has transformed my spiritual and mystical vision of the world. Through it and through the grace of the Mother, I have discovered that when deep, passionate, pure love is the architect, inspiration, and guide of the emotional, sexual, and mental experience between two beings, then what takes place in both beings is a profound healing at every level and nothing less than the gradual alchemical fusion of the entire self. In this alchemical transformation—whose terms, laws, and miraculous visions and possibilities Miranda Shaw explores with real wisdom—the heat of love, of consecrated passion, is what I would call the Shakti, the divine fire that ensouls the body and embodies the soul, and so gradually and marvelously melts together all divisions between inner and outer, spirit and matter, heaven and earth.

I have begun to taste that liberation of all the senses simultaneously into their bliss-ground and bliss-essence and to know more and more simply and spontaneously that natural immersion in the Mother, in sacred unity, that comes from adoring another human being and being adored by that person in this way. And I have come to realize in the process that all the old patriarchal distinctions between sacred and profane are in fact lies designed to keep a body-denying priest-and-master class in power. There is in fact—and this is the great tantric discovery—no separation between human and divine love, because all *real* love is divine, and divinely powerful and transformatory.

Keeping a true vision of this great tantric work is, however, difficult. Most Eastern and Western philosophies have conspired to degrade sexuality, and we therefore have to chart a reverent and refined balance between denial and shame on one hand, and pornographic license on the other. To create the alchemical vessel in which tantric transformation can take place—this Shaw and the many marvelous texts she quotes makes clear—both beings have to be entirely dedicated to using their experience of mutual love as a way of celebrating and entering into the divine beauty and glory of the universe. Mutual honor and mutual respect at the most profound level are essential for that trust to be engendered in both people, without which the kind of revelatory merging that tantric practice aims to produce cannot take place. If these laws are strictly and humbly observed, and if everything that is done between two beings in tantric relationship is repeatedly offered to the divine, then ordinary (and, dare I say it, quite guru-free) miracles are possible. This kind of sacred marriage will become, as I have said, more and more the site of the tantric encounter and one wonderful way for the Mother to initiate us into her directly, in the ground of ordinary life.

One of the reasons—perhaps the main reason—I am now convinced that Meera wanted to split me from Eryk was so that I would not discover this great tantric secret that I could only discover by embracing my sexuality and his and our love. Many, if not most, of the gurus who are preaching denial of the body and of sexuality are trying to keep their disciples divided, frustrated, and dependent on them. If seekers were to enter their bodies and find the kind of divine human love that I am talking about and live it, they would not be in need of a master-disciple relationship. They would be living a direct communion with the Mother. There are hardly any true couples in ashrams; a true, tantric couple forms a unit of "ordinary" divine presence and divine power that needs no authority and no guidance, except those of the inner master, the soul. One of the reasons, both conscious and unconscious, that all the patriarchal systems have been sex-fearing and sex-hating to some extent or another is because they have understood that complete physical and spiritual love, tantric love, is the source of the divine human freedom that no power on earth can control or destroy. This tantric love initiates both people naturally in the rhythms of the Mother; there is no need for any external authority of any kind.

*I agree with what you've been saying. Yet in the marketplace, in Western society, it's very difficult to maintain the aliveness of this ecstatic tantric communion with a daily life. Do you have anything to say about that?*

I agree. I think that there's no substitute for real spiritual practice of a very ordinary, very humble kind. I don't think there are any quick routes. I do think, though, that practicing the tantra in the way that I have suggested gives enormous strength and illumination to life, and inspiration. But that inspiration still has to be integrated into ordinary life, and the best way to integrate it into ordinary life, I find, is through daily, simple meditation practice.

To return to tantric sexuality for a moment, I feel that the human race's understanding of sexuality is as limited as the our understanding of the physical universe. In a hundred years' time, our current ideas about sex will seem as outmoded as our ideas about matter. How could a largely misogynistic and homophobic world learn to understand the full nature of sexuality? The freedom from all the old divisions that the Mother is offering is going to give us access to essential new information, new experience, that will, I am certain, help immediately in our healing and illumination, and in our liberation from all the forms of constricting authoritarianism.

*It's been a disappointment to me to see that some of the worst misogynist and homophobic language comes from women.*

Even though they suffer under it most obviously, women can be as trapped in the patriarchal system as men. I know, unfortunately, many women who are misogynistic and homophobic. This is a tragedy because in being so, these women are helping to perpetuate the very structures that denigrate and imprison them.

No one sex has a handle on the revolution of the Mother. In my experience I have not found that women always *automatically* understand the Divine Mother better than men. Both men and women are being called upon to change profoundly in the revolution of the sacred feminine, for the simple reason that both men and women have been degraded and limited by patriarchy, its panic-stricken strictures on sex and the body, and its bias toward transcendence.

For a long time I believed that we would be guided into the coming reign of the Mother by women gurus. Now I see clearly that the great majority of them have been—consciously or unconsciously—co-opted by the patriarchal system that I believed they were trying to help us transcend. They are, I have come to see, Jehovahs in drag.

Take Meera, for example; her "advising" me to separate from Eryk shows clearly that she is homophobic, whatever she or her followers may now claim. You have only to read her *Answers* to see that she has no understanding whatsoever of the spiritual and illuminating potential of sexuality. She is not merely homophobic; she is also, in the good, old Indian way, misogynistic. She has bought the ancient Hindu patriarchal vision of women as subservient to men, wives obeying husbands absolutely, in everything. She has also repeatedly said that she does not think that there is any real problem of child abuse in our culture—when the facts, and so many of our own experiences, prove the opposite—and that one of the reasons that the world is decadent is because children do not always obey their parents. She has never publicly said anything against the caste system in India, and when she is there goes by its rules entirely, just as Anandamayima did. What has happened recently—the fact that Meera has denied again and again that she told me to leave Eryk and made me out a crazy liar (with the help of all-too-willing disciples) proves that she is more interested in conserving her own power than in telling the truth.

This passion for power is purely and dangerously patriarchal, as indeed is most of the rest of Meera's philosophy and practice. Much the same could and can, and at last, thank goodness, *is* being said about the great majority of the other women gurus. These women are not representing the Divine Mother, they are representing themselves and perpetrating a dead system in the process. Their masquerading as the divine sows immense confusion and blocks the full radical power of the Mother's love.

Think for example, of how a patriarchal system like the Catholic Church uses *its* "mother," Mother Teresa. She is a very holy person, but she keeps going all the various lunacies and lies of the Church. She doesn't say anything against the Pope's crazy attitude toward overpopulation, although living in Calcutta she cannot but see what misery and disaster it creates. She doesn't ever stand up to the Pope's lunatic attitudes to sex, although she could easily as a woman have a much more healing, intelligent, and loving attitude toward the body. Mother Teresa has been co-opted by a patriarchal power system, and is produced regularly whenever they need a bona fide saint.

In fact, when you analyze what Mother Teresa is saying, it is keeping alive nearly all the patriarchal fantasies that are causing the destruction. The same is unfortunately true with many female gurus. They're not beginning anything new, they're saying the same old stuff. They may alter it a little to get new disciples, but in fact, their practice is the same old patriarchal authoritarianism, the same old patriarchal hierarchy, the same old patriarchal denial of the body, the same old patriarchal misogyny, the same old patriarchal homophobia. What a devastating disappointment!

*Isn't it just as devastatingly disappointing that you, for example—and thousands of others—initially bought and are still buying the stuff of these gurus?*

Of course. *Everyone* is being exposed and unmasked by this revolution of the sacred feminine. There would be no gurus without people who are, like I was, hungry to play the disciple, just as there would be no criminals without policemen and judges. There would be no so-called "Mothers" without thousands of people anxious, as I was, to play children in the unhelpful—because regressive and narcissistic—way.

The devastation I have been living through these last months has compelled me to see clearly how my own need for a "good mother," my own desire for transformation on the cheap and for pretending to autonomy while in fact longing for authority, conspired, all together, to keep me an all-too-willing "victim" of a woman I now see not as an enlightened "mother" but as potentially dangerous. What I am waking up to in this catastrophe a lot of other people are also waking up to. Many more will, as the present light rain of guru-scandal deepens into a full-scale monsoon. The next five years will see a torrent of scandals and most of our current spiritual jails will be shattered. This will be agonizing, but in the end will enable people to take the direct path to the *real* Divine Mother, the path that I am now dedicating my work to help open up.

The Divine Mother is asking all of us, I believe, to dissolve our addictions to power of all kinds. Dissolving those addictions necessitates the most radical, unsparing, and unflattering analysis of all those forces, inner and outer, that keeps them going. Anyone who wants to take the direct path will have to undergo—and sustain—this severe self-analysis. *Any* addiction to power of any kind blocks enlightenment because it blocks love. That is simple to say, but hard to understand and even harder to practice continually. But I believe that the Mother is asking nothing less of us, and that if we respond to her an amazing new era of freedom for the whole human race can begin.

*If the guru system does not work, how will spiritual transmission take place?*

I think that one of the things we're trying to do here in the name of the Divine Mother is to reimagine what spiritual transmission might be like and reimagine what spiritual community would be like. It's my contention that if spiritual transmission was, as Eastern traditions claim, only between master and disciple, from enlightened master to enlightening disciple, then we might just as well all go and throw ourselves into the sea. There are hardly any enlightened masters. The scandals are raging all around us. The system is falling down around us. And if the only way of achieving spiritual community is to go into some sect, or to join a not-enlightened master and their sectarian followers because it gives us an illusion of security, it would be a disaster also, because in the search for truth, in the search for reality, we have to forgo that kind of false consolation.

I think that there are many solutions. I think that what I am trying to propose is a new paradigm that looks to me like this: First, direct contact with the divine, not through anyone but through a naked exposure of your true self to the true self of the Divine Mother, in whatever aspect you worship her. Secondly, a group of devoted friends, spiritual seekers, who really support each other. They might have different vows, different ways of approaching reality, but they will meet to pray and practice together, support each other, and share democratically their wisdom. Why do we have to have the old paradigms of master and disciple, ashram and guru? This is all the past.

What I'm discovering as I go around the country talking to people and holding workshops is that when you trust a group of people, when you invoke the Divine Mother and trust the Divine Mother to be there, when people open to each other gently and speak with each other, miracles take place. Instead of people looking to some master to bring them wisdom, they start to find and share a connection with their own divine wisdom. Instead of people going to so-called "enlightened beings" for guidance, we can actually go to each other, because we are all fragments of the Divine Mother. Everyone has their own life-wisdom, which a patriarchal system of spiritual authority has decried, denied, and degraded. What we all have to do is to learn how to be together, to listen to each other, to honor each other's sacred wisdom, to learn from the different aspects of the Divine Mother that each of us are. This will be the real spiritual revolution. In fact, it's the only way in which the spiritual transformation will get through.

If we rely on the "enlightened" masters to do it, we'll be here forever. If we rely on the transmissions to come through that way, we'll all die ignorant. If we rely on the old systems of authority, we will simply be keeping alive the old patriarchal vision, the dependence on someone else to tell us what to do instead of enacting what is necessary now, which is to honor the sacred wisdom of every being, listen to the tender emergence of that sacred wisdom, and pool it together, in groups, in "tribes," not with leaders, but with guides or friends—friends who admit their imperfections, guides who admit that they may have got things wrong, who admit that they've got huge areas of "shadow" that they're still working on and that they need the help of everyone else to deal with. If that were the case, everyone would feel liberated to talk to and with everyone else and to share, because we would all feel that we have something to contribute, *which we do!* Each one of us has got something important to give and each one of us has got to learn how to listen to the truth of everyone else.

This is the new paradigm, this is what the divine feminine is bringing in. It's difficult because it means that we have to stand on our own together in many deep ways. It's also heartwarming, because when you do relax into others, instead of projecting your fantasy onto some self-proclaimed master, what you discover is how incredibly wise life is, how the Mother surrounds us at all moments. When I lost Meera, the quote-unquote "mother," I discovered the Mother all around me. She was in friends who supported me through this terrible time, she was in a lot of amazing, flawed, tender women and men who came forward, always with different kinds of gifts. She was in intuition, in dreams that guided me, in visions that she showed me. I suddenly realized that I had been focusing my mind and heart and soul on an illusion, on an idea, whereas in fact the Mother was dancing and bubbling and helping and laughing and extending compassion from absolutely everyone and everything around me. What was taken away was a false image and what was placed in its stead was a living revelation of the holiness of all beings and of life itself. I think that this revelation of the holiness of all beings and life itself is the real revelation of the moment, the crucial one. Secure in that revelation, we would all learn what the Mother is, I believe, trying to teach us—how to stand on our own together.

*I love that phrase you just used: "Standing on our own together." It sounds to me like a real marriage of masculine and feminine.*

Exactly! That's such a beautiful point. The "masculine" has its nobility of solitude and its nobility of really owning up to and being responsible and really taking care of one's own progress; and the "feminine" points to our interconnectedness, to a link with everyone else, and the sacred wisdom of everyone else. The sacred marriage of "standing on our own together" is the future.

*If the time of gurus and ashrams is, as you claim, coming to an end, how will we create a sacred environment?*

I would like to begin answering this by saying that most of the ashrams I have known and visited are *not* sacred environments where people progress; they're places in which people regress—to blind adoration, spiritual vanity, sibling rivalry, mirroring and parroting of the so-called master—and in my experience, I have to say, sadly, that I have seen very little real spiritual progress made in them.

The question of how to create and sustain a sacred environment is of course a vital one. We cannot look to outside institutions any more, to churches or temples or ashrams. The urgency of the situation demands that we ourselves, in the intimacy of our own homes and solitude, become spiritually creative, become pharmacists of our own bliss, poets of our own development, inspired and guided by the supreme poet, the Mother. There are many ways of creating for yourself a sacred environment and each person must find the way that works best for them, within the terms and range of their spiritual personality. I myself find being in nature inspiring, and music and religious poetry of all kinds are marvelous ways of keeping centered in the divine. Very simple meditative techniques help, too—like keeping up a river of prayer in the heart, or meditating whenever you feel distracted or anxious. Serving others or giving to others also helps keep you in an atmosphere of sacredness. We must stop relying on others to provide inspiration, and learn how to inspire ourselves. If we do, we prepare a ground in which the Mother can continually act to guide and enliven us quite simply and directly. Just try this sincerely and you will see its truth.

Anyone who finds the secret of self-inspiration, who connects with the divine simple ground of her or his own inherent creativity, gradually becomes free and cannot be controlled by any political or religious authority. The sacred democracy of the Mother will be a gathering-together of free creative beings, of divine children who have learned to be always attuned to her in the most ordinary details of their lives. Needless to say, this direct path demands *more* passion, *more* truth, *more* concentration, more real inner work, and more consistency than a path which consciously or unconsciously relies on someone or something else to do things for you. My experience increasingly is that when people are invited or given permission to be spiritually creative in this way, they quickly unearth in themselves unexpected and very exciting resources of imagination, passion, and love.

*What do you feel about the Tibetan tradition of lineage?*

I was talking to Ken Wilber recently. We had a long talk about
the problem of transmission in this time. He is going through
the same kind of crisis of awareness that I'm going through,
understanding that all the guru lineages are in great danger
now, and really trying to think of new forms of transmission.
We were talking about the Tibetan tradition and I was talking
about this amazing meeting with Thuksey Rinpoche in Ladakh,
in the mountains, and Ken said that what we had asked of the
Tibetan masters was that they come out of their agrarian world
into a post-industrial world, and that the system of guru-
initiation, guru-transmission, that worked in the agrarian world
—because everything was already arranged for it, in a hierarchy—could not work in ours. In that world, there was a whole
tradition based on checks and balances that made it very difficult to get away with rubbish—there was your master, there
were your fellow disciples and all the people who had achieved
realization all around you, who could say, "You're full of you-
know-what. You can't do it like that." So there was a whole
set of checks and balances and ways of really testing people.

What has happened in our situation is that it's become a
free-for-all in which there are very few checks or balances, and
in which almost anybody can get away with almost anything
because of the lack of a tradition, and in which the tradition
of lineage itself, as recent appalling scandals show, no longer
works and cannot work in such different modern conditions.
The next years will make this painfully clear.

Ramakrishna knew, I think, that the guru-system would collapse (and needed to) and that's why he made the point again
and again in his teaching to go directly to the divine. He fore-
saw the confusion, the chaos, the lack of standards, the lack of
any real transmission in this particular age, and realized that
the Divine Mother had provided a solution for it—direct contact with her, with the energy of divine love through simple
prayer, simple meditation, simple service that would bypass this

need to get trapped in different kinds of magical illusion or moribund transmission systems.

My thinking about gurus and talking about gurus doesn't simply arise from an intense personal crisis, which many of you know about, but arises also from a very deep spiritual crisis which is shared by many different mystical thinkers in the world at the moment, and which has to do with a crucial problem. This is: How can the mystic knowledge that humankind now needs be transmitted? How can it be given to enough people quickly enough for them to seize with joy and rapture and confidence and courage its essential awareness without cheapening it? How can it be given without destroying the sense that there are many different stages of purification, surrender, work, and discipline to be got through before real knowledge can flower? What a master traditionally was there for, apart from representing the enlightened life, was to give the student a continual check, a continual sense that they haven't quite got there, that there's still a lot of room of integration to be done, that there have been certain realizations, but there are other kinds of things that need to be accomplished. That was what the traditional enlightened master was there to provide—a constant reality check.

But in a situation like ours, what are we to do? How are we to get this mystic knowledge over without cheapening it, and how are we going to get it over in a democratic way while acknowledging the need for standards, even a kind of inner hierarchy? If you do not keep the gravity and complexity and knowledge of difficulty that the old hierarchical traditions "discovered," anybody is given license to say "I am God, I am enlightened, everything that I do is God-like, is enlightened." This is the reverse of spiritual wisdom; it is another kind of free-for-all. So you have the guru free-for-all and then you have everybody dancing naked in the moonlight saying they are enlightened. Both are crazy. This is why a mature working-out of the direct path— one that honors both the subtlety of past traditions *and* the necessity of connecting directly with the divine—is essential.

*What are the signs of recognizing a true guru or a real spiritual guide?*

Well, in the Tibetan tradition it is said that you should test your guru for a very long time, and you should look at them and watch them from every possible angle and really try to catch them out. If you do, then leave them. The other thing the Tibetan tradition says is that you should practice with someone at least twelve years before you wholeheartedly accept them as your guru.

For myself, I think that there are three very clear signals that a guru or guide is not awake. One is if money is involved. I don't mean that there shouldn't be any money involved, often when people are setting up a dharma retreat or something like that, there must be a reasonable fee collected from participants just so that occasion can take place. But if there is a large amount of money involved or continual drains of money, then I would be suspicious. I'll also say that any kind of sexual exploitation reveals the presence of a lack of freedom and, I think, is extremely psychologically dangerous. I don't buy for a moment this notion that some people seem to accept, that it's all right for a guru to sleep with their disciples. The Dalai Lama was asked a year ago if there was anyone he knew of who was free enough to be in a state of emptiness and be tantrically transmitting when they're having sex with one of their disciples. He said, "No!" If anybody knows, he knows. So that means all of this so-called "tantric" justification of sleeping around is just so much bullshit and should really be taken as a sign that the "master" is exploitative.

The third thing, I think, is that there should be no attempt to direct the life of the disciple, to interfere in any way with the choices of the disciple. Nearly all masters will tell you that one of the telltale signs of falsity is the desire to manipulate lives. A guide can give advice, can suggest, but even then should do so with tremendous discretion. The guide is there to represent enlightened love, and to go on representing that in every situation. Not to tell you what to do, not to direct you without being asked, not to make it impossible for you not to do certain things; the guide is there to *be*, and you are there to drink from that ecstatic being and nothing else. If there is anything else going on, if you're being asked for money or sexually exploited or being in any other way, however subtly or charmingly, psychologically manipulated, then get the hell out, because I would say that you're in the hands of somebody who wants to use you in one way or another.

The other thing that I would say, from my own experience, is to be extremely skeptical about great experiences as proof of the divinity of the master. I have realized through reading and through talking to many real practitioners and mystics that a so-called master can have extraordinary powers and give marvelous experiences without being at all enlightened. I think it is important always to remember Ramakrishna's dismissal of occult powers and his continual prayer to live not in power but in pure love. I think that prayer represents a very clear kind of statement to the world. What Ramakrishna is saying is: Don't be hooked on powers, or on the sensation of great experiences, or on the person you imagine to be giving you those great experiences—they may be a sign of magic, of occult manipulation, but not in any way of enlightenment. They may be a sign of powers being used to take you over, to use you, to manipulate you, to enthrall, seduce, and enchant you, and not at all signs of the direct wisdom that liberates you. If you're with a supreme magician who wants power and has extraordinary powers to be able to give you all sorts of mind-boggling exciting experiences and "wow" you with them continually, a part of you may come to crave that. A part of you may come to be thrilled by that, a part of you becomes addicted to that, and that addiction becomes a source of their hold over you, because we're all susceptible to becoming addicted to extraordinary experiences. We all want them. But that isn't enlightenment. A great many famous gurus are not enlightened beings, but occult magicians, as Ramakrishna said. People go on worshipping them because they become hooked on the drug of "experiences" they are pushing, and in a time like ours when nearly everyone disbelieves in the occult, or is simply ignorant of it, or is too afraid to even imagine it, such occult manipulation has immense power.

I'd like to say, too, that an authentic guide admits mistakes. One of the things that I most admire about the Dalai Lama is that the Dalai Lama often admits the mistakes he has made when they're pointed out to him. Just recently, and this is a wonderful example and very relevant to what we're saying, a nun got up at a meeting of teachers in Dharamsala and said, "Imagine, Your Holiness, that when you went into a temple, all you saw around you were female Buddhas, and imagine that you had to sit at the back, that the women just herded you into the back. Imagine that you had to bow to a nun all the time even if she had been only ordained the day before, and you had been a monk for years." She went on and on, dramatizing the plight of women in Buddhist tradition, and at the end of her speech His Holiness just put his head into his hands and wept and looked up, saying, "What can I do now? What shall I do? Tell me." That is the authentic voice of awakeness, because it says "I don't know everything, but I'm listening. When you tell me something that strikes the note of the real, I adjust everything that I have learned up to that very moment to change everything, if necessary, to put this new richness of the truth into practice."

The enlightened mind isn't omniscient in any way that we know or can imagine, because it's not interested in omniscience. It is endlessly receptive, endlessly sensitive, endlessly awake to the sound of love, and endlessly able to be flexible enough, humble enough, awake enough to put that sound of love into practice in the different circumstances presented to it.

*What do you feel about recent examples of "crazy wisdom" gurus like Trungpa or Rajneesh?*

They are, I believe, dangerous examples to follow. Trungpa died an alcoholic at forty-seven, I think, leaving in charge of the whole of his movement his regent Ösel Tendzin, who slept around with many people, some of whom contracted AIDS from him. He thought that the sacredness of the teachings would prevent anything from happening. He himself died of AIDS a few years ago and had infected at least two other people, which threw the whole of Trungpa's world and movement into total confusion. You have to ask yourself the following question: How could anyone who was fully enlightened put in charge of the whole movement someone who was going to do something that crazy, that obscene and terrifying? I cannot accept any of the explanations myself, and I cannot myself accept any of the explanations that this behavior was an enactment of an extreme form of "crazy wisdom."

I do not believe that a truly enlightened person would behave that way. I believe that what Trungpa did was a terrible mistake. It does not mean that he wasn't a genius—he was. It does not mean he did not write amazing books—he wrote some important, illuminating books. It does not mean that he did not help many people—he did. In the words of Rick Fields, "I never knew anybody who did more harm or more good." I think that is probably the wisest thing ever said about Trungpa. Nobody who ever meets Trungpa from his books doesn't feel the impact of his wild brilliance. But what actually happened shows that he couldn't have been enlightened, I think. What he did was a disaster for Tibetan Buddhism because it really fed into Chinese propaganda that Tibetan masters are nothing but reprobates and debauchés who do nothing but have sex, get drunk, and commit blind, mad acts in the name of "awakening."

As for Rajneesh, I think his realization was great in certain ways. I think many of the books are brilliant. I think Rajneesh got certain things right. His understanding that the West had to accept sexuality and that it had to really put that acceptance of sexuality into practice, that it had to bless the body, is very valuable (although his homophobia is an inexplicable stupidity). But Rajneesh's own practice and his building-up of enormous wealth, and what he allowed to go on around him—there were murders, people were killed!—shows, I believe, that he was not in any meaningful sense enlightened. The excuse for Rajneesh was always that he was in such a "deeply enlightened state" that he didn't know what was going on and so he couldn't be held responsible for it. This is nonsense. Masters must be accountable for what goes on around them, or they are not really masters. What does it mean to say that someone is enlightened when what's going on around them is devastating and harsh and cruel and criminal? Either the master is not enlightened and is passively allowing this, or is actually participating in it in some way and is actively criminal.

As for Rajneesh, I think he had a very strong realization, but it was in no sense a complete one. I think he had a vision of power, but not one of compassion. I think he was corrupted like so many gurus are corrupted—by the adoration of their own disciples. He got crazier and crazier and let himself go further and further into believing in his own omniscience until madness rained around him. I see him as a gifted and brilliant tragic failure.

In general, I think that nearly all of what passes for "crazy wisdom" and is justified as "crazy wisdom" by both master and enraptured disciple is really cruelty and exploitation, not enlightened wisdom at all. In the name of "crazy wisdom" appalling crimes have been rationalized by master and disciple alike, and many lives have been partly or completely devastated. The next few years are going to have to see a hard-nosed reevaluation of this whole area, and the reintroduction of sober and sobering criteria at every level of the spiritual enterprise. I myself believe that guru-abuse has now reached epidemic proportions; it is a kind of spiritual cancer that is destroying from within the spiritual health and independence of thousands of seekers. I also believe that the time is coming when international legislation will be necessary to curb the unchecked power and force of the false gurus and their occult power corporations. What will also be needed is the setting up of foundations and centers where people who have been abused can go for real comfort, free legal help where necessary, and sustained spiritual assistance from others who have survived spiritual abuse in the name of "crazy wisdom" and who have established a healthy direct relationship with the divine.

These last months have made it painfully clear to me how little help a person who tries to protest the cruelty of a guru can expect from anyone. His or her fellow disciples will be in denial and will frequently join the guru in demonizing the one who has begun to see through the illusion. Close gay friends who were actually with us in Thalheim and witnessed Eryk's and my agony have supported Meera's version that Eryk and I are lying. This has been for me the most tragic betrayal of all—it shows just how deep guru-manipulation can be, and how mind- and heart-numbing.

Besides, the whole spiritual world in general is still very unsophisticated as to what is really going on. Vague "New Age" beliefs in the "paradoxical" nature of spiritual teaching and in moral relativism and the lust to see "teaching" in the most arbitrary criminal activities of the so-called enlightened master actually conspire with the madness and cruelty. How many well-meaning psychiatrists and meditation teachers and amateur mystagogues have told Eryk and I that Meera's appalling treatment of us can only be part of her "divine plan" for both our lives and that we will one day be grateful for having our lives nearly ruined by her. This may have helped *them* sleep at night or justify spiritual abuse in their past, but it has revealed to both of us the arrogant cowardice and poverty of response of the so-called spiritual world. This kind of falsely sophisticated "comfort" actually abets the spiritual criminals that modern gurus often are, allows them to continue their games without any kind of intervention or check. A great waking-up is ahead. A lot of people are going to be very ashamed of what they have allowed to go on in the name of "crazy wisdom" and "enlightenment." I often think of the intellectuals in the Thirties who lauded fascism and communism only to wake up years later to the price of their praise, the cost of their long blindness. I hope that our awakening will not cost so much or be so staggered and protracted.

*Isn't there a danger in your stance of being the institutional rebel, the "anti-guru" guru?*

Of course. I spent fifteen years of my life serving the guru-illusion; I don't want to spend the next fifteen years deconstructing it, or being trapped in a posture of anti-parental rebellion. This is why I am attempting to give here a very detailed and I hope independent account of the direct path.

To be betrayed by your so-called master is a death, and in this case, as in other cases of radical abuse, mourning has its stages of agony, depression, necessary and wholly justified revolt. Healing is when you can stand on your own in direct relationship with the Mother. Every day that passes confirms me in the truth of the new and marvelous directness of the relationship with her I am uncovering and coming into. What I am trying to do here is share the ordeals and possibilities of that relationship, as I have experienced them. In this I am taking Ramakrishna and Aurobindo as my guides and brothers.

Because I played Sternberg to Meera's Dietrich in my various books and lectures about her, and was instrumental in making her world-famous, I feel I have a karmic responsibility to witness to what I have discovered about her and others like her. I don't feel that I am addicted to that witness, nor conditioned by it. Witnessing what I and a great many others have suffered in the guru-prison will help me and I hope others to become free. It is that freedom from *all* limiting and controlling kinds of authority that I want to live, espouse, and help flourish. Any critique I give here is not an end in itself, but a means to this new end.

I am also fully aware that until people are open to this new freedom (which means that they will have gone through and learned enough internally), *talking* about it may not always be

of immediate use, Truths take time to penetrate, especially great
and scary truths that are radically disruptive of the prevailing
order. Think of what the Communists in Russia had to go
through, realizing only gradually and agonizingly, and with
many comings and goings, how deeply they had been gulled
and manipulated for years. Some *still* cling to the old system.
The intellectuals of the Twenties and Thirties that I was talking about earlier woke up to the realities of Marxism in very
different ways. For some, like Sartre, it took almost thirty
years—so much of their self-identity had been invested in the
illusion. The guru system is, I am certain, doomed; it will fall,
but that fall will take time and there is a lot of complicated
messy suffering ahead. As it falls, there must be another vision
in place to help people. I am working on trying to understand,
live, and transmit that vision. Many other seekers are also now
involved in this painful and beautiful work, and I am convinced
that we will eventually be vindicated. Vindication isn't in the
end all that important, except as a stepping stone to greater
freedom. What *is* important is that anyone who does take the
direct path to the Mother takes it with as much knowledge,
discrimination, courage, joy, and passion for service as possible. This is what I am trying, with my limitations, to model,
not as a guru but as a seeker who has made mistakes and is
starting to learn from them, and as a child of the Divine Mother
who is waking up to the glory of my own—and everyone else's
—inheritance.

All gurus are of course also invited to The Divine Mother's
great feast—but as children, not "masters." The liberation she
is preparing is a liberation for "masters" and "gurus" as well.
If Meera and others like her can wake up to the appalling spiritual and karmic dangers of their positions and have the courage
to step out of the illusion they are propagating, there is no doubt
that they can taste this freedom. They are her children, too.
Even gurus can become free, if they pay the necessary price!
For the Mother, *nothing* is impossible!

*Where do we find real evidence of the power of this direct path you say the Mother wants to open up to us?*

In the *Upanishads* it is said: "The Atman chooses those to whom the Atman reveals itself." Which means that enlightenment is a kind of dazzling random gift by the divine to a part of itself. In a very crucial passage in his *Gospel*, Ramakrishna says he imagines God as a child who has a whole heap of gems in front of him and is sitting by the roadside. All sorts of people come and beg the child to give them the gems, all sorts of serious seekers come and beg and beg, and say "I've done this and that, I've been on this retreat and that pilgrimage, I've done a thousand million purifications," etc. The child doesn't yield any of the gems to these seekers, but then somebody comes along and walks past the child, just walks airily on, and the child runs laughing up to them and gives them all of the jewels. This is Ramakrishna saying that if you think you can limit the divine play, if you think you can organize the whole business of enlightenment, if you think you can tame and train the divine to do exactly what you want, to summon it into your system, your master, your way of doing things, you're crazy.

The divine is a child at play and it will illumine who it wants to. What you *can* do is to open yourself spaciously to that outrageous possibility and just relax in divine love. That is a marvelous way of going about it. So, we have it from the very highest authority (and you know how I love authority!) saying that it can happen like that and that it *does* happen like that. I think a great deal now about the Christian saints and the whole extraordinary legacy of sanctity in the Christian church—none of the saints followed an embodied master. They had guides and friends, but they were essentially meeting the divine directly in naked love. They were essentially meeting the Christ-core of their own spirit, the enlightened core of love, in direct naked exposure to it in prayer, in service—and *this* is what woke them up. Awakening fell upon them. St. John of the Cross didn't have a guru, he had Christ exploding in his mind, and so can we if we allow Christ in. If we allow the Buddha or Krishna or the Mother in, they will explode in us.

I think one of the great, great functions of Christianity at this moment, of the way in which the Christian saints were enlightened, is to show that this outrageous possibility of direct contact, direct transmission from the heart of light to the human heart, is possible. Where was St. Francis' guru? No guru— Christ. Where was Teresa of Avila's guru? No guru—Christ. They both knew direct transmission, direct from the divine to the human heart. Where was Mohammed's guru? No guru— direct transmission from the divine. The Mother can do it, and in a time like this of extreme danger, she is doing it like crazy, only we're not doing it with her. Every conceivable kind of opportunity is being given us to wake up, including terminal catastrophe, which should be a mirror in which we should see exquisitely and completely what needs to be done, both in our souls and politically.

Do you see what I'm saying? It's very hopeful, this vision. It doesn't destroy the old vision, it just says that it had its time, its place, its culture and conditions. We have thousands of stories that prove its validity, but we are in different cultural circumstances, in a different time, a very much more dangerous time when a vast awakening is necessary, and that means that we have to each of us take responsibility for a direct relationship with the divine and really plunge into it. I know how difficult it is to establish direct relationship and I know how much it costs; it costs, in fact, far more than the relationship with the guru. It costs total nakedness, it costs real work, it costs constant exposure, but it is possible, and wonderful.

*You helped write* The Tibetan Book of Living and Dying. *What relevance do you think it has to the sacred feminine?*

When I think about the revolution of the sacred feminine, when I think about this great mystical awakening that has to happen, what I think about are people having available to them

major, very important, very simple yet powerful kinds of meditation techniques and visualizations that they can use to transform their minds and hearts. That's why I devoted many years
to that study and to that particular book, so that those meditation systems, those forms and techniques, could be given to
the entire world. Sogyal and his tradition wanted to do that,
so that's why I worked with them. I saw from my experience
with Thuksey Rinpoche that the Mahayana Buddhist path is a
profound Mother-path. It is a Mother-path because of its understanding of the Mother-experience, of this vast experience of
being held at all moments and at all times in the shining void
that is the Mother. It's a Mother-vision because it's a vision of
total interconnectedness, of the interconnectedness of every
being and every event, every thing. It's a Mother-vision because
of its emphasis on compassion and because at its core it has a
very powerful vision of enlightened service, of service to others enacted out of a vision of emptiness and compassion, out
of the marriage of wisdom and compassion. This is the vision,
in other words, of the bodhisattva, the one who gives up total
enlightenment to stay and work in the world of suffering.

All these aspects are crucial to the Mother-revolution, to the
revolution of the sacred feminine. Mahayana Buddhism has at
its core this central, ecstatic, illumined perception that samsara
is nirvana, and nirvana is samsara—they are *not* separate, not
two: we are it and as it, always, now. So I've been trying to give
this comprehensive, explosive awareness of the Mahayana and
why it is so crucial to us. And, as I have said, why it is crucial,
too, is, that out of this amazing wisdom an amazing complexity of really valid techniques has been created—techniques that
really work to transform the mind. That's why this wisdom tradition is so vital. Christians have read *The Tibetan Book of
Living and Dying* and have been tremendously inspired by it.
Hindus have read this book and gotten tremendous inspiration. People who have no religion at all have started to use the
meditations in the book when they are dying and have had
direct experiences of the nature of mind and reality. Clear truths

are made available through them that can now be shared by
everyone in this great mystical revolution. These meditations
will remain valuable long after the lineage system that helped
transmit them is dead.

*You have talked about the importance of preparing for an under-
standing of emptiness. What is this preparation?*

In the Tibetan tradition, the more profound recognitions of
emptiness are only "allowed" to those who have purified and
clarified themselves sufficiently so as not to misinterpret them
or put them into the wrong kind of practice. The Tibetans have
been very aware of the dangers of knowing that things are inherently empty before the entire being has been consecrated to
compassion and purified by meditation. Knowledge of emptiness without a fully-developed sense of compassion and dedication to service can lead to disastrous amorality justified in
the name of "emptiness."

This raises a larger question: How do we on the direct path
exercise the same kind of scrupulous self-control that was traditionally exercised in the master-disciple system? There are
different stages in mystical growth and different kinds of dangers that belong to each stage. The duty of anyone who decides
on the direct path is to become as acquainted as possible with
*all* the different mystical systems so as to build as comprehensive, subtle, and rigorous an awareness as possible of what we
might call the "hierarchy" of mystical development. This can
be done without a master; it requires, however, a real sense of
inquiry, *passionate* inquiry, and real learning.

Having a direct relationship with the divine does not mean
short-circuiting any of the stages of mystical unfolding. We are
all going to have to go through these different stages, and we
are all going to have to study all the traditions to get as much
precise help as we possibly can to understand in detail their
natures. And we are all going to have to be humbly vigilant to
help each other not to get trapped in any of the fantasies and

subtle illusions of these stages. This is by no means an impossible task, as many of those who support the master system blindly, even in its present state of decay, pretend. The Divine Mother will give direct inspiration to anyone searching sincerely, and as Ramakrishna said, "One ray from the light of the Mother works miracles." Taking our own inner development into our own hands is a very complex act, one that involves ultimate courage and ultimate responsibility. There will never be any substitute for hard work, deep discipline, and extensive humble learning. If the grace of the Mother is continually invoked and if all the difficulties are continually laid at the feet of the Mother, help will always be directly given, as Ramakrishna and Aurobindo make clear.

The "hierarchical" understanding of the old mystical systems can be incorporated successfully within the "democratic" structure of the new forms of transmission, but only if all of us who are developing this path take the time and trouble really to learn—and go on learning—from the precision of the wisdom of the past. As Vaclav Havel said, "To run a democracy takes *more* skill and understanding, not less, than running an authoritarian regime." The kind of freedom that the Mother is opening up to the whole human race is one that will have to be continually safeguarded by knowledge and humility.

*Can you say something about Tara as the Divine Mother?*

In the figure of Tara, you have a fully enlightened female Buddha. Tara is described in some Tibetan Buddhist texts as having been born from a tear of the Buddha of Compassion. If you actually look at the sacred texts of Tara, it's quite clear—and it also quite clear from the practices in which she is invoked, from the rituals and the forms of the rituals by which she is invoked, and from the sacred importance that is given her in many Mahayana Buddhist sects—that Tara is considered nothing less than a fully realized, totally enlightened female Buddha. In some texts it is said that she made the choice to come back in a woman's body, because Buddhanature is nongendered, and because most Buddhas had taken birth in a male body, so she decided to show that it could also be done in a female body, from a different perspective, one that had been neglected. So "it" came back as a "she" to do the work of salvation.

So, in the exploration of the opening up of Tara to the world, of this aspect of the Divine Mother, we have yet another of the forms of the Goddess, of the great empowering form of the Goddess radiating her enlightenment through the whole of the Mahayana tradition, the whole of the Tibetan tradition. She radiates it as Tara in Tibet, as Kwan-Yin in China, as Kannon—there are many names for her. But she is unmistakably realized, and she is unmistakably female. That is a glorious contribution to the whole search for the sacred feminine and its use. "Tara" means "star"; she is also said to be the liberator, the savior, the one who rescues in times of danger, and her mantra *"Om tare tuttare ture svaha"* is one of the mantras that really gives total protection. Tara is invoked in many of the highest tantric practices as the giver of the wisdom of emptiness, the giver of the final wisdom, the final understanding, because it comes, as I have been saying, from a radical union of samsara and nirvana, emptiness and form, heaven and earth. It's the feminine that gives that union.

Tara represents the sacred force of compassion that unites emptiness and form, this world and the light manifesting it. That sacred form and force of compassion results in the endless employment of sacred skillful means to help beings struggling in illusion recognize their own liberated nature. That is who Tara is. She plays a very deep part in Mahayana Buddhism, and exploring what Tara's nature may mean for the future will be very much the task of many Buddhists now. I foresee that we are going to have a Tara revolution, a Tara revival, a Tara explosion. It's going to bring into Mahayana Buddhism a whole flood of new creativity and insight. It's going to be a source of wonderful strength, because there it is: this wonderful force of feminine enlightenment, waiting to be used in a new way, with new intensity.

Let me end by evoking an old Tibetan Buddhist prayer to Tara, Female Buddha, Force of Protection, Wisdom, and Compassion; a prayer which expresses with awe and passion the full extent of her divine power:

> With your eyes that flash like lightning,
> Heroine, *Tare Tuttare*
> I bow to you, who sprang from the corolla
> Of the lotus of the Buddha's face.
> With your beautiful face of love
> Round like the circle of an autumn moon
> I pay homage to you, as you hold a lotus-blossom
> And turn out your hand in the mudra of gift-giving.
> With *tuttare* you spring us from the prison of samsara!
> With *svaha* you pacify all defilement!
> I bow to you, Divine One, as you open the gate of Brahma
> With your original all-powerful Om!
> I pay homage to Tara, the Mother,
> The Mother of all sentient beings
> Who protects the entire world
> From the eight great terrors.
> Gods and demigods lay down their crowns
> At your lotus feet.
> I pay homage to Tara, the Mother
> Who saves us from all poverty and danger.
> May I and all sentient beings
> Live directly in your sublime presence.[13]

## Notes

1. Sogyal Rinpoche, *The Tibetan Book of Living and Dying*. Edited by Patrick Gaffney and Andrew Harvey (San Francisco: HarperSanFrancisco, 1993).

2. Andrew Harvey, *A Journey in Ladakh* (Boston: Houghton Mifflin Company, 1983).

3. *A Journey in Ladakh*, pp. 206–208.

4. Quoted in Ken Wilber, *Eye to Eye: The Quest for the New Paradigm* (New York: Anchor Books, 1983), p. 194.

5. Quoted in Wilber, *Eye to Eye*, p. 297.

6. Wilber, *Eye to Eye*, pp. 297–298.

7. Quoted in Wilber, *Eye to Eye*, p. 299.

8. Quoted in Wilber, *Eye to Eye*, pp. 300–301.

9. Quoted in Wilber, *Eye to Eye*, p. 306.

10. From *Buddha Mind: An Anthology of Longchen Rabjam's Writings on Dzogpa Chenpo*. Edited by Harold Talbott (Ithaca, New York: Snow Lion Publications, 1989).

11. Milarepa, quoted in Sogyal Rinpoche, *The Tibetan Book of Living and Dying*, p. 40.

12. Miranda Shaw, *Passionate Enlightenment: Women in Tantric Buddhism* (Princeton, New Jersey: Princeton University Press, 1994).

13. Author's translation.

# Chapter Nine

# The Tao and the Mother

*The Tao is the Way, the Way behind all ways, the principle
underlying all principles, the fact underlying all facts. Taoism, in its broadest sense, is the search for truth and reality.
In a narrower sense, it is the original knowledge tradition
of China, but the narrowness of this definition is growing
more acute day by day, as Taoism has already in the last
couple of centuries extended some of its influence in the
West to nearly as diverse an array of areas of human inter-
est as it has in the East.*[1]

IT IS IN THOSE moments or hours in life when we enter, without knowing why, the space of a vast mysteriously ordered
calm, as beyond hope as it is beyond despair, that we glimpse
the Tao and know ourselves immersed in completely and moved
by its laws and rhythms. These are always moments or hours
when we are—for whatever reason—sprung gently clear of
ourselves, of everything we think of as our mind or our biography, or even everything we remember or have formulated of
our mystic awareness of things. Something, as it were, *vanishes*
us and what remains is an Eye in which everything that is appears shining in the light of a love so deep and calm we know
it to be the love at the heart of all things, that infinitely stable,
ageless love beyond all concepts and words, around which all
things revolve and in which all things are soaked as if in tears
of recognition, wonder, and joy.

No words have or ever could describe the astounding fresh purity of these entries into our true nature and the true nature of all things, for the simple reason that these entries are always effected in a silence that is itself the condition and law of the mystery that it reveals. In such times, the Tao looks at the Tao through our eyes and feels, sees, intuits the Tao with all our concerted awakened senses; the Mother gazes at herself through the eyes of the child, who then, through the accumulated grace and power of such awakenings, learns to become the mother of that inner divine child that is waiting to be born in him or her. The mystery of the divine alchemy of the Tao opens for us and begins its slow, intricate work of transforming all of our scattered being into its at once in-gathered and quietly out-streaming self. Liu I-Ming, one of the greatest of all the Taoist master-children, writes in his *Awakening to the Tao:*

> After people are born, the primal is mixed into the tempo-ral, and the temporal is mixed into the primal. Considering this mixture and adulteration, if we do not refine away acquired artificialities, then the primal will not return. If we borrow the temporal to refine the primal while using the primal to transform the temporal, when the temporal is com-pletely transformed and the primal is completely whole, this frees a radiant pearl whose light pervades heaven and pen-etrates earth.
>
> Then you may soar straight up or go straight ahead, go against or go along—everywhere is the Way. When your achievements are complete and your practices are fulfilled, you break through space, fly to heaven in broad daylight.[2]

Those who have awakened to the Mother, who have birthed the Divine Child in themselves, have always a certain look. Dol-phins and whales have this look; a dog I saw dying in a ditch outside a hotel in Delhi had this look; an ancient tortoise I swam with in the waters of Hawaii had this look; Ramana Maharshi, Ramakrishna, Aurobindo, and the furry extravagant gentle Taoist immortals in the paintings of China have this look. It is the open, calm, loving shining look of the Mother, of the Child who sees the Mother in all things and events and at all moments.

To grow that gaze, to allow its slow unfolding in us, to allow it to take possession of all our faculties and powers and to turn all of them into it, and to become one with it and one with the One that it is always seeing, is the goal of human life, the "radiant pearl whose light pervades heaven and penetrates earth." A *dzogchen* master calls this look "The Immaculate gazing at itself," and it is the unmistakable (and unfakable) sign of one who is arriving at the enlightenment-field, the light-field of the Tao, arriving in the Mother with more and more of the Mother's own humility and love and wonder and boundless, spacious strength. Only the fully awakening divine child can awaken it completely and sustain it at all moments, even through the agony of death, as Ramana Maharshi did and St. Francis and Chuang Tzu are said to have done. This gentlest and strongest of all looks is the only gaze that can be called triumphant, because it has outstared change, outstared all turmoil and evil and even death itself to see the Face of the Tao, the Face of the Mother, streaming through and in the Real at all moments.

* * *

The immense richness and profundity and profound practical usefulness of Taoism, of the Taoist vision of reality, is best approached tangentially, poetically, with all our physical and spiritual senses turned to that dark silence behind and beyond all concepts. The *Tao Te Ching* warns us: "The Tao that can be *tao*'ed is not the Tao," which means, among many other things, that making *any* conceptual system around defining the Tao— making a *Way* out of it ("Way" is of course another meaning of "Tao") reduces it and so betrays it. Lao Tzu tells us:

> The Tao that can be told
> Is not the eternal Tao.
> The name that can be named
> Is not the eternal name.

The unnameable is the eternally real
Naming is the origin of all particular things.
Free from desire, you realize the mystery.
Caught in desire, you see only the manifestations.

Yet mystery and manifestations
Arise from the same source.
This source is called darkness.

Darkness within darkness.
The gateway to all understanding.

This "darkness," "the gateway to all understanding," the
source of all manifestation, the hidden-behind, the unnameable, is the Mother.

There was something formless yet complete
That existed before heaven and earth;
Without sound, without substance
Depending on nothing, unchanging,
All pervading, unfailing.
One may think of it as the Mother of all things under
     heaven
Its true name we do not know.

To be in tune with the supreme mystery of the Mother, of
the source, of the Tao, is the goal of Taoism, a goal which can
never be formulated or conceptualized, a goal that is itself an
ever-expanding, always more liberating mystery. From this
increasing in-tuneness with the Mother, the reward of constant
purification and discipline and the application of techniques of
all kinds to clarify the body and nervous system and to fast the
mind and heart of the fantasies that keep them ignorant, arise
a magical spontaneity, *tzu jan* (what the Hindus call *sahaja*),
the mysterious, wholly natural joy of the divine child who rests
in the dark fecund silence of the Tao, the Mother, and who is
forever free from the need to impress, convince, or wield power
of any kind.

Chuang Tzu writes:

Nan-po Tzu-k'uei said to the Woman Crookback "You are old in years and yet your complexion is that of a child. Why is this?"

"I have heard the Way!"

"Can the Way be learned?" asked Nan-po Tzu-k'uei.

"Goodness, how could that be? Anyway, you aren't the man to do it. Now there's Pu-liang Yi—he has the talent of a sage but not the Way of a sage, whereas I have the Way of a sage and not the talent of a sage. I thought I would try and teach him and see if I could really get anywhere near to making him a sage. . . . So I began explaining and kept at him for three days, and after that he was able to put the world outside himself. When he had put the world outside himself, I kept at him for seven days more, and after that he was able to put things outside himself. When he had put things outside himself . . . he was able to achieve the brightness of dawn, and when he had achieved the brightness of dawn, he could see his own aloneness. After he had managed to see his own aloneness, he could do away with past and present, and after he had done away with past and present, he was able to enter where there is no life and no death. That which kills life does not die; that which gives life does not live. This is the kind of thing it is: there's nothing . . . it doesn't welcome, nothing it doesn't destroy, nothing it doesn't complete. Its name is Peace-In-Strife. After the strife, it attains completion."[3]

At home in the Source, at one with the Tao, the divine child acts in the world of the "ten thousand things" with the calmness, freedom, spontaneity, gaiety, and abandon of the Tao itself, of the Mother. At home in both the transcendent and the immanent, in the darkness, in the light, and in the play of the light in matter, balancing the yin and yang, the feminine and masculine forces of the psyche and the universe, the child "breathes with his heels," "makes oneness his house and lives with what cannot be avoided," knows "the ten thousand things belong to one storehouse and life and death share the same body." Refusing all the lures of the path of transcendence—simply to ascend above existence and deny the world and the body—the child refuses also all the temptations of descent, of a merely this-worldly celebration of nature and time and impassioned physical life, and lives in a mysterious and radiant balance of both from a peace beyond both, simultaneously awake in all possible interlinked dimensions with skill, humor, and abiding unmediated joy.

That this is not in any sense an abstract ideal or one that "floats" above the exigencies of the most ordinary mundane existence is stressed again and again in Taoist texts. *This* life is the divine life when lived to the rhythm and in the luminous spirit of the Tao; *this* body is the body of heaven when its needs and laws are respected and its strength constantly nourished from the dark milk of peace, from the milk of the dark silence that is always flowing from the breast of the Tao; *this* moment is eternity when known and lived as the music of the changeless. Whatever activity is undertaken in the inspiration of the Tao will radiate a mysterious swift balance and effectiveness, because it will be instinct with the secret power of the universe itself and in harmony with it.

This story of Chuang Tzu marvelously illustrates the spontaneous mastery that is the reward of the discipline of attuning one's whole being to the Tao:

> Cook Ting was cutting up an ox for Lord Wen-hui. At every touch of his hand, every heave of his shoulder, every move of his feet, every thrust of his knee—zip! zoop! He slithered the knife along with a zing, and all was in perfect rhythm. . . .
>
> "Ah, this is marvelous," said Lord Wen-hui. "Imagine skill reaching such heights!"
>
> Cook Ting laid down his knife and replied, "What I care about is the Way, which goes beyond skill. When I first began cutting up oxen, all I could see was the ox itself. After three

years I no longer saw the whole ox. And now—now I go at it by spirit and don't look with my eyes. Perception and understanding have come to a stop and spirit moves where it wants. I go along with the natural makeup, strike in the big hollows, guide the knife through the big openings, and follow things as they are. So I never touch the smallest ligament or tendon, much less a main joint."

Cook Ting goes on to "explain" his mastery:

"A good cook changes his knife once a year—because he cuts. A mediocre cook changes his knife once a month—because he hacks. I've had this knife of mine for nineteen years and I've cut up thousands of oxen with it, and yet the blade is as good as though it had just come from the grindstone. There are spaces between the joints, and the blade of the knife has really no thickness. If you insert what has no thickness into such spaces, then there's plenty of room—more than enough for the blade of the knife to play about in. That is why after nineteen years the blade of my knife is still as good as when it first came from the grindstone.

"However, whenever I come to a complicated place, I size up the difficulties, tell myself to watch out and be careful, keep my eyes on what I am doing, work very slowly, and move the knife with the greatest subtlety, until—flop! the whole thing comes apart like a clod of earth crumbling to the ground. I stand there holding the knife and look all around me, completely satisfied and reluctant to move on, and then I wipe off the knife and put it away."

Appropriately moved and excited, Wen-hui exclaims:

"I have heard the words of Cook Ting and learned how to care for life!"[4]

The feudal lord and master learns from the lower-class cook how to "care for life." The Taoist revelation has the inherent robust anarchic radicalism of the Mother. All beings appear as her in her, but it is the humblest and most unpretentiously disciplined and receptive who live her mystery most completely.

Chuang Tzu described Taoism as a religion without doctrine, without dogma or institutions, whose "transmission is not recorded in the history of the world." What can be recorded in history after all is only the fragmented dance of concepts, arranged in pleasing but always artificial orders. The radical wild sweet naturalness that is the aim of Taoism and the reward of direct intimacy with the Mother looks like foolishness to the brilliant, anarchy to the moralistic, heresy to the "religious," laziness and self-absorption to the "political," nonsensical paradox-for-paradox'-sake to the "rational." They all in different ways laugh at it, but as Lao Tzu said, "If there were no laughter, the Tao would not be what it is." Its spontaneity and power laugh forever beyond all our ideas of the Tao, waiting for us to drop our clothes of pride and dogma to enter into that wise receptive nakedness of heart and mind where its intuitions dance in and through us naturally, teaching us simultaneously how small we are and how miraculous.

Because of their profound reverence for the dark source, the Tao, the Mother, and their profound respect for all the laws and rhythms and interlinked arisings of nature and events, the Taoist sages stressed again and again, and with subtlety that is always inspiring, the necessity of taking the *feminine* path into truth. No other mystical revelation has celebrated so richly and so emphatically the calm glory of the way of the sacred feminine or made it so clear that without developing the feminine qualities of intuition, openness to mystery, caring for life, capacity to sink again and again into that rich receptive peacefulness that is the lifespring of all mental and spiritual energy, no complete relationship either with the Absolute or with life itself can be established. In this, Taoism is very close to the wisdom traditions of the Hopis, Yamomamis, and aborigines, and in fact may historically draw much of its knowledge from ancient shamanic traditions and practices that have long since vanished. It has preserved through the long patriarchal agony the calm

mystery of the knowledge of Origin, of the original knowledge
of humanity's immersion in the Mother, and we need its wisdom now more than ever:

> Know the male, but keep the female
> So becoming the universal river-valley.
> Being the universal river-valley
> One has eternal virtue undivided
> And becomes again a child.
>
> Gravity is the root of lightness;
> The quiet is the master of the hasty.

Because Taoism is not limited to an understanding, however exalted, of the spirit of things but "seeks reality in the *body*
as it lives" (Chuang Tzu), the Taoist adept is encouraged to
think of himself or herself as holding the True within his or her
own being, as a mother with child. Birthing that child—which
in Taoist practice is synonymous with enlightenment, with
"eternal virtue undivided"—can only be achieved through the
radical cultivation of a feminine nature, one whose essence is
attention, quiescence, surrender, practical compassion. Chuang
Tzu tells us of Lieh Tzu that after his illumination by Hu Tzu,
he

> ... concluded that he had never really begun to learn any-
> thing. He went home and for three years did not go out. He
> replaced his wife at the stove, fed the pigs as though he were
> feeding people, and showed no preferences in the things he
> did. He got rid of the carving and polishing and returned to
> plainness. ... In the midst of entanglement he remained
> sealed, and in this oneness he ended his life.

Chuang Tzu adds, describing unforgettably the subtlety of feminine mystical awareness:

> Do not be an embodier of fame; do not be a storehouse of
> schemes; do not be an undertaker of projects; do not be a
> proprietor of wisdom. Embody to the fullest what has no

end and wander where there is no trail. Hold on to all that you have received from Heaven but do not think that you have gotten anything. Be empty, that is all. The Perfect Man uses his mind like a mirror—going after nothing, welcoming nothing, responding but not storing. Therefore he can win out over things and not hurt himself.[5]

To know the masculine and yet maintain the feminine is completed in the *Tao Te Ching* by following sentence: "To know clarity and yet maintain obscurity is to become the measure of all things." Out of and in that obscurity, that deepest humility and continual holding-open of a space of inner emptiness, the divine child, the ultimately free human divine being, is born.

This feminine attitude was not simply, as the story of Lieh Tzu makes humorously clear, a *spiritual* direction; as Kristofer Schipper tells us in his superb book *The Taoist Body*:

> [T]he female attitude must also be constant in *daily life*. This is laid down in instructions to the masters, as seen in *The One Hundred Eighty Commandments for Libationers*, the religious leaders of the liturgical organization of the Heavenly Master: one must be cheerful, never raise one's voice, never stare, carry arms, hunt, or amuse oneself with cars and horses, and, sure sign of antivirility, never urinate while standing.

Women themselves were treated in Taoism with greater and more comprehensive respect than in any other of the major mystical traditions. In the book of Chuang Tzu there were many women among the initiates.

> [T]he movement of the Heavenly Master [a later development of Taoism] was organized on the basis of absolute equality between men and women who, as Libationers, shared in equal numbers the leadership of the liturgical organization. The Heavenly Masters themselves shared their duties with their wives. In the dioceses there were as many female as male masters. This balance was fundamental, even

in the practice of perfection, inasmuch as the highest degree of initiation—that which qualified the adept for the rank of master—could only be obtained by a man and a woman together, as a couple. Celibacy was unthinkable.[6]

In the China of those times,

> [A]ll the lords had harems. Education of women was virtually unknown. The marital situation of the wives was extremely precarious, especially in the absence of any male children. Official morality embodied an outright misogyny.[7]

What, then, to make of a religion that ruled out polygamy, made women the intermediaries, if not the keys to initiation, and allowed them the status of master in the same way as men, which implies a high degree of education? The origins of such an organization can only be found in a liturgical context where femaleness was predominant.

So the Taoist celebration of sacred femininity was not simply a spiritual or intellectual one; it was practical and radical as well, daring to implement the rich balance of the Tao in reality as well as in inner practice, so attempting to end that split between male and female, feminine and masculine, heaven and earth, mystical awareness and political and economic practice that still plagues our thinking about the divine.

Every being, then, attempting to enter his or her own deepest truth, is a mother pregnant with a divine child, a child who has to be birthed through tenderness, patience, infinite and repeated surrender beyond all thought and concept to the rhythms and laws of the universe.

> Can you keep the turbulent *p'o* [negative forces],
>     prevent them from leaving; embrace the One
>     without its leaving you?
> Can you control your breathing and make it soft as a
>     child's?
> Can you purify your vision of the mystery so that it
>     loses all distortion?

> Can you, by Non-Action, watch over the people and
>     rule the [inner] land?
> Can you by opening and closing (at given times) your
>     natural gates, realize your female nature?
> Can you, by Non-Knowledge, let the white light
>     penetrate all the regions of the [inner] space?[8]

Chuang Tzu says:

> I tell you the supreme Tao. This is the essence of the supreme
> Tao: Confused! Obscure! This is the principle of the supreme
> Tao: Chaotic! Silent! No sight, no hearing; in silence embrace
> your spirits and your body will become spontaneously sound.
> Be calm, be pure, do not overburden your body . . . and you
> will enjoy Long Life! . . . I keep the One so as to remain in
> harmony![9]

This "keeping of the One so as to remain in harmony" is
the essence of the path of the sacred feminine, the clue to the
sacred marriage, the fusion of masculine and feminine in the
dark silent depths of the psyche to produce the child. And as
Taoism with its physical and meditative techniques (t'ai chi
chuan, chi gong, and a host of others) makes clear, "keeping
the One" is the work of the whole being and a whole lifetime,
a work that becomes more and more grounded, earthy, and
practical, more powerful and transformatory as it learns in ever-
deepening lessons the Mother-art of surrender; more and more
transcendent as it pays ever-more intuitive attention to the
rhythms, needs, impulses, and laws of the immanent.

As Ko Hung, a great third-century Taoist mystic, writes:

> He who knows the One has accomplished everything.
> He who knows the One knows all.
> For him who does not know the One, there is nothing
>     he can know.
> The Tao reveals itself first of all in the One.
> It is therefore of incomparable value.

If we know how to preserve it, the One is there;
If we neglect it, the One is lost.
If we turn towards it, we find good fortune;
If we turn away from it, we meet disaster.
Those who know how to keep it will experience
  endless joy.
In those who lose it, life will dry up, their energies
  exhausted.[10]

To the Taoist, knowledge of the Mother, and living attuned
to it in all the details of physical and spiritual life, is essential
on every level. The body cannot survive if the spirit is not in
harmony. The world cannot live in peace if each being in it is
not satisfied in the Tao, resting in strong peace against the breast
of the unnameable Mother. Anything that is accomplished outside the laws and rhythms of the Mother will be unbalanced,
exaggerated, and will perish; all knowledge that is not knowledge of the Tao is exhausting and vain; the joys of a direct naked
relationship with her are the only lasting joys, both in the physical world and in that light-world that everywhere interpene-
trates, manifests, and sustains it. When that relationship is
established in the sweetest and most radical humility imaginable, all needs—physical and spiritual—are met immediately,
naturally, casually, normally, with the miraculous appropri-
ateness and ease that belongs to the love of the Mother and her
all-embracing, all-balancing, sober, and blissful knowledge.
Hung Po tells us:

That is why in the books of the Immortals it says:
If you want to obtain Long Life, you must know how
  to keep the One!
Think of the One, and if you are hungry, the One will
  give you food.
Think of the One, and if you are thirsty, the One will
  give you drink.[11]

The aim of human life, to the Taoist, is a conscious return to
the Mother and the birthing into reality through that return of

the inner divine child. The name "Lao Tzu" means, wonderfully and revealingly, "Old Child." All liberated human beings, all human beings freed to enter the Tao and breathe and walk and sleep and make love in its serene wild calmness, are "old children," naturally at serious play with all the other children of the Mother, wanting and working unhurriedly for their good in all things, released from all claims to "enlightenment" and all need for fame or power, at home here at last, children at home in the house of the One, the great Tao—womb of the universe.

This sublime vision, in its sanity, depth, humanity, wise humility—this passionately and wittily egalitarian vision comes closer than any other I know to incorporating and embodying the mystery of the Mother. For that reason, perhaps, this vision is the hardest for the Western mind to grasp, simply because it cannot be "grasped" in any known conceptual sense but has to be uncovered, discovered, intuited, lived from the beginning in a spirit of mysterious poetic reverence. From its earliest for-mulations—in the *Tao Te Ching*, the *I Ching*, Chuang Tzu's always astonishing writings—Taoism derails and mocks the intellect's need for the security of definition, dogma, hierarchy. Anyone who claims to understand the Tao and be a master of Tao immediately and comically exposes his fraudulence.

Living in the Tao is an art which goes on and on perfecting itself in illumined patience up to, and—who knows?—beyond the last breath of this or any other life. The highest and most evolved beings are "old children" who have learned enough to know beyond a shadow of a doubt that they know nothing and are content with that non-knowing, for from it every useful kind of secondary knowledge bubbles forever as if from a hid-den—and inexhaustible—fountain. All they know and need to know is that not-knowing is the gateway into the unnamue-able, into her, into the Tao, and that over many years of sus-tained practice in the midst of life it forms a conduit whereby gnosis can gradually flood each moment with its humor and its bliss, its wise practicality, and its ordinary divine poetry.

Like all poetry that arises from a mystical tradition, Taoist poetry has the taste, the *rasa*, the perfume of the understanding (or *not*-understanding) that inspires the whole revelation. Not surprisingly, then, it is poetry of the ordinary divine, of holy particulars, of the subtlest and calmest imaginable flashing-out from the heart of reality of the Presence. For the Taoist, as we have seen, life as it is lived in harmony reveals a constant divine ground and joy and bliss and self-evident meaning, for in its mysterious and paradoxical beneficence the Tao has made the "world of the ten thousand things" the playground of the poet-in-the-heart, the divine child.

This sense of the continuing poetry of the divinity of the ordinary is the great contribution of Taoism to the revolution of the sacred feminine, and is a continual gentle challenge to everyone to refine themselves sufficiently to hear the music of what happens. It is this supple, subtle, infinitely graded and open-souled and open-hearted refinement of attention to being that is the crown of the sacred feminine, its richest and most marvelous and useful "child," for with its growth installed in us all of life increasingly reveals the presence of That, of her, of the Tao, and so births in us calmly the truth of our divine identity with the Tao and all things.

As Loy Ching-yuen writes so beautifully in his great work, *The Book of the Heart:*

> To know the Tao
> meditate
> and still the mind.
> Knowledge comes with perseverance.
>
> The Way is neither full nor empty;
> a modest and quiet nature understands this.
> The empty vessel, the uncarved block;
> nothing is more mysterious.
>
> When enlightenment arrives
> don't talk too much about it;
> just live it in your own way.
> With humility and depth, rewards come naturally.[12]

Boiling up the soup of immortality takes hours on the
    stove,
like learning the Way: just one method—
Practice diligently:
Heaven is within the grasp of all.[13]

## Questions and Answers

*You have been talking a great deal about action in this dangerous world to save the planet. How can the Taoist understanding of non-action help us?*

Any action, however passionate or just, that isn't also simultaneously rooted in divine peace, in the peace of the Tao, will almost certainly engender fresh difficulties. Which does not mean that we have to wait until we are perfect to act—that is another subtle evasion—but that *as* we act in life, we must also always be working on tuning our deep selves to the laws and rhythms of the Tao.

This will help us preserve and nourish ourselves from the breast of the Mother. To fight for the preservation of the planet in the Mother's love we will also need her tirelessness and her spacious depth of perception. This is why a mystical activism is the only kind of activism, I think, that can succeed in a crisis as extreme as ours. Only an activism informed subtly as far as possible with the Mother's wisdom can be effective; only an activism informed as far as possible with the Mother's peace can continue—even in derision, violence, horror, failure, even, if necessary, through final defeat.

Chuang Tzu tells a story of seeing an old man fall into a cataract and come out safely downstream. The old man, when asked to explain how he did this, simply said: "Plunging into the whirl, I came out with the swirl. I accommodate myself to the water, not the water to me." Accommodating ourselves to the water—the whirling waters of destiny, individual and collective, demands authenticity, honesty, and capacity for surrender, just those virtues that Taoism celebrates so richly and knows so wisely how to cultivate in balance.

The beautiful poetic definition that Alan Watts gives of *wu-wei*—non-action—in his great book *Tao: The Watercourse Way*, can help us here:

"The Tao does nothing, and yet nothing is left undone."
These famous words of Lao-tzu obviously cannot be taken
in their literal sense, for the principle of "nonaction" (*wu-
wei*) is not to be considered inertia, laziness, *laissez-faire*, or
mere passivity. Among the several meanings of *wei* are to
be, to do, to make, to practice, to act out; and [it can mean]
false, simulated, counterfeit. But in the context of Taoist
writings it quite clearly means forcing, meddling, and arti-
fice—in other words, trying to act against the grain of *li*.
[The innate "grain" of things.] Thus, *wu-wei* as "not forcing" is what we mean by going with the grain, rolling with
the punch . . . taking the tide at its flood, and stooping to
conquer. It is perhaps best exemplified in the Japanese arts
of *judo* and *aikido* where an opponent is defeated by the
force of his own attack, and the latter art reaches such heights
of skill that I have seen an attacker thrown to the floor without even being touched.[14]

Learning the secret of *wu-wei* and the calm strength and
effectiveness it gives all forms of life and action is the reward
of opening to the Tao and letting it teach you. This teaching
beyond dogmas or words does not breed passivity at all, but
the kind of strength no evil or cruelty can defeat. In our apocalyptic time we all of us need this strength more than ever, and
need to know that wisdom, and its simple techniques, both spiritual and physical, that can help us grow and sustain it.

*You described Taoism as mastery of balance. Can you tell us
what you understand about yin and yang and their relation in
ourselves and the universe? How does this help you better understand the mystery of the sacred feminine?*

Just looking at the yin-yang symbol has been a source of continual inspiration and guidance for me in my journey. In it I
find represented with unmatched simplicity and directness the
highest wisdom of the Mother.

In this symbol, the "dark" (the yin, the feminine) and "light" (the yang, the masculine) are equally contained within a circle, that circle, the Tao, that embraces and contains, yet mysteriously transcends both. The yin and yang are divided not by a straight line but, very importantly, by an S-curve, a curve that itself often seems to me like a signature of the Tao.

Go on looking at this symbol and what do you see? You see that the wisdom that invented this symbol—or "found" it—does not separate the white and the black, dark and light, by a straight line that would engender clearly delineated and "absolute" opposites. In fact, the distinction is *provisional,* alternating like an electric current, continually shifting and changing; continually, if you like, at play, as the changeless Tao is at play in the parade of the "ten thousand things." What is even more revealing is that the black and the white—the feminine and masculine—each contain the other as if in embryo, and the force of the curve sends your mind *around* the circle, and does not allow it, as Anne Baring and Jules Cashford point out in their book *The Myth of the Goddess:* "to become fixed in one part or another nor to begin at any particular place." They go on:

> Consequently, we are directed to understanding yin and yang not so much in terms of opposition, but rather in terms of complementarity, where the separation of each from the other makes possible the perception of both at once. Insofar as there is difference, there is mutual dependence; the sense of movement created by the alternations of color and shape, and further, the way that the movement changes the more intensely it is contemplated suggest that here we are in the presence of principles or realities that escape precise definition and exact application. In the West this perception is made easier for us because the words and symbols of yin and yang have no previous association or public reference, so we cannot resolve the tension of the paradox by reducing it to something already known and explaining it away conceptually. What we have to do instead is experience what we habitually separate too distinctly in a new way; that is,

not as opposites that tend to conflict, but as complements that tend to relate. Following this model, we would have to consider any problem that arose not as one of finding a resolution to conflicting opposites, but one of discovering the just or appropriate relation between them, which would inevitably redirect us to their underlying identity.[15]

I wanted to quote Anne and Jules at length because this is a passage that has helped and continues to help me a great deal, for it demonstrates in the subtlety and precision of its insights the *movement* of the sacred feminine, of that intuitive wisdom that can constantly attend to the "grain," the *li*, of the mystery of life and not ever seek to impose on it what Keats called "the irritable reach" of pseudo-reason.

This infinitely subtle and robust, simultaneously mystical and hard-nosed actual wisdom is the gift of Taoism to us. You see its balance—that is the balance of the sacred feminine—in all aspects of the Taoist vision: in its understanding of the interlinking at every level of body and spirit, heaven and earth, transcendence and immanence, humility and sublimity, what we call "good" and what we call "evil." What such a wisdom demands of us is not a surrender of categories or discrimination, but their utmost *refinement* through clear-eyed gazing at the Real, a refinement so wise and alert and "empty" that it can see exactly what is happening at every moment without prejudice or the dubious consolations of righteous (and excluding) judgment. Again, this does not mean that cruelty, madness, viciousness are not recognized as such—but just that their relationship to *everything else* that is also going on is allowed to be known in all its complexity. It is only such refinement that can keep us supple in catastrophe, because only its eye can detect the location of that mysterious exit always there—even in the blackest, darkest darkness—the hole of "white" in the densest blackness through which we can climb into Origin.

How do we apply this kind of refinement to the present crisis? If we continue to see all those who oppose the kinds of radical changes we find necessary as "evil," we will miss every opportunity of really communicating with them. The yin-yang symbol reminds us uncomfortably that a part of our clarity (the deepest part, the Buddhanature part, in fact) is in them, and that their "darkness" is also in us. They *are* us and we *are* them. From that recognition of essential unity with all beings and things—with everything that happens, however horrifying— grows the kind of real humility and patience that can, if anything can, truly communicate with the destructive.

For myself, another way I try always to use this sacred feminine wisdom of balance, this mysterious understanding of the underlying identity of opposites, is to go on even in chaos and agony trying to find points of light, of hope, of encouragement. In the worst, most atrocious darkness there is always new light trying to be born; the darkness is part of the alchemy necessary to give birth to this light. That doesn't in any way excuse the works of this darkness; this is very important, and the Taoist masters insist on the ordinary moral distinctions of common sense as well as a higher awareness of paradox—unlike some modern New-Agers who obliterate all distinctions and so abet the work of evil—but it does breed in the heart and mind a kind of ruggedly serene hope, that hope that St. Paul means in Corinthians when he says "Love hopeth all things."

I see the apocalypse that we are living through as also, potentially, a birth—the birth of a new ordinary divine humanity, free from all structures of authority. Without a terrible smashing of *all* illusions, political and religious, such a birth simply will not be possible. What the Mother is asking of us all is, first, to see just what a terminally dangerous situation we are in, to wake up to that fully and with no false consolation; and then to see what an extraordinary new possibility is struggling to be born amid so much strife, horror, and blood. Rooting all our being in her, as the Tao helps us to, we can then focus all our powers to try and help this possibility to be born inside and around us. And as we struggle and fight and try, we will also be reminded by the wisdom of the sacred feminine that we must continue the constant work on ourselves not to incorporate

into our struggle the very features of the darkness we are fighting—its cruelty and intolerance, its blind and useless anger.
Only those who take the humble risk of continually "empty-
ing" themselves of everything they think they know will go on
being fed the kind of supple knowledge that can help even in
the most terminal and seemingly tragic situations.

*How does this feminine wisdom help you and Eryk understand
what has happened with Meera?*

It helps me most of all to preserve a sense of the whole meaning of the experience *without* in any way stopping making the
necessary distinctions to understand and judge what has happened and is happening.

This is what I see, with the help of the light of the Mother:

To survive my childhood and the wreckage of my relationship with my own mother, I had to, in this life, find the Divine
Mother in a human form. In the condition I was in, I wasn't
able to go to her directly. So my life and destiny brought me
to Meera. I have since seen that Meera is in no way the Mother,
although she is *playing* the Mother. But because initially her
"impersonation" of the Mother was convincing enough, I could
project onto her my overwhelming subconscious needs for an
absolutely *good* mother. The passion of this projection, the
passionate and fifteen-year-long adoration that this projection
engendered and sustained, were what provided the force of
truth necessary to awaken me partially in those years of being
with Meera. It wasn't Meera who was awakening me, but the
Mother. Meera, who thinks she can control the Mother by
playing her, is just another player—as we all are—in the great
game of Mother. She is in fact further from the Mother than
most of the other players because she dares to imitate her, and
of course fails.

*All* awakenings are done between the child and the Mother
directly, however it may appear otherwise. The Mother uses
whatever she needs to accomplish this—sometimes even a false

guru. Many mystical stories in all the traditions make it absolutely clear that a false guru can appear to illumine a real disciple. Let me explain myself further. There is a story that Ramakrishna, who knew *everything* about false gurus, told quite often. A sincere disciple was spiritually in love with a charlatan. He repeated with the most intense devotion the name of that charlatan as if it was the divine name. The passion of his devotion was so great that the divine flooded him with real powers, real *siddhis,* one of which was the ability to walk on water. Seeing his disciple walking on water one day, the false master (who of course knew deep inside that he was a fake) was heartened. "I can't be such a fake after all," he thought to himself, "if the power of my name is so great!" Overjoyed, he ran to the river, and, chanting his own name, attempted to walk on the water. Naturally, he sank like a stone.

This is a very profound story. It shows clearly that it is the quality of the disciple's *adoration,* not necessarily the authenticity of the master, that provides the fuel, the Shakti, for awakening. The Tibetans say that if you worship the master as a Buddha, you will get the blessings of the Buddha. Even if the master is an absolute rogue, thief, liar, maniac—if you worship him or her as the Buddha then the blessings of Buddha-nature will somehow get through to you.

However, the *full* awakening *cannot* take place with a false master. You can only go a certain part of the journey through the passion of projection. There comes a time when you are either stuck in that projection or the Mother shatters it ruthlessly to let you out of the subtle cage that it has erected around you, even while it has begun the process of your liberation.

Since Meera is not in any shape, sense, or form the Divine Mother on earth, my continuing adoration of her, even in the face of growing secret doubts and fears and real objections to some of the things I saw her doing, was increasingly trapping me. I had publicly proclaimed her as *the* Mother in *Hidden Journey* and when the crisis struck in December 1993, I was about to go all over America with her on tour as her spokes-

person. Kali intervened and showed me with shattering and agonizing clarity the truth about what she is, a truth that the horror and lies and pathological excesses of these last months have
only confirmed. All at once, the light of the real Mother came
up without any need of mediation and showed me that Meera,
in asking me to leave Eryk, become heterosexual, and write a
book about how she as the "Mother" had transformed me into
a heterosexual—couldn't, under any circumstances, even the
most broadly interpreted as paradoxical, be either enlightened
or the Mother. It was purely a power play to keep me in her
control and to stop me from progressing further into a dimension where I would see her for what she is, without consolation
or illusion. The fact that she went on to lie continually, even self-
contradictorily, about what had happened, thereby exposing me
and Eryk to the demonization of her panic-stricken disciples—
some of whom knew full well what had happened but reinforced
her abuse out of fear or deranged fanaticism—made it pro-
gressively clearer to me that not only was Meera *not* the Mother,
but in playing the role so convincingly and with such occult and
psychic powers at her disposal, she was actually dangerous and,
to put it mildly, "not on the side of the good."

Even in the worst moments of what happened, however, the
feminine sacred wisdom has kept me awake to the great new
possibility trying to be born out of this nightmare, both for
myself and Eryk and for all those who have chosen to wake up
with us (and thank God there are many who see that we cannot possibly be lying about all this and have no reason to do
so). In my most acute anguish—and this kind of betrayal of
the child by a so-called mother is one of the greatest sufferings,
really a rape of the soul at the deepest and most horrible level—
I have always been prompted to understand that the removal
of the false icon that Meera is was a necessary preparation for
the arrival of the direct unmediated Mother in her gathering
splendor. And that what this catastrophe would prepare in me
if I survived it was a wholly new understanding of the Divine
Mother, the one that I am now sharing, an understanding of

the Mother beyond name or form. Through the wisdom of the
underlying balance of opposites, I have been able to see that
this horror was—*is*—a birth and try to focus my faculties on
helping that birth as far, as bravely, as lucidly as possible, whatever anyone else might think or say or do.

I want, however, to say here that the wisdom of the sacred
feminine has also helped me become clearer in this situation,
has helped me face the worst, not without trembling, but without falling apart into madness or despair. What that wisdom
has shown me is that Meera and those like her—and there are
many in the contemporary guru-circus—are actually *essential*
to the great awakening that is being offered to us.

By playing the Mother and failing, Meera did me a terrible
good deed: she woke me up against my will to the *real* Mother
that needs no mediation *ever*. This was not in any way Meer-
a's teaching; it is absurd to imagine that she would in some way
organize this horror and these lies simply to liberate me—such
a Pyrrhic compliment is unthinkable from one who in the last
few months has by default whipped up a hate-campaign against
me and Eryk and so manipulated several of her disciples to acts
of what can only be described even by the most merciful of
intelligences as real unadulterated malice and evil.

Meera's great gift to me and the gift of this whole scandal
to anyone who cares to follow it is *not* that she is some great
"crazy wisdom" teacher who can make even horror shine out
with the revelation—that is the kind of dangerous pseudo-spir-
itual rubbish that lets the criminal among the gurus get away
with anything—even pedophilia and murder, as in certain recent
cases. What Meera revealed by her initial actions and the manip-
ulations that followed on them is exactly what the Mother that
she pretends to incarnate *is not*. Despite herself—and such is
the wit of the Mother—the one who is faking the Mother serves
her great purpose because she exposes to anyone who has the
courage to look into this abyss exactly what the Mother is not
and could never be, although for the purpose of the game the
Mother is of course appearing as Meera, just as she is also

appearing as Castro and Ceaucescu and all the other criminals who keep the "plot" going.

The Divine Mother is not homophobic for a start; she would never under any circumstance work to destroy the true and deep love that exists between two beings of any gender; she is not anti-sexual because she knows that tantra truly pursued can illumine the whole ground of ordinary life. She does not need houses and mansions and jewels and a corrupt mystique of avatarhood, and lies and occult powers and elites and core-groups, and lies and more lies. Meera is doing the whole spiritual world a great favor if only we can be brave enough to accept it: she is playing the *shadow*-Mother, the negative projection of the Mother; not the real divine Kali, but the fake human destructive Kali-shadow. And in doing so, ruthlessly (but also badly because so obviously cynically and self-contradictorily), Meera has given me a definitive education—without meaning to—in what the Divine Mother is now trying to reveal. What a terrible marvelous joke! And as I grow daily through the grace of the Mother in the beauties and joys of the direct child-relationship with her—inspired and helped at every stage by my brothers and sisters in her—the hollowness of the guru-game becomes ever more comically evident to me, and the possibilities that arise when we move beyond its temptations and false satisfactions ever more immense.

What the wisdom of the sacred feminine has also revealed to me in this crisis is that to go forward I have to dissolve in myself all the panic, fear, need, hunger for power, and narcissistic longing for sensations, bliss, and experiences that kept me and keeps others hooked on a magician like Meera. As long as the shadow of these different weaknesses are in me I will either be a prey to the kind of slavery I was in for fifteen years, or worse, unconsciously open to *repeating* them in another situation, to play the "anti-guru guru," for example, which would be a defeat as well as very boring indeed, and not just for me! By making me face up to and analyze the things in me which linked me subconsciously to her and enabled her to manipulate me at every level, even to appropriate the partial awakening I had through the real Mother's grace as *her* working, this catastrophe has helped me, at long last, to *begin* to begin to become a real authentic child of the Mother, of the One who is everywhere and in everyone and everything. This I now see is wild, marvelous grace and I will spend the rest of my life trying to learn and increasingly embody its lessons.

*How does this experience of Meera and your greater awareness of the direct mystical teaching of the Mother, through the Tao, for instance, change your understanding of enlightenment?*

What I am now beginning to understand—and I think the deepest and wisest teachings of all the traditions confirm this—is that "enlightenment" is not, even in the most subtle sense, a static state or achievement. Anyone who claims to be enlightened shows *by that very act* that he or she *cannot* be enlightened, because to enter the real enlightenment-field, the love-field of the Mother, is to enter a mystery of growth and expansion without end and therefore beyond any definition. The only beings who can really negotiate this field are like Ramakrishna or Lao Tzu: "old children" who are too lost in joy and humor and bliss to care about any kind of power. Anyone awake to the Mother in this field needs nothing, nothing at all, except to do good helpful work and keep on listening to and loving others and life. Any attempt to *use* any of the stages of this awakening freezes the growth of the adept. Most gurus are not in any way free from the system of greed and power they claim to transcend; they are trapped at the highest occult levels of it, condemned to a pointless game of manipulation whose strings are not seen by those who have not attained the *siddhis* necessary to see them. The divine child does not need followers or dogmas or money or ashrams, or even to be loved and appreciated by others, because he or she knows by thousands of daily signs and ordinary miracles that he or she is loved directly by the Mother of the Universe. And so he or she is free, free especially

of the need to *say* they are free or use the shining of that freedom to attract and enslave others.

When I say he or she is free, I mean of course that he or she
is *increasingly* free, because what I am understanding is that
freedom, like the divine love of which it is the direct emanation,
is infinite. As we grow in the Mother we grow more free and
playful and gentle, and if we are really growing in her, not just
pretending to be, we shed more and more masks and all the
consolations and privileges of *any* kind of status. This is what
the Taoists understood with such anarchic humor; returning to
what Lao Tzu calls the "uncarved block" is not something that
you could possibly "exploit" or would even want to. Having
the Mother, you already have everything. Having the Mother,
and knowing and loving her more and more in the ground of
ordinary life—recognizing and saluting her there at every
moment—frees you to live and be just what you are, without
artificiality or pretense or any need for recognition. This glorious freedom is what the Tao is always holding out to us, if only
we can love and work hard enough to dissolve in ourselves all
the barriers that prevent our true Tao-nature from shining out.

Gurus claim, of course, to be in this state. But their claiming of it exposes comically their exclusion from it, and the
actions that always follow on such a false claim reveal to anyone clear-eyed enough that they must be lying. Would an "old
child" need organizations, donations, the whole circus-appa-
ratus of masterhood, let alone to lie and manipulate and rewrite
history and keep secret bank accounts in nooks and crannies
all over the world? Of course not! Real awakening, I am slowly
discovering, is more humble, more funny and casual, and far
more egalitarian and radical.

*And available to anyone?*

Yes, absolutely! One of the reasons I revere Taoism is its insistence that if you work hard enough you can come into the most
illuminating possible relationship with the Tao. There is no

elaborate and complex stuff in Taoism about past lives and karma and reincarnation, no postponement to other lifetimes of the necessary work of transformation. The Great Alchemy can be done now, in ordinary life, by anyone of any race, religion, gender, sexuality, physical appearance, economic or social status, anyone at all who is prepared really to work hard enough and to look for real and usually very humbling guidance from the mystical texts and fellow travelers along the Way. Taoists love and respect superior adepts and value immensely their wisdom and direction but *never* divinize them. Everyone in the end has to do the great work alone and together with all other beings and the Tao herself.

I find this view at once sobering and exhilarating. All magical consolations are revealed by it as what they are, and that is humiliating—but a gentle challenge that is also an invitation is laid down to *everyone*. As Liu I-Ming says in *Awakening to the Tao,* and I think he is speaking directly here, as the Taoist sages so often are, with the direct uncompromising but generous voice of the Mother:

> If you have the will, study [the Tao] widely, question it closely, ponder it carefully, understand it clearly, carry it out earnestly; multiply the efforts of the ordinary person a hundredfold, and you can actually master this Tao. Even if you are ignorant you will become enlightened, even if you are weak you will become strong—no one who has done this has ever failed to reach the realm of profound attainment of self-realization.[16]

It seems to me that the Mother is saying to us now, uncompromisingly and generously: "You are now grown up enough to leave behind all the props and dogmas and face me directly and enter into my realm directly. I will give you every grace and help and my light is always streaming toward you at every moment to help you. *Now do the real humble no-nonsense work* on every level!"

Without hundreds of thousands, perhaps millions of us

accepting this advice and taking up the challenge of direct empowerment, I do not believe the planet can survive. All the other ways are obviously failing us, but in this massive and heartbreaking failure an entirely fresh path is opening—and it leads directly to the freedom of all beings, the claiming by all beings of their inherent divinity, and the enactment of that divinity in love-in-action in every arena of the world. This, I am convinced, is the revolution of the Mother.

*It is becoming clear to me that the path of the Mother is simultaneously both transcendent and immanent, that it is, as the Taoists say, a mysterious balance between the two. Could you comment on this?*

The Mother is asking us to see the transcendent in the immanent and the immanent in the transcendent, to know the timeless in time and live time in the timeless, to love the spirit in the body and the body in the spirit, to be, as the Taoists would say, "companions of heaven and companions of earth together," and so be whole, be her.

A meditation of Liu I-Ming puts this mysterious balance perfectly:

> The body of heaven is extremely high. Open, round, immeasurable, it is boundlessly vast. Covering everything, containing everything, it produces myriad beings without presuming on its virtue, it bestows blessings on myriad beings without exception or reward....
>
> The earth is very thick. Lowly, above all else, it bears everything and nurtures all beings. It can bear even the weight of the great mountains, and it can endure even the erosive force of great waters....
>
> What I realize as I realize this is the Tao of emulating heaven and earth.

Liu I-Ming goes on to explain what he means, in words whose simple but hard-to-enact wisdom are timeless:

If people can be open-minded and magnanimous, be receptive to all, take pity on the old and the poor, assist those in
peril and rescue those in trouble, give of themselves without seeking reward, never bear grudges, look upon others
and self impartially, and realize all as one, then people can
be companions of heaven.

If people can be flexible and yielding, humble, with self-
control, entirely free of all agitation, cleared of all volatility,
not angered by criticism, ignoring insult, docilely accepting
all hardships, illnesses, and natural disasters, utterly without anxiety or resentment when faced with danger or adver-
sity, then people can be companions of earth.

Liu I-Ming sums up this balance in this way:

With the nobility of heaven and the humility of earth, one
joins in with the attributes of heaven and earth and extends
to eternity with them.[17]

It is precisely this sublime and practical balance of "nobility" with "humility" that is, I believe, the wisdom of the sacred
feminine, of the Mother. Both of what Ken Wilber calls the
"Ascending" and "Descending" mystical philosophies betray
her mystery—the former by their emphasis on transcendence,
the latter by their over-insistence on immanence, on *this* world.
Many of those who claim to be worshipping the Mother at the
moment are worshipping either, as I have said, a "Jehovah in
drag," a purely transcendent Mother-dictator beyond the universe, an idealist projection; or are worshipping the Mother as
"Nature" or "Life" without her transcendent qualities and
powers. It is the fusion of *both* of these ways of worship that
will produce the real path to the Mother and the real revolution of the Mother. The revelation of her transcendent glory
will constantly illumine that of her immanence, and the revelation of her presence in immanence, ground, earth, will help
embody her transcendent powers and laws. This is how the
Mother's reign of love on earth will be brought about.

*You said in your exploration of Mahayana Buddhism that it is
essential now to combine the "hierarchical" knowledge of the
various stages of mystical awakening which the mystical religious traditions have given us with a new radical democratic
form of transmission. Do you find such a balance in Taoism?*

To lose the brilliant and exacting precision of the mystical traditions and their knowledge of the various stages of mystical
growth (with their attendant dangers) would be disastrous.
There are no shortcuts to her and to be "aware" of the Mother
actually, to *see* her light and *know* it saturating and illuminating everything, real work and discipline have to be undertaken.
Yet if these are undergone in what I see as an outmoded guru
system, the full simplicity and impact and egalitarian potential
of awakening will be diffused and the sacred energy that a massive world-awakening could release will be swerved from its
true goal of fighting to preserve the planet and establish justice.

In Taoism I see a real and valuable attempt to combine "hierarchy" and "democracy," to combine the most scrupulous possible understanding of the difficulty of authentic transformation
in the Tao with an opening of the secrets of that transformation to anyone willing to work for it, not in ashrams or monasteries but in the ground of ordinary life. Many of the greatest
Taoist sages were bums or cooks or candlestickmakers, not
priests or "masters," and they relished their relaxed status with
a joy almost as mischievous as that of the Mother's. The Mother,
as anyone who is beginning to know her knows, delights in
overturning all worldly and mental categories and privileges.

One of the constant figures of fun in Taoist texts is the
"Sage," usually poor old Confucius, so preoccupied with his
own "enlightenment" and dogmas that he sees and knows nothing real and lives in the name of "wisdom" nothing but vanity. Often he is woken up by some cook or itinerant hunchback
or sometimes even—Heavens!—a *woman!* Taoists know that
the wisdom of the Tao is everywhere and often flashes to us in
the most anarchic ways and from the unlikeliest of places and

people. Alertness is all. The Mother can and does teach directly in any situation.

What you need to know next may jump at you from a road sign or advertisement or be sung to you over a car radio or shouted after you by a drunk in the street or told to you in a joke by a three-year-old child. Human categories of "sacred" and "profane," "righteous" and "unrighteous," "evolved" and "unevolved" distort mystic reality, *her* reality, which is infinitely more polymorphous, comic, forgiving, nonelitist and all-embracing than anything the human intellect could ever imagine, or want to, because it is too simple and accessible at all times to anyone willing to open to see it.

*Has your study and absorption of the Taoist mystics deepened or extended your inner knowledge of tantra?*

Yes. The Taoist mystics, like the Mahayana and Hindu tantrics, make it clear that sexual tantra is very much more than a physical or emotional path; the whole of life and the whole of being are involved and the inner fusion of "masculine" and "feminine" to birth the inner divine child is the goal. As Schipper writes in his magisterial *The Taoist Body*:

> [The] Inner Alchemy [of Tao] puts sex at the center of its practice, just as it locates sex in the very center of the body.... There, Fire from the heart (represented by a young girl, i.e. *yin* being born from *yang*) and Water from the kidneys (a boy, *yang* born from extreme *yin*) meet. Sex is no longer concentrated, or confined, to the genital organs, nor is it [only] a matter of the heart or of the mind; it is *united at the Center* and from this Center it radiates and spreads through the whole body. Love thus engages the body as a whole, merging all the organs and all the functions.... All the faculties of the senses: our eyes, nose, breasts, hands, come together in total participation.[18]

Like all practitioners of the holy and transforming tantra

that is one of the supreme gifts of the Mother to humanity, the Taoists know that it demands a discipline every bit as exacting and precise as the most ascetic practice—the discipline of purification of the whole nervous system, body, and emotional past so as to clear all obstacles between the two practitioners, and the disciplines thereafter of the greatest mutual compassion, reverence, honor, and divine respect. Tantra mirrors in the ecstatic relationship between two beings the dance of yin and yang in the Tao, and is in the highest and deepest sense the "making pregnant" of each other by the other through the inner fusion of yin and yang, feminine and masculine, that takes place in both, "embodying the soul and ensouling the body," and so in gradual miraculous stages brings both beings into conscious unity simultaneously with each other, their own deepest ground, and the ground of all things.

Degraded or superficial visions of tantra stress merely sexual excitement, which is only a part of the real tantra. The aim of the real tantra is to take the "heat" of sexual ecstasy, the Shakti, and illuminate the whole of life through it, thereby pacifying the negative emotions and bringing both beings into a more and more tender daily harmony, a more stable and rich and exquisite mutual honoring and poise that reveals itself as a *divine* poise and honoring, a mirroring in human life of the secret divine life of the Tao, of what St. John of the Cross called "the tenderness of the Life of God."

It can never be emphasized too strongly—and the Taoist masters as well as the Mahayana and Hindu yogis stress this again and again—that for the Great Alchemy to succeed, *fidelity* is the law, the key. The vessel must be sealed to create the crucible in which both beings can slowly be "cooked" and made tender enough to be eaten by the Tao. Fidelity is the sealing of the vessel. This is why this tantric alchemy was usually practiced by Taoists only in married couples, in couples where both people were consciously on a spiritual path and devoted and faithful to each other. The kind of acute delicacy and sensitivity on every level simultaneously that has to be working continually for the tantra to be effective is simply not possible without absolute trust, and such a trust can only be engendered by respect and total fidelity. Schipper again:

> These are the two stages of Keeping the One: the preliminary stage and the union through intercourse. The first stage demands strict discipline and regularization, a point by point harmonizing, as though a harp with ten thousand strings were being tuned. Then follows the playing, a flood of sounds which sweep us like a wave, a moment of utter passion, an extreme tension that comes apart in abandon, a fall toward the origin of things.[19]

And after that "fall toward the origin of things," there comes the work of "mixing" that glimpse of Origin and the sweet deep wild rich heat that radiates from it into the ground of ordinary living so they can go on acting there at ever-increasing depths of compassion and humor. Then the whole of life begins to be set in all its dimensions to the music of human divine love.

I would like to say one more thing that my meditation on Taoism, and on the richness of the yin and yang symbolism in Taoism in particular, have given me. What I am understanding is that the authentic tantric partners form together the yin-yang symbol, a circle, an egg, if you like, of divine human completion. Put simply, both people love both the yin and the yang in the other, both the "masculine" and the "feminine," equally and totally. In my love for Eryk, I love him both as a "man" *and* as a "woman" and he loves me with the full passion of his masculine and feminine sides. The tantric awakening we are beginning to live takes place as a dance of yin and yang at very level and in every dimension. The fact that our masculine and feminine sides mesh so completely together allows our *inner* masculine and feminine to start to mesh deeply within us and to begin to heal past agony, rejection, abuse, and chronic imbalance, and through that healing to effect what I can only describe as a "mutual birth into the Tao."

I am talking about this here because I believe this tantric

awakening is part of the revolution of the Mother, an essential part of the revolution to come. Any couple—heterosexual or homosexual—who take vows to realize this balance of yin and yang within themselves through love in her, and protects those vows with fidelity and respect, will be slowly awakened in their ordinary lives to the highest, wildest, and sweetest truths of the divine presence. This will bring the springtime of love to the human race. Consciously or unconsciously, nearly all the religious and mystical systems now in place are trying to prevent this springtime, for the obvious reason that when it greens the earth, the authority of the ayatollahs and popes and gurus and experts and politicians will be rubbled.

A human race released into divine normality will no longer need to be fed dogmas and policed by various subtle forms of fear; everyone will be staring into the smiling face of the Mother-in-Life directly, individually and together. The whole patriarchal system is rooted in fear, denial, and degradation of the feminine. A tantric awakening could only take place through a complete worship of the feminine in life, a total honoring of women and a freeing all beings from any traces of homophobia. Once this wild luminous secret—the secret of the possibility of this *darshan* in ordinary life—really gets out and is begun to be lived and believed and spread between human beings, the patriarchy will begin to crumble, because all its old separations and shibboleths and all its games of power will be unmasked as corrupt, dangerous, cruel, and above all—and this is the Mother's best joke—*unnecessary*.

The last thing the patriarchy could now afford is widespread divine practice of heterosexual and homosexual tantra. Heterosexual tantra would necessitate a revalorization of women at every level—because it simply cannot be practiced without women being given *full* respect and autonomy which would have to stretch into all political and economic arenas as well. Heterosexual tantra would also mean, obviously, the transformation of men, who in meeting and honoring their feminine side in their female partner would also be meeting and honoring the feminine side in *themselves* and so beginning the great mystic transformation spoken of in the Tao when Lao Tzu says "know the male but keep to the female." This would in the end result in a much richer, more whole, both more adult and more childlike male whose whole being would be sensitized and therefore far more aware of what is happening in the world and far more empowered at every level to do something about it. Homosexual tantra would heal gay and lesbian communities, reveal to others everywhere the grandeur and dignity of true homosexual passion and its spiritual power and nobility, and open up to all beings vital new information and energy. Who knows what tribes of linked sacred couples—hetero- and homosexual—could accomplish with the divine knowledge, strength, and passion acquired in their tantric practice? A wholly new kind of activism could emerge from such linked unions and from the enactment of their divine health in reality.

The Mother is now releasing the necessary secret information to the whole of humanity about how tantra can and should be practiced. But just as it is important when developing the new democratic forms of spiritual transmission not to abandon the precise understanding of the stages of mystical growth inherited from the mystical traditions, so it is essential in the coming worldwide dissemination of the truths of tantra to retain what the secret tantric yogis of all traditions know: that tantra has *laws,* real and severe laws which have to be honored for the alchemy to work. Breaking them not only makes transformation impossible; it can actually endanger both people in every way. To betray the person with whom you are taking the tantric journey is, as all the traditions warn us, worse than murder. "Normal" murder kills the body; betrayal in such a relationship can kill the whole being.

All the healing freedoms that the Mother is now offering and making available to humanity in our present state of crisis demand that we all grow up as fast as possible to honor their terms. If we want to take the direct path into her we will have to be *more* disciplined, more knowledgeable, and more humble than on any other path; if we want to practice tantra, we must honor the splendid rigor of its laws. In this the Mother is not repeating the repression of earlier traditions in a new form. She is at one and the same time freeing us and making us completely responsible for—and aware of—the price of awareness and discrimination and continuing humility that keeps that freedom authentically divine and authentically transformatory.

## Notes

1. Thomas Cleary, Preface to Liu I-Ming, *Awakening to the Tao* (Boston: Shambhala Publications, 1988), p. xi.

2. Liu I-Ming, *Awakening to the Tao*, pp. 75–76.

3. *Chuang Tzu: Basic Writings*. Translated by Burton Watson (New York: Columbia University Press, 1964), pp. 78–79.

4. *Chuang Tzu: Basic Writings*, pp. 46–47.

5. *Chuang Tzu: Basic Writings*, pp. 94–95.

6. Kristofer Schipper, *The Taoist Body*. Translated by Karen C. Duval (Berkeley, California: University of California Press, 1993), p. 128.

7. Schipper, *The Taoist Body*, p. 129.

8. Quoted in Schipper, *The Taoist Body*, p. 138.

9. Quoted in Schipper, *The Taoist Body*, p. 149.

10. Quoted in Schipper, *The Taoist Body*, pp. 130, 131.

11. Quoted in Schipper, *The Taoist Body*.

12. Loy Ching-yuen, *The Book of the Heart: Embracing the Tao*. Translated by Trevor Carolan and Bella Chen. (Boston: Shambhala Publications, 1990), p. 47.

13. Loy Ching-yuen, *The Book of the Heart*, p. 42.

14. Alan Watts, *Tao: The Watercourse Way* (New York: Pantheon Books, 1975), pp. 75–76.

15. Anne Baring and Jules Cashford, *The Myth of the Goddess: Evolution of an Image* (New York: Viking Press, 1991), pp. 674–675.

16. Liu I-Ming, *Awakening to the Tao*, p. 78.

17. Liu I-Ming, *Awakening to the Tao*, pp. 3–4.

18. Schipper, *The Taoist Body*, p. 154.

19. Schipper, *The Taoist Body*, p. 155.

# Chapter Ten

# Mary Our Mother

*Remember, O Most Holy Virgin, that it never was heard in any age that anyone turning to your protection was abandoned.*
—Bernard of Clairvaux

*The greatest sin is to rebel against the Motherhood of God, and to refuse to recognize me as the Mother of all human beings.*
—The Virgin to the Children at Fatima

*He who finds Mary finds every good.*—Raymond Jordano

*God is our father, and above all God is our Mother.*
—John Paul I

*When He named Mary ... He desired His heart might leave His chest. For He declared that this sweetest of names was like a honeycomb melting in the inmost depth of His soul.*
—Henry Suso

IN THE LATE AUTUMN OF 1993, Eryk and I were staying in a hotel in Mahabalipuram, South India, by the sea. Late one afternoon, Eryk came in smiling (he had been on a visit to the town) and put a large brown paper parcel by me on the bed where I had been resting, nursing my bad back. "Open it now, I can't wait," he said. I did so, as a deepening silence filled the room. What I discovered in the parcel was a foot-high statue of the Virgin holding the young Jesus, made by a local craftsman out of light-gold mango wood. The Virgin is carved as a tender, strong, big-hipped country woman in a simple sari. She has a face at once withdrawn and forceful, the face of a woman who understands and endures without false sentiment.

As I sat gazing at the simplicity and strength of the statue, Eryk told me a story that he had never told me before. "You know," he said, "that I have an old friend in Belgium who saw the Virgin in one of her apparitions there in the Thirties." I nodded. "Well," he said, "one day I was standing with him in the schoolyard where she had appeared in the tree, and my friend said 'I haven't told many people this, and you won't find it in the Vatican records of what the Virgin said to us. On the second day, when we saw the woman with light whiter and fiercer than summer lightning around her in the tree, I, as the one boy, was urged by the two girls to go forward and ask her who she was. As you can imagine, I was trembling. I summoned up all my courage and asked haltingly, remembering my catechism, "Are you the Immaculate Conception?" The woman smiled and said, "Call me by whatever name you want—I am your Mother."'"

Light from the open door to the beach had fallen on the carving, making it glow a ripe, soft gold, like the sands of the Mahabalipuram seashore. Tears came to my eyes. "You know," I said, "She looks here very much like the first Indian nurse I had as a child, a big warm Indian woman who cheated at 'Snakes and Ladders' and whom I loved." "What was her name?" Eryk asked. "Mary," I said. "She was the cook's wife and a Catholic from Kerala."

Eryk and I sat a long time watching the late sun first glow and then fade on the statue. My tears continued to fall quietly. So much had suddenly become clear.

Late that night I wrote at length in my notebook:

"I am your Mother" the woman in the tree said to the child. And that is who the Virgin is, the Mother, *the* Divine Mother, the *full* Divine Mother.... I look at her statue that Eryk had made for me here in the place where I have always been "taken forward" by the Mother, and all the faces of *all* the Mothers are in the strong face of the country woman with a sari around her head. Tara is there, so are Durga and Saraswati and Kali. So are Kwan-Yin and Isis. And so are the Aborigine and Kogi and Hopi mothers, the mothers of Polynesia and South America. The woman of the statue could be a Bulgarian peasant, or Caucasian, or from Africa or Malaya. Mary is the Mother, all human mothers, and all Divine Mothers. How could I not have *seen* it before?

I went on:

Just look at this statue and you know that the "myths" about Mary's passivity and obsessive "purity" *must* be wrong, a convenient patriarchal fiction, a way of keeping corralled the great power of the divine truth invested in her. This Mary is passionate, strong, ripely sensual, a full and complete woman like the first early Byzantine or Romanesque Virgins. Her "purity" is the innate purity of great dignity and love and has nothing whatever to do with *physical* virginity. She is the Universal Mother, the mother of all beings, the mother especially of nature and the earth, a mother made from the sweetest wood of all, the wood of my childhood in India.

And yet there is a difference, a major and marvelous difference between this revelation of the Mother and all the others and until today I hadn't really grasped how powerful that difference is. Durga, Kali, Saraswati are divine beings and emanations, powers of light; Tara is a bodhisattva whose effectiveness breaks all barriers of time and space; but Mary is a *woman*, a simple strong woman of the poor. Mary *lived on earth*. Mary suffered every conceivable difficulty and drawback *here on earth*. There is no suffering she does not know, no humiliation she hasn't endured. She is the most human, most poignant, most moving face of the Mother because she has *lived* here and knows everything about the hardship and injustice and agony and heartbreak and folly of human life. Anything we suffer she understands. She suffers with us, in us, as us. Any separation between her and us is only our ignorance, our fear, the shadow we cast on ourselves through despair.

And something else becomes clear as I sit up tonight looking at the statue by candlelight as Eryk sleeps. This statue is of a woman who stands firmly on the earth and who loves the earth and who honors the beauty and sacredness of life in all its aspects and who protects innocence and beauty. This statue is of a woman who is always strong and who can be fierce, of a woman who both stands for and asks for justice and equality and real naked, simple compassion; who says, as Christ says in his last words in St. John's Gospel: "Feed my sheep, feed my lambs." For the first time I really understand the Magnificat tonight and see that it is not the sweet interior prayer that we were always taught to believe it was. It is a call for social transformation, the ending of injustice, an end to poverty, the transforming of *this* world into a living mirror of God's beauty and justice and love.

"He hath showed strength with His arm; He hath scattered the proud in the imagination of their hearts. He hath put down the mighty from their seats, and exalted them of low degree." Mary is the first Christian revolutionary. She remains a permanent calm revolutionary of love, of active love.

Moved by what I was discovering, I walked out into the moonlit night and stood by the sea. The sea itself seemed to be saying her name. I returned and wrote:

I realize that *all* the powers of the Mothers, of Tara, Durga, Kali, are in Mary. She has Tara's sublime tenderness; Durga's inaccessible silent calm force; the grandeur and *terribilta* of Kali. But Mary is also a woman, a poor woman and a human mother. In her the full path of the sacred feminine is lived. In her we have a complete image of the Divine Mother, an image at once transcendent *and* immanent, otherworldly and this-worldly, at once mystical *and* political and practical.

In Mary the Divine Mother comes to earth and lives on earth and lives the passionate, strong, serious, simple, and transforming life that shows us all how to live. Mary is the bridge between heaven and earth, between the human and the divine worlds, between human and divine justice.

What more important task could there be for anyone on a journey into the Mother than to come and love Mary, to see her in her *full* power, outside the narrowing definitions of those myths and dogmas that have seemed to worship her but have really limited and constrained her? What more important restoration could there be than the restoration of Mary to her full truth and power and glory and passion for justice? For in restoring Mary to her full mystical and political truth we would also be restoring the sacred feminine to its full intensity. In allowing the complete mystical and practical truth of Mary to emerge in our minds and hearts we would be revivifying the whole Christian tradition, and re-envisioning the entire vision of Christ, because seeing Mary as the Divine Mother would help us to see Christ too as every much the son of the Divine Mother as the Divine Father. Seeing that would release Christianity from its patriarchal stranglehold and restore the mystical purity of its passion for fraternity and sorority, for equality and social justice and service.

Mary is the hidden force and secret of Christianity, and until her force—the force of the Divine Mother—is revealed and uncovered in the Christian story its whole truth cannot be present. Just as Christ is the Son of God, Mary is the Daughter of God; just as Christ is also one with the Holy Spirit, so is Mary; Mary is in union with the Source just as Christ is. The current all-male model of the Trinity is absurd. The sacred feminine has to be seen as penetrating *all* aspects of the Trinity.

One reward of the long journey into Eastern mysticism

and into all the different traditions of the Mother that I have
taken is that it makes very clear what the truth of the Trinity is: the Source must be feminine as well as masculine (as
well as beyond both). The Spirit is both feminine and masculine; and in fact the Spirit was worshiped as feminine by
the early mystics. It makes no sense to have only a *Son* of
God especially when there is a Daughter crucial to the story.
Mary is the force of the Mother-aspect of God made manifest in time, and as such is one with the Trinity in all its
aspects, when they are expanded, as they must be, to include
the sacred feminine at every level and in every dimension.

I felt my understanding becoming clearer and clearer:

The Catholic and Orthodox traditions may claim to adore
Mary but until the full glory of her presence is recognized
that adoration is really a golden prison, a way of pretending to hallow Mary while ensuring that the full force of the
feminine power streaming through her to the world is dampened and restrained, especially in its aspects of justice and
service and love of the poor. As long as Mary is "dampened," Christ is also, because if the full majesty and urgency
of her appeal for justice is unheard, the full majesty and
urgency of Christ's teaching about the Kingdom and of the
necessity of making *this* world a mirror of God's justice and
of realizing the laws of love *here* will also go conveniently
ignored. The Son will come back only when the Mother is
fully present; the full wildness of Christ will only return
when the full strength of his Mother and the full passion of
her hunger for change is acknowledged.

If there is a "second coming of Christ" in the hearts of
humankind—and how can the West be transformed without it?—it will come hand-in-hand with the return of the
Mother. It is Mary the Mother who gave us Christ, who
bore him and still bears him in the soul of the heart and who
can bear him again in the human heart. The fundamental
truths of Christ's teaching—about the futility of all forms

of power, about charity and humility and purity of heart and service to all beings—are the truths of the Mother, and when she is recognized again, they too will be.

I finished writing and looked across at the statue of Mary lit now by candlelight. This time I noticed her hands—big, knobbly gardener's hands, not prissy at all, the hands of a woman who cooks and digs and washes clothes. And I remembered the hands of the Mary who had loved me as a child, as they ground *marsala* on the roof, as they dressed me for school, pulling my shirt over my head and tying my shoelaces and cramming scrambled egg sandwiches into my knapsack. I could see my Mary now—with her betel juice-stained grin, the patches under her arms where she sweat, her screams when I rolled over onto her purposely in the night. "Call me by whatever name you want— I am your Mother." I felt my heart beating very fast, as if on the threshold of a mystery. "I am being given back Mary," I wrote in large, shaky letters in my notebook. "I am being given back Mary where I first found her—in India—and I am being given her back at a time when I can at last see who she is."

The words I wrote that night were more prophetic than I could then know. The next months were to bring me to Mary in a way I had never anticipated. When at the end of December 1993 Meera asked me to leave Eryk and to write a book about how her force had transformed me into a heterosexual, she revealed to me that she could not possibly be the Divine Mother on earth as I had believed her to be for fifteen years. The Divine Mother could not be homophobic and could not be destructive of real love and could not want to assert her power at the expense of the ruin of two beings. In the terrible despair and desperation that Eryk and I both felt in the last days of December in Germany, one thing became clear to me: We had to leave Thalheim as soon as possible and we had to go to be with Mary. I said to Eryk on New Year's Eve, "We have to go to the real Mother now and ask for her protection. Let's leave in two days and go to Beauraing and Banneux."[1]

I knew—and I did not know how or why I knew so certainly—that our best hope of surviving the horror of what had
happened to us was to put ourselves under Mary's truth, to
turn to her compassion and strength. The anguish that we were
both living through made it seem inevitable that we should turn
to the one who had known all pain and who had also suffered
rejection and humiliation. In my last nights at Thalheim, I kept
seeing the face of the statue Eryk had given me, alternating with
the face of my old nurse Mary, and kept hearing in my heart's
ear the words: "It is time to come home now. It is time to come
home. I am your Mother, your true Mother. It was I who was
initiating you all along and it was I who you were loving in
Meera, projecting onto Meera. It was I who you were loving
through her. Now the projection has been ended, the idol of
me has been destroyed. Come and see me as I am."

We drove first to Banneux and then to Beauraing in savage
winter rain under glowering skies. I found myself for the first
time praying to Mary with my whole being. I remembered an
old Jesuit priest I had met in Ephesus saying to me, "With Mary,
just speak directly and simply. Just *speak* to her. She is your
mother." I felt too shattered to be anything but direct. I prayed:
"Help us. Save us. Help us. Save us," for hours and hours. And
I prayed: "Show me the *real* Divine Mother. Show me the *real*
Mother." And I prayed: "Forgive me. Forgive me for not seeing. Forgive me my vanity, my ignorance." For I remembered
on that journey that the very first time I had knelt to Meera I
had seen in my mind's eye the Velazquez painting of Mary as
Queen of Heaven (the one in the National Gallery in London),
and had heard the words "I am the Queen of Heaven" in several languages. At the time I had taken that as a sign of Meera's
greatness; now I realized it had been a *warning*, one that I had
not only ignored but totally misinterpreted, going on to become
the virtual creator of what I now was starting to see as a dangerous cult. I remembered too that in the year of partial awakening I had celebrated in *Hidden Journey,* I had spent a month
in Montreal. One morning I had been reading about Mary's

appearances in Medjugorje and a white light filled the kitchen where I was sitting and I felt her presence. I planned to write about it in the book but had cut it at the last moment, ostensibly not to "offend the Catholics," but I now saw it was because I had again not heard the message I was being sent.

The only thing that kept me from feeling paralyzed with guilt was the certainty that the Mother was unconditional love. Whatever I had done, or ignored, or created, or allowed, I could still and would always be her child. I remembered another thing the old Jesuit in Ephesus had told me: "Mary never refuses anyone. She is everyone's first and last resort. If you were to distill the love from everyone's heart into one heart, that heart would only be a thousandth as loving as hers."

I am glad we arrived in Banneux and Beauraing in the rain. They are not glamorous places and to see them in the cold winter light made them even more real. Eryk said, "Mary rarely appears in wonderful places but nearly always in the middle of the banal to transfigure it." Weatherbeaten middle-aged women and men in anoraks stood silently in the small chapel in Banneux gazing up into the face of the statue of Mary. They were not New Age seekers or crystal gazers or channelers; they were ordinary people come to commune with their Mother, and the downbeat sublimity of their simplicity and faith, and the intimacy of the way they looked at her, shook me. "How simple it is," I kept saying to myself, "How simple the real contact with her is!"

When we arrived at the schoolyard in Beauraing where the tree in which Mary appeared still stands (now with its beautiful white statue), the rain was coming down hard and we were alone, alone with her. Eryk and I stood in the rain before her and wordlessly gave ourselves over to her and into her hands. Peace and joy filled both of us, and an astonishing lightness. Eryk and I went into the chapel by the side of the yard. He went up to the altar, bowed, and removed two white roses from the vase in front of Mary. He kept one for himself and handed one to me. "Now we wear *her* rose," he said. "And she is our Mother now and our love is in her protection." As he said those words, a great wave of joy swept me and I knew they were real, a real message from her to us through him. Whatever the Catholic Church might have to say about homosexuality, I knew then that the Mother of all beings cares only about the truth of love, and that the Mother who saw her own son dismembered by the cruelty of prejudice has a special love for all those who are lonely or oppressed or in danger. I went out again into the rain and knelt to Our Lady of Beauraing and her extended open arms and her glowing gold sacred heart and said, over and over, "Bring me to your truth. I am your child now."

The next day Eryk and I were back in Paris and he took me immediately to the chapel in the Rue du Bac where Mary appeared to Catherine Labouré in the 1830s. A week later we had gone on pilgrimage to Bruges to worship the Madonna of Michelangelo; two weeks later we were praying at the shrine of the Black Madonna in Chartres. The moment we arrived back in San Francisco in February we went to the Mission and worshiped Mary there, day after day. Our lives became a continual meditation on and prayer to her. She gave us many astonishing signs that she was with us. When Meera started to lie about what had happened and disciples who were with us in Thalheim either betrayed us or cultivated a sudden "amnesia" and our lives were plunged into a storm of evil, we clung to Mary with all our hearts and minds knowing that adoration of her was our only protection. I started to read as many of the old Marian mystics as I could—Bernard of Clairvaux, Alphonsus de Liguori, the Curé d'Ars, Louis-Marie Grignion de Montfort—finding in their devotional insights support and elaboration of everything I had begun to glimpse and live. "With whom can we compare you, O Mother of grace and beauty," writes St. Bernard. "You are the paradise of God. From you springs the fountain of living water that irrigates the whole earth."

In the middle of March, I had a powerful dream in which it was made clear to me that new knowledge about the Mother was being given to me. At the beginning of the dream, I was at the entrance of a Baroque church; I met two suave young Jesuits and asked them, "Can you show me the Mother?" They looked amused at this and said, "Oh, you mean the old BVM?" I nodded and they took me on a tour of all the statues of Mary— very gilt- and angel-ridden—that they had. They were polite and so was I, but I felt embarrassed because every time I looked at one of the statues all I could see was a heap of dirt. I heard an inner voice say: "The Mother has left the Church." Eventually the two Jesuits and I parted and I found myself in a field where there was a huge purple, red, and yellow billowing circus tent, very much like the *shamayanas* of my Indian childhood. I heard chanting and mantras and suddenly felt excited. I thought, "Perhaps here I will find the Mother."

I went in and shuddered. There was Meera in the corner in one of her expensive saris and gold and diamond earrings giving *darshan* while her disciples were actively snarling at the disciples of two other well-known "Mothers," one Indian and one American. The entire atmosphere was cinematic, showy, hysterical, as baroque as the statues in the church I had left. I knew that these imperious, over-dressed women were only *playing* the Mother, and playing her for fame and power and money, and I felt disgusted and full of guilt at the part I had played in bringing people into this charade. I heard the words, spoken gently but sternly: "How could the real Mother wear diamonds when half the world is starving? How could the real Mother want adoration and cars and houses and devotees? If the Mother *were* in a body on earth, wouldn't she be serving the poor and the starving and not surrounding herself with bankers and rock stars?" The voice went on and on, detailing all the ways in which the figures in front of me were desecrating the compassion and passion for justice and equality of the authentic Mother. Eventually I could stand it no longer and ran out of the tent, sweating and in great pain and confusion.

I ran through the streets of what appeared to be a deserted town and came at last to a barren plain with a small hill in the center of it and a small two-room farmhouse near it. Around the farmhouse was a small ragged field with only a little grass in it and an old donkey who stood flicking the flies off his back with his tail. Suddenly, I felt calm. I had stopped looking for anything or anyone and all I wanted to do was sit down. I found a small rock and as I was about to sit I heard the creak of a door. I looked up. The door of the small farmhouse was opening. There, in the half-light, stood an old haggard peasant woman in black. She stopped and looked at me a long time and until I die I will never forget the intimacy, tenderness, and sober absolute compassion of that look. It was *her*, alone and simple and poor and one with all nature and all beings and an old woman. She lowered her head and walked a little crookedly and unsteadily into the light. She was carrying a pail of water in her right hand and she walked slowly over to the old donkey, to give it a drink. I thought as she held the half-blind face of the donkey to her own and closed her eyes, "Perhaps it was on this donkey that her son rode into Jerusalem." I awoke and wrote down the words that I heard inwardly: *"Know me in my simplicity and awake to my love and my justice."*

In the marvelous early morning that followed the dream I vowed to serve Mary in any way I could and asked to be led forward into her truth. I knew now that it was a truth of the strongest imaginable simplicity and the simplest imaginable love, and of the justice that arises naturally from them both. I knew that in Mary the full Divine Mother was appearing in the humblest and most poignant way imaginable to wake up humanity to where she is—in the naked open heart and the actions streaming from it, in the Sacred Heart and its passion to see the whole of life restored to the truths of love and justice. No other Mother would have such devotional power over me, deeply though I reverence Kali and Durga and Tara, because no other face of the Mother is so completely turned toward humanity, the humanity of this terrible moment of agony and apocalypse, when the whole world needs more than ever the clarity of the good heart and the simple natural response and the helping hand and the mind and heart tuned to the sacred silence of justice—justice for the animals trapped in the burning forests and polluted seas, justice for the poor and the starving, justice and equality and compassion for every kind of being down to the last useless aging donkey as in my dream.

Empowered by the dream, and by everything both Eryk and I were experiencing of the healing and protective power of Mary, I turned more and more deeply to her for help at all times, help and support and inspiration, and meditated more and more constantly on Mary's role and purpose in the great Christian revelation. I came to understand that the reason why I had been on such a long journey into Hinduism and Buddhism and Sufism was to be able now to see Mary's silent and unvoiced majesty. to realize the highest mystical truths hidden in her that for so many Christians was nearly completely obscured by the Church, to recognize her in fact as the full Divine Mother with all her powers, her righteous anger as well as her tenderness, her passion as well as her peace. I realized once and for all that the conventional image of Mary as submissive, passive, and cloyingly sweet was an absurdly partial vision of who she is, one that had little to do with the immense force that I am coming to know in the core of my heart and life.

So, full of this need and fresh vision and passion, I plunged again into the story of Mary, her astonishing story as recorded in the Gospels and by the great Christian mystics and visionaries. I kept clear in my mind everything I had learned about the Mother from my journeys in the other mystical traditions that celebrate her so that I could see her in this one, and very soon I found myself happy and amazed at what I was discovering. Everything becomes so much more clear when you know who Mary is and what she represents—even the hoariest dogmas reveal themselves as imperfect, one-sided stammering attempts to register her greatness.

Take the dogmas of the "immaculate conception" and the "virgin birth," for example. When you really investigate them by the light of mystical love and knowledge, you see that they are attempting to describe in patriarchal language (and in a way that has done immense harm to women, to sexuality, to the body) a real mystery, one of the central mysteries of the presence of the Divine Mother and the creation she is always spinning out of her body of light—her and its perpetual *freshness,* her "virginal" purity, the purity and freshness of her eternal rose garden when seen with the eyes of impassioned, clear, and wondering love. When the eyes of love open in the subtle body through the grace of the Mother and of everything and of everyone she has made, they see the "freshness" Gerard Manley Hopkins speaks of when he writes: "There lives the dearest freshness deep down things."

That "dearest freshness," the hidden, pure, inviolable lifespring in all things, is her. All things appear wet with the source when seen with true love, wet with the light-water of the source, of her. And that is what is meant essentially by Mary's "virginity." As the Mother, Mary's heart and mind are always turned in adoration toward the divine and toward divine reality, and both are always concentrated, always pristine, clear mirrors in which the light of truth can keep flowering. Such "virginity" and the strength it brings (another interpretation of "virgin" — *parthenos* in Greek—is one who can stand alone, one who needs no support) are one with love, and love's deepest source and secret. This virginity has nothing to do with physical purity; the theological obsession with Mary's physical virginity has been a long, sad, disastrous red herring which has separated her from other women, conspired in the general Christian debacle of body-hatred and actually *blocked* the force of Mary's real purity.

When you think about it, such a misinterpretation is not surprising in a church addicted to hierarchy and authority. True "virgin" perception, the insight into the actual nature of things that mystic initiation brings, can be uncomfortable, accurate, scathing, and demanding. The eyes if the real Mother, of the sacred feminine, are lucid and unsentimental as well as loving; their purity is an X-ray that reveals every hypocrisy, every illusion, every authoritarian ploy, every inegalitarian masquerade, every falling-away from truth. This virginity has inherent in it a Kali-like piercing-through of veils and fantasies and games, which the patriarchy could not afford and so muffled and narrowed and tried—consciously and unconsciously—to control by adoration. It is time for the real purity of Mary to be reinstated in every heart, so that every heart can become her throne of wisdom and pillar of justice, so that the living connection between the mystical virginity of perception of the real world and its real sacred relation with action and justice can become evident. As any unbiased reading of the Magnificat makes clear, Mary was on the side of the marginal, the defeated, the scorned, and the poor in a very unmetaphorical sense. The pure eyes of her love saw the misery of the world without any consolation, precisely because they also saw the total holiness of all created things and the plan of divine love that the Father-Mother had willed for the creation since the beginning. Mary wanted the reign of God on earth, just as her son would, and it is the potentially scalding and revolutionary *demand* in this desire that the Church's dogmas have stifled and covered over.

The old version of Mary as passive and submissive is a lie. Look deeply at the story and you see in it a woman of immense strength, surrendered to God but not submissive; humble, patient, tender, infinitely focused on and burning with real love, but never passive. As the French mystic Meubert put it: "This Virgin so tender is the most indomitable of women. There never was a man so full of strength and character as this woman." What immense strength it took to accept Gabriel's message and the long agony she knew being the mother of the chosen one would be; what fortitude and persistent courage it took to live the life that unfolded, a life of wandering, exile, danger, poverty. She had the strength to raise her son in savage circumstances (no sooner was he born than the whole family had to flee massacring soldiers) and she had the strength to let him go when he needed to wander and learn free from her, and she had the strength to accompany him throughout the agony of his death. I see her at the crucifixion not wringing her hands but *witnessing* her son's pain and standing in it, standing at the core of his and her suffering, so that as he writhes in agony and dies she can feed him her peace, her strength, her faith, her never-failing trust. The Curé d'Ars said: "Mary is our Mother twice. She gave birth to humanity twice—once at the Nativity and then again at the foot of the Cross." What she did at the foot of the cross was to help Christ become a mother like her, to become on the terrible childbed of the cross the mother of a new humanity by consenting to being torn apart and allowing himself to die into the darkness out of which the light of the resurrection and of a resurrected humanity was born. She witnessed his suffering and fed him the wisdom she had acquired from the long crucifixion of her life, that subtler crucifixion that she had shared as his mother and as *the* Mother. Christ and she became one in the terrible mystery of the birth on the cross, one in the transforming wisdom of surrender and absolute love for all beings of the Mother, *his* Mother.

This most nonpassive and marvelous and inspiring strong role continues inexorably after Christ's death, resurrection, and ascension. Mary has to remain to become the mother of the early Church and so of all Christians. She has to stay on to suffer more persecution, wandering, exile, poverty, and to be the mystical center of strength, the Tower of Ivory in which the early disciples could find protection and guidance and refreshment. She is in the upper room at Jersualem, the center of the mandala of the disciples, when the Comforter arrives in fire. It was because of Mary's "unspeakable intensity" of appeal and prayer and longing, Leo the Tenth tells us, that the Paraclete came down, that the Holy Ghost came down in tongues of fire in that "upper room" at Pentecost and began its Great Work in the heart and souls of all those who turn to Christ for guidance.

And just as Mary was crucified with Christ, both in subtle terms because of the deeply painful life she had to lead to succor the Revelation and in more obvious ways—through the terrible grief of watching her son defiled, degraded, and dismembered—she also shared in the glory of power of his resurrection, and in a way that clearly reveals her role—the role of the sacred feminine—in the mystery. Christ died on the cross and was reborn in a light-body that appeared to his disciples to signal his eternal conquest over death and the path he had opened for the divine light into the heart of human nature, nature, and matter. It was left to Mary the Mother to extend and deepen and further that path that her son had opened up.

One of the meanings of the Assumption—the taking-up of Mary bodily into heaven—must be that for the twenty-some years after Christ's death Mary remained to integrate more and more completely, more and more steadily, the light with matter, transforming the whole of her being entirely in the process and so earning the human and divine right to take her own body uncorrupted into the divine directly. And to take with it, by radiant implication, the whole of the subtly informed and transformed matter of the universe, a universe whose subtle laws had been forever altered, first by the magnificent fierce love and courage of her son's death, and then by the equally magnificent and persistent lonely courage of her continuing of his light-work, her calling-down of the light into this dimension and this world, into its every corner and nook, down even in the most recalcitrant cells of the body.

What Mary did, in the silence of total love and total witness and in the splendor of total surrender to the spirit, was to *unite* in her own being and body heaven and earth, matter and spirit. It is this ultimate sacred marriage that is celebrated in the myth of Christ welcoming and marrying his mother in heaven. She as the Daughter of God, as the Mother, had completed the work he as the Son had been sent to do. Only the Mother in him could have accepted and endured the appalling terms of the transformation, and only the Mother in her could have accepted and endured the long mysterious work of "marrying" all dimensions between "human" and "divine," "here" and "there." This vast double yoga and divine dance of Mother and Son is the mystical secret of Christianity.

The word "mystical," however, can be misleading because it can suggest an other-worldliness foreign to both Mary and her son, and to the core-truth of the Christian revelation that remains as devastating as ever. This core-truth is that the kingdom of God is *here* and lies all about us and can be seen and known by love—and must be—and then must be *enacted* with the same passion, unwavering intensity, and integrity as Mary and Christ did. All the long gloomy talk about "original sin" and the irredeemable fallenness of the "city of man" serves only to obscure this essential visionary truth and perpetual challenge. The Mother and her son came to show us a revolutionary new way of enacting and witnessing love in action in the world, not simply to alleviate suffering and "render unto Caesar what is Caesar's" but to conspire with the inner will of grace to change everything and to change everything utterly—to transform the world and life in the world into a direct representation of God's love and God's justice. For this most noble purpose, both Christ and Mary gave everything, everything up to and beyond the end, and showed us forever that the only way to conspire with this possible future is also to give everything for it. What I know of Mary's inner mystical force tells me that it is for this change on earth that Mary is working—for an end to pollution, an end to the brutalization of nature, an end to injustice, cruelty, hypocrisy of all kinds, an end to homophobia and misogyny and sex- and body-hatred; the end of anything, in fact, that prevents us as human beings from acknowledging our own inner divine nature and the divine splendor of the planet we are in such imminent danger of destroying.

This is why Mary has been appearing with such regularity over the last 150 years—because she cares, and cares absolutely and passionately; she cares personally and with a tremendous suffering intimacy for the future of humanity and of the planet. From the beginning, she has been warning humankind of the disaster that awaits us if we do not turn back to love and holiness and prayer and action-in-truth. Her warnings go far beyond the confines of what we call Christianity or what we know of the Church. She has again and again said that she is the Mother of all human beings, the universal Queen of Peace.

Of all the representations and aspects and "faces" of the Mother, Mary is the most urgently concerned with us and our fate—because she once shared it, and, as the Queen of Heaven and Earth, shares it still with a passion of tenderness that anyone who turns to her simply will feel and experience, a passion of tenderness that is also an immense force of protection. As the medieval mystics knew, the Queen of Heaven is also the Queen of Hell, and no demonic power can withstand under any circumstances the strength of her love. Thomas à Kempis tells us: "Evil spirits are terrified of the Queen of Heaven and fly from the sound of her name as if from fire. At the very sound of the word 'Mary' they are prostrated as if by thunder." Alphonsus de Liguori writes: "Mary is said in the sacred canticles to be 'terrible' to the infernal powers as an army in battle array, and she is called 'terrible' in this way because she knows very well how to 'array' her power and mercy and prayers to the discomfiture of her enemies and the benefit of her servants." Bernard of Clairvaux informs us: "As poisonous reptiles fly from flowering vines so do the devils fly from those fortunate souls in whom they perceive the perfume of devotion to Mary."

Such language may be quaint, but the reality of the worldwide struggle between love and evil it alludes to is not. And in that struggle, on whose outcome the future of the planet depends, the power of divine love and truth of the Mother in her aspect as Mary is one of the most devastating and transforming weapons of all, and coming to know that and know it for certain, is an immense grace, extended now and always, to everyone whatever their faith. As Hildegard of Bingen wrote of Mary:

> O greening branch
> You stand in your nobility
> Like the rising dawn.
> Rejoice now and exult
> And deign to free the fools we are
> From our long slavery to evil
> And hold out your hand
> To raise us up.

And as the great sixth-century Akathist "Hymn to the Virgin as Theotokos" by Romanus the Melodist hymns her in her full divine glory:

> Rejoice, lightning that lights up our souls!
> Rejoice, star that causest the sun to appear!
> Rejoice, thou through whom the creation becomes man!
> Rejoice, bridge that conveys us from earth to heaven!
> Rejoice, access of mortals to God!
> Rejoice, defense against invisible enemies!
> Rejoice, key to the gates of paradise!
> Rejoice, radiant blaze of grace!
> Rejoice, thou through whom we are clothed in glory!
> Rejoice, pillar of the fire guiding those in darkness!
> Rejoice, key to the kingdom of Christ!
> Rejoice, impregnable wall of the kingdom!
> Rejoice, thou through whom we obtain our victories!
> Rejoice, healing of my body!
> Rejoice, salvation of my soul!

## Questions and Answers

*It seems to me, listening to you over these weeks, that there is
a danger in both the patriarchal and matriarchal visions of the
sacred feminine. The patriarchal either ignores or idealizes the
Mother, and the matriarchal roots her too deeply in the world,
in nature. In her aspect as Mary it seems we are being led toward
a new fusion, more radical than either.*

Exactly. The patriarchal vision of the Mother exalts and tran-
scendalizes the feminine from a secret fear of its power, and
tries, whether consciously or unconsciously, to distance the
demands of its sacred tenderness, urgent clarity, and passion
for justice by mythologizing and distancing it. The tendency of
modern matriarchal revivals of the Mother, on the other hand,
insists excessively on the Mother as *only* immanent. The full
glory of the Mother is that she is at once both transcendent *and*
immanent, the source of love and love-in-action.

What has to take place now in our reimagining of the Mother
is a fusion of the best and wisest of the patriarchal and matriarchal visions of her. This will engender a more majestic, comprehensive, and, as you say, *radical* vision than either. Out of
the sacred marriage of these two visions will come a fresh vision.
one that combines mystical knowledge of the transcendent
Mother with a radical political vision of the Mother-in-time,
and shows them to be two side of the same love.

In a rediscovery of the full glory and power of Mary lies, I
think, the great hope for the West in making this sacred marriage at the heart of the Christian tradition in such a way that
both revolutionizes that tradition and reveals and makes active
in the world its innermost mysteries. When Mary is seen as the
human face of the Divine Mother and the full urgency and
authority of her message is understood, then a massive new
force for change on every level can enter time.

What has to be seen clearly is the *revolutionary* nature of

the *fusion* between eternity and time that both Mary and Christ
are living out and the *demand* that arises from this fusion. That
demand is nothing less than to enact the holy kingdom *here*,
to make divine love active here and in every arena and institution and thought and emotion and political decree.

The tendency has been with both Mary and Christ to either
"transcendentalize" them or make them both into super-ethi-
cal social workers, thus defusing the power that comes from
their being both in eternity *and* in time. The power that streams
from grace into time is the greatest and most transformatory
power of all because it is the divine power. This is the power
that must be used in the highest sense to transform first the
heart of the world and then the practice of all beings in the public arena. The key to access to that power and the loving and
humble use of it lies in the adoration of Mary, of the Mother,
since it is in the heart of the Mother that heaven and earth, love
and justice, are united.

*How can this adoration be completed in Christianity?*

Mary must be given her rightful place in the Trinity. It is essential now that the fullness of the Motherhood of God be admit-
ted and celebrated by every religion and mystical tradition and
in the most complete possible way, otherwise the dangerous
imbalances that have contributed to our current catastrophe
will continue. In Christianity, for example, the Trinity must be
expanded to reveal a rich and secret feminine component that
incarnates itself in the story of Mary.

Christian mystics have always stressed the unique relationship that Mary has with the Holy Spirit who "marries" her and
with whom she in some sense becomes one through humility
and adoration. But now it is time that Mary is seen also as the
immanent source and the Daughter of God, as complete a par-
ticipant in the full life of the divine as her son.

Such thoughts, though still radical, are not new. In a sense
they are a culmination of that process that began early on in

the development of Christianity when a need for the presence of the sacred feminine led to an honoring of Mary and a gathering around her of the titles and attributes of Isis, Cybele, Athena, and Demeter; an honoring that flowered in the Councils that named her "Theotokos," "Mother of God," and culminated in the ratification of the dogma of the Assumption in the Fifties. Now it is time to go further and reveal the full splendor of her identity. As Peter Damian said of Mary: "All power is given to you in heaven and earth." As Germanus said: "You are the mother of true life." As Bernadine of Siena said: "At the command of Mary, all obey—even God."

This recognition of Mary as the Divine Mother is essential because if Mary is not completely recognized the force of the sacred heart that is active in her and through her in her son will be dampened and muffled and her power will go on being imprisoned in a golden cage of controlling patriarchal "adoration."

*What do you mean by the "force of the Sacred Heart"?*

When the true mystic heart is contacted and awakened and opened and made the guide and controller of the human body, soul, and mind, then a force of loving action floods reality, and this force has the full divine power of divine love and the full precision of discrimination. It is to awaken this force, to birth this Christ-heart, that Mary came and still comes to anyone who calls on her sincerely.

The difference between the patriarchal yogas of transcendence and the Mother's yoga of fusion lies precisely in the greater importance that the Mother places on the awakened heart. This is not a sentimental emphasis at all. The Mother is not sentimental. It is an emphasis on praxis, on *embodying* the light and on acting continually and wisely and passionately from its lived truth in the world.

In many patriarchal yogas the ultimate aim is to live from the center above the head in the light, and to guide all things from that transcendence. In the yoga of the Mother this is a preliminary stage, the first stage. What has to happen in the Mother's yoga is that all the *chakras* are opened one by one until they are all open together—including the topmost *chakra* called by the Hindus the *sahaswara*. Then the "marriage" of illumination with matter, awakening with all the thoughts and emotions and movements of the physical apparatus, has to be undertaken. This is hard as it involves a total sincerity and total dedication and a taking seriously of time and nature as divine truths in themselves.

As this marriage progresses, the awakened heart, the heart-*chakra*, becomes more and more the balancer of the whole spiritual and physical work. The naked adoring heart becomes the site of the sacred marriage between the spirit and the body, the fountain of love-in-action, the "Mother" of active divine childhood.

Mary's Sacred Heart was transmitted to Jesus and his whole teaching arose out of its wordless passion. All those who undertake the adventure into Mary are in effect asking the Mother to engender in them her sacred heart, that power of love that springs from the love of the divine and the love of justice that arises naturally when the world is loved and the beings in it and their misery, ignorance, and suffering are seen without any false "religious" consolation. The awakened sacred heart is awake, simultaneously, to the glory of the divine that floods it ever more intensely as it expands ever more intensely its powers of adoration, and to an exposure, as naked and unsentimental as possible, to the agony of the world. From this double exposure, this double vulnerability, comes a vision that sees heaven and earth as one and knows divine love as the yet unexpressed law of worldly life. From this double exposure and double vulnerability arise, too, a commitment to root and ground the light here in the world in every action of life and in a transformation of the human world through justice.

Peter Chrysostom puts it clearly: "A gentle woman housed God in her womb and asked as its price peace for the world, salvation for those who are lost, and life for the dead."

*How does your devotion for Mary fit in with what you have been saying about tantric sexuality? Mary, after all, has traditionally been represented as above sexuality, as almost puritanical.*

This has been a disaster, one that has encouraged a wrongheaded and cruel dismissal of the body, and fostered an ignorance of the great mystical understanding hidden in lovemaking when it is consecrated and divinized by authentic love.

When the "virginity" of Mary is seen, as I believe it must now be seen: as an expression of the freshness and inviolability of her mystic force and of her extreme purity of mind, heart, and soul, and not in any way as a merely physical description—then Mary and the Mother-force streaming through her to the world will be released from all puritanical interpretation. Mary is the queen of true love, the queen of the healing and transforming energies of sacred Eros, the queen of tantra, not merely in its highest and most ethereal aspects but in its aspect of blessed sexuality. In this too, Mary is the full and fully empowered Mother come to heal her children of all false shame and guilt and self-hatred and to dissolve all barriers between beings, and between beings and the creation. As St. Bernard says of her: "Read and read again, as often as you want all that is said of her in the Gospels, and if you can find the least trait of severity recorded of her, then fear to approach her. You will never find this . . . so run to her with a heart full of joy."

It is essential to remember, too, that the first miracle that Christ did—prompted and urged on and supported by his mother—was to turn the water into wine at the marriage of Cana. For me, the changing of the water into wine symbolizes the transformation of the ordinary banal consciousness into mystic passion, and so the changing of the ordinary sexual into the sacredly sexual. Read from this perspective, the story of the marriage of Cana becomes one in which the Mother through the grace of her son transforms the limitations of ordinary marital relationship into the deepest and widest and most revelatory kind of bliss, so revealing the divine meaning of marriage. Marriage is meant to be the place where the fundamental sacred energies that create the universe can be unleashed and understood within an entirely protected and honored atmosphere of mutual honor and fidelity, and both people are designed to be transformed by its real experience. This real experience—of the human divine Eros in all of its facets and powers and healing joys—is what Christ is giving by changing the water into wine.

Since the moment when Eryk handed me the white rose from the altar at Beauraing I have known and felt in every way that Mary blessed and protected our love. When Eryk and I got married we consecrated our whole marriage to her. Our lovemaking is dedicated by both of us consciously to Mary, and she has flooded it again and again by every kind of joy and bliss and illumination and sacred insight. We have both known her intimately as the queen of tantra, as the blessing Mother who wants her children to live the fullest joy in every dimension, and to link all the dimensions together in an experience of that joy that is always birthing them all, that is her. There is nothing puritanical about this force of healing that flows from the hands of Mary to all lovers who dedicate their love in fidelity and serious truth to her. There are rules and laws, as I have repeatedly said, of mutual honor and above all of fidelity—of mind as well as body—but the freedom that the grace of Mary the Mother opens up, the freedom that her force fuels and expands and that her grace makes more and more electric and revelatory, is a boundless and divine freedom.

What Mary wants, it seems increasingly clear to me, is a world of achieved and loving couples, of couples wholly dedicated to each other in her. Such couples can be heterosexual or homosexual; whatever the churches may say, the Mother is not anti-sexual or homophobic—how could she be? All Mary cares about is real love, and the truth of love, and her force is always given unstintingly to the protection and fostering of authentic love, because authentic love is one of the highest ways of honoring and embodying the divine. Her grace is entirely

given to those who, through fidelity and surrender and prayer
to the Mother, cultivate the noble mystical sensuality that honors the divine in the other and honors the reflection in pleasure
of the joy that births the worlds. Such couples are the core-units
of the revolution of love-in-action that the Mother is bringing
to the world. They cannot be co-opted by any system of spiritual or political authority; their own happiness is the source
they draw from and so they need no dogma nor controlling
guru nor priesthood; their mutual religious surrender automatically transforms where they live into small temples of love,
intimate shrines to her; the healing ecstatic energy that streams
from one to the other in the sweet heat of true tantra frees both
people gradually from childhood neuroses and sexual guilt and
opens both to the joy and pain of the world and the necessity
of serving other beings and sharing the joy that is now embodied and real.

The true fully divine and human Mary, the Mary that the
mystic child devoted to her comes to know, is at the heart of
this great spiritual and sexual revolution. Without healing the
body and making the body a site of spiritual insight, there can
be no healing and preservation of nature. The Mother knows
this, Mary knows this, and her energy of love is streaming out
everywhere to anyone who can invoke it. Just as there is a tantric
Kali and a tantric Durga and a tantric Tao, so there is a tantric
Mary whom the devotee can humbly and ecstatically connect
with and derive protection, succor, and holy inspiration from.
I am convinced that many Christian mystics have known this
over the ages—the alchemists especially—but could not say so
overtly for fear of misunderstanding and ecclesiastical persecution. Now the time has come to say it openly and with great
gratitude. Everything that the Goddess has Mary has; everything that the Mother is Mary is, and invested in her are all the
healing powers, including the powers of sexual healing that are
so crucial to the current spiritual revolution, that are invested
in the Mother.

There is a further secret that I believe Mary now wants to

be made available to the world. This is, simply, that when love-making is permeated by what you might call the Mary-element—the element of surrender, sweetness, and holy intensity of service—then the entire tantric process becomes a Mary-process, a way, that is, of giving birth to the Christ-heart in both beings. The whole experience "Marys" both beings, turns both into the "Mary" of the other. Each partner becomes the mother of the divine child, the Christ, in the other. This is not a metaphorical or poetical statement, but a precise, mystical-scientific one. The Mary-heat of true passion births the Christ-heart in both partners and tantric sexuality, when dedicated to her, reveals its highest meaning as childbirth, as the birth in both psyches, minds, hearts, and bodies of the awake and inte-grated divine child. I have no doubt whatsoever that Mary is the midwife of this process, or better still, the source from which the sacred fire that performs the alchemy streams, and streams continually.

When sincere Christians and devotees of Mary grasp the full meaning of what I am saying here there will be a world-wide sigh of gratitude and relief, and awe. The Mother is much freer of "moral" and "ethical" controls than we imagine, and so much holier and purer than any merely moral or ethical imagination can possibly imagine. Hers is the purity of total love, the purity of the desire that rises from total love to see all of her children illuminated and whole in the ground of ordi-nary life, fully divine and fully human, with nothing left out, and nothing left unlit by the truth of love.

*What do you feel is the relationship between Mary and Sophia, the feminine force of divine wisdom mentioned in the Old Testament?*

I agree wholeheartedly with the great Russian mystics such as Soloviev and Bulgakov that Mary is the created Sophia, the cre-ated manifestation of Sophia, the holy wisdom underlying all spiritual knowledge. The grace that the Sophian mystics claim for Sophia has three aspects—a mystical aspect leading to mystical union with the divine; a gnostic aspect, communicating gnosis to human beings; and a magical aspect, whereby human beings in union with the divine will can accomplish works of divine magic—understood in the highest sense as works of redemption and healing. All of these three powers of grace also belong to Mary and are part of her working in the world.

Sophia comes from the Hebrew *Chokmah*—"wisdom." Three books of the Hebrew Bible are designated as "books of wisdom" for they refer to the figure and teaching of Sophia—Proverbs, Job, and Ecclesiasties (some add the Song of Songs). Two other books from the Apocrypha also fall into this field—Ecclesiasties, or Sircah, and the Wisdom of Solomon. Sophia is eternally associated with Solomon, who achieved with her a relationship at once mystical, gnostic and magical. In Wisdom 8:2 Solomon speaks of Sophia in a way that Bernard of Clairvaux and Alphonsus of Liguori would speak of Mary: "I loved Sophia and sought her out from my youth, and I sought to take her for my bride, and I became enamored of her beauty. When I come into my house I find rest with her ... and in assiduous communing with her is understanding."

In Wisdom, Solomon goes on to describe what Sophia has taught him: "A knowledge of the structure of the world ... the alternating solstices and changing seasons ... the cycles of the years and the constellations ... the nature of living creatures and behavior of wild beasts ... the violent force of winds and human thought ... the varieties of plants and the virtues of roots. I learned it all, hidden or manifest, for I was taught by Sophia by her whose skill made all things."

These quotations make clear that Sophia is the feminine representation of the wisdom of God in all things, a name of the Mother in fact, and a way of approaching and celebrating Her mystery at the heart of the patriarchal Jewish revelation. In the Akathist hymn to the Blessed Virgin, Mary is referred to as the "spiritual temple," "a tabernacle of God, the Word" and is addressed, "O You, who surpasses the wisdom of the wise."

Mary is clearly seen as wiser than Solomon, and as a still more perfect container for the glorious power of Sophia. Until recently, the liturgical readings on the festival days of the Virgin in the Catholic Church were drawn primarily from the Books of Wisdom. The Cathedral of Holy Sophia in Kiev, in the Ukraine, and the Cathedral of Holy Sophia in Novgorod, Russia, with its famous and beautiful icon, were both dedicated to Mary. In the Christian story it is clear that Mary is the incarnation of the Sophia-aspect of the godhead.

The pinnacle and masterpiece of Sophian theology is the teaching of the threefold divine feminine, "The Sophian Trinity—Mother, Daughter, Holy Soul." In this beautiful and wise scheme, the Mother is seen as the ideal substance and foundation of creation, the power or force of its being, the spiritual origin of all matter. She is, as Rudolf Steiner says, "the ocean of light in which your soul lives." The Daughter-aspect of this divine feminine trinity is wisdom, Sophia. It is this Daughter-aspect that the Sophian mystics see as being incarnated in Mary (just as Jesus is the incarnation of the second person of the Trinity). As Bulgakov writes: "The most holy Mother of God is the created Sophia ... therefore she is exalted as 'more honorable than the Cherubim, more gloriously incomparably than the Cherubim' and *a fortieri* holiest of the human race.... Wisdom is at one with the most holy Mother of God, who is the summit of Creation, the Queen of Heaven and Earth." As the Daughter, Sophia—Mary—has in this vision a profound union with the "Holy Soul," the Sophian term for the divine feminine force of presence known in the Old Testament as the *Shekinah*, that force of the mystery of love that, among other things, gathers communities of spiritual seekers together in both devotion and direct inner knowledge of the divine.

In this Sophian Trinity, the Mother, then, is the power or force of the being of creation; the Daughter (counterpart to the Son as the Mother is to the Father) is the reason of creation, its ultimate meaning, truth, and justice; the "Holy Soul" is the "spirituality, holiness, purity, and beauty" of the creation. For the Sophian mystics, the two trinities are not mutually exclusive, but mutually interdependent, interlocking, and mutually penetrating.

I have elaborated the ideas of these mystics because I honor them and find in them a rich journey towards the feminine understanding of the divine in Christianity. Soloviev's three great experiences of Sophia that provided the impulse for his whole life's works are in my opinion genuine revelations of the power of the Mother in our time. As Soloviev writes;

> Let it be known; today the Eternal Feminine
> In an incorruptible body is descending to earth.
> In the unfading light of the new Goddess
> Heaven has become one with the depths.

I have two reservations, however, about this wonderful body of mystic thought. The first is that I see no need for an alternative Trinity; instead the present "model" has to be expanded to include the sacred feminine on every level. In doing this work, Soloviev's understanding and that of the other Sophian mystics will be invaluable, but I do not believe that he and they have prepared the final synthesis, which can only come, I believe, when Mary is acknowledged as the full incarnation of the Mother-aspect of God.

This brings me to my second "objection." In the Sophian scheme Mary is the Daughter, Sophia, the Incarnation of Wisdom. I said at the beginning that I agreed wholeheartedly with this and I do. I merely want Mary's presence in each aspect of the Trinity *in all its aspects* to be understood and celebrated. She is as much the Mother and the Holy Soul as the Daughter to me (and to many other mystics who experience her fullness). This full Mary, accorded the full majesty of divine grace and power is, I believe, the "goddess" in whose "unfading light" Heaven will become "one with the depths."

There is a danger in Sophian mysticism of etherealizing the sacred feminine; the vision of Mary as transcendent and immanent, as at once Queen of Heaven and a poor struggling woman—her essential and miraculously human mystery—grounds and roots and makes actual and active the sacred feminine in a way that I believe is now essential.

It is my belief that a comprehensive vision of Mary as the Mother in time, the Mother who suffered as us and with us without any veil and separation, takes us even further into the mystery of the Mother-aspect of God than a vision, however glorious, of Sophia, which still remains, however marvelously, abstract. Mary concretizes, crystallizes, embodies, enacts, demonstrates the sacred feminine in time and matter, and I believe that the relationship we can have with her includes and goes beyond any we may have with Sophia.

I find that the naked relationship with the embodied Mother in Mary compels me into a naked relationship with reality, reality *as it is,* in all its bliss and suffering, and draws me deeper and deeper into that fusion of heaven and earth, holiness and matter, that is the clue to the new transformation.

In Mary, as in Christ, the divine is related to every conceivable aspect of human life, and the duty to realize the divine in every aspect of life—including grief, loss, humiliation, and death, and also including political and economic choice—becomes urgent, passionate, and, in the highest sense, inescapable. I think the intensity and practicality of focus that comes from living that demand of the Mother in time is crucial to the changes that the Mother wants for the earth, and that any formulation of her force, however noble and beautiful, that remains un-embodied prevents the full explosion of love and justice that she is trying to release.

*Do you believe that the figure and symbol of the Black Madonna, which so many modern feminist theologians and mystics and psychologists are turning to, helps us deeper into the mystery of Mary in our time?*

Absolutely. For me the Black Madonna is becoming increasingly the key to my devotion to Mary the Mother.

The suffering of this year and my experience of Eastern mysticism, especially of Kali and the Kali-aspects of the Mother, have brought me to the Black Madonna and helped me to begin to see and feel the divine power of this image of Mary. It is, I am beginning to see, one of the most majestic, powerful, all-comprehensive, and moving images of the Divine Mother ever imagined by humankind, and a perfect image on which to focus devotion for Mary in all of her aspects—as Queen of Heaven, Queen of Nature, Queen of Earth, and as a suffering, brave, dignified, mystical, and practical human being who struggled and wept and prayed with us and who struggles, weeps, and prays with us and in us still.

I am coming to see in the Black Madonna three main and only superficially contradictory aspects of Mary: first, Mary as the mystery of transcendent blackness, the blackness of divine mystery, that mystery celebrated by the great Aphophatic mystics, such as Dionysisus Areopagite, who see the divine as forever unknowable, mysterious, beyond all our concepts, hidden from all our senses in a light so dazzling it registers on them as darkness; second, Mary as queen of the fertility of nature, queen of tantra and all natural fertile engendering processes in the external and internal worlds; third, Mary as Jacopone da Todi's *"donna brucciata,"* the burned, seared, anguished, but infinitely strong and dignified human mother who has learned and embodies the ultimate secrets of mystical and personal suffering. In the Black Madonna, in the mystery and magnificence and force of this image, Mary appears as all three of her crucial aspects as Divine Mother.

The Black Madonna is the transcendent Kali-Mother, the black womb of light out of which all of the worlds are always arising and into which they fall, the presence behind all things, the darkness of love and the loving unknowing into which the child of the Mother goes when his or her illumination is perfect; the Black Madonna is also the Queen of Nature, the blesser and agent of all rich fertile transformations in external and inner nature, in the outside world and in the psyche. And she is as well the human mother blackened by grief, but ennobled and made adamant by the secret mystical knowledge she has won from agony and is representing with dignity. All of the different energies and powers of Mary are present in all of their different levels and dimensions and inner relations.

Because Mary is represented fully in this image, when we contemplate it we are gradually initiated through the Black Madonna into the full nature of our divine childhood in her. The human seared mother accompanies us in our worst anguishes and humiliations, representing that endurance and faith and surrender that are the clues to their transmutation into wisdom. The Queen of Nature blesses us and all the movements of our nature, making them whole and rich and fecund with her dark fecundity, and strong with her strength that is rooted in the depths and mysteries of natural processes and rhythms, rhythms of creativity, transformation, and birth. The transcendent mysterious dark Queen of Heaven constantly inspires us and leads us forward and upward into the highest mysteries, while showing us in other of her aspects that are also simultaneously present how to ground, root, demonstrate, live, and embody them.

In this time of tragedy and worldwide catastrophe, the Black Madonna for me offers the least illusionary and most empowering vision of the Mother I know. Anyone who turns to the Black Madonna with devotion will experience what I am experiencing—an immense force of protection, an immense alchemical power of transformation through both grief and joy, and an immense inspiration to compassionate service and action in the world. From the darkness of her eternal mystery flows those graces that divinize nature and life and give the courage to enact the laws of that divinization in every arena of life. All of those who accept the Black Madonna's challenge to "hope, believe, endure all things" in the service of an alchemical transformation of the body, nature, and the whole of life on earth will also be protected with that divine power that is hers, that power the Marian mystics celebrate when they call Mary the Queen of

Hell. The Black Madonna is this aspect of Mary also, Mary as Queen of the Underworld, Mary as that force of pure suffering mystical love that annihilates evil at its root and engenders the Christ-child in the ground of the soul even as the world burns; Mary as the full blazing power of the Divine Mother in her creative *and* destructive aspects, which nothing, *nothing at all,* can destroy.

Saint Cosmas of Jerusalem said: "While I keep my hope in you invincible, I shall be safe. I will fight and overcome my enemies—inner and outer—with no other buckler than your protection and your all-powerful help." James the Monk said: "You, O Lord, have given us in Mary arms that no force of war can annihilate."

*How do you think it is best to adore Mary the Mother so as to ensure that this power you talk of protects and works through us?*

Paul VI says of devotion to Mary that "it makes a soul free with the glorious liberty of the children of God." I believe that the simplest ways of adoration are always the best. Mary does not need long words or elaborate meditations.

The best way I have found—and all the Marian mystics testify to this—is to go to Mary directly, to speak to her directly with no fuss, no decoration, no shame. She sees and knows us better than we see and know ourselves; no aspect of our grief is foreign or disgusting to her; whatever we have done she always loves us and always with the same love.

I find three very simple kinds of adoration useful. First, the rosary. Anyone who has not practiced the rosary hasn't any idea of what power it has to transform the ground of experience. I try to keep up the "Hail Mary" always in my heart, as a continual whisper of my being toward her and find that this prayer, done sincerely, has every kind of tantric power—the power to bring the light down directly, the power to draw inspiration into the mind and heart, the power to give immediate access to protection and courage, the power to infuse the entire being with the fire of love.

Secondly, I find that meditation on specially sacred images of Mary help. The images I find most powerful are the Black Madonnas of Einsiedeln, Montserrat, Chartres, and Valcour, and our Lady of Beauraing and the Virgin of Guadelupe. Just looking at them with love fills the heart, mind, and body with confident peace and strength. I use these images too in simple forms of meditation in which I imagine them alive in light and streaming toward me health, insight, courage, passion, and truth. Each morning, I sit before our Lady of Beauraing and ask her as simply as I can for what I need for the day, like a child would ask his mother. This I find bathes the whole day in her divine presence.

The third way of adoration of Mary is the one that Therese of Lisieux put so beautifully: "Do works of charity. That is the best way of paying a visit to Mary." Serving others is the quickest way to be in her presence, serving others with honor and respect and love, the love of the Mother. If we want to experience fully the love of the Mother, we must—it is one of her laws—enact it incessantly in works of charity and works of justice. We should do all things, as Louis Grignion de Montfort says, "by Mary, with Mary, in Mary, for Mary." As we gradually learn to do all things "by Mary, with Mary, in Mary, for Mary," her living divine presence becomes a continual companion and source of strength, so that we come to begin to know what the Curé d'Ars meant when he said, "I have so often fetched water from her spring that there wouldn't be any left if it were not inexhaustible."

It cannot be emphasized too strongly that the way to Mary is through her own simplicity, humility, and directness. In the deepest and highest sense, she is far less interested in adoration than imitation. The Mother doesn't just want to be loved; she wants that love to be made active in all things and in all moments so that the reign of her love can begin on earth.

Louis Grignion de Montfort characterizes the spirit of Mary

as "zealous and prudent, humble and courageous, pure and fecund." It is this spirit that adoring her births in us. In this spirit we can do anything; with the force and intelligence of this spirit we can survive all dangers and transmute all terror and anguish into grace. De Montfort cries out: "When will it be that souls breathe Mary as bodies breathe the air?" St. Ambrose prays: "Let the soul of Mary be in each person to glorify God there; let the spirit of Mary be in each person to rejoice there in God." Through adoring Mary we become one with her, grow something of her Mother-power and Mother-spirit in ourselves and come through grace to participate in her life of joy and glory. This is not theology; this is experience. Try it and you will see for yourself.

This is the process as I understand it; the child invokes the Mother's love; the Mother pours her love and grace into the child; the child is slowly divinized, and when this birth into divine childhood that is also divine Motherhood is complete, the new child becomes a mother—a mother of love, of service, of loving action in every way and in every arena. With Mary, no intermediaries, priests, gurus, "experts" are ever needed, are necessary or even desirable; direct, naked contact is available at all moments and in all circumstances. Mary can do anything, if we let her, and will, if we open to her as she is always open to us—simply, naturally, tenderly, completely. The great reward of adoring her is to come to know her in this all-healing intimacy, the intimacy in all dimensions of the real and full Mother, the Divine Mother who is also human, and "closer to us than our jugular vein."

Where I live in San Francisco, I go often to the shop of a Mexican grocer who worships Mary. One day we were talking about the Mother and he said, pointing to a picture of the Virgin of Guadelupe he has taped above his counter, "I always go to her when I need anything. With that one you can be sure she'll listen. She *always* listens." I was moved because I saw just how simple his relationship with her was. "So you speak to her exactly as you do to your real mother?" I asked. He looked at

me as if I were crazy, and then said slowly, as if spelling out the
words to a dim-witted child, "She *is* my real Mother!"

*In talking about Mary, you stress a great deal her role as "Queen*
*of Justice" and her power of protection. Can you say more*
*about that?*

I believe that the understanding of Mary as the Queen of Justice, and of the Divine Mother as showing us through Mary
that she wants a complete transformation of the terms of this
world, is crucial to the revolution of the sacred feminine. There
can be no real spiritual revolution in the name of the Mother
that is not also a passionate and loving reconstruction of all
the terms of life for all of her children and all beings.

There can be no transformation in the name of the sacred
feminine without a passionate, strong, deep commitment to
saving the forests, ending pollution, and putting a stop to the
false use of power in all its forms, political and spiritual. That
is why the force of the Mother has been contained, derided, or
forgotten—because it is a force that makes an extreme demand
on us to claim our divine identity as her children and then to
act from that awareness in all areas of life. Justice is one of the
holiest names of the Mother and the commitment to political
and social justice in every way and in every form is essential
now if the planet is to be preserved.

To this transformation, Mary is a great guide. A true reading
of the Magnificat reveals just how impassioned her desire for
justice is, and how literal and unmetaphorical: "He hath shewed
strength with his arm; he hath scattered the proud in the imagination of their hearts. He hath put down the mighty from their
seats, and exalted them of low degree. He hath filled the hungry
with good things; and the rich he hath sent empty away."

All of the revelations of the Mother in all of the traditions
have something beautiful and sacred to reveal to us about her;
what Mary in her life and mission reveals to us of the Mother
is ultimately important now in this catastrophic age. What she

reveals is the thirst, the divine thirst of the Mother, to see the world transformed into a living mirror of her love and justice. It isn't enough simply to worship the Mother; her demand that people should live in love and radical equality with each other and radical wonder at nature has to be heard and implemented, and done so with seriousness and simplicity of heart if the world is to be given a chance to survive.

In many of her apparitions Mary is shown weeping, initiating us into one of the greatest of all the mysteries of the Mother's nature—showing us that the Mother *cares*, cares for us more than we care for ourselves, cares for the condition of the world and finds the cruelty, exploitativeness, and ignorant insane injustice of human beings to each other and to nature intolerable. It is this passion for change, *real change of real conditions,* that fueled Mary's life on earth and fuels still her mission to the world.

The knowledge that the Mother is a revolutionary force is crucial knowledge, a crucial key to the future, and in Mary you see clearly this revolutionary appeal for justice on all levels. Christ's teaching on the kingdom and on the need to deconstruct all forms of power and to live in equal love to all arose directly from Mary's inner knowledge of the relation of love to justice. This aspect of Mary is becoming increasingly evident to her devotees all over the world—to the liberation theologians and radical Christian communities of South America and Italy, to mystics of all kinds who turn to her beyond dogma.

As Leonardo Boff writes in his magnificent chapter "Mary: Prophetic Woman of Liberation" in his book *The Maternal Face of God:*

> In the *communidades de base* (base communities) [in Brazil], wherever the political dimension of the faith is discussed, a special appreciation of Mary's role of denunciation and proclamation *(denuncia y anuncio)* of prophecy and liberation, stands out as a key aspect of the people's devotion to her....
>
> Christian ideology ... has had a difficult time deciding between not ascribing any importance to Mary's prophetic

words [in the Magnificat], superficially so male and so strange-sounding on the lips of a woman, and spiritualizing them—bestowing upon them a meaning calculated to reinforce the privileged position occupied by Christians here, or even simply applying them to "the others" (Jews, pagans, or "forces of evil"). In any event, they have not been applied to the Church or to Christians. As a result for centuries, Christianity has rendered the critical, liberating content of the Magnificat impotent. It is our task, then, to develop a prophetic image of Mary—an image of Mary as the strong, determined woman, the woman committed to the messianic liberation of the poor from the historical social injustices under which they suffer.[2]

I would add: not only of the poor, but of the animals being burned alive in forests, the fish being murdered in the polluted seas. And it is not only Christianity that has to make this effort to actualize justice, but *every* religion. We all have to hear the voice of the Mother in Mary's plea for transformation in this world; we all have to hear the anguish and pleading in the voice of the Divine Mother to feed the starving, protect the environment, transform the conditions of justice and power for the billions of people living in poverty. Coming to know the Mother is coming to know the furnace of her loving heart, a heart that cannot rest so long as one creature is in unnecessary pain, or one child goes hungry at night, or one whale develops a mysterious wasting disease. What the Mother is revealing to us through Mary is that what we need at this moment if the situation is to be saved is a love like Mary's; a love that is, as Boff writes, "in solidarity with the suffering and with those who suffer with them—an intelligent love that looks for concrete, liberating steps to take to develop relations of justice among human beings."[3]

Why I have emphasized Mary's power here is to make as clear as I can what I am beginning to understand through Mary —that the divine grace of the Mother and her divine protection are always given to those who fight for a new world, for the authenticity of love and the truth of justice. The emulation that Mary wants from us far more than adoration is a mirroring of the passion and always active compassion of her life, the whole turning of ourselves toward the service of other beings and the tireless working on behalf of humanity for real substantial change.

I have found that the Mother floods all those who turn to her with power, insight, and love to help them endure such work in the world, and protects them with the full majesty of her grace. Knowing just how powerful that grace always is and how sure that protection always is in the middle of hurricanes of evil is essential for all seekers now. Without the Mother's heart we will not see the full catastrophe of what is happening; without the Mother's grace and protection we will not be able to endure the kind of harsh, difficult, gritty, practical service we will all have to do with our individual gifts in and for the world. The times are terrifying and the necessary work exhausting; only by rooting ourselves in her protection will we be able to go forward. But the hope is that her protection and grace are always given. Mary has made it clear that she will be with us always. That is what she says at the end of nearly all her messages: "I will be with you always." Always, in whatever circumstances, trials, ordeals, crucifixions. Always—even if we destroy everything and ourselves.

*What would Christianity be like if it accepted and venerated Mary as the full Divine Mother?*

If Christianity could open itself to the full transforming sacred force of the Divine Mother in Mary it could also at last, at long last, open itself to the force of Christ. Because they are the same force. Mary is Christ and Christ, Mary; they are united so intimately in every dimension that one is entirely in the other. St. Bridget says: "As Adam and Eve sold the world for an apple so did Mary with her Son redeem the world as it were with one heart."

The return of the Mother is also the return of the real Christ, the Christ who preached not an otherworldly kingdom but the kingdom of justice *here,* not an ethereal compassion, but an extreme, passionate and practical one. This is the return of the mystical and pragmatic Christ, the full son of the Mother as well as the Father, the Christ that has the authority and wholeness and completeness of the son of the Mother-Father and is the sacred androgyne that has fused in its being male and female, heaven and earth, prayer and action, divine love and human love, divine law and human justice. The gift of this Christ in the soul is Mary's gift; opening to her grace is allowing this Christ to be born in the soul, mind, heart, and body in his full fiery joy and truth. As Louis Grignion de Montfort said: "Jesus is everywhere and always the fruit and the son of Mary . . . and Mary is everywhere the real tree that bears the fruit of life and the real Mother that engenders it."

De Montfort also wrote: "It is through Mary that the salvation of the world began; it is through Mary that it must be brought to consummation." I believe that the second coming of Christ can only come through Mary, just as his first appearance came through her. Through the awakening to and of the sacred feminine that is being made available to the world in its potentially final catastrophe, a full knowledge of Christ is also being made available, of a mystical androgynous Christ, the Prince of Love and Justice, and an immense force for the most radical change imaginable—the transformation of this world into the kingdom, the living of the life of grace and love here on earth in the name of the Father-Mother. This is the Christ that the Church has been blocking for two millennia and it is this fully empowered radical and empowering Christ who shares the passion for this-worldly justice of his Mother, who shares her anguish at disaster, who shares her seeing-through of all false modes of power—*including religious ones.*

When the Mother is seen and known in Mary, the Mother-love at the heart of Christ's teaching will also be uncovered and the teaching he gave revealed as perhaps the most complete of all the teachings of the sacred feminine—because at once transcendent and immanent, at once mystically profound and focused on this world and its terrors and pains. The revolutionary fusion of love and justice that forms the heart-core of Christ's teaching is a Mother-teaching streaming from Mary, the Mother. Christ voices and articulates what Mary is; Christ voices and articulates the silence of the sacred heart that she has transmitted to him and will also transmit to us, if we let her, so that we can become one in the ground of our entire being with both him and her, and so co-revolutionaries with them in the only revolution that can save us now—the comprehensive political and spiritual and mystical and active revolution of the Mother.

Just as Mary gave birth to Christ in history, so she gives birth to him in eternity, in the ground of our souls; just as she sustained Christ's growth in time, so she sustains and nourishes the life of Christ in us, by every kind of tender grace and protection. Loving Mary helps us to become the mother of our own inner Christ, helps us to give birth to the radical Christ in ourselves and feed, nourish, preserve, and sustain him and enact the laws of his love and gnosis in reality.

When Bede Griffiths was in his final illness, he kept saying, "Serve the growing Christ! Serve the growing Christ!" The best way to serve the Christ growing in everyone and in history—the Christ which must grow and become more and more present in the ground of everyone's soul, heart, and body for history to be transformed—is to serve, love, and adore his Mother. She will birth him in us in all of our faculties, in the transformed body as well as the transformed heart, mind, and will. And she will teach us how to serve him in ourselves and in others. And she will teach us how to become him, and her-in-him and him-in-her, so that at last we can know and live and enact the total intimacy that he had with her and her with him, here, in this world, in this body, and also in eternity.

"O Jesus alive in Mary be alive in us," cries Louis Grignion de Montfort, "And May the Kingdom of Mary come so that Yours can come." It is the same kingdom that both Mary and

Christ want—the kingdom where there are no more poor, where there is no more cruelty and exploitation and injustice, where the forests are safe and the seas clean and the world protected, and human life and human love recognized as utterly sacred and holy. Catastrophe is at last bringing us to the time when we can no longer hide from the demand of Mary and her Son for us to transform everything in the name of divine love and to see justice done in every area of life.

> Rejoice, flashing symbol of the Resurrection!
> Rejoice, rock that has refreshed those thirsting for life!
> Rejoice, shelter of the world broader than a cloud!
> Rejoice, robe of freedom for the naked!

## Notes

1. Beauraing and Banneux, Belgium. At these two sites, there have been miraculous sightings and signs of Mary's presence on earth.

2. Leonardo Boff, O.F.M., *The Maternal Face of God: The Feminine and its Religious Expressions*. Translated by Robert Bar and John W. Diercksmeier (New York: Harper & Row, 1987), pp. 188–189.

3. Boff, *The Maternal Face of God*, p. 202.

# Chapter Eleven

# Christ the Mother

IN THE ANGUISH of the massacre of half a lifetime's spiritual illusions that followed my leaving Meera, I turned, as I have already written, to the Mother in her aspect as Mary. In turning to Mary, I discovered I was also turning to Christ, to a Christ I had half-suspected was there, the full mystical-radical Christ, the Christ of St. Francis and the Curé d'Ars and Mechthild of Magdeburg and the liberation theologians, the Christ who is as much the son of the Mother as of the Father. Through rediscovering Mary as the full Divine Mother, I discovered for the first time, with awe and amazement, the overwhelming presence of the sacred feminine in Christ himself, discovered intuitively and mystically, in the core of my mind and heart and body, what Louis Grignion de Montfort meant when he wrote: "Jesus and Mary are united so intimately that one is entirely in the other," and what St. Bernard of Clairvaux meant when he wrote in one of his bursts of adoration of Mary the Mother: "By You we have access to the Son: Grant that we may receive Him by You who through You was given to us."

To receive Christ through Mary is to receive the Christ of the mystics, the Christ who, while rooted in the Father, in transcendence, loved this world with the humble passion of his mother, *the* Mother, and in his own person, teaching, and life-journey lived not only the Father-path of transcendence but also embraced the whole of existence and struggled to redeem all of it with the intensity of the Mother. To receive Christ through Mary is to see and know him as the sacred androgyne, the divine child-self, the sacred androgyne within each of us waiting to be born through and in the Mother.

Many years ago in South India I had my first intimation of this. I was in Mahabalipuram, alone, meditating before a statue I love of Shiva Ardhanarishvara—that representation of the Absolute that is half-male, half-female, half Shiva, half-Parvati, which I had for a long time realized was the aspect of the godhead I was most drawn to and the inner clue to my own mystical evolution. I had long known that in this complete and subtle representation of the Absolute, India had succeeded in "imaging" the sacred androgynous nature of the fully awake divine child of the Mother, the being that fuses the masculine and feminine in the psyche and so achieves alchemical absorption into reality. As I gazed at the ancient worn-gold statue of Shiva Ardhanarishvara in the late afternoon light, something astonishing happened. For a moment, instead of Shiva standing there, I saw Christ, the resurrected Christ, relaxed, smiling, opening his gold shirt to reveal a vast gold-red heart. This Christ was even more feminine than the statue of Shiva Ardhanarishvara—not effeminate, but extremely, powerfully gentle, suffused with a free passion of love. He smiled at me a blinding smile and then disappeared. I wrote later: "Christ is man-woman, Mary-Jahweh, the coincidence of all opposites and their burning-point, the diamond-point of committed love on which they dance forever in harmony." A new depth in my love and inner knowledge of Christ had been opened.

Then, just recently, two months after leaving Meera, I went to Mass at St. Ignatius in San Francisco with a ninety-year-old woman whom I love. Before we went into the church she took my hand and looked in my eyes, "Do you love Christ?" she asked me. "I know you have explored many religious traditions, but," and she repeated the question, *do you love Christ?*" I found myself saying, "I have loved Christ all my life, ever since my mother first read me the Gospels. My first poems, at six or seven, were love-poems to Christ. I was a chorister between the ages of nine and eighteen and Christ filled my heart. Once in South India. . . ." My friend interrupted me and took my hand firmly, "It is time for you to rediscover Christ, to invite him back into your heart. I don't mean the Christ of the ideologues, I mean the Christ that is a lover of lovers." A "lover of lovers" . . . the phrase was suddenly so poignant that my heart dilated and I remembered the smile of the transformed statue years before. Then my friend and I entered the church. We were late and the service had already begun. As we were finding somewhere to sit I heard the priest say words I had either never heard before or never noticed as part of the Mass: "Mother," he said solemnly, holding out his hands, "Mother, reveal Thy Son."

Because my heart had already been opened by my friend and the words she had spoken on the steps, the priest's words came to me with the shock of initiation. "Mother, reveal Thy Son." I heard a voice say in me inwardly: *Until the Divine Mother is welcomed back into the heart of Christianity and into every part of the Trinity and until Mary is known and celebrated as the Mother's face in time, no one will really understand Christ, and the radical force of his love will go on being blocked.* It continued: *When Christ is revealed by the Mother as her son, the full range of his passion for justice and service and the full truth of his passion for this world and its healing will also stand revealed, in all its inescapable unconditional demand.* Two phrases from the Marian mystics I had been devouring swam into my mind. The Curé d'Ars wrote (and continually repeated in his sermons): "The way to Christ is through Mary, through the Sacred Heart of His Mother that is His heart also." And St. Bernard, in his commentary on the Canticles, in a phrase that had wounded me by its strange beauty, wrote: "Suck not so much the wounds as the breasts of the Crucified." These phrases went on circling each other in my mind, drawing me deeper and deeper into their field of revelation.

Next day, attempting to clarify what I was discovering, I found myself writing:

When the priest said, "Mother, reveal Thy Son," a veil was burnt away and for the first time completely I saw—beyond thoughts, emotions, concepts—really saw that only the Mother can reveal the full Christ. Only when we have invited back and reintegrated the sacred feminine with every aspect of our perception and action will we begin to see who Christ really is and has always been—the complete sacred androgyne, the full son of the Father-Mother, the one who more passionately and demandingly than any other of the great mystic liberators of humankind fused in the depths of his own being, and in his teaching and example, the Father, the Ground, the Source, the Witness, the Transcendent, with the Mother; to give birth, through his own agony and resurrection, to a vision that marries both. Christ's, then, is a vision of transcendence *and* immanence, of love *and* service, divine absorption *and* action, mystical passion *and* the most total imaginable call for actual transformation here on earth, a transformation of *everything* that prevents the realization *here* of the Father-Mother's laws of justice and love.

As I wrote, it became clear why this astounding truth had been either consciously or unconsciously obscured:

What Christ discovered in his "double" enlightenment from the Source and the living Mother was the most radical of all visions and solutions—a nuclear force in fact, the fire of divine love that streamed from her and his heart to burn away everything in the world that created separation. Christ's real vision, rooted simultaneously in a totally clear knowledge of the nature of God and in the most scathing analysis of the nature of the world, allows no possible escape. All authority is menaced by it, all injustice arraigned, every human "solution" that is either merely activist or merely quietist accused and derided and exposed, all spiritual comforts and consoling dogmas exposed as evasion. Christ's synthesis of divine and human love and divine and human law shatters all norms and barriers and categories and potentially unleashes into this life an unparalleled force of critical passion fueled by divine energy—just the force that could revolutionize society in a way the patriarchy never wanted.

This nuclear Force, this second discovery of Fire that Christ made (and is) has now to reenter the consciousness of the world, otherwise the synthesis that the Mother is trying to effect cannot inspire and remake the West. To rediscover Christ as the Divine Child of the Mother and the Father is to begin to release this outrageous love-force, this fire of the Sacred Heart. Releasing this fire worldwide is what the Second Coming will be—not a return of Christ from without, but an explosion of Christ from within hearts tuned by contemporary catastrophe to be ready at last to hear the full demand of Christ's hunger to see this world mirror God. Blake wrote, "Jesus Christ is the Son of God and so am I and so are you"; this truth has now not simply to be mouthed but experienced and enacted. Christ came—and comes—to "Christ" us all, to enflame his lovers to love and act as he did, with passion, abandon, and love of justice and healing in all of its forms.

The Second Coming of Christ can only come through and by the Mother, for the return of the honoring of the Sacred Feminine and the return of the honoring of the Sacred Heart that Christ is and engenders in anyone who turns to him are the same thing, are the same seared, naked, boundless fire of sacred tenderness for every form of life, are the same clear-eyed, unconsoled, and impassioned call for justice at every level and in every arena, are the same willingness to give and suffer anything and everything to transform the conditions of this world, are the same unwavering mystical and radical vision of the Kingdom as being already here, as being already the complete human-divine truth of our earthly condition and experience, waiting only for us to be brave anguished and illuminated enough to donate everything to bring it into being. "Mother, reveal thy son."

I finished writing and sat in meditation. After long quiet-
ness, I heard the words, *I Christ am the Mother. I am Her. No
separation between my flesh and hers, my heart and hers, my
will and hers, my love and hers. No separation. I am the Mother.*

This inner message drove me to dive headlong into a tradition I already knew existed—the mystical tradition of worshipping Christ as the mother that runs underground from the
Greek fathers through the great Cistercians of the twelfth and
thirteenth centuries, into Juliana of Norwich and other four-
teenth-century female mystics such as Mechthild of Magdeburg
and Marguerite of Oingt. One of the Cistercian fathers, Guer-
ric of Igny, wrote, recalling St. Bernard:

> The Bridegroom has breasts lest He should be lacking any
> one of all the duties and titles of love. . . . He is a father in
> virtue of natural creation . . . and also in virtue of the author-
> ity with which He teaches. He is a mother, too, in the ten-
> derness of His affection, and a nurse.

St. Anselm of Canterbury wrote:

> Jesus, Good Lord, are You not also a mother? Are You not
> like that mother who, like a hen, collects her children under
> her wings? Truly, Master, You are a mother. For what oth-
> ers have conceived and given birth to, they have received
> from You . . . You gather under Your wings Your little ones,
> Your dead chicks seek refuge under Your wings. By Your
> gentleness, those who are hurt are comforted by Your per-
> fume, the despairing are reformed. Your warmth resusci-
> tates the dead.

The Carthusian prioress Marguerite of Oingt speaks of
Mother Jesus in this way:

> Are You not my mother and more than my mother? The
> mother who bore me laboured in delivering me for one day
> or one night, but You, my sweet and lovely Lord, laboured
> for me for more than thirty years. Ah . . . with what love

You labored for me. . . . But when the time came for You to be delivered, Your labor pains were so great that Your holy sweat was like great drops of blood that came out of Your body and fell on the earth. . . . Ah, who ever saw a mother suffer such a birth! For when the hour of Your delivery came You were placed on the hard bed of the Cross . . . and Your nerves and all Your veins were broken. And truly it is no surprise that Your veins burst when in one day You gave birth to the whole world.

This tradition did not merely end in the fourteenth century or the Reformation. It continues secretly on into the mystic writings of Louis Grignion de Montfort, who exclaims, in the late eighteenth century:

Jesus is entirely in Mary and Mary entirely in Jesus; or rather she is no longer "herself" but is all Jesus only; you could separate light from the sun more easily than Mary from Jesus. So that you could call our Lord Jesus of Mary and the Holy Virgin Mary of Jesus.

This knowledge of the mystical androgyny of Christ, of his fundamental connection with the Mother, inspired also the greatest saint of the nineteenth century, the Curé d'Ars. The Curé d'Ars in his own life realized Christ the Mother, lived out in a long grueling love-agony of service and healing and witness what he knew of Christ's divine motherhood and the demand so total an example of Mother-love as Christ's placed on all who love and follow him. When the Curé writes of Christ's motherhood he does so with the naked authority of one who has known and lived it. "The heart of Mary," he writes, "was the spring Jesus fetched the blood from with which he redeemed us." When I went to Ars last September and walked through the pitifully bare rooms in which the Curé had lived his life of dedication to others, that remark kept returning to me and I knew that it provided one clue at least to his own indefatigably passionate compassion.

Mary's spring of heart-blood was where Jean-Marie Vianney too drew the strength, the courage, the intensity to carry on his humble mission of love, despite all the opposition and derision he encountered on all sides. What else but his continual experience of the divine motherhood of Christ could have helped him endure the life he led? Mary and Christ the Mother poured through him their healing gifts and their passion for justice and their power of love that knows no barriers, that "hopes and endures all things."

No one, in fact, has ever described this motherhood of Christ more simply or beautifully than the Curé d'Ars:

> Our Lord is on the earth like a mother that carries His child in His arms. This child is naughty, kicks its mother, bites her, scratches her, but his mother doesn't only pay total attention to the child. He knows that if He leaves the child, the child will fall because he cannot walk alone. This is how our Lord is: He endures our dreadful treatment of Him, He bears all our arrogance, He forgives us our stupidities, and He pities us, despite everything we are and do.

It is impossible to understand Christianity without realizing that the vision given to us by Jesus Christ is permeated, saturated, irradiated, and illuminated at every level by the most direct possible vision and understanding of the divine feminine. Christ's whole journey is rooted in the motherhood of Mary, in the strength that she gave and fed him. There is a marvelous late fifteenth-century Italian painting in which Mary is shown lying quietly in a bed; from her breast an immense tree grows. On that tree, which is green and in full blossom, is Christ hanging on the Cross. What that image suggests to me is that everything that Christ did, everything that he was, everything that he gave to us, everything that he said and transmitted, came out of Mary's great silent, majestic heart, her sacred heart, her heart that, in the most profound mystical sense—"that understanding of the immanent sacredness of everything"—was the foundation of his entire pilgrimage, his entire journey.

You cannot understand Christianity until you realize that the Christianity that we have been given is a betrayal of everything that Christ said and did. Christ did not come to announce himself as the only son of God, he did not come to announce himself as the only perfect one. He did not come to found a religion in which he would be adored as a divine being. What he came to do was something much more radical and powerful, much more extreme, and very much more necessary. He came to exemplify the divinity of every single human being and to give to the human race the outrageous possibility of a direct divine relation with God: a direct gnostic ecstasy which would also be an ecstasy of service and justice. As he says in the Gospel of Thomas: "Whoever will drink from my mouth will become as I am and I myself will become that person, and the things that are hidden will be revealed to him." The Gospel of Thomas also relates that "His disciples said to Christ, 'When will the Kingdom come?' And Jesus said, 'It will not come by expectation. They will not say, "See here," or "See there," but the Kingdom of the Father is spread upon the earth and men do not see it.'"

Christ came to help all of us to see the kingdom, to open our eyes to love. To bring us directly into the divine presence here on earth in all the ordinary splendor of our ordinary lives. In the Gospel of Thomas, Christ also says: "If those who lead you say to you 'Look, the kingdom is in the sky' then the birds will arrive there before you. If they say to you 'It is in the sea' then the fish will arrive before you." The kingdom of God, Christ makes clear, is an *inner* revelation, a stage of naked self-discovery: "Rather the kingdom is inside of you, and it is outside of you. When you come to know yourselves, then you will be known, and you will realize that you are the children of the Father."

When you really begin to see that Christ's mission was to help us realize our direct relation to God and to bring about the reign of love and justice here on earth—for recognition of the kingdom would inevitably be followed by enactment of its

sacred laws of healing, compassion, interrelationship, and justice—and to meditate on this, then everything appears different in Christianity. Everything changes. You realize that the
fatal mistake, the fatal shift, was the shift from seeing Christ
as the divine messenger of our own divinity to an unapproach-
able and magnificent "son of God" beyond all our powers of
understanding and praise. No one has ever analyzed this crucial mistake better than Jung, who examined our projection
onto all so-called divine beings, not just Christ.

Anne Baring and Jules Cashford's commentary on Jung's
passage illuminates our entry into it:

> By a strange and tragic twist of "fate" the numinous ground
> within the human being which was approaching the thresh-
> old of consciousness in many individuals and was personi-
> fied by Jesus as a teacher of Wisdom, was lost as Jesus was
> transformed into a god to be worshipped. Instead of the
> ground *within* the soul being recognized as divine, and related
> to the underlying divinity of the whole of life, the old literal
> pattern of the worship of a god was emphasized and the
> separation between consciousness and its ground was per-
> petuated. Immanence was tragically sacrificed to transcen-
> dence. Christians were taught that as long as they believed,
> belonged to and obeyed the Church, they would be redeemed
> by the sacrifices of Jesus' death on the Cross. And so, as
> Jung has pointed out, the divine image came to stand *out-
> side* man and woman, rather than within.[1]

Now listen really deeply to what Jung has to say, because
in this passage is the tragedy of our civilization:

> The demand made by the *imitatio christi* [the imitation of
> Christ]—that we should follow the ideal and seek to become
> like it—ought logically to have the result of developing and
> exalting the inner man. In actual fact, however, the ideal has
> been turned by superficial and formalistically mind believ-
> ers into an external object of worship and it is precisely this

veneration for the object that prevents it from reaching down into the depths of the soul and transforming it into a wholeness in keeping with the ideal. Accordingly, the divine mediator stands outside as an image while man remains fragmentary and untouched in the deepest part of him.... An exclusively religious projection may rob the soul of its values so that through sheer inanition it becomes incapable of further development and gets stuck in an unconscious state. At the same time it falls victim to the delusion that the cause of all disaster lies outside and people no longer stop to ask themselves how far it is in their own doing.[2]

So as it has developed, Christianity lost not only the Divine Mother, it also lost the outrageousness of the real message of Christ, the messenger. It has betrayed both because they are inextricably related. What was the Mother announcing then, as now? She was announcing the possibility of the direct relationship with the ground of God and of humankind's becoming divine in this life. When you deeply apprehend what is actually said in the Bible, what Christ is actually saying, then you realize that there has never been an apostle of the sacred feminine more passionate, more extreme, more beautiful, more ferocious, and more loving than Jesus Christ. Christ came to dissolve, destroy, and end the patriarchy. But to protect itself, the patriarchy took the glory of Christ's passion and his sacrifice and made a "Church" around it, thereby entombing and shutting off forever the violence and the beauty of the outrageously radical vision that he had come to give the world. By imprisoning Mary in a golden cage of adoration and by turning Christ into a god, the Church ensured that the naked demands of the sacred feminine—for a world transformed into the living image of love and justice—would be muffled and castrated, and so continued to crucify Christ again and again and to act as a screen against his force permeating and transfiguring the world.

When the Buddha was dying, his disciples came to him and

said, "How should we commemorate you?" With his remaining strength, the Buddha put the palms of his hands on top of each other, meaning that to commemorate him after everything that he'd tried to teach them was like heaping one emptiness upon another. The disciples took took that sign and made of it the shape of the *stupa*. Liberators come to us, announcing the good news of our divine identity, and what do we do? We usually kill them, and if we can't kill them, we kill them in another way: we create religions around them. We make them into gods so that we do not have to face the fierce demands that they have come to ask of us, demands to embrace and enact our divine identity and alter the whole of life. This god- and religion-making is the source of all limitation and all the mutilations of our divine identity.

Of all humankind's betrayals of its liberators, its betrayal of Christ is the hardest to bear. To create a clutch of hierarchical, misogynistic, homophobic, dogmatic churches in the name of the "lover of lovers," the one who Teresa of Avila called "the wild and broken-hearted prince of love," is an almost demonic enterprise and one that has blinded us for centuries.

Look again with fresh eyes at the Sermon on the Mount. There is no purer, clearer, more radical and complete statement of what the sacred feminine is than the Sermon on the Mount. In this most crucial of his teachings, Christ reverses all the patriarchal values, all the values of the world being born around him, reverses all the masculine values of power, exploitation, and domination; reverses all his—and our—culture's fascination with toughness, hardness, harshness, violence, and authority. The Sermon on the Mount is entirely about the feminine virtues of humility, patience, tenderness, and kindness. Christ is speaking as a male divinized by the Father-Mother, initiated into the transcendent force, and into the Mother's—*his* Mother's—radical knowledge of the power of powerlessness, the infinite force of humility. The kingdom he is revealing is the Father's *and* the Mother's:

Blessed are the poor in spirit, for theirs is the kingdom
of Heaven.

Blessed are those who mourn, for they shall be
comforted.

Blessed are the meek, for they shall inherit the earth.

Blessed are those who hunger and thirst for
righteousness, for they shall be satisfied.

Blessed are the merciful, for they shall obtain mercy.

Blessed are the pure in heart, for they shall see God.

Blessed are the peacemakers, for they shall be called
sons of God.

Blessed are those who are persecuted for
righteousness' sake, for theirs is the kingdom of
heaven.

I have been in the place where Christ is said to have delivered this sermon, a very bare chapel in Tabka, Israel. Its win-
dows give out right onto the Sea of Galilee. Standing in that
chapel and reading the Beatitudes in Latin on the walls, alone,
the revelation came to me that the landscape in which Christ
delivered this message to the world is an intensely maternal
landscape. The sea in front of the chapel is a glittering, pale
beautiful blue, Mary-blue, and all these warm, maternal, brown
dark hills are around it, like breasts caressed by Israel's pure
light. Christ gives this message of the divine feminine in a landscape that embodies its humility and its open loveliness, and
his message reflects that humility and loveliness. Moses gave
the law against the bare landscape of Sinai. Christ announces
the paradoxical rules of entry into the kingdom of love and
justice in a landscape redolent of the gentleness and strength
of the Mother. That landscape and the Mother are speaking
through him. He is her clearest, sweetest, fiercest voice, and the
truths that he announces are the truths she has always sustained.

"Blessed are the poor in spirit, for theirs is the kingdom of
heaven." They are "poor" in spirit because they are empty of
vanity and pride, empty of all those dogmas that would prevent

them from entering here, from being present here in love, and so in the kingdom of heaven.

"Blessed are those who mourn, for they shall be comforted." Blessed are those who dare to feel; who dare to suffer cruelty, oppression, and injustice; who dare to protest, who dare to say the sacred "No." Blessed are they who dare to take all the pain of life into themselves and face it without slick political or spiritual evasions. They shall be comforted, because in mourning itself, in grieving itself, in opening out and up to the pain and difficulty of life and to the pain and difficulty of what we have made of life, is the source of healing and the source of that just action that comforts and consoles.

"Blessed are the meek, for they shall inherit the earth." The earth, and the life that we live on it, does not belong to the powerful, because they feel and notice and understand nothing; blinded by privilege, they have their agendas, plans, and dogmas. Only the meek can really enter the truth of life. Only they can really know what earth they are on. It is they who come to know the great secret of the Mother: that life is an unbroken flow of normal miracle. It is they who inherit the earth, and only they, for the earth can only be known by the humble, attuned to its rhythms and laws and to the rhythms and laws of nature and life. The proud, the vain, the angry and violent, are all trapped in their various mind-hells that are really states of living death. Only the humble ever really arrive here, because they learn to share the humility of the Mother herself, of that universal love that is as present in the smallest ladybird as in the Andromeda galaxy, and that is always kneeling before all its own creations in adoration and tenderness.

"Blessed are those who hunger and thirst for righteousness, for they shall be satisfied." The real approach to spiritual truth and spiritual knowledge is to let yourself hunger and thirst for righteousness, to take up the feminine position of need, the feminine position of admitting that you need help, and asking for help to transform the conditions of the world. Christ blesses those who do, blesses those who hunger and thirst for righteousness and go on doing so, because by that perpetual hunger and by incessant thirst, they create the energy that the divine can use to help birth the kingdom, that kingdom of living actual justice of the Mother and her child that Christ wants on earth, which can only be created by human beings working humbly and with radical passion with the fire of grace.

"Blessed are the merciful, for they shall obtain mercy." This is profound, one of the most subtle Beatitudes, and it is very rarely dwelt on. Christ not only talks about mercy, again and again, but exemplifies mercy in how he lived. He says, "Blessed are the merciful, those that are merciful, blessed are they for they shall obtain mercy." They will taste mercy because the universe will support them in their work of mercy. When fate brings them into darkness, destiny will also surround them with the healing powers of the Divine Mother, the protection of the Divine Mother. As Simone Weil wrote, "There is something in the universe always on the side of the 'good.'" That "something" the merciful will know consciously and feel its astounding force of courage and protection.

"Blessed are the pure in heart, for they shall see God. Blessed are the peacemakers, for they shall be called sons of God." The sons of God, according to Christ, are not the powerful, are not the ones who "win," are not the violent, are not the punishing. They are the peacemakers, the bringers of balance and harmony. Has the vision of the Mother ever been put more clearly and absolutely? What is the sacred feminine but that force of boundless unconditional love that is always looking for reconciliation, forgiveness, and peace, and knows how to secure them?

The other aspect which is crucial to an understanding of Christ, of just how outrageous Christ is and how feminine in his outrageousness, is his understanding that love is worth nothing unless it is enacted. All these teachings are worth nothing unless they are at every moment put into action, just as he did. Christ did not merely speak in parables, he offered up his entire life as a sacrifice, a sacrifice that remains a perpetual accusation and challenge to all lesser intentions. Every second, every movement, every thought was offered up by Christ in devotion to the world. He never ceases to give birth out of love, to make love live in healing, in miracle after miracle. If there is anything that the sacred feminine is, it is love-in-action, love birthing itself in action incessantly. And if there is any life, *any life,* that has exemplified that birthing with such purity of passion, it is Christ's. Christ says in the Gospel of Thomas, "If you bring forth what is within you, what you bring forth will save you. If you do not bring forth what is within you, what you do not bring forth will destroy you." Enacting love, embodying the truth of love, is, then, literally a matter of life and death for every individual. Everyone has to become a mother of new life, or die. The whole universe is summoning us to this active motherhood that is the source of all real life.

In the Last Supper, just before the terrors and the agonies of the Crucifixion came upon him, Christ said, "Take, eat, this is my body. This is my blood." There is no cold, abstract "intellect" in that, no male separation, no cult of transcendence, no trying-to-go-somewhere-else, no hiding behind immortality or visionary ecstasy or "enlightenment." Christ is saying, "Look at the horror and the glory of life, enter right into the fire, and burn as love in the fire, as I am doing. When you share this great sacrament that imparts this divine identity to all of you, do not go to it in some otherworldly ethereal way; remember— *this is my body, this is my blood."* Christ's demand is naked, maskless, passionate, transcendental and immanent, mystical and physical. Christ corners us with the inescapable intensity of his demand to give everything as he did; to stake, as he does, our blood and bodies on the building of the kingdom in reality. Christ does not say, "This is my philosophy, and these are my dogmas." He does not say, "These are my twelve commandments and this is my church." He says, "This is my body, this is my blood." He is asking us all to sacrifice ourselves to make love real. This active love is the Mother's love, and its glory radiates through the Christian tradition when it is properly and deeply understood.

You hear that glory in another celebration of the divine feminine, in I Corinthians 13, in which Paul sums up everything that he has learned of the essential nature of Christ, from his visionary connection with Christ. He sums it up in a vision— not a philosophy, not a dogma—but a vision of love, that love that led Christ (and Paul himself) to risk and suffer everything.

> If I speak in the tongues of men and of angels, but have not love, I am a noisy gong or a clanging cymbal. If I have prophetic powers and understand all mysteries and all knowledge, and if I have all faith so as to remove mountains but have not love, I am nothing. If I give away all I have and if I deliver my body to be burned but have not love, I gain nothing.

Listen to these words, how radical they are, how they sweep away almost everything that we believe we want: the powers, the knowledge, the understanding of the mysteries; all the psychic experiences and sensations. Paul, and Christ through him, is saying, "Get rid of all of that. All of that is potentially vanity and self-absorption and narcissism." The only way into the burning presence of the divine is by loving with every cell in your body, mind, heart, and soul, and living that love and embodying it.

> If I have prophetic powers and understand all mysteries and all knowledge, and if I have all faith so as to remove mountains but have not love, I am nothing. If I give away all I have and if I deliver my body to be burned but have not love, I gain nothing.

In all religious literature, there is nothing I know as radical and absolute as that. Only love-in-action matters, only that, all the rest is sentimentality. Then, Paul turns to describe what love is:

> Love is patient and kind. Love is not jealous or boastful. It is not arrogant or rude. Love does not insist on its own way,

it is not irritable or resentful, it does not rejoice at wrong, but rejoices in the right. Love bears all things, believes all things, hopes all things, endures all things.

If there was one sentence that really sums up the life of Mary—and of her child—it is this: "Love bears all things, believes all things, hopes all things, endures all things." That is the core of the unshakable, patient, all-bearing, all-enduring, all-understanding love of the Divine Mother.

Paul goes on:

Love never ends. As for prophecies, they will pass away. As for talents, they will cease. As for knowledge, it will pass away. For our knowledge is imperfect, and our prophecy is imperfect, but when the perfect comes, the imperfect will pass away. When I was a child, I spoke like a child, I thought like a child, I reasoned like a child. When I became a man I gave up childish ways, for now we see in a mirror dimly, but then face to face. Now I know in part, then I shall understand fully, even as I have been fully understood. So faith, hope, love abide, these three. But the greatest of these is love.

When the full urgency and agony and passion of Christ's vision of love and love-in-action breaks upon the mind of the world, the world will really be transformed because we will finally have come into the kingdom and know that it is here, that we are in it, that we *are* it.

This complete mystical passion of Christ, this complete mystical vision, is not found in the Gospels as we have them, although there are amazing traces of it in John and Luke especially, and in what comes through Paul. It is found, however, in a very startling way in the Gospel of Thomas. This text was discovered in the late Forties and translated in the late Fifties. It is thought that this text was derived from a group of sayings collected by Christ's own brother, James. The history of Western civilization would have been different if we had had these original ecstatic, gnostic, mystical sayings of Christ as the foundation of our knowledge of him, instead of what the later Gospels gave us. If we had known that Christ is the sacred androgyne, the yogi-son of the Divine Mother and the Divine Father, revealing the divinity inherent in all of us; and if we had known that Christ at no moment separated earth from heaven, body from spirit, sexuality from sanctity, at no moment separated the heart from the mind, and the mind from the soul, and the soul from the body—if we had known these things, then this long patriarchal ghastliness, the huge terrible destructiveness of modern culture might never have taken place.

I want to share with you from the Gospel of Thomas three extraordinary Logions (sayings). In the Gospel of Thomas is a complete vision of the Sacred Father and the Sacred Mother, an entire vision of the burning bliss of being, an entire vision of the absolute holiness of this life, this creation, this world, this body.

Before unravelling Logion 77, which goes even deeper than the Sermon on the Mount into a vision of total sacredness and immanence, let's look at Anne Baring's introduction to the Gospel of Thomas in her and Jules Cashford's *Myth of the Goddess:*

> In 1956, Professor Gilles Quispel discovered the Gospel of Thomas in Cairo and realized that it contained material from the Jewish tradition, and, most significantly, that it was related to the earliest Jewish-Christian congregation in Jerusalem. Scholars now accept that this Gospel transmits the original Aramaic sayings of Jesus that were preserved by the members of his brother James' group, and that this was one of the earliest sources drawn on for the sayings in the Gospels of Matthew and Luke. One or more members of this group went to Odessa and established a centre of teaching there, and the Gospel of Thomas transmits the essence of this teaching.... There are many familiar passages in the Gospels of the New Testament in which Jesus

speaks of the embodiment of Sophia, the divine light of Wisdom, but there are other places from the Gospel of Thomas that are not so well known.[3]

And Logion 77 is one of them. Listen now to its full madness. In it you will hear, in five short lines, the whole message of the sacred feminine:

> I am the light that is above them all.
> I am the all.
> The all came forth from me, and the all attained to me.
> Cleave a piece of wood, I am there.
> Lift up the stone and you will find me there.

In those five lines, Jesus moves from transcendence to the most tiny, naked, burning, simple, ordinary, banal immanence and shows you that the eternal light and the tiny slug under the stone are one and the same, forever and ever. And more, that the person who observes that, feels that, knows that, is one with the all, one with the one beyond all barriers and dogmas, one with both the transcendent source and the creation.

"I am the light above them all." The utter transcendent light of the divine Father-Mother. "I am the all." All the great mystics have shown us this, that everything that is, is finally what we are. But Christ goes on and puts the definition of being the all in a very maternal way. He says, "All came forth from me," I am the source that gives birth to everything. Let us recall that the Divine Mother is not just the ground of reality, and not just the energy, the Shakti, that the ground is manifesting to create, but is also the culmination and consummation of the process of evolution, the place to which all the universe is spiraling up in all of its transformations. This is what Christ is saying: "I am the all. The all came forth from me . . ." the light gave birth to the cosmos, " . . . and the all attained to me."

The all *attained* to me. The *all* actually arrived in me, in the "I," in the eternal light. This is a way of saying that everything is totally sacred, everything is holy, as Blake says. When the masks go, when the Mother gives us the revelation of where we are, when we finally arrive here, we see that "the all has attained to me," that just by being here, we are in her. We are in the light, present and immortal, all in one burning, sacred moment. As Christ says in another saying; "Penetrate the present depth." In Logion 77 Christ goes ever deeper and wilder, and as if to say, "If you don't believe me—*cleave a piece of wood"*—of *wood!*—the dullest, least significant kind of thing, the perfect image for a carpenter's son. "Cleave a piece of wood, I am there."

The eternal godhead is as present in a bit of chipped wood as it is in the choirs of seraphim and cherubim.

"Lift up the stone and you will find me there." As Christ said in the logion with which this chapter began, "The kingdom is here, only we do not see it." Christ is not talking about other worlds, dimensions, spheres. He was in ultimate reality here and trying passionately to transmit the final vision of the Divine Mother, her final gift which is to arrive here on this earth, in this body, and to know this life as a totally sacred experience lived always as Blake puts it, "in eternity's sunrise."

In the next logion I have selected, Logion 22, Christ gives the ultimate statement of the whole process of sacred alchemy in the feminine. In this brief saying is the entire alchemy of the Father-Mother, the entire alchemy of the sacred androgyne, the entire alchemy of what happens within the spirit as it comes to be absorbed into and becomes one with the ground of all things:

> When you make the two, one, and when you make the inner as the outer, and the above as the below, and when you make the male and female into a single one, so that the male will not be male, and the female not be female, then you shall enter the Kingdom.

Christ is speaking here as a realized sacred androgyne, one who has combined all of the different aspects of reality in the transformation into total sacred androgyny. He is saying: "Make the two one"—life and death one, body and spirit one, heaven

and earth one, make them one by fusing them in gnostic understanding, vision, and sacred action. And when you make the
"inner as the outer," you know that what you are staring out
at is yourself, your most divine self, manifesting in a billion different ways. You *know this,* you're not just reading it on a page
or imagining it; you know it because your spirit has been through
the hundred thousand fires necessary so that it can actually see,
feel, and taste it in every second. When you have seen that the
"inner is the outer, and the outer is the inner," you have dissolved the final barriers that the ego-mind erects to try and prevent you from discovering that huge secret: the living kingdom
of God.

Christ is also saying, "When you make the inner as the outer,
the outer as the inner, the above as the below," you realize that
all this nonsense about dogmas and hierarchy is so much mind-
made slavery, that, as Heraclitus says, "The way up is the way
down, and the way down is the way up." You can find sacredness everywhere, and instruction and fundamental forms of
teaching everywhere, and that what is normally thought of as
profane is also sacred; what is normally thought of as unholy is
also holy. Really strip away the categories and concepts of what
enlightenment is, of what spiritual achievement is, of what it
means to climb the rungs of the understanding of emptiness.
When you stop buying all the theories and philosophies and
actually enter into the full mystic outrageousness of the divine
presence that is beyond all names and forms, then you will know
that you have gone beyond duality. You will know that the mangy
old dog dying in the gutter is as sacred as the Dalai Lama, as the
Dalai Lama himself well knows. You will be free. You will be
free because you belong to no system, you have come into the
full splendor of God's own wild love for all things, and your
original self at the same time, "When you make the inner as the
outer, and the outer as the inner, and the above as the below."

And Christ goes on, "and when you make the male and the
female into a single one, so that the male will not be male, and
female not be female"—this is very profound and subtle, and

points to the truth of what is meant by a revolution of the sacred feminine. Such a revolution is not about the "feminization" of everything; it is about the mysterious, fecund balancing of all dualities. It is the bringing of everything into so true a relation that what we now think of as "masculine" is transformed by its contact with what we now call the "feminine," and what we have thought of as "feminine" is transformed and irradiated by its contact with the "masculine," so that both enter into a completely different stage of richness, unity, and radical fertility.

The only symbol that comes close to expressing this is the yin-yang symbol. In the yin-yang parts of both elements are present in each. One part is black, one part is white, and in the white there is black, and in the black there is white. If you are really looking at the symbol, your eye cannot rest, because the white tapers into the black and the black soars into the white. It draws your eye around and around, in its endless cycle of the two parts that are one. What you then enter is the dynamic unity of reality in which both "feminine" and "masculine" are continually transforming each other, and transforming into the other. This is the meaning of the sacred androgyne: to be one with the ground of reality, to be the divine child, to be free, both the masculine and the feminine deeply fused, and so become one that both includes and is beyond them. When you have made the male and female into one, so that the male will not be male, and the female not be female, then you shall enter the kingdom—because the kingdom will be blazing around you and you yourself will be the kingdom. You will be divine, naturally, normally, and simply, you will know and feel and see everything as divine, and you will see the whole world radiating, literally, normally, in the divine light of your own love because you will have reconciled in yourself the two aspects of the godhead, the Father and the Mother, and be one with the godhead they both spring from, and be always acting in love, for love, radiating the kingdom with every thought and action.

This unity Christ came to reveal and to live out. That is what the Christ-force is attempting to initiate us all into in the world.

Listen now to a great Christian mystic, Juliana of Norwich,
in her meditation on Jesus as the Mother. It's a woman's meditation, and it took a woman, really, to understand this aspect
of Christ in both its transcendence and its practicality:

> Jesus is the true mother of our nature, because He made us.
> He is our mother, too, by grace, because He took our cre-
> ative nature upon Himself. All the lovely deeds and tender
> services that beloved Motherhood implies are appropriate
> to the second person. In Him Godly will is always safe and
> sound, both in nature and in grace, because of His own fun-
> damental goodness. I came to realize that there were three
> ways of looking at God's Motherhood. The first is based on
> the fact that our nature is made. The second is found in the
> assumption of that nature, the fact that God and Jesus took
> on nature, so that in the generosity and the abandon of that,
> there begins the Motherhood of grace. The third is the Moth-
> erhood of work, which flows out over all by that same grace.
> The Motherhood of love in action, the length, and breadth,
> and height, and depth of it are everlasting and so is His love.

Juliana goes on:

> A mother's is the most intimate, willing, and dependable of
> all services, because it is the truest of all. None has ever been
> able to fulfill it properly but Christ; He alone can. We know
> that our own mother's bearing of us was a bearing to pain
> and death, but what does Jesus, our true mother, do? Why
> His love bids us to joy and to eternal life. Blessings on Him.
> Thus He carries us within Himself in love, and He is in labor
> until the time has fully come for Him to suffer the sharpest
> pangs and most appalling pain possible and in the end He
> dies. Not even when this is over, and we ourselves have been
> born to eternal bliss is His marvelous love completely sat-
> isfied. This He shows in that overwhelming word of love
> that He said to me [in the visions Juliana received] "If I could
> possibly have suffered more, indeed I would have done so."

This fine and lovely word, Mother, is so sweet and so much its own that it cannot properly be used of any but Him, and of Her who is His own true mother, and ours.

I have already described how Eryk and I left Meera and Thalheim after our horrible suffering there and went immediately to the places where the Virgin appeared in Belgium, Banneux, and Beauraing.

It was in the first place we stopped—Banneux—that I began to realize that the new journey into the real Mother that was beginning would also necessitate a complete revisioning of Christ. Something marvelous and strange happened. After worshipping in the shrine where Mary had appeared and washing my face and hands in the icy sacred spring nearby, I went into the local shop that sold religious souvenirs. There I found, to my astonishment, the complete version of an image of Christ that I had once found in a New York thrift store and had loved for years. My picture had only the uppermost part of this particular painting of Christ; now I saw the whole body.

My whole being shook and tears came, for what I saw in that ramshackle souvenir shop, I knew, was the full Christ. In the complete painting, Christ is standing with his hand raised in blessing, greeting, and warning; his face is grave, majestic, and intimate, male and female, all at once. From his heart—which he is pointing to with his right hand—streams not one by two rivers of light. It was on these two rivers of light that my mind focused. The one flowing to the right is the white light of the source, of the Father. The other, which flows in sweet passionate radiance to the left, is the pink light of the Mother, a pink light that I had seen several times in vision and knew as the light of the Mother's love, compassion, and infinite tenderness. This is the Christ of St. John's Gospel and the Gospel of Thomas, the Good Shepherd and the sacred androgyne of Logion 22, the divine savior and the earthly brother-in-love, the sacred child of both the Father and the Mother, the image of the completely awake, active, mystical-practical child of God.

The brief vision that I had had years before standing before
the statue of Shiva Ardhanarishvara in Mahabalipuram found
its abiding and revelatory consummation in this image that I
knew I was being given by the Mother as an inspiration, clue,
command, and challenge. I realized, in fact, that the meaning
of what had happened in Thalheim (a meaning, I hasten to add,
unintended by Meera) was to restore me not only to the Mother-
as-Mary but also and simultaneously to this full and complete
and androgynous Christ that was—and is—at once the really
revolutionary Christ, the Christ whose passion for transformation of reality has to be reawakened now in the world, and the
truth of my own identity, and of the identity of all human beings.
Here, before me, at the heart of the Western tradition, was an
image that fused all the various profound mystical intuitions
that my long journey through Eastern mysticism had engendered
in me, and pointed mysteriously beyond them to a radical, passionate, inescapable, fiercely demanding truth of love-in-action
now, here, in the world. The Mother had taken me on a long
and frightening journey through various ordeals and illusions
to this return to her in Mary-in-Jesus and Jesus-in-Mary, this
revelation of her presence at the mystical heart of the faith of
my childhood and my ancestors and my civilization.

I realized then how we must all rediscover Christ. It does
not matter if we call ourselves Christian or not, that is not
important. To come into contact with the astounding force of
love-in-action that is Christ is essential at this moment in the
transformation of the West. The Eastern traditions have wonderful things to offer us, astonishing revelations, vast depths of
mystical understanding, but they largely lack what Christ brings
to the table of the world: a burning sense of present action, of
present love, an absolute insistence on justice. In the mandala
of the sacred masters (and there are many of them in that mandala coming from all religions and all parts of the world), I
believe that Christ represents the burning broken heart, the
heart that was pierced as his mother's heart was pierced, and
from that heart is always streaming out the light of the Mother

and the light of the Father, the light of gnosis and of gnosis-as-action. We cannot go forward as a civilization until we have found the way to welcome the Mother and Christ right back into the center so that we can begin to live, really for the first time, what they came to give us: our own divinity in love and truth, in love and the making real of love as an end to all cruelty, pollution, injustice everywhere.

Let me return now to Christ himself and his life. When Christ is seen as the sacred androgyne child of the Father-Mother and as the one who fused with unique intensity the Father's transcendence with the passion of the Mother for charity and justice, then the actual shape and meaning of his earthly journey becomes much clearer. In many ways he can be seen as journeying into the Mother, into himself becoming a mother, into, as Marguerite of Oingt made clear in the passage I quoted at the beginning of this chapter, giving birth on the terrible bed of the cross to the new humanity and the new creation. Resurrection is childbirth, the birth of the new world; and to give birth to the new world, Christ had to become completely a mother, to learn and embody the power of total love, to embody, in its fullest, most dreadful, and so most powerful sense, the power of humility, of surrender, of total gift. Like a mother who gives birth, he had to consent to be torn apart. To become a mother he had to incarnate in every way the Mother's knowledge of the power of powerlessness, the power that arrives when every form of human power—political or religious—has been given up in the name of love, the power that subverts the patriarchy from within and unveils and dissolves all its desolate and suicidal games. Jesus had to consent to be stripped of every "masculine," patriarchal support, of any support at all, to embody and discover the radical divine power of rebirth that springs straight from the dark and burning heart-core of the Mother.

So what happens—and must happen—in the process leading up to the crucifixion is that Jesus is stripped, terribly, again and again, of any remnant of masculine or patriarchal identity—of his name, his role, his message, his mission. Everything goes, until he is nothing but pure pain and pure love on the cross, until he is nothing but *her* sacred heart, open forever in an abandon of embrace. At that moment Christ becomes one with the Mother and can give birth to the new humanity. She is standing there by the cross, feeding him her mystical strength so that he can enter into the absolute darkness, the essence that she is also. His great act is one of consent to this surrender. He and his Mother become one, and that moment is the resurrection, the new humanity is born; matter baptized in the darkness of the Mother is reborn in the light of the source. Heaven is pulled down into every cell of earth and love knitted in blood and light to every atom.

A German scholar of Aramaic told me about recent research that underscores what I am saying. He told me that Jesus may have been punning on the cross. Let me share with you the full brilliance of the pun. Just before he dies, Jesus cries out, *"Eli, Eli lama sabactrani,"* which is translated in the "authorized version" as "My Lord, My Lord, why hast thou forsaken me?" Apparently, the meaning of the Aramaic word *sabactrani,* "forsaken," might also be interpreted as "glorified"—"My Lord, My Lord, why has thou *glorified* me?"

By tasting total abandonment and forsakenness, total loss, by being stripped of everything, any conceivable kind of power that the ego, even the subtlest spiritual ego, could want, anything that he could cling to or hope for, any kind of dignity that could remain; by being totally devastated, demolished, disintegrated, dissolved, destroyed, Jesus was—and knew himself to be—at the last moment glorified, so emptied by agony that nothing remained but that glory, but her. At that moment he went into the darkness and he saw that he was both simultaneously abandoned and glorified.

The entire human race and the planet is at a similar moment of paradox. All the old structures and systems of transmission are burning before our eyes. Even in this appalling destruction, however, we are not being abandoned, but are being brought closer to the nuclear secret of our own divine identity—that secret that all the mystical truths have been trying to give us, that we have evaded time and time again by creating religions and dogmas and theologies around them. Everything has failed, but our divine identity waits to glorify us in the darkness of total loss. We have nowhere else to go but into our divine truth, because human madness stands revealed, and we are visibly dying in it and from it.

Richard of St. Victor, one of the greatest medieval Christian mystics, wrote a book called *On the Four Degrees of Violent Charity*. He divided the steep stairway of love by which we travel to union into four steps: the betrothal, the marriage, the union or wedlock, and the fruition of the soul:

> On the first step, the soul is awakened, and on the second it is made on fire with love. In the third, the soul passes beyond significant or ecstatic events and is initiated into the steady divine light [what is normally thought of as enlightenment]. The soul passes utterly up into God and is glorified in God.

Most mystic diagrams end there, in the transformed union, but Richard of St. Victor saw clearly that the marriage of the soul and its origin could not be a barren ecstasy:

> In the fourth stage, the soul, the bride, after being caught up into such final delight, is humiliated below herself, [these are his words; remember that he is meditating on Christ.] accepts the pains and duties of love, after enjoying its sublimest raptures and becomes a source, and a mother of new life.

The bride of God, the *"sponsa dei,"* he says, becomes the *"mater divinae graziae,"* the mother of divine grace, a fountain of fertile tender activity, a center of transcendental energy, a creator of spiritual families who co-labor with God in the divine life. That is what our time is calling us all to be, the Mother's fountains of radical confidence, co-creators with him and her of a new world.

Richard of St. Victor's is a vital diagram, because it doesn't
end in the attainment and possession of a state, it ends in an
abundance of charity, of love and energetic action in the world.
The "mother of divine grace" is what Christ himself became.
The whole journey of the soul in Christ is toward that divine
motherhood in which the Christing of the soul results in becoming a mother and a source of transcendental energy, action, and
love.

The spiritual revolution that is trying to be born will not be
born unless the true mystic Christ returns; and the true mystic
Christ cannot return without the Mother, for Jesus and Mary
are two aspects of the same immense transformation, two sides
of one vast transformatory yoga of love in which all things are
reborn in the fire of the Mother's presence and passion. It is to
that transformatory yoga of active divine love that everyone
now, whatever their religion, is being called.

Any vision that is not rooted in the transcendent will inevitably fail because it will not know how to be fed by the invisible or inexhaustible springs of grace; any vision not also rooted
in the immanent will also fail, because vast political and economic changes have to be effected at every level and very wisely
and very fast for us to have a chance to survive. In Christ's journey, in Christ's fusion of Father and Mother, love and action,
prayer and justice, heaven and earth, body and soul, we have
a permanent revolutionary example which up to now we have
done everything to avoid enacting, including creating church
after church in Christ's name that have served only to dampen
and divert the full outrageous force of what he was and always
is at the heart of every human heart, at the core of every human
self.

There is talk everywhere of "spiritual revolution," but there
can be no useful spiritual revolution now without the clearest
and most demanding possible vision of justice and action. Any
vision—however exalted and with whatever distinguished a
pedigree—that does not simultaneously bring us up against the
full brutality of the unbearable facts and also give us an active

response to them, is frivolous. Christ's demand to give our "blood" and our "body" and to follow him onto the cross of passion and sacrifice in the service of love remains the wildest and fullest demand that has ever been placed on us.

On whether we can respond to it in all of its aspects, divine and human, mystical and political, understood and embodied simultaneously and together, depends the future of the West and of the planet.

## Questions and Answers

*What parallels are there between what you are saying and alchemical tradition?*

It was in the alchemical tradition—as well as in the writings of certain great mystics such as Eckhart—that the secret knowledge of Jesus being not a god but the inherent divinity of every human being was preserved, often against tremendous opposition. The alchemists, as Jung pointed out so eloquently, were mystic pioneers of integration and individuation; what they aimed to engender through their mysterious processes was to produce the "philosopher's stone," which is really the healed and divinized being, the one who has become "Christed." Alchemical gold is a symbol for the divinized and integrated self, the self that has been through the ordeals of all the various stages—the *nigredo, calcinatio, mortificatio,* etc.—in order to, as Jung said, "make the darkness conscious." With all its previously unconscious faculties raised to divine truth, after repeated harsh shattering, the self is regrouped around its divine core, and so achieves the "sacred marriage" between the inner masculine and feminine, soul and body, heaven and earth.

This mirrors exactly what I have said about Christ's enterprise, and I think one way of understanding alchemy is to see it as a Mother-science, as another way the officially rejected sacred feminine had of being present at deeper levels. It has all the qualifications for a Mother science—a passion for integration at every level and in every dimension, a deep awareness of the sacredness of matter, an ability to embrace and use processes of destruction and grief and decay for transformatory purposes, a knowledge of the divinity of life itself and of the divinity waiting to be awakened in humanity. Many of the alchemical texts contain extensive references to the healing and transforming powers of the Virgin in particular and the Mother in general.

I find too that the alchemical model of the mystical journey helps me in retrospect to understand Christ's journey more deeply and confirms my awareness that it is a journey into the Mother as well as a journey in the Father. In fact, I think the alchemists knew this without necessarily needing to put it into the language and in the way that I am doing. They knew that the glory and uniqueness of Christ's passion was his embrace of the terms of human life, his embrace of matter and reality, the extraordinary courage of his hunger and his willingness to undergo all the necessary ordeals to realize his goal to bring the whole of life into the light. So the alchemists developed a three-part schema of transformation which is clearly an account of the tantric Mother-change that I have been describing in different ways throughout this book.

The first stage is *separatio*—the separation through purification and spiritual discipline of the spirit from the body, so the spirit can know itself and its divine transcendent source. This is where many patriarchal models of enlightenment end—in the vision of the divine light at the end of this stage. But for the alchemists, as for Christ and the Mother, the *separatio* is only the first stage, a vital first step—since without living experience of the transcendent no divine human life is possible—but it is *only* a first step. After it comes a stage which has been called various names but which is essentially a stage of descent, a stage in which the light that has been seen and known as the transcendent source is painstakingly and in great danger and difficulty invoked, drawn on, and "married" to life, to matter, to earth, to the unconscious.

As Dorn writes in his *Physica Trismegisti,* "In the end it will come to pass that this earthly, spagyric birth clothes itself with heavenly nature by its ascent, and then by its descent visibly puts on the nature of the center of the earth, but nonetheless the heavenly center which it acquired by the ascent is secretly preserved." Correspondingly, after the baptism and the temptation in the desert, Christ did not "leave" or remain in the secure glory of transcendence; he "came down" into the plains and began the huge Mother-labor of marrying the transcendent to the immanent in direct healing action that was to sweep him forward onto and beyond the "childbed" of the cross into the full divine birth of the resurrection.

This "descent" involves necessary ordeals—ordeals in which the old self is shattered repeatedly, dissolved, broken down so that it can be remade, "resurrected" around and in the deathless "gold" of real awareness, the awareness of the divine child born from the sacred marriage of heaven and earth, the Christ-awareness in which "here" is known and lived as the kingdom. As this "marriage" between soul and body and heart and mind becomes ever more complete, stage two merges into stage three, the stage of the *res simplex,* the "simple thing," where the now integrated and divinized self mysteriously becomes one with the simple ground of the whole cosmos, just as Christ became one with the entire universe in the resurrection and ascension. In this stage, the life of the perfected individual self flows and merges into the cosmic divine life. As Flamel puts it, "The water of the river flows into and merges with the sea."

What the alchemists have understood, I think, is the "scientific" nature of Christ's journey, the way in which its different stages exemplify exactly the workings of transformatory grace. They have understood that Christ's life is a diagram, a living organic map of transformation in the Mother. The eighth of the *Emerald Tablets* (a central alchemical text) puts this enterprise—the enterprise of the Mother—perfectly: "Ascend with great intelligence from earth to heaven and again descent to earth, and unite the powers of higher things with lower things. Thus you will receive the glory of the world and darkness will fly about you."

Christ came to give us the glory of the world and to show us how to find, honor, and embody it. He said, "Take up your cross and follow me." This the alchemists interpreted most profoundly as a call to the courageous facing of everything dark, stubborn, and intractable in the psyche and in matter, a call to the "crucifixion" of the false, perverse, limited, and unconscious self so that its true "resurrected" being could be realized. What the alchemists are essentially offering to anyone who accepts their challenge and analysis is what Christ is inviting us to—Divine Motherhood, to become "mothers" through undergoing the complexity and pain and grace of the process of transformation, "mothers" of our own secret Christ-self. They are inviting us to give birth to our inner Christ, and in the way that Christ himself "gave birth" to his self. The system they developed is at least as subtle as the Hindu and Mahayana mystical systems, and more useful now in many ways because of its exacting sobriety, its emphasis on birthing heaven here, its brave insistence on divinizing and integrating all aspects of human life, its continual stress on humility by being the architect of all real progress, and its celebration of the virtues of the most exact—and exacting—kinds of inner lucid illusionless observation. Alchemy also offers a very moving account of the direct path and of the subtle miracles that spring from persistent and radical trust in the holy spirit and in life as the Mother.

*How has your study of and immersion in the Christian tradition affected your understanding of the guru-disciple relationship?*

It is an astonishing fact that all the great Christian saints and mystics, from St. Paul to the Curé d'Ars and beyond, were initiated directly by the Holy Spirit, by God. There is a tradition of spiritual guidance within the Church and the mystical tradition, but never ever of deifying the adept.

The directness of the Christian path is one reason why I believe the Christian mystics are helpful now. They know the rigors and dangers and temptations of the direct path, know from sometimes harsh and always demanding inner experience just how much passion, clarity, and discrimination are needed to establish authentic contact with the divine. They also knew just how dangerous were occult powers, which wanted either

to exploit transformation or to prevent it, and had to learn to
protect themselves. The Christian mystics, from the Desert
Fathers on—precisely because they were on the direct path,
the path of the heart-to-heart transformation—had to develop
an extremely sober, no-nonsense vision both of the mystical
path itself and of the nature of mystical development. No Christian mystic ever claimed that the creature becomes God in mystical experience, only that a union in the ground of the soul
is possible.

The Eastern propaganda that a guru is essential for enlightenment is simply not true, and the whole magnificent proces-
sion of Christian saints proves quite the opposite, and encourages
by the intensity of their example anyone now who wants to go
to God directly.

*Is the sacred androgyne Christ you have been describing also
a tantric Christ?*

Yes. To birth the sacred androgyne in the soul and mind and
heart and body is the sign of tantric truth and mastery, the ultimate reward of a tantric discipline. The Christ I am describing
is a tantric master yogi-child, the one who finally and forever
married masculine and feminine, heaven and earth, and so
opened to the whole race the nuclear secret of its divinity and
the potential divinity of life on earth.

Any couple who consecrate their love to Mary and Jesus will
find, as Eryk and I am finding, that the Christ-fire enters into
and irradiates their lovemaking at every level. And this is not
just metaphor; the "green fire" of the Holy Spirit, what Hildegard of Bingen described as *"viriditas,"* is nakedly visible when
pure love is present and its effects are palpable at every level—
physically, in healing the pains and awkwardness of the body,
those places which false shame and guilt have hidden for decades;
emotionally, in revealing the all-encompassing dance of love in
the universe; and spiritually, in slowly but astoundingly birthing
both partners into the beginnings of Christ-consciousness.

What happens in the consecration of sexuality to Christ is that its essential Christ-heat is released; the Christ-heat that is the outstreaming of the completely open sacred heart and also the secret life-sustaining energy of the body, is now made alive, vivid, ecstatic and above all conscious. It is seen and known as one force, one central sacred directly initiatory force that has no divisions nor boundaries, and springs and flows and streams always from the Father-Mother. The aim of tantra-in-Christ is to awaken this Christ-Force, the force of love, and to permeate and saturate consciousness and ordinary life with it, and so grow "love's body" both spiritually, physically, and practically.

When Christ changed the water into wine at the marriage of Cana he was, I am convinced, blessing and consecrating the tantric tradition. Anyone who undertakes with someone else the work of sacred marriage in Christ's name will find himself or herself being sustained and illumined at extraordinary depths by his grace and fire-presence, will discover in fact many outrageous and transforming alchemical truths quite naturally and in a rhythmic divine-human order which unfolds simply and superbly. What happens is that both partners in a true tantric marriage open to Mary and Christ become their own and each other's "alchemists," give birth to the Christ in the other, become "mothers" of the other's divine child and in learning to "mother" the other with fidelity and compassion also simultaneously learns how to "mother" their own whole Christ-child into being. This process is an inexhaustible mystery, one that many will soon be uncovering and living in the reign of the Mother.

The hideous body- and sex-hatred, misogyny, and homophobia of most of the churches founded in Christ's name have obscured the tantric Christ and so prevented the Christ-force from doing the great and sublime work of sexual healing that it is empowered to do. Christ's is that Mother-love which dissolves all false shame, all false guilt, to renovate the whole of life in the *viriditas,* the "greenness" of the spirit. Where better to train this sacred healing-fire than on the dark places of sexual pain and wounding that are the source for so many of us of our deepest neuroses and fears, and some of the most fertile breeding grounds of cruelty, horror, and violence?

When the love of the sacred heart is allowed to inform and direct and saturate all forms of love, it transforms them all into its divine passion, ecstasy, and intensity, and not through denial at all—as the "church fathers" would always have it—but through acceptance and consecration. Consecrated human love *becomes* Holy Communion, and Christ's words, "Take. Eat. This is my body, this is my blood" reveal another dimension of simple miracle. Human divine lovemaking becomes the place where Christ is known and felt and seen and tasted, again and again; becomes a Christ-fire in which the old self is repeatedly immersed to burn away more and more of its falsity, hypocrisy, self-protective inhibition, secret self hatred and demonic contempt for the radiance of the body. It becomes, in fact, the site of a "simple" resurrection, the Alembic in which the "philosopher's stone" of Christhood is most naturally engendered. I am convinced the alchemists knew the sacred sexual secrets—some texts talk of a "mystical sister" or "mystical brother" being essential in the last stages of the quest—but they could not talk about them in their time because of its general sex-madness and sex-hatred. Now, thank God, these saving secrets can be shared; they are the bread and wine of the new communion between beings in the Mother.

*What does the Christian tradition have to say about the occult?*

The Christian mystical tradition's extreme sophistication about and awareness of the tremendous dangers of the occult stem from Christ himself. Look again at the three temptations Satan tempted Christ with in the desert; each of them are an invitation to another aspect of occult mastery, occult power. Christ refuses all occult powers and all power that does not spring directly from the heart of divine love, just as Ramakrishna did, and for the same reason—occult power is as potentially demonic as any other form of power.

Christ's critique of all forms of power-over-others is total and devastating. He knew that only the power of love could change anything and that any other power—or the search for it—blocked, distorted, and perverted that central divine and fundamentally egalitarian sacred force. Certainly Christ had extraordinary powers himself, but he used them with great economy and humility, in the service of other beings, and *never* to dominate or manipulate others.

In many ways, Christ took great pains not to be worshipped as a "guru": he continually referred those he had healed to the divine law and he moved from place to place, never allowing a cult to be built around him. This was because Christ wanted at all costs to avoid being separated from humanity, since what he was trying to give humanity was not "himself" but the relationship he knew with the source, the Father-Mother. He wanted people to awaken not to him, to a personality, but to their own divine relationship with God. Because his illumination was complete, it was empty of any need to prove or be anything; the Gospels make it clear that Christ's only desire was to give away the love he knew and was continually, and so awaken all beings to a revolution of love, a revolution that would sweep away all hierarchies, religious and political, and bring truth, consolation, and justice to everyone, not in "his" name but in the name of the love of the Father-Mother.

From very early on Christians were warned of the dangers of the occult, of "ministers of evil" masquerading as "angels of light." Christ himself warned them, as did Paul and St. John the Divine in Revelations; warned them continually and passionately of the amazing simulacrum of virtue that the demonic can be and of how one of evil's best disguises is in the clothes and rhetoric of holiness. These warnings alerted the Christian mystical tradition from the beginning and it is one of its greatest strengths that from the earliest Desert Fathers, from Macarius of Egypt and Clement of Alexandria right through Eckhart and Angela of Foligno to St. John of the Cross, Teresa of Avila, and later Therese of Lisieux and Elizabeth of the Holy Divinity—a tradition of amazing discrimination persisted to guard and protect and inform the aspiring soul.

This system is subtle, fierce, and complex and should be studied by every seeker, whatever their path, because in it vital distinctions are made at every level and in every dimension between the "occult" and the "divine," between spiritual powers that are used to enchant and control—or worse, to allow the infiltration of pride and evil—and spiritual powers that flow directly from the heart of divine love and deepen the soul's experience of love and humility. The Desert Fathers particularly are masters of this kind of essential discrimination and know very well that one effective way of snaring the fledgling soul is to dazzle it with its own powers and make it drunk on pride. Such drunkenness on mystical "sensation" makes the soul easy prey to the dark powers.

Because of the extremity of their passion to unite with Christ and the light, the Desert Fathers also developed the most scrupulous and sober ways of discriminating real experience from experience that is mixed with falsity or frankly prompted by the demonic. Later mystics—I think of St. John of the Cross and Teresa of Avila—built on these insights to develop very precise ways of telling when a vision was a vision and not a hallucination; when voices, for example, came from the source and not from the subconscious or the dark, and when mystical progress was real and not imaginary.

Essentially, all Christian mystics bring to the test of spiritual experience the "test" of Christ's own example. They all ask themselves and us: "Do your experiences make you humbler or do they not? Do they open you more to serving life and others as sacred beings, or do they not?" However "great" the experience seems, if it leads to any form of pride, even hidden and subtle, it is not divine. Any manipulation of another in any way through "spiritual" powers acquired on the ascent to God is, as Christ made clear, dangerous—and all the more dangerous because it is a blasphemy against the real holy spirit that always seeks to nourish love, not power.

Very few modern seekers understand, or dare to understand, the occult, the domain of what Hindus call the *siddhis,* the power to alter reality acquired on the ascent to God. Very few modern seekers have bothered to read the chapters in St. John of the Cross, "The Ascent to Mount Carmel," for example which discussed with scorching precision all the various kinds of subtle perversion that can defile mystical experience and tempt the adept.

Very few modern seekers have acquainted themselves with the teachings of the other mystical traditions—Sufi and Hindu, for example—or the letters of Sri Aurobindo, in which he clearly and with great painstaking wisdom tries to define from his perspective how the destructive powers that want the death of the human enterprise try to unnerve, exploit, appropriate, and invade spiritual transformation. For most modern seekers, the occult is an embarrassing topic, one to be dismissed as quickly as possible.

This is a disaster, because not understanding the occult and not being made aware of its astonishing powers—as I well know to my own cost—opens you up to being their perfect victim. Thinking you are having "divine" experiences given you by a "divine being" makes you easy guru-food. Most modern gurus—the vast majority—have embraced what Christ refused in the desert—embraced the occult powers that promise fame, money, power and more power. Most modern seekers are so hungry for sensational experience, so passionate for visions and trances, that they are easily manipulable by those who know how to "send" experiences. Any serious student of the occult will tell you how easy it is, after a certain stage, to send experiences and to hook others on your powers, and how this is not in any sense a sign of divinity but in fact of something close to the opposite. The vast majority of gurus are now occult magicians, power-mongers masquerading as "angels of light." They are, in fact, Mafiosi of the soul. When this fact is recognized widely, as I believe it will be in the coming years, the support of the contemporary guru system will be destroyed and its manipulation on subtle levels revealed as the psychic murder it is.

Seeing this without consolation or illusion is crucial at this moment because millions have been ensnared by occult manipulation, and being ensnared in this way cannot lead to true divine transformation, to the kind of transformation that is essential if the world is to survive. On the highest spiritual levels a war is now being fought for the future of the human race— between the occult "dictators" operating in the name of the divine who really want only their own glory, fame, and power, and who together, as Soloviev said, "make up" the Antichrist, and the real children of the Mother who want the release of the human race from all unnecessary hierarchy and lust for power, who want the true divine human life to be available to all. The greatest weapon in this war is clear discriminating intelligence, and it is hard to sustain. The Christian mystics again and again warn us of how easily the mind perverts or exploits truth, of how easily we can be seduced away from humility, of how subtle the difference is between a vision that initiates and one that confirms us in our own self-love. The "New Age" needs to heed their warnings in sober and sobering detail or millions will continue to be gulled by master-illusionists and continue to feed by their adoration the power-mania of cruel "occult corporations" that in their domain are as dangerous to the future as the industrial corporations are.

Horrible recent experience has confirmed to me that St. John's vision in Revelations of a "demonic Pentecost" in the "last days" is not some sort of sick poetic license, but something very like the actuality of the situation we live in, where magicians who materialize watches are treated as avatars, known pedophiles and sexual sadists are worshipped as enlightened beings, and false "divine mothers" who have the occult power to give sensational visions and experiences use the adoration engendered in the ignorant to increase their own fame and wealth and to protect by any means whatsoever their own power. Facing the extremity and evil of this situation has involved, in my own case, a shattering of every kind of naiveté. The great transformation that the Mother is trying to engender in the human race—the transformation of the direct path—has to be protected by the clearest, canniest, and shrewdest possible discrimination, otherwise it could fail and the human race die out.

*What do you think are the essential contributions of the Christian mystical tradition to what you call the revolution or return of the Mother?*

The great and central Christian teaching is the radical humility of Christ, a passionate and loving humility and the service that incessantly springs from it. This radical humility is the humility of God, that divine source that cradles everything in its arms of light and attends to all things with unfathomable tender love. All the high insights of the Christian tradition stem essentially from the humility of Christ's example, and this humility remains permanently radical in its implied rejection, as I have said, of all powers and putting-on-of-airs, and in its emphasis on the necessity of always flowing out in love in fertile and creative action and service for other beings.

This humility of Christ stems, as many mystics knew, from his relation to his mother. Ruysbroeck wrote in *A Mirror of Eternal Blessedness:*

> Although Mary was chosen above all creatures to be the mother of God and the Queen of Heaven and Earth, she nevertheless chose to be the handmaid of God and of all the world.... In the same way, her Son, our dear Lord Jesus Christ, who is both divine and human, after He had consecrated the blessed Sacrament, given it to His disciples, and received it Himself, wrapped a linen towel around Himself, knelt before His disciples, washed their feet, and dried them with the towel, saying "I am giving you an example, that as I have done to you, so you also should do in service to one another."

Ruysbroeck adds in a later passage:

> What is higher than the Son of God, yet what is lower than
> the servant of God and of all the world, Christ Himself?
> Again, what is higher than the Mother of God, yet what is
> lower than the handmaid of God and of all the world, Mary
> Herself?

To begin to experience this burning and sacred humility of
Christ and his Mother is to lose permanently any taste for power
of any kind, especially any kind of spiritual power that could
lead to vanity or self-inflation. Humility, as Ruysbroeck wrote
in *The Spiritual Espousals,* is "an interior bowing of the heart
and mind before the transcendent majesty of God." Christ and
Mary's humility is shattering—it shatters every human pretension, every human kind of pride and self-image. It shatters
to release anyone who contacts it into the boundless and bar-
rier-less life of the Mother-Father, of life itself.

From this central sacred and mystical fact of the necessity
of humility and service comes a mystical tradition whose greatest examples and writings made very careful spiritual distinctions which we need now more than ever.

I have already spoken of the Christian traditions' very careful and scrupulous understanding of the occult and how important that now is. Now I wish to speak of three other linked
sacred insights of this tradition that I myself have found invaluable in my journey into the Mother and which I believe are crucial. First, the insistence throughout the Christian tradition on
the difference between the Creator and the Creature, and on a
union-in-separateness or communion-in-love that mirrors in
the human soul's relation with God, the interrelation of the
Trinity; secondly, the vision of enlightenment as in no sense a
static or permanent achievement but the entry into a necessarily endless and infinite expansion toward the good, a vision
which begins with St. Paul and finds its supreme articulation
in the Gregory of Nyssa's "concept" or "discovery" of "*epectasis,*" which I will explain later; third, a corollary vision of

enlightenment or holiness, or what Ruysbroeck calls the "Super-essential Life," as being not one of solitary contemplation or mystic ecstasy alone but being, like Christ's, a life in which the highest mystical understanding is at all moments wedded to service in the world, to the flowing-out in charity and wise action and works of justice toward all beings. Each of these three linked insights seem essential to me, essentially sobering and humbling, and to have the perfume of the humility of the Divine Mother and of her practicality and love.

The distinction between Creator and Creature is, I am beginning to see, essential for the true mystical quest because it roots the seeker always in the humble ground of awe. The danger of the Hindu and Buddhist Mahayana systems is that they can encourage a too-easy equation of the human with the divine, a too-facile merging between the human and the divine that can lead to a dangerous inflation and the kind of ruthless and self-deluding cruelty that many modern gurus—and seekers—practice in the name of their own "divinity." Because Christ himself never claimed to be God—only to be one with the Father-Mother and dependent on them—the true Christian mystic never claimed to be God either.

Christ came to show the way to divinization of the self but the process was always seen as immensely difficult and the distinction he himself made was always maintained between the godhead and everything that streams from it. The humility this kept alive in the Christian mystic's heart allowed for the possibility for ever-greater progress, and for a continuing refusal to confuse being God with "deification," the process of "divinizing" the being. This is a vital distinction because there is always work to be done on the self, even after major mystical illuminations, and the best way to do this work is to preserve at the subtlest level the distinction between God, the Mother, and the child.

The human psychosomatic apparatus has limitations—of time, of perception—and God is always beyond any categories or concepts that even the most refined and soul-inspired intel-

lect can impose. Keeping that knowledge of ignorance alive
always in the mind, soul, and heart ensures that the Mother
can always lead you forward. Believing you are "deified" already
prevents you from doing the necessary grueling and sobering
work to prepare and embody real transformation. We are surrounded in the "New Age" with so-called masters and seekers
who confuse minor illumination with total divinity and who
use the heady rhetoric of the *Upanishads,* the *Bhagavad Gita,*
and other sacred texts to justify vicious behavior. The Christian mystics' caution and continual awe before the unknowable
and ineffable divine presence seems more than ever necessary.

In the Christian model, union with God is possible but it is
a union in which the person is not obliterated but completed,
in which individual "personhood" is not dissolved in ecstasy
or trance but perfected, brought to uttermost fullness in the
always-surpassing fullness of God—a union-in-separateness
where the ground of the soul becomes conscious of its oneness
with the ground of being but where the limitations of finitude
and all perception are also humbly and soberly acknowledged.
A growth in God in this model is always a growth in humility,
in sacred love of others and of the world. There is, of course,
the danger—which many great Christian mystics have not
avoided—of excessive mortification and self-hatred and self-
rejection when considering God so absolutely beyond all human
thoughts and enterprises. But at its sanest and wisest, in St.
Bernard of Clairvaux and Teresa of Avila and Ruysbroeck, for
example, such a vision of God's boundless grandeur serves
always to balance the human being, simultaneously to initiate
him or her into the truth of transcendence *and* the truth of finitude, and so keep him or her sober, alert, compassionate, awake
to every inner impulse that appropriates or exploits the truth.
This wise balance I see as the Mother's balance, and essential
on the direct path with all its dangers of inflation.

The truth that naturally flowers from such a vision—of
enlightenment or the "real life" as being an endless expansion—
*epectasis*—in and toward the God, the beautiful and the holy—

also seems to me essential now. The Sufis say that there are two journeys, the journey *to* God and the journey *in* God. The journey to God is finite; the journey in God is endless, because God is endless. This central sacred truth is accepted and developed to unparalleled heights of love and abandon by Gregory of Nyssa, who in his vision of *epectasis* adds something essential to the human understanding of enlightenment.

Briefly, Gregory of Nyssa maintains in his *Life of Moses* and in his sublime commentary on the Canticles that the holy life is one of boundless expansion. There is never any end to the journey into God, because God is infinite, unknowable, forever and always beyond any stage we might reach, at any level in any of the worlds and dimensions. Evolutionary development through greater, always greater love and surrender is always possible at every level: there are always new heights of gnosis to scale, always new mountains of naked love to climb, always further and finer degrees of knowledge to reach and then transcend. This wonderful, both humbling and expanding vision, shared in part also by Rumi a thousand years later, coincides with everything honest mystics come to learn and with what science is revealing of the always-changing, always-transforming and expanding nature of the universe itself. I believe it to be the most truthful as well as the most ecstatic model of divine transformation that I know, and one that illuminates marvelously the journey into the Mother that, as Goethe, and of course Ramakrishna and Aurobindo, knew, leads us "ever upward" in ever-expanding spirals of adoration and transformation toward an ever-attracting and ever-further-withdrawing source of love and wisdom.

As so often, Ruysbroeck, perhaps the greatest of all Christian mystics, expresses this vision with precise and majestic eloquence, in his section on wisdom in *The Spiritual Espousals:*

The fruitful Unity of God abides above the unity of our powers and *constantly* calls us to likeness to God in love and virtue. For this reason we are *at all times touched anew,* so that we might always be renewed *more and more* and become more like God in virtue. At each new touch our spirit falls into a state of hunger and thirst and wished in this storm of love thoroughly to savor and penetrate this groundless abyss in order to find satisfaction. This gives rise to a never-ending, ravenous striving *which never reaches its goal.* . . . When we meet God, the heat and light are so infinitely intense that all spirits fail in their activity and melt away in the love which they experience in the unity of the spirit. In this ground of felt love there lives that welling vein which is the illumination or interior activity of God which *at all times moves and urges us on,* draws us inward, and makes us flow forth with new works of virtue. [Italics added]

I think this vision of "endless progress" is essential for the transformation asked by the Mother now, precisely because it explodes all patriarchal pretensions of being "enlightened." In this vision, no one is permanently "enlightened," some people enter through devotion and grace what could be called the "enlightenment-field" and what they learn there is awe, humility, and how to go on opening more and more passionately and selflessly to divine grandeur and love. The holy life becomes then a life of ever-deepening adoration, ever-growing humility, ever-more all-encompassing charity. No static fixed point in this journey could ever be celebrated as "enlightenment" without misrepresenting the whole nature of the journey. This law of "eternal progress" or "eternal evolution" applies, as Gregory and his great successor Dionysus the Areopagite make clear, not merely to life here on earth but to all the angelic orders and to whatever worlds may be beyond them. The transcendent, Gregory claims, remains always at the same magnificent distance from us at whatever point of illumination we find ourselves, always drawing us forward and onward.

What this means of course in worldly terms is that the pretension of so-called masters to complete enlightenment is rubbish, a theatrical and exploitative statement, and not in any way a mystical one. In the vision of Gregory and his successors, there are only learners and lovers, not "masters." The greatest "master" of all, Christ, was after all a servant of all, and as his astounding story shows, he rested nowhere but pressed on and on, burning his life away in ever-deeper embraces of the real and of the world, in ever more startling and searingly humble dedications to the service of all beings.

This brings me to the third great linked sacred insight that I believe everyone, whatever their path, needs to learn from the Christian mystical tradition—the necessity of service. There is a pronounced tendency in the higher stages of the great Eastern mystical systems to denigrate action. Even as great and wise and illumined a child of the Mother as Ramakrishna "bought" the standard Hindu line that the higher you grow, the less you do or have to do. Nearly all the patriarchal visions of enlightenment have at their core a promise of release from action, or from the fruits of action, as in the *Gita*, which in fact has a more heroic vision of the spiritual life, as Aurobindo made clear. Christ and the Christian tradition implicitly reject this essentially conservative view. Christ himself never ceased to pour himself out in loving action after his illumination; indeed he transformed his entire self into one long act of love and service. I am convinced that Christ knew about karma and reincarnation but did not teach them because he knew that they could both be used to justify sloth and the status quo—and the destruction of spiritual sloth and the status quo were essential to him if the kingdom was to be created not merely in the mind but also in practice. For Christ, the only real proof of illumination was in the love and service of others; the only true sign of the love of God was in the love of humanity and in the indefatigable search to see justice done.

This perfect and revolutionary balance—you might call it a "nuclear" balance—between love and action that we see in Christ and his life and example was often lost in a religious institution that came to stress monasticism and ascetic withdrawal, but the greatest of the Christian mystics—St. Paul,

Teresa of Avila, Ruysbroeck—always knew that, in Teresa's typically succinct phrase: "Martha and Mary must combine." In Ruysbroeck, this sense of balance reaches its highest and most complete expression. "When love falls in love with love and each is all to the other in possession and in rest." Ruysbroeck tells us, in *The Sparkling Stone,* that the object of this marvelous ecstasy is not a permanent self-loss in the divine darkness, a "slumbering in God," but "a new life of virtue, such as love and its impulses demand." "To be a living, willing Tool of God, wherewith God works what He will and How he will" is the goal of transcendence described in the last chapter of *The Sparkling Stone.* "Then is our life a whole, when contemplation and work dwell in them side by side and we are perfectly in both of them at once."

In her book *Ruysbroeck,*[4] Evelyn Underhill, commenting on this wonderful passage, writes:

> Then the separate spirit is immersed in and part of the perpetual creative act of the Godhead—the flowing forth and drawing back, which have at their base the Eternal Equilibrium, the unbroken peace, wherein "God contemplates Himself and all things in an Eternal Now that has neither beginning nor end." On that Unbroken Peace the spirit hangs; and swings like a pendulum in wide arcs of love and service between the Unconditioned and the Conditioned worlds.

She adds:

> So the Superessential Life is the simple, the synthetic life, in which man actualizes at last all the resources of his complex being. The active life of response to the Temporal Order, the contemplative life of response to the Transcendent Order are united, firmly held together, by that "eternal fixation of the spirit": the perpetual willed dwelling of the being of man within the Incomprehensible Abyss of the Being of God.

No age has needed this vision of the Christ-balance, of the necessity of flowing out from inner truth and vision to acts of love and work and justice more than ours. No so-called "spiritual revolution" has needed Christ's injunction to serve more than our own, where narcissism and the whoring after false gods, and self-inflation are so criminally, sadly, and frivolously rampant.

Unless all of us learn from Christ how to combine mystical love with active love and how to give everything in every dimension simultaneously to try and secure the establishment of the laws of love in this world, then this world will die out. The catastrophe of our time is calling on us to be indefatigable servants of love and justice, and on how earnestly and with what discrimination and passion and humility we respond to that call depends the success of the transformation the Mother is calling us to and so the future of the planet.

### Notes

1. Anne Baring and Jules Cashford, *The Myth of the Goddess: Evolution of an Image* (New York: Viking Press, 1991), p. 626.

2. Carl Jung, quoted in *The Myth of the Goddess,* p. 626.

3. Baring and Cashford, *The Myth of the Goddess,* p. 629.

4. Evelyn Underhill, *Ruysbroeck* (London: G. Bell & Sons, Ltd., 1914), pp. 184–5.

Chapter Twelve

## *Conclusion*

*Come, let us go for a walk, O Mind, to Kali, the wish-
    fulfilling tree
And there beneath it gather the fruits of life.*
—Ramprasad

*The only God that exists, the only God in whom I be-
lieve ... my God the miserable, my God the poor of all
races.... So long as even a single dog in my country is
without food, my whole religion will be to feed it.*
—Vivekananda

*The Tao is centered and straight. To practice the Tao it
is imperative to rely on worthy action. Only when you
are imbued with worthy qualities and also act on them
do you become real.*           —Liu I-Ming

*The Way of Sages is to be magnanimous yet stern, strict
yet warm, gentle yet straightforward, fierce yet humane.*
—Lao Tzu

*Without the God*
        *there is no Goddess,*
*And without the Goddess*
        *there is no God.*

*How sweet is their love!*
*the entire universe*
        *is too small to contain them,*
*Yet they live happily*
        *in the tiniest particle.*

                                    —Jnaneshwar

*Remember, O most gracious Virgin Mary,*
*That never was it known*
*That anyone who fled to your protection*
*Implored your help*
*Or sought your intercession*
*Was left unaided.*
                        —St. Bernard of Clairvaux

THERE IS VERY little time left. The next few years are going to reveal the full horror of what we have done to the planet and to ourselves. How much time do we have? Twenty years at the utmost, twenty years in which to undergo a vast transformation of all our ways of thinking and acting, twenty years in which we will have to make major decisions in every arena or abandon the fate of the world to chaos. And if we do not change? The human race could die out in unimaginable suffering, and take most of life on the planet with it.

Any spiritual vision that does not ask us to calmly face the appalling facts is, I believe, whether consciously or unconsciously, conspiring in our infantilization and so in our destruction. I am often asked whether I am optimistic or pessimistic about the future. I reply that both optimism and pessimism are now luxuries we can ill afford. Optimism is crazy, given the facts—the facts of overpopulation, environmental destruction, the pollution of the air and water, the facts of escalating nationalism and tribal hatred, the facts of still-continuing nuclear proliferation, the facts of obscene frivolity and denial in all of the media of the nightmares we face. There is nothing whatever to be optimistic about. Yet pessimism is also crazy; it just conspires with catastrophe by imagining it to be inevitable. Catastrophe may be likely, but it is never inevitable.

The only response that I find honorable in this potentially terminal situation is that of dedicated love. Whatever happens, whatever horror or destruction unfurl upon the world, however terrible the suffering of human beings and nature becomes, such a response keeps the heart open and keeps alive courage and compassion. This response of dedicated love, committed love, of love-in-action, springs directly from the sacred heart of the Divine Mother, of the Mother of the cosmos and the Mother within us. "I am the Queen of Peace," Mary says again and again as she appears; peace can only be engendered by love and sustained in love-in-action.

The essential message of the Divine Mother to us can be summed up, I believe, in the following Ten Sacred Suggestions. I have called them "suggestions," and not commands or commandments, because the Mother does not issue commands. At all moments in our relation to her, we are left free—free to rise through her grace into our own human divinity and take the journey into her love, or free to deny her and her laws and destroy ourselves. Not even the Mother can help us if we do not wish to be saved; not even the Mother can help us if we turn from her help. Everything now depends on us, on the authenticity of our sincerity, on the passion and wisdom with which we turn to the divine.

I have tried to impart the flavor of these suggestions as richly and comprehensively as possible. On how deeply and fully we *imagine* the Mother depends how much strength, courage, and inspiration we can draw from her. Incomplete imagination of her will lead to incomplete contact and incomplete help. It is crucial now, with such worldwide disaster and agony, not to repeat any of the past mistakes, exaggerations, or limitations of our understanding of her. We need the largest possible vision of the Mother and of her relationship with us and of how we can sustain, interpret, and enact that relationship. All the clearest insights and highest awakenings of all the traditions that celebrate her, however partially, have now to be fused together. She is calling on us to unite in one all-embracing and all-encompassing knowledge all the separate ways of knowing her. Neither a purely transcendental vision of her nor a purely immanent apprehension of her can help us now; we need *both*, fused in a sacred marriage of truth.

We need Ramakrishna's vision of the all-transcendent Kali and the aboriginal celebration of the wallaby as the guide to motherhood; we need the Sufi understanding of the transformatory powers of suffering as well as the Mahayana Buddhist knowledge of the void-as-Mother and the sacred mystery of the Tao. We need a restored Mary and a restored Christ. We need, in fact, all the help we can get in order to make conscious the full radical range of the great and healing mystery of the sacred feminine, that mystery we have betrayed for so long but must now reclaim in its completeness and complete challenge, or perish.

These, then, are the Mother's Ten Sacred Suggestions as I understand them now in my journey into her:

1. I am the Mother. I am both transcendent and immanent, source and all that streams from it. I am one with all things in creation and one in boundless light within and beyond it. Adore me.

2. Adore every being and thing, from the whale to the ladybird, as life of my life. I am appearing in everything as everything.

3. Honor yourself humbly as my divine child, and see, know, and celebrate all other beings as my divine children. Whatever you do to or for anyone, you do to or for me.

4. See through constant practice of adoration that nature is the sacred body of my sacred light, and do everything at all times to honor its laws that are my laws and to protect it from destruction. I and you and nature are one love, one glory; protecting nature is protecting yourselves.

5. Dissolve forever all schisms and separations between sects and religions. Whatever you adore is a face of me, and everyone is on his or her own unique path. Know that there are as many paths as there are people.

6. Dissolve forever through repeated holy inner experience of my unity all barriers between what has been called "sacred" and what has been called "profane." Know the whole of life as my feast. Realize ordinary life as an unbroken flow of normal miracle.

7. End all hatred of the body, all guilt and sexual shame, and discover and celebrate my sacred Eros in all its ecstatic connections and revelations. Preserve its purity and power, in my name, with truth and fidelity and mutual honor.

8. Unlearn all the "religious" propaganda that tries to tell you that you need intermediaries in your relationship with me. I can be contacted by anyone, anywhere, at any time and in any circumstance, simply by saying my name, however you imagine it. No intermediaries—no gurus, priests, "experts"—are ever needed. You and I are always, already, one.

9. Do not make of my worship another dogma, another mind-prison. Remember always there is no "Mother" without the "Father," no "Goddess" without "God." I do not want a new religion in my name; I want the whole of experience on the earth to become holy and integrated in love. I want the return of harmony and sacred peace and balance, the union of the sacred marriage at the great-

est depth, and in everyone, of "masculine" and "feminine," "earth" and "heaven," body and soul, heart and intellect, prayer and action. Men are as much my children as women; the wound of the loss of the Mother is felt by women as well as men. Any separatist or prejudiced or one-sided attempt to worship me worships only a distorted image of me. Dare to know me in my full majesty and all-encompassing humility, and know that there is never any end to the journey into me and that the conditions for that journey are ever-deepening faith, radical trust, and radical humility.

10. If you trust and love me, put your trust and love into action in every aspect of your life—emotional, sexual, spiritual, social, political—with my passion, my clarity, my unsentimental practicality. Know that my revelation is a *revolution*, a revolution that demands calmly a transformation of all the terms and conditions of life on earth. Establish justice for all in my world, in my name, and in my spirit of all-embracing, inexhaustible compassion. Let no one be poor, or discriminated against; may all sentient beings everywhere be cherished and safe and protected from harm by law and by love. Turn to me now and I will fill you with all the grace, strength, courage, and passion you need to transform the world at every level into a living mirror of my truth, my love, and my justice. If you truly love me, change everything for me.

How can we most richly, wisely, and comprehensively respond to the Mother's Ten Sacred Suggestions? When I first wrote them down, I had a sudden inner vision of a burning gold heart with five flames leaping from it. I heard the words: *This is my Sacred Heart in you, and the five flames are Five Sacred Passions.*

These Five Sacred Passions are: The passion for the divine beyond forms, the transcendent source; the passion for nature

as the immanent manifestation of the source, instinct everywhere with its glory; the passion for all sentient beings and all
human beings; the holy passion for one other human being, a
tantric passion devoted to tantric transformation in the Mother;
and finally, focusing and fulfilling all the others, a passion for
*service* and *action*. All Five Sacred Passions draw from, enthuse,
infuse, strengthen, sustain, and inter-illuminate each other. Lived
together in every dimension for her and *in* her, they represent
the full alchemical force in reality of divine human love. Living them together, alone and together, is what will help us transform not only ourselves but the world.

> *Let my Sacred Heart become yours.*
> *Live and act from my love.*
> *Risk everything while there is still time.*
> *Give everything while there is still time.*

The First Sacred Passion—the passion for the source, the
transcendent, the transcendent Mother of Light—fuels all the
others. While it is true that the patriarchal bias toward transcendence has resulted in a destructive rejection of women,
nature, and the body, it is also true that contemporary overemphasis on the immanent can cut us off from those sources of
transforming power that are the gift of the invisible and transcendent. It is from the one beyond all forms, names, dogmas,
and concepts that the light of grace streams; if we do not love
origin passionately, It cannot send us the strength and inspiration
we need, and need all the more intensely now as catastrophe
deepens. To be in continual loving contact with the transcendent is vital for the stamina and illumined wisdom we need to
survive. As Ruysbroeck reminds us in his *Mirror of Eternal
Blessedness:*

> At the beginning of the world when God resolved to create
> the first human beings, God said ... "Let us make the human
> being to our own image and to our likeness." God is a spirit
> and so God's word is God's knowledge and God's action is

God's will. God has created each person's soul as a living mirror, on which God has impressed the image of God's Nature.... Our created life is one, without intermediary, with this image and this life which we have eternally in God. That life which we have in God is one in God, without intermediary.... We thus live eternally in God and God in us, for our created being lives in our eternal image.... This eternal image is one with God's wisdom and lives in our created being.

For this reason the eternal birth is always being renewed, and the flowing forth of the Holy Spirit into the emptiness of our soul is always occurring without interruption, for God has known, loved, called, and chosen us from all eternity. If we resolve to know, love, and choose him in return then we are holy, blessed, and chosen from all eternity. God ... will then reveal his divine resplendence in the topmost part of our soul, for we are his kingdom, in which God lives and reigns. Just as the sun in the heavens pervades and enlightens all the world with its rays and makes it fruitful, so too does God's resplendence as it reigns in the topmost part of our mind, for upon all our powers it sheds its bright, brilliant rays, namely, its divine gifts: knowledge, wisdom, clear understanding, and a rational discerning insight into all the virtues. It is in this way that the kingdom of God in our souls is adorned.

To connect profoundly with the transcendent source, the transcendent Mother-Father, is not to devalue immanence in any way, for when we come to see the Mother as Ruysbroeck's "resplendence as it reigns in the topmost part of our mind," then, as Ramakrishna also said, and in fact all the Mother-mystics make clear, we also see and know reality as entirely saturated and radiant with her glory. We come to know that nature is entirely holy with her, is in fact her body. "God's grandeur," Gerard Manley Hopkins wrote, "will flame out, like shining from shook foil." Nature *is* that "shook foil" from which the grandeur of the Divine Mother is continually and incessantly flashing, if the eyes of love are open in us. From this immanent knowledge of her splendor in every fern and dolphin and wave and rose and deer and hippopotamus and orchid and wind-swept sand dune arises, then, the Second Sacred Passion—the passion for nature. It is this that Ramakrishna was living and expressing when, after his vision of Kali as the light-conscious-ness pervading and manifesting all things, he "threw flowers in all directions." It was this sacred passion for the blazing of the source in all created things and for the humility of the source's presence in and as all things that possessed St. Francis of Assisi and made him talk with sparrows, wolves, snakes, tur-tledoves, and all the elements as his brothers and sisters and equals, that led him to that state in which, as one of his biog-raphers tells us, "worms kindled in him infinite love." This sacred passion for nature is not something we can afford to leave to the saints; we must all know it, live it, and act from it now if we and nature are to survive. When we know nature as the Mother's body and everything in nature as utterly sacred, then, and then only, will we do everything in our power to pre-serve, honor, and protect nature.

Knowing the "resplendence" and its radiant dance in nature is not, however, all we must do; we must also know all sen-tient beings as her, and see, know, and celebrate all human beings, whatever their caste or creed or color or gender or sex-uality, as her divine children, each unique, each holy, each loved unconditionally by the Mother. From this Third Sacred Pas-sion—the sacred passion for all sentient and human beings—the passion of the bodhisattva, of the Sufi lover, of all those who give themselves to Christ to be "Christed,"—arises that loving knowledge of our interbeing with all being, of our total and fundamental interconnectedness with everyone and every-thing in the entire cosmos.

Unless all of us now realize at greater and ever greater depths of truth and integration this Mother-law of interdependence, and unless we translate its truth into action at every level and in every arena, humankind will not survive. Christ said: "Feed my sheep"—his sheep are *our* sheep. The animals perishing in the burning forests are burning in us; the old woman dying alone and abandoned in Rio or Los Angeles or Calcutta is dying in us; the acid rain falls on us when it falls on the trees; it is into ourselves that we release clouds of deadly chemicals and it is in ourselves that we bury nuclear waste that no known technology can contain. We are implicated in every life and every death, in every injustice, in every crime, in every casual premeditated or unconscious brutality. Allowing this Third Sacred Passion for all beings to begin to awaken in us is a terrifying experience, one that many celebrate but few want to live, because this awakening shows us that there is no escape anywhere into any mystical state or other world from this tremendous responsibility of love. All our fantasies of "progress" or "spiritual transformation" will not save us—and cannot— if we do not see, know, explore, and enact more and more fully, comprehensively, and passionately our interconnection with absolutely everyone and everything. Such an opening to her web of love, however terrifying, however demanding, however devastating to all our private agendas and notions of separateness, is now essential. There will not be any significant turning-around of our contemporary catastrophe without it.

In the Fourth Sacred Passion—for one other human being with whom we live in consecrated tantric communion, in sacred marriage—the Mother brings us the tender opportunity not merely to go on *talking* about healing the split between body and soul, but actually to do it. When consecrated to her and protected by fidelity, the sexual, spiritual, and emotional passion for another being becomes the site of an encounter with her in every dimension and at every level, the site of an always-unfolding empowering *direct* teaching by her of us in the ground of our daily lives. A massive worldwide healing of sexual pain is now essential if human beings are to be freed to love themselves and honor the body and so love and honor nature. Through exercising this Fourth Sacred Passion in and with all the other passions, human beings will discover, without any need of any church or dogma or intermediary, the *unity* of the Mother, her radical blessing of *all* of life, her love-presence in all things, and so taste ever more deeply their own divine human power and freedom. Couples—heterosexual or homosexual—who allow themselves to experience this tantric teaching (and submit to its necessary rules of mutual honor, service, respect, and, above all and always, fidelity) will find that psychological and spiritual suffering are greatly diminished through it, that revelations dance naturally around and in them, and that humble self-reliance in and for her becomes increasingly instinctual and increasingly joyful. I am living this great teaching with Eryk in her and for her and know that its promise is genuine.

All of these four Sacred Passions lived separately or together could become decadent, narcissistic, or escapist if they are not *always* linked—and felt and known to be linked—to the Fifth Sacred Passion, which focuses and fulfills them all—the Sacred Passion for service and for love-in-action.

"Those who are near to me are near the fire," Christ tells us in the Gospel of Thomas; those who are near to the Mother now are near to her great fire of change. The return of the mother, I have continually argued in this book, is not merely a revelation but also a *revolution*—a call to emotional, sexual, spiritual, social, economic, political revolution. Daring to allow the fire of the Mother into our lives is daring our lives to burn away in that fire, to be transformed continually to reflect ever more richly and intensely the Mother's laws of love and justice.

It must never again be forgotten, as it has been forgotten for millennia, that one of the Mother's holiest names is Justice. To awaken the Mother's sacred heart in us is to awaken a passion to serve, honor, and protect all of nature and all living beings. The human race will not really be honoring the Mother until every starving person is fed; until every homeless person is housed; until every sick and poor old person has free access to medicine; until every woman everywhere is free from all kinds of oppression; until every human being everywhere, whatever his or her sexuality, feels free to love openly; until, in fact, *all* the man-made distinctions between white and black, male and female, poor and rich, straight and gay, are radically transformed so as to express in both individual and social, spiritual and political ways, the equal love of the Mother.

Every sea must be cleaned for her, every ravaged forest restored, every endangered species—including those parts of the human population facing a kind of selective genocide—protected, every commercial arrangement that threatens the creation in any way forbidden. The force of the Mother is a revolutionary force of love that works incessantly to break down *all* barriers and separations in the name of love and hungers to see *this* world become the stable paradise it already is in her mind of truth. Unless we serve this force, and will and strive to put into living practice its unsparingly radical injunctions, we are not loving the Mother but a watered-down personally tailored version of her that can only keep us trapped in illusion and the world on its headlong rush toward annihilation.

The revolution of the Mother demands of each of us unstinting service. And what does such service mean? It means dedicating our every gift and power, our every prayer, our every thought and emotion and perception, to the welfare of others in the world. It means having the courage and patience to learn all the dreadful facts about what is happening and how we all of us conspire in what is happening. It means taking *personal* political responsibility on local, national, and global levels, alone and together. It means scrutinizing who we vote for, who we give power to, and holding them to their promise of change. It means realizing, once and for all, with no false consolation of any kind, in just what terrible danger we are and how each of us will have to dedicate our entire being and intelligence to focused, thoughtful acts of loving service to all, if we are going to have a chance to survive.

It may mean in the near future taking to the streets all over the world in a massive peaceful but adamant protest against what the politicians, generals, and corporations are doing. It may even mean being prepared to die. The service the Mother is asking of us in this catastrophe is as humble, supple, many-faceted, loyal, indefatigable, and extreme as hers. If we claim to love her, or to know her love, that claim must be made good in tireless love-in-action using all of our gifts and resources; and it must be fed, illumined, balanced, and informed, as I have said, by all the other Sacred Passions.

And when these Five Sacred Passions live in us and we in them, then we will be living the full human divine life in the Mother and we will be awake in her sacred heart and living and acting from it and with its blessing and serving power.

> *Know that my revelation is a revolution.*
> *Establish justice for all in my world.*
> *If you truly love me, change everything for me.*

There is very little time left.

The dark forces that want the human experiment to fail and the world to be destroyed are everywhere more and more powerful, subtle, deadly, and ingenious. But the Mother is always in us and with us, and her strength will never fail us. "I am with you always," Mary has said again and again. "I am with you always."

And, as St. Bernard of Clairvaux reminds us, the Mother and her power is always, *always,* there to be drawn on in love's name:

> When you follow Her you do not take a wrong turn.
> When you pray to Her you do not lose hope.
> When She occupies your mind, you are sheltered from error.
> When She holds you up, you cannot fall.
> When She protects you, you do not fear.
> When She leads you forward, you do not get exhausted.
> When Her star shines on you, you arrive at the harbor of Liberation.

*Interviews*

# Introduction

*One word of truth outweighs the whole world.*
                                        —Mandelstam

I AM FREQUENTLY ASKED, "Do you forgive Meera and what her disciples did to you?" Yes, I forgive them, and my heart is clear. Neither Eryk nor I, however, have any desire for any kind of "reconciliation." There is nothing further to be said between any of us. The cruelty has been too extreme, the lies too atrocious, the evil too terrifying. Both Eryk and I wish no one harm but we wish for the rest of our lives to have nothing further to do with any of the people in this last year who have tried to destroy our careers, our marriage, our lives. We have survived, by the grace of the Mother, and we wish to be left to live our love in peace.

I forgive Meera; I see her clearly at last as she is—trapped in a lie of being a divine being which now she cannot escape and is condemned to protect by any means available. Everything she did to me and Eryk will come back to her. Karma is accurate and inexorable, and among the greatest crimes are those that she has committed—imitating the divine, exploiting and abusing the devotion of those who adore you and put their trust in you, and lying repeatedly in such a way as to attempt to destroy other beings. It is only a matter of time before the cult she has created splits apart and her game is further exposed. Meera has butchered the great love I had for her;

451

but I still pray that when her fall comes she will be able to learn from it.

As for the disciples who participated with all-too-willing enthusiasm in the orgy of denunciation and cruelty that followed on Meera's lies—I forgive them also, and with a clear heart. I know, however, that many of them knew exactly what they were doing, knew that I was not lying and had no reason to do so, knew that Meera was not "omniscient" and had made mistakes before in the past, and still went ahead to try and destroy Eryk and myself. A vicious, callous, and sophisticated system was set up by a group of ex-"close friends," that included anonymous letters, death threats for nearly a year, horrible telephone harassment, visits to New York publishers to discredit Eryk's and my work, attempts to have me thrown out of my job in San Francisco, relentless public and private calumny—the complete cocktail, in fact, of cult violence, demonization, and attempted destruction. No words of mine can convey how horrifying it was to live such an experience. Nothing was too low or too disgusting or too cruel for them to attempt in their passion to silence us. All that such behavior did, however, was to increase our resolve to testify, since it exposed just how dangerous the Meera cult is. All I can pray now is that none of the people who participated in this evil will suffer as much as Eryk and I did, when the inevitable consequences of their actions return to them.

I here thank those among them who, repelled by what they were being "persuaded" to do, turned to Eryk and myself in secret with affidavits and letters admitting in detail what was going on, and telling us all the names of those involved, here and in Europe. Their courage helped to save our lives and I am grateful. Eryk and I have made the choice not to use this information to destroy anyone else in the spirit of those who wanted to destroy us, but the fact that it exists and is now known to exist, and in such appalling detail, protects us.

With the help of many friends, scandalized ex-devotees of Meera and well-wishers from all over the country, Eryk and I have amassed a comprehensive dossier of affidavits, testimonies, transcripts of revealing conversations, copies of which have been placed in banks here and in Europe with lawyers and with reliable influential friends. A group of those who believe in us have gathered together to protect our legal rights both here and in Europe. Eryk and I have already had occasion to press certain legal claims in a way that sent a firm message to everyone concerned that while we did not wish to meet evil with evil, we had no intention of being annihilated by injustice and would defend our rights in every appropriate way. I here want to thank, from the bottom of my heart, all those friends who helped us, our lawyers, here and in Europe, and the authorities with whom we have worked.

*       *       *

The first interview reprinted here was published in the September/October 1994 issue of *Common Boundary.* I shall always be grateful to my friend Rose Solari for her courage in interviewing me and in standing by Eryk and myself through everything. Every attempt was made by certain chief disciples of Meera to block publication, but the result of such patently manipulative attempts to prevent the truth getting out only made the editorial staff of *Common Boundary* even more adamant in their decision to go ahead. Certain disciples even went so far as to claim that Carol Ricotta, quoted by Rose Solari in her introduction as another example of someone who had experienced Meera's homophobia, was Eryk's sister! This tragicomic allegation was soon cleared up when Ms. Ricotta offered to send a complete witnessed transcript of her conversation with Thalheim, and Eryk's real sister sent her passport documentation to the offices of *Common Boundary.*

When the interview appeared, hell broke loose. Our death-threat quota went up, as did the abusive telephone calls (this time noted by the proper authorities). Anyone anxious to depress themselves by studying the current level of pathological denial among many disciples of the "New Age" should read the subsequent January/February 1995 issue of *Common Boundary*. I can only hope that those who wrote such letters—including some distinguished "teachers" who should have known better—are now ashamed of themselves. Lending authority to a demonization of Eryk and myself, who had already suffered, exposed them in a way they cannot have intended. Fortunately, in subsequent issues, sanity has returned as readers from all over America, angered by the attacks on us, wrote in not only in our defense but in defense of all rights to speak out about abuse. I thank all those who wrote in so intelligently and urge everyone now to be vigilant. I know of many cases of terrible abuse where ex-disciples of this or that "master" are too terrified to speak out; Eryk and I both pray that our example—and the example of Rose Solari and *Common Boundary*—will encourage a more realistic, outspoken, and urgent discussion of these crucial issues. Eryk and I also hope that the many influential teachers who *are* aware of the extent of the current abuse stop keeping their wary, self-protective silence on the subject. Not to speak out now is to conspire with horror and the destruction of hundreds and thousands of souls.

I want to thank Rose Solari and *Common Boundary,* too, for checking so thoroughly, even remorselessly, all my "allegations." The fact that they withstood such assiduous fact-checking makes it clear now that if Meera and her cohorts wish to continue with their lies the burden of proof is now upon them. I shall take any further attempts to defame myself or Eryk in public or in private as criminally liable. We have been patient and understanding in the face of this cruelty, but the facts are now in. Anyone who wants to ignore them does so at their own legal peril; Eryk and I consider that they have no more right to implicate us in their ignorance.

The second interview, with Catherine Ingram, appeared in the July/August 1995 issue of *Yoga Journal,* and it takes some of the themes of the first into another dimension. I thank Catherine for her acumen, sympathy, and courage, and I thank *Yoga Journal* for printing my exact words.

I want here to urge every reader to take seriously what I have said in this interview—and throughout the book—about the occult. In this last year, I have talked at length with several world-respected "white" occult adepts (in both America and Europe); they have all confirmed to me what I was learning and have distilled here. The occult, I discovered almost too late, is terribly real and terribly dangerous, and the opportunities for manipulation on a vast scale are all-too-available in a world like ours that is blinded by its vanity of "reason" and has no real information about these matters. Many ex-cult members and victims of abuse and occult manipulation have thanked me for the research I have done, but there is a great deal more to do. I urge here that all those who know the truth about occult manipulation by gurus should now speak up, in detail, and save lives.

Anyone who wants immediate information should read *The Gospel of Sri Ramakrishna,* the chapters on experiences and visions in St. John of the Cross' *Ascent to Mount Carmel,* and suitable excerpts from the *Philokalia.* The *Letters* of Sri Aurobindo are also very helpful. Any seeker now who is not informed in detail on this subject is in real danger.

In reprinting these interviews and in finishing this book I think with great sadness about all those thousands of fellow seekers who have been abused by so-called "masters" and either been brainwashed or intimidated into silence, or simply could not find anyone willing to listen to their story. I was well-known enough to be listened to, and supported enough by loving friends and an infinitely brave husband to be able to endure to witness the truth, and have it heard. I would ask here that anyone reading this should not waste the anguish that Eryk and I have suffered. Listen with calm open hearts to what we are saying and have the courage to believe us. May a new and liberating truth, *her* truth, grow from our grief.

Last year, an old friend, who personally witnessed some of the death threats we were receiving, wrote to us: "Go on telling the truth always, whatever happens. Even if they kill you for it, and they may. Even if they kill you, they cannot kill the truth, and others will live from it and you will live in them."

I have lived to tell our truth, and I bless the Mother for everything she has given. I have witnessed as clearly and as responsibly as I can. I put my faith now and always in the One who has never failed me, and I know that she will protect me and Eryk through everything, because we turned to her, and we have loved, and believed, and been honest. Those who witness her majesty and mercy can never be defeated in the only dimension that ultimately matters—that of her truth.

# On Divine Responsibility

When I rang the doorbell of the apartment where Andrew Harvey was staying in Washington, D.C., I felt more than a little intimidated. An Englishman born in India and educated at Oxford, Harvey became, at 21, the youngest Fellow in the history of All Souls College. Success as a poet, novelist, scholar, and teacher came early; so, however, did discontent with the intellectual atmosphere he lived in—what he refers to as "the concentration camp of reason." His subsequent spiritual quest led him back to India and resulted in two of his best-known books: *A Journey in Ladakh* (1983), an account of his studies with Tibetan Buddhist master Thuksey Rinpoche, and *Hidden Journey: A Spiritual Awakening* (1991), which tells of his relationship with the Indian woman known as Mother Meera, who followers claim is an avatar, or a divine presence on earth.

In the last ten years, Harvey has become known for his role as Mother Meera's spokesperson, spreading her ideas in the West. Even his most recent books, published early this year— *Dialogues with a Modern Mystic,* a question-and-answer book on spiritual and social issues coauthored with *Common Boundary* contributing editor Mark Matousek, and *The Way of Passion: A Celebration of Rumi,* in which he translates and

Adapted from an interview with Andrew Harvey by Rose Solari, in *Common Boundary,* Volume 12, Issue 5, September/October 1994, pp. 32–39. Used by permission.

457

comments on the poems of the thirteenth-century mystic and poet Jalal-ud-Din Rumi—reflect his relationship with Mother Meera: She is quoted in the former volume, and the latter is dedicated to her and Shams-i-Tabriz, Rumi's teacher. Perhaps because Mother Meera herself rarely speaks—the centerpiece of her practice is *darshan,* or "divine transmission," a ritual in which devotees kneel before her and look directly into her eyes for guidance or enlightenment—Harvey's name had become, in spiritual circles, inextricably linked with hers. But shortly before his meeting with *Common Boundary,* he broke with Mother Meera and with the spiritual system that he had practiced and written about for the last fifteen years. Harvey, who once believed that the wisest and safest path involved commitment to one teacher and one tradition, now advocates a wholly different approach: the direct relationship of each individual to the divine.

In this interview, Harvey gives some of the reasons for his split with his former teacher. The strongest, and the most controversial, of these has to do with what Harvey describes as her homophobia. Harvey himself is openly gay, and he recently married Eryk Hanut, a French photographer. Harvey says, in fact, that it was his entrance into a committed, public relationship with Hanut that precipitated the end of his link to his former teacher.

When asked about Harvey's allegations. Mother Meera, reached at her home in Thalheim, Germany, said through a translator that she is "not opposed to homosexuality." She referred further inquiry to James Thornton, a devotee of hers and executive director of Positive Futures, an organization formed to combine environmentalism with spirituality. According to Thornton, "Mother [Meera] fully accepts and appreciates homosexuality as a normal and good way of being human.... Why else would she ask me, a gay man, to speak for her on this issue?" He added. "People with AIDS have come to her by the dozens and received nothing but her blessing."

Yet Harvey's experience seems to be not an isolated one.

Early this year, Carol Ricotta, a lesbian follower of Mother Meera's, called the teacher to ask for a blessing on Ricotta's relationship with her lover. "She answered that she didn't want to bless such a union because she disapproved of my way of life," says Ricotta, who lives in Belgium. "I was told that I should give up the girl I live with, get married, and have children." Ricotta, who had been a follower of Mother Meera's for a couple of years and had made a pilgrimage to Thalheim for *darshan,* was shocked and hurt. "I used to call her Mother," Ricotta says, "but I don't call her that anymore."

Despite the controversy surrounding his break with Mother Meera, Harvey seems barely to have broken stride—teaching, promoting his new books, and speaking whenever possible of the benefits of walking a guru-free spiritual path. Any fear one may have of being overwhelmed by his intellect is dissolved almost immediately by his warmth; although fiercely articulate, he is also accessible, and the depth and confidence of his Oxford education are softened by his poet's heart. Harvey seems to have been able to reinvent his life—not once but twice—by trusting his instincts.

The evening following this interview, he spoke at the Smithsonian Institution in Washington, D.C., on "The Goddess Experienced," a lecture in which he explored aspects of the Divine Mother from various religious traditions. He combined readings from his own books and from Ramakrishna and Rumi with descriptions of what he sees as possible if we combine the wisdom of pre-Christian, matriarchal cultures with the intellectual advances of the patriarchy to create a "third stage," a divine marriage of masculine and feminine. Although his message entails a drastic redefinition of the connection between spirituality and politics—which he sees as essential, given environmental crises that threaten to destroy all species—perhaps the most radical aspect of Harvey's message is also the simplest: Only the transforming power of love can make the salvation of the human race possible.

Rose Solari: *You've written so much and spoken so eloquently about your relationships with your spiritual teachers. In many of your books you talk about the necessity of having an advisor or teacher. Why do you feel that having a teacher is so essential?*

Andrew Harvey: Actually, I've changed my opinion since I wrote those books. I think that I have greatly exaggerated, and that most traditions have greatly exaggerated, the necessity of a spiritual teacher. I now believe that what we need is a direct relationship with the divine, a direct empowerment by the divine, a direct going to the Divine Mother for the love, peace, bliss, and energy to transform oneself. So I'm very much looking now for ways—simple ways—to make that possible. This is what I'm trying to transmit at the moment.

*What led to that change?*

I left my teacher. I have left Mother Meera, separated completely from her. I no longer believe that she's an avatar.

I have realized that many of the gurus who claim, for example, to represent the sacred feminine are in fact just Jehovah in drag. They are reproducing the old patriarchal hierarchies, the old patriarchal lies, the old patriarchal ways of dominating, ruling, and accruing personal power and fortune. The revolution of the sacred feminine—which is what I've devoted my entire life to—can now, I believe, only happen if we get rid of the old guru model, if we empower ourselves, if we establish a direct relationship with the Divine Mother herself, who is willing to initiate us directly. This new way of getting in contact with the Divine Mother is, I'm convinced, the way that the great spiritual transformation will happen.

*How does one directly contact the divine and transform oneself without a mediator?*

It's very simple. It's so simple that it's shattering. The way to do it—the way it's been done in all major religious systems— is by three things. First, by direct prayer—sincere, loving, passionate, fervent prayer—and the simpler the better. If you can say the name of God in the heart, then God will come to you in whatever form you address God. Ramakrishna said this again and again. He said, "Don't go through masters or through me. Go directly." The Divine Mother wants to initiate you directly.

The second is through simple forms of meditation—at least half an hour in the morning and half an hour at night of silent, tender meditation, which opens the heart and allows the divine to come in. This has immense transforming power.

The third thing is service. We must serve, honor, and respect every living being—every flower, every fern, and every leaf— as a divine event. Through service—respect for everyone and everything that comes to you—you train the mind and heart to learn their divinity and the divinity of all things.

Those three things together—prayer, meditation, and service—will take you right into the heart of a direct relationship with God. That is the secret that religions and gurus have tried to appropriate for themselves. They all say, of course, that they are trying to empower us, but in fact if you look at the ways in which their authoritarian systems work, they're not trying to empower us; they're trying to manipulate us.

*Can you give me an example?*

The sacred feminine is unconditional love, and yet many of the women gurus who represent the sacred feminine are, in practice, homophobic. I separated from Meera because she wished to break up my relationship with my lover, Eryk; she said that I had the choice of either being celibate or getting married to a woman and, when I got married, writing a book about how the force of the Divine Mother transformed me into a heterosexual. She then set about censoring my new work, *Dialogues with a Modern Mystic,* removing all homosexual references, forbade me to sell the video of my life the BBC had made, which contained one fleeting reference to my sexuality, and told me to withdraw an interview on gay spirituality I had given Mark Thompson for his book *Gay Soul*.

I went through a period of tremendous suffering and confusion, thinking that all this might be a divine teaching of some kind. But after deep self-questioning, and considering the appalling details of what unfolded from every angle, I realized it wasn't a divine teaching of any kind. It was pure prejudice—a conservative, cruel, and dangerous prejudice—and I was certainly not going to follow it because it would have meant the end of everything that I believe in, and Eryk's and my complete spiritual destruction.

*Yet Mother Meera must have known about your sexuality.*

She seemed to have been accepting of it initially. But what had happened was that I'd become famous, I'd become her spokesperson, and she didn't want to have a homosexual spokesperson. Besides, in meeting Eryk, I had met real love, and so was no longer alone, melancholy, fixated on her, and always manipulable. To keep me where she needed me, she had to try to destroy any life not centered on her.

*How do you think it was possible for you to have believed in her to begin with?*

I have begun, in these last months, to unravel my relationship with her. I think that gurus aren't the only ones to blame for the ways in which we've put them into positions of power. We are also to blame, because we're looking to reproduce the glory of our imagined childhood, we're looking to have magical solutions to our lives, we're looking to have a totally divine being to love in a totally simple way, and all of this is hooey and illusion—and narcissism, too.

Gurus really may believe that they're doing God's work,

which of course makes them near crazy and very dangerous. They really may believe that they are divine, and so therefore that they can do anything and manipulate people's lives in whatever way they want. But we are also to blame for letting them believe that and for feeding them the kind of undiscriminating adoration that enables them to go on believing that and doing what they want without any check of any kind.

I discovered that there were three components to my obsession with Meera. First, there was my desire for a perfect parental relationship. Often our guru represents the parent we had the worst relationship with, and I had a difficult relationship with my mother. Meera reproduced in a higher dimension that ancient childhood relationship, and I fell for it again.

The second thing was that Meera represented India for me. I was born in India and was forced to leave that country when I was nine to come to school in England. A long period of unhappiness followed. Meera was for me India—India in its essence, India in its sweetness. Also, I'd hated my family's imperial engagement there and felt very guilty about it as a child. So by serving a largely unlettered, "simple" Indian woman, I was both half-consciously expiating the karmic sins of my family and having a final and exquisite revenge on my family.

The third thing, which also comes out of my relationship with my mother, is that I had always been fascinated by powerful female stars. And in a sense, Meera is the Garbo of the spiritual Hollywood. She is the one who is rarely seen, the mysterious one who never speaks, and I fell in love with this ultimate kind of control. I fell in love with the ultimate star.

I see, too, that all of this hooked into a profound need, in my own nature, to be a messenger. I had to reintegrate myself after a shattering childhood and after seeing through the illusion of worldly success. I needed to find a stunning role, and the most stunning role you can find is to be the angel messenger of an avatar. So my unconscious narcissistic desire was fueled and fed by her. Her need to have someone be that and my need to be that coincided exactly.

*It must have been devastating when it ended.*

It's been a huge and shattering disappointment for me, a sav-
agely heartbreaking experience, especially since Meera has compounded her initial cruelty by lying about what happened, so
as to attempt to discredit Eryk and myself. This has put us both
in great spiritual and physical danger. But the experience has
also been liberating because it has made me define what the
sacred feminine is. It has made me come to understand that trying to attain liberation by worshipping a so-called divine being,
which is essentially a system of projection, doesn't work. It
gives you certain experiences and even certain visions, and I've
had those experiences and those visions. But to liberate yourself, you have to enter into a relationship with your own divinity without any master, without any intermediary.

   The patriarchy can well afford 150 divine mothers who keep
alive the old lies of the patriarchy. That's exactly what the patriarchy would want, wouldn't it—imitation divine mothers keeping alive the old lies and, in the name of the Divine Mother,
selling the lies of the patriarchy. That's what I've come to understand is mostly going on, and it's a very frightening system. It's
much too dangerous and much too late to be with these people, because what's at stake is a reevaluation of the entire mystical relationship with the sacred feminine, and there could be
no more important thing at the moment.

*Why at this moment?*

Well, I see this as the age of Kali. Kali is trampling every illusion—political, emotional, sexual—every construct, every concept, including all the religious, mystical, and spiritual ones.
They're all going because they're all inefficient. They haven't
worked; they haven't got us into a direct relationship with ourselves and with nature. If they had, we wouldn't be destroying
nature.

   What we're all living through is massive disappointment

after disappointment. Kali is doing this because she wishes to shatter us free of our enslavements. She wishes to bring us into a final adult relationship with the divine, to hear us say, "You and I, Mother, are one. I'm your directly empowered, sacred, heavenly child. Give me what I need."

What is trying to get born is a human race free of the old slaveries to systems; even the mystical systems have to go because those are the last illusions, the last cinemas of samsara. They will have to go because there's a completely new, radical relationship being formed. It is already being formed in the mind of the Divine Mother, and the human race is being brought up to that, is being shattered to that outrageous possibility. If we can get to that direct relationship with her, then she can directly initiate us and give us the divine energy that we will need for this great transformation.

We've got to learn both how to stand alone and how to work together humbly in unhierarchical, democratic ways. We've got to learn how to respect ourselves and each other, and not just to choose three or four people, three or four avatars onto whom we project all our needs and divinity. I've got to learn to see the divinity in you, and you've got to learn to see the divinity in me, nakedly and directly, and then we have to live and act from that reality. That's the real relationship—that's the relationship that will provide the sacred energy of transformation.

*It sounds like a real celebration, too, of the fact that we're embodied creatures.*

That's the whole thing—the sacralization of the body, the real honoring of the body. I've had all the out-of-body experiences that an accomplished escapee can have. I've seen flashing lights of every kind. But what I'm really just beginning to have is the in-body experience—the experience of the integration of the light with every moment of ordinary life—including the radiance and holiness of sexuality, the sacredness of sexuality.

The sacred feminine is the experience of life as the normal flow of unbroken miracle. That experience contains, embraces, celebrates, ennobles sexuality. It's lethal and obscene to keep alive the old patriarchal fears about sexuality. What is needed is for the body to be blessed. Why? Because we're in it. Why would we be here if we weren't meant to love and celebrate our bodies, and to ennoble and irradiate the joys of the body with the wisdom of the soul, and to find out that sexuality can be the physical grammar of the lovemaking of the soul? That's what we're here to find out.

*And our traditional religions have failed to lead us to that?*

The patriarchal religions separate the body from the spirit. In doing so, they keep alive all the old sexual prejudices. But when you finally learn how to love and celebrate your body and your sexuality, it's then that the full miracle of life becomes obvious to you.

It is then, too, that you understand that nature is also your body. That is a crucial understanding for the human race now, because we are destroying nature. Why are we destroying nature? Because all the religions have taught us that our bodies are fallen and irrelevant and a block to spiritual progress. Therefore, nature is by implication fallen, irrelevant, and a block to spiritual progress.

What we need now, and what the Divine Mother is offering us, is a vision of the holy splendor of the body-spirit and of nature. That is the complete, the full, the glorious revelation, and it's the only revelation that can heal these appalling thousands-and-thousands-of-years-long wounds—sexual wounds, emotional wounds—all of which have come from our separation from our bodies and from nature and their natural sanctity.

We have perhaps twenty years in which to save the environment. How are we going to save the environment unless we realize where we are?

*Where are we?*

We are in a sacred dance of light and love. That's where we are. Our bodies are doing that sacred dance. Nature is ablaze in that sacred dance. And if we're thinking all the time about getting out of our bodies, how will we ever turn to bless nature?

*So there is no division between our souls and our bodies, or between ourselves and nature?*

There is absolutely, at no moment ever any division.

*Because you're also a poet and a fiction writer, how do you connect the path of being an artist with your spiritual path?*

I think being a poet has been the prime energy of my mystical search. It has also been a drawback, because I think my own passion for poetry was probably what led me into announcing Meera as an avatar. My desire to see her in the most extreme and gorgeous terms was probably what enabled me to purvey that illusion, which I'm deeply sorry for because I think it has misled a great many people and done real harm.

The danger of being a poet is what Plato says it is—that a poet lets the longing run away with reality. If I'd been less of a poet and more of a scientist, I would have realized that it was my energy of adoration that was creating this illusion, and not her power. I would have realized also that she could be someone with many powers and not be anywhere near enlightenment.

So I'm very aware now of the dangers of being a poet, of the dangers of that visionary, ecstatic view of the world, because I musn't allow that ever again to interfere with the sobriety of real judgment. I hope that after this shattering experience, I will have a greater sense of the responsibility that belongs to a mystic.

*How do you define the word "mystic"?*

A mystic is someone who has a naked, direct relationship with
the divine presence, direct cognition of the godhead. I used to
believe that there were very few real mystics; I now believe that
everyone is a closet mystic. Everyone has deep glimpses of the
divine in dreams, in lovemaking, in exalted moments of friendship, in moments of aesthetic ecstasy looking at a great painting or listening to music. We're not taught to recognize these
as glimpses of the godhead by this culture, and so we forget
them or half-ashamedly hoard away their memory and don't
acknowledge, don't share them.

*So every one of us has glimpses of the divine?*

All the great teachers have been trying to tell us that each of us
is divine. What we have done with all the great teachers who
have told us this is the worst possible thing: We've made them
into the founders of religions. Christ said this, and we killed his
message by building Christianity around it. The Buddha gave
us this vision, and what did we do? We created Buddhism around
it. So that the outrageousness and the splendor and the radicalism of the message would be covered over and contained and
tamed by the edifice of religion, by the disciplines of religion.

We can't afford that taming of the outrageousness of the
truth anymore, because we need—each one of us on the earth
needs—to face up to our divine responsibility. To say that everybody is a mystic puts a tremendous responsibility on everyone
to live up to the honor and beauty of that relationship with
God. It puts a tremendous responsibility on everyone to transform the ground of their ordinary living into a divine ground.
People much prefer to feel that there are only three or four
accomplished mystics, or that if you want a mystical experience you have to go through this guru or that church, because
it actually takes off the pressure.

What we need to do is to put on the pressure. I think the
Divine Mother is saying, "Get rid of all of these illusions, get
rid of these religions and these gurus. Own up to what you are.

Face it directly, own it directly, suffer it directly, claim it directly, be it directly, alone and together, and save the planet."

I think we had this relationship once with the world, and I think we can see it in the ancient matriarchal traditions, the first stage of our existence. Then there was the second stage, the patriarchal stage—with the growth of the hero myth, the growth of dissociative righteous forms of thought. Now we're entering the third stage, which is not a return to the matriarchy. That isn't possible. Patriarchy taught us some very important things. What we're entering now is the era of the sacred marriage, the union of the masculine and feminine in our psyches, in ourselves, in nature, in the world—the era where a direct relation with the divine will result in direct action in every arena of life, the era of engaged and passionate enlightenment.

*I was wondering how you might see us taking that union into the political arena. I was intrigued by the conclusion of* Dialogues with a Modern Mystic, *where you make a call to readers to go out into the street and reform the world.*

First of all, what has to be done is to reimagine what the sacred feminine is. It embraces life. It longs passionately to preserve life and to make *this world* the mirror of the justice and love of the Mother, and therefore to transform political conditions: to transform the conditions of the poor; to transform the media, which is just an avalanche of trash pouring into our minds; to take on the burden of altering all the industrial relationships between the nations; to take on the burden of using technology to clear away pollution; to pull down the whole worldwide concentration camp of reason and fear and guilt we live in, and establish justice, harmony, and balance—not merely intellectually or spiritually but actually, in terms of the conditions in which we live, in terms of the conditions of the environment.

What I see happening in the next fifteen years is that there will be terrible ecological disasters, and the facts of our devastation of nature will become more and more obvious and more and more painful. At that moment, it's very important that there be in place spiritual friends who can say to the world, "We have all got to get onto the streets now." People protested against the war in Vietnam in the Sixties, and amazing things were done because of the power of their civil disobedience. What is needed is for everyone who cares for the future of the world to take to the streets in a massive, worldwide civil-dis-obedience movement. People must join together and come out— onto the streets in Washington, the streets of every capital city all over the world, and say no to pollution, no to the prolifer-ation of nuclear arms, no to the destruction of the earth.

The situation cannot go on in the way that it is going on. We are being given a message: Transform or die out. None of the governments are taking this seriously. We have to take it seriously.

*So you envision a spiritual revolution that leads directly into social activism?*

There is no spiritual revolution worth the name at this moment. There isn't a revolution that is passionately concerned with poverty, with justice, with the end of the destruction of the envi-ronment. Without that, what is happening is not a spiritual rev-olution. It's a masturbation of the soul.

Meanwhile, the politicians are in a dream of their own power. The gurus are in a dream of their own power. The majority of spiritual seekers are really looking for a little bit of aspirin rather than enlightenment, because the last thing they want is to be enlightened and therefore to be in a state of love in action towards the world. So we're in a terribly dangerous position in which the narcissism of the people in power and our own narcissistic desire for security in a terrifying world coincide and collude.

I'm not leaving myself out of any of this criticism. I feel impli-cated in this escapism because I've been one of the purveyors of it. What was lacking from *Hidden Journey,* lamentably, was the

sense of the political dimension of action. So I'm not saying I've
been awake; I've been asleep. But 99 percent of the other Western seekers on the planet have also been asleep, because I know
many of them, and I tell you, I've heard their snores.

*It sounds as though the changes you've gone through in the
past year have been liberating. Has your marriage been part of
that process?*

Marriage—the contact with a real human being and with real
human love—has absolutely transformed my life. I'd been so
battered as a child and so disappointed in love in my twenties
and thirties that I thought that the only relationship with any
hope was the kind of exotic, intense, subtly sadomasochistic
relationship I had with Meera.

But there's nothing more redemptive than a real relationship with another human being. There is nothing more difficult and more spiritually transforming, because you're really
compelled to take responsibility for every breath, every action,
and what you do profoundly influences the other person's life.
So you have a very direct teaching in responsibility. And also,
you have a very direct teaching in unconditional love, because
if there is true love, it is unconditional.

I've been blessed with somebody who really does love me
unconditionally and who is the most honest person I know. To
be with someone who is not playing any games is a tremendous spiritual education. Eryk has taught me more than anyone I've known simply by being completely himself and by
forcing me to be completely myself.

What is revealed through deep love of another being, and
the responsibility of that love, is the inherent sacredness of
everything in life. In a real relationship, you see how everything, at every moment, is at stake. And that is exactly what
life is like: At every moment, everything is at stake. So you're
initiated into the sacred intensity of life in its most normal
aspect.

What a wonderful thing we are, just as we are. What wonderful revelations we can, just as normal, flawed human beings, bring to each other. Those wonderful revelations are the revelations of the Divine Mother. They're the revelations of ordinary, divine love. I've seen through the illusions of religious power and found God in my own house, and that's where God is. That's where God always is.

# Teachers and Seekers

B ORN IN INDIA on June 9, 1952, Andrew Harvey spent his first six years in wondrous fascination of a world where one saw "the miraculous in the commonplace," and where visions of deities abounded. This enchantment dissolved at age six and a half, however, when his parents sent him to a boarding school a thousand miles from home, "baptizing me in despair." At nine years old he went to live in England with his grandparents. Though his mother was of British descent and his father part Indian and part Scottish, they had always lived in India and would not join Andrew in England for another five years. In his homesickness, Harvey spent his school years throughout the Sixties attempting to "Indianize" everything about his life.

In 1970 Harvey won a scholarship to Oxford and in 1973 became one of the youngest fellows in the history of All Souls College, considered the most prestigious academic institution in England. But for the next seven years his spirit starved. He was sexually confused, had taken to drinking, suffered insomnia and nervous hysteria, and had thoughts of suicide. In this desolation he fled to the only sanctuary he had ever known—India—and spent seven months in Pondicherry, where he developed a rev-

Adapted from an interview with Andrew Harvey by Catherine Ingram, in *Yoga Journal,* Issue 123, July/August 1995, pp. 56–63, 152–153. Used by permission.

erence for the teachings of Aurobindo and once again felt whole. He then returned to England and went on to a teaching fellowship at Cornell University in New York, but again he faced the same old gloom. His meditations grew listless; academia seemed pointless. Any talk of spirit in that atmosphere sounded like "expounding upon the genius of the wheel in a world of user-friendly computers." At a particularly low point, he received a letter from a friend in Pondicherry telling him that he must come there at once to meet a most extraordinary young woman.

In a bare white room on Christmas Day, 1978, Andrew Harvey met a seventeen-year-old girl known as Mother Meera. She was totally silent but placed her hands on each side of Harvey's head and gazed into his eyes. This was the beginning of a devotion to her that lasted fifteen years. Harvey felt that Mother Meera was the Divine Mother incarnate.

This period of his life also marked the onset of Harvey's complete immersion in the great mystical teachings of the world. In addition to his readings of Aurobindo, he studied the Mahayana philosophies, classical Buddhist sutras, the Madhyamika scholar Nagarjuna, the great mystic poets of Sufism, and many others. He particularly embraced the works of Jalaludin Rumi, after studying in Paris with Eva de Vitray-Meyerovitch, one of the world's foremost translators of Rumi.

His scholarship inspired a prolific outpouring of his own. Since 1978 he has produced nine books of poems, three novels, seven books of translations, and four works of nonfiction. In addition he has edited two books, including *The Tibetan Book of Living and Dying* by Sogyal Rinpoche. In 1993 Harvey was the subject of a BBC documentary called "The Making of a Mystic," and in the same year the *New York Times Magazine* profiled him in a piece entitled, "The Merry Mystic." But, it was also in this year that Harvey's world turned upside down in agony.

His book *Hidden Journey*, which had been published two years previously, had described his meetings with Mother Meera and proclaimed her as an avatar. The book was widely read and spread Mother Meera's fame throughout the world. In 1993, however, Harvey came to a point of total estrangement from Mother Meera in a controversy publicly disputed on both sides. Though he experienced many misgivings in the latter phase of his involvement with her, his final break resulted from his feeling that Mother Meera disapproved of homosexuality in general and of his relationship with photographer Eryk Hanut in particular.

Since that time Harvey has undertaken a scathing critique of the guru-disciple system as one of the remaining bastions of authoritarian societies and a "block to the true and direct relationship with the Divine Mother." His forthcoming book, *The Return of the Mother,* contains much of this critique as well as an in-depth exploration of the sacred feminine. Harvey has also turned his attention to the inspiring relationships he had with Thuksey Rinpoche of Ladakh and Bede Griffiths of India (both now deceased) as models of authentic spiritual guides.

Though the period of disillusionment with Mother Meera pained him, the wind is in Harvey's sails again. After fourteen years in Paris, he recently moved to San Francisco, where he teaches courses on Rumi, Christian mysticism, and Ramakrishna at the California Institute of Integral Studies. He continues to explore the world's mystical traditions and has recently forged into Jewish mysticism, which he refers to as "this-world" divinity. He also travels and leads workshops that are "devoted to working out a new form of spiritual transmission in which people empower themselves in their own divine potential." But perhaps his greatest passion in life is his relationship with Eryk, which in 1994 was formally consecrated in a marriage ceremony in San Francisco attended by a hundred friends.

I agree with Andrew Harvey that it is time to jettison most of the patriarchy's antiquated ideas of transcendence as escapism, enlightenment as static, and guru as omniscient. I am also aware of appalling stories of abuse by gurus and teachers in our own time.

Nevertheless, for over twenty years my own experience with

teachers, some of whom are considered to be gurus, has been almost entirely positive. I have profound gratitude especially to H. W. L. Poonjaji, who pointed out and manifested the greatest treasure of all—the simple truth of Being—and who wanted nothing in return. With most of my teachers I was able to take the best and leave the rest, and the best was transforming. I am therefore inclined to honor our inheritance of the more inspiring aspects of traditional systems while allowing that it is now time to move forward into more mature relationships with our teachers and with those who come to us for advice. But when I say to Andrew, "Let's be careful not to throw the baby out with the bath water," his response is, "There is no baby in the bath water anymore; it's just bath water." Nevertheless, there seems little doubt that with the coming of the Dharma to the West, there has been a maturing of seekers over these past few decades that is precipitating more democratic relationships with teachers and a deculturalization of our understanding of Dharma. As Carl Jung said, "One does not become enlightened by imagining figures of light, but by making the darkness conscious."

For the past year or more I have read and reread Harvey's books *The Way of Passion* and *Dialogues with a Modern Mystic* (coauthored with Mark Matousek). Prior to our interview, I attended a day-long workshop he held in Portland, Oregon. To my delight, I found in him the person I had imagined from reading his books. He is a passionate man. He laughs and cries easily and tends to burst into song or poetry at the slightest provocation. I also noticed, as I watched him work, a great humility, kindness, and constant affirmation of others' unique visions. He demonstrated by example those very qualities of a spiritual friend that he now feels are appropriate for our time.

The following interview took place over a three-month period in late 1994 and early 1995 in Portland and San Francisco.

Catherine Ingram: *You have said that when you were pretending to be mad everyone thought you were wonderful, but now that you've truly gone mad, they consider you dangerous. Why is that?*

Andrew Harvey: Because the real madness is the embrace of one's own and everyone else's complete freedom and equality before God. When you are doing that, you are doing what Christ and the Buddha and all the real mystics have done. Think how the whole human race has conspired, while adoring them, to eliminate their message.

I think that we are now facing an entirely new era of enlightenment, an era of passionate enlightenment, in which enlightenment will not be seen in the old way as detachment, as an escape, as a way of fading out from existence, as a way of being separate in poised peace, but will combine the ancient and original knowledge of the ground of Being with a very radical commitment to life at every point—emotional, physical, political—to save the planet and transform the quality of life on it. And we don't need any gurus for this. I've come to believe that most of the masters and gurus are actually the patriarchy's most brilliant way of keeping these always-revolutionary truths of divine identity and equality under wraps. The last thing the patriarchal societies have ever wanted was for women or homosexuals or the untouchables or the poor to get hold of these truths, because then all power elites would crumble. And unfortunately the guru systems have nearly always been indirect servants of power.

*Do you think there are any redeeming elements to those systems? After all, many of us have benefited from them whether we are still involved in a relationship with a master or not.*

Whatever successes they have had, and they've had real successes, they've also conspired with that infantilism and that incessant desire for authority that has kept the human race trapped and unempowered. If you take that along with the fundamental body-denying schizophrenia and imbalance toward transcendence of the patriarchal notion of enlightenment which all these people are serving, whether they are male or female (and it has been so disappointing to see that so many women gurus turn out to be Jehovahs in drag), you realize that they are not revolutionizing the system, not radically undermining its folly by bringing in a new sacred perspective from the feminine, which would say "Let's admit that we have bodies, let's find the divinity in the body, let's consecrate sexuality, let's adore nature and preserve it."

In fact, to preserve their power as so-called divine beings, they just repeat all the shadow fears and sexual taboos of the patriarchal tradition, with its decadent rhetoric of the world as illusory. They pretend that they don't have a body, because the body is going to give the continual lie to their claim to divinity in the patriarchal way of understanding they claim. Then because the followers, to preserve their fantasy, believe the guru has transcended all physical needs, they cannot face the shadow side of the all-too-human guru, and the guru himself or herself is discouraged from facing that shadow side as well. And this results in, as we know, disaster after disaster.

*Yes, in recent months we've seen a new eruption of scandals involving Asian teachers and abuse of sex, money, and power. It is becoming clear that there are areas of psychological development and relational experimentation that were missed by many of the Asian masters, either because these areas of development were not fostered in their cultures or were thought to be transcended in the master. Do you think it would be possible for us to, just as we go to a therapist for psychological needs, go to gurus or masters for spiritual understanding and not expect them to be psychologically developed?*

I'm beginning to doubt even that. I wonder what use is this transcendent knowledge that they claim to have if, in fact, it results in manipulation. Let's face it, what's going on is much more than people sleeping around and misusing funds or whatever. It is abuse of a very profound kind. It is child abuse. It is abuse of someone in their most defenseless position, because no one is more defenseless than a devotee rapt in adoration before a master. So what kind of wisdom could they possibly have if they are first indulging in that kind of abuse and then denying it in sometimes criminal ways? We really do have to face the full extent of their failure, and that is very painful, because we then have to face our illusions about them and the ways in which we colluded with them in our hope for magical solutions and transformations on the cheap.

*Yet people are having extraordinary experiences in the presence of masters, experiences of bliss, openings, visions. What accounts for these experiences?*

I am going to say something which might shock you, but it is my belief that 90 percent of the so-called masters in the modern world are not enlightened at all but are in fact occult magicians. The occult magician will use his or her occult powers to ensnare the devotee in a posture of adoration by feeding them visionary experiences, which may seem to open things up for the devotee but actually keeps one dependent on the guru. It's a kind of drug pushing, as dangerous on the spiritual level as cocaine or heroin is on the physical. Because people don't know the difference between the divine and the occult, nor how accurately the occult can mimic the divine, nor how easily occult powers can be cultivated by the unscrupulous and ambitious, they take these powers and experiences to be unmistakable signs of divine presence and go on worshipping as divine these people who have, in fact, shown that they are neither good, nor kind, nor humble, nor generous.

They cannot truly help anyone because they are not free themselves. They are not free because they have chosen power, not love. They are the heads of occult power corporations, trapped at the highest level in the very system of greed and illusion they claim to see through and transcend. It is time to look at the guru system in terms of an all-comprehensive critique of power. The search for any kind of power kills the sources and centers of love and so blocks all access to real enlightenment.

*And wanting power over anyone is only possible if there is a belief in separation, which is the antithesis of what most of these people espouse.*

Oh yes, the cleverer gurus are always saying, "You are divine." They ape the highest truths while running fascist organizations that thrive on intimidation, lies, secret core elites, and the rewriting of history to suit whatever they want to be told about themselves.

*Aside from occult powers, what about the simple projection that occurs on the part of the devotee? I can't help but think of girls fainting in front of the Beatles.*

Well, the whole society is run on a star system, the entire media is dedicated to creating star systems, and the guru system as it has developed in the West plays neatly into this. We must now look at our fascination with power, our own hunger for power, our delight in the satisfactions of visionary excitement rather than in the rigor of the real mystical life. We must do a major self-psychoanalysis with regard to this.

*What do you think it is in our psyche that so makes people want to project their divinity onto another?*

I think the fundamental rationale behind this projection is terror. I think people are mortally frightened of naked contact with the divine, of claiming their fullness, of being totally authentic and responsible for every waking and sleeping moment of their lives. Projecting their divinity onto someone else who is all too willing to accept that projection is a secretly convenient way of getting out of the appalling responsibility of becoming divine and acting as a divine human being in the world, which means an endless disruption of one's life and the perpetual scrutiny of one's motives. This kind of surrender is always exposing you and dissolving whatever certainty you have in order to draw you deeper and deeper into its passion and its love. But this is a terrifying prospect, and people will go to masters and gurus and pay them anything, give them anything, even their children, if they will live out the burden of our own unlived sanctity. So we then find ourselves the prey of people who are in many cases much less divine than their ardent devotees.

I think there is another aspect which is also in keeping with the star system, and that is, if you are projecting adoration onto someone, you yourself start to shine with the reflected luster of that projection, so you experience a covert self-adoration. You are now decorated with a little aura of sanctity that you didn't have to earn. This is corrupt, because if you were really to own those qualities that you are projecting, you would have to be responsible for them.

Coming close to truth demands rigorous goals of service and real charity. To be hooked on the experiences that adoration brings, without enacting and incarnating that adoration in service and charity, is fundamentally not to be adoring God but to be adoring one's own spiritual ego. There is so much suffering, and there is so much help each of us could give. It is shocking to me how little the so-called new age is doing to help out and how little the gurus talk of environmental or social transformation, or political justice, or any kind of service. The only service most of them talk about is service to them!

*There are some notable exceptions, in my opinion, such as His Holiness the Dalai Lama; my own teacher, Poonjaji; and others. After all, it is the existence of real gold which makes selling the counterfeit possible.*

Though there are exceptions despite the system, I think the guru system, as it is now, is flawed at its core. Anyone in that system is going to run extreme dangers, whether they are the guru or the devotee. I think the next five years will see a massive shattering of the idols. What is now a light summer rain of scandal is going to become a blizzard. The guru system in its current state of dangerous corruption will be revealed.

*The sadness in that vision is that many people may then turn away from Dharma, from the love and the mystery, and just abandon themselves to samsara, chasing their desires and resisting their fears in a dog-eat-dog world.*

Yes, our current orgy of credulity may be succeeded by an even more dangerous orgy of nihilism and cynicism, an orgy that the culture at large is longing to throw anyway. And that's why it is so important that a group of us who have been through the fire of disappointment in the guru system and the fire of facing our own collusions, follies, and lusts to project should try now to model a radical, practical, and humbly direct relationship with the divine. I am extremely disappointed with those Western adepts who are adopting the Eastern models of masters, who are playing the stars of the spiritual world and parading a sub-Hollywood glamour. That is the opposite of what is needed now and a profound failure of spiritual intelligence. For, adopting any of these old dying forms is to keep their blocking effect alive. That's why it is important to go through the pain of this critique, so that a group of us will be able to say, "I find my relationship with the divine to be enough; I don't need any intermediaries; I'm serving, and I'm making mistakes, but I'm living my own life in this direct relationship, and you can too. The suffering that you are going through in facing the death of the guru illusion is real suffering, but get over it, learn what you have to learn, and come and join us as equals in this celebration."

*But in a way, that puts one in the role of teacher, if even to say, "I know what you're going through; I've been through it." Do you think there is any place for spiritual mentors or guides?*

Of course, it would be absurd to say that we weren't to revere anyone, weren't to respect the spiritual achievements of anyone, that we weren't to sometimes go to others for advice, or that we weren't for particular purposes to have spiritual guides and friends and teachers.

*What would be the criteria for a healthy relationship with a spiritual guide?*

What I have understood after years of meditating on this comes out of a very positive relationship that I had with a great Christian saint, Bede Griffiths, at the end of his life. I realized that Bede had got the relationship of spiritual friend exactly and perfectly right, because he was in a clear and humble relationship to God. So in thinking about what it was in this relationship with Bede that was so inspiring, I came up with the following. A real spiritual guide never, ever, tells you what to do. Ramana Maharshi said, "He who instructs an ardent seeker to do this or that is not a true master. The seeker is already afflicted by his activities and seeks peace, rest, and quiet." A guide may suggest, may try and draw out something they know to be there already, but they will never interfere with the karmic course of your life. They will be a source of support, encouragement, radiance, tenderness, and generosity, but never of control.

The second point—and this is crucial—is that a real spiritual friend would never claim complete enlightenment. A great guide might want to witness supreme spiritual and mystical experiences that they had had, but if those were true experiences, they would have created in that person a fundamental awe and humility before the divine which would make him or her scrupulously aware of precisely those things in himself or herself that had not yet been transformed. Everyone who enters the enlightened field realizes that enlightenment is endless transformation. It is not static. Gregory of Nyssa calls this "epectasis," endless opening. Rumi speaks of transformation being a glory that goes on from light to light.

So anyone who is in the enlightenment field is, by definition, aware of all the mountain peaks of gnosis that they haven't climbed, all the love that they haven't grown when faced with this massive, vast, insanely powerful and beautiful presence. What a real spiritual friend is trying to do is to send you wild with love of That. Real spiritual friends are trying, as Rumi is in his poetry, to communicate to you a fatal attraction, not for them, but for That. A real friend knows that when you are nakedly in contact with the Divine Mother in every moment, in every rose, in every face, in every breath of wind, it is so much more vast, ecstatic, and transforming if there is no name or form between you.

*So if one calls oneself free in referring to perhaps a lack of identification with one's personal story, this is not by your definition the end game.*

I think one should be very suspicious of anything anyone says. I think it's more important to see what they do, how they act. Is their freedom transformed into passionate daily service of other beings, into radical humility before the universe, into a visionary tenderness?

I think that the true spiritual guide admits that he or she is still in process, that they are always aware of their own shadow and of the limitations of their upbringing, their cultural conditioning, their particular religious views. The true spiritual guide never claims to be unified with the divine. The human being can merge with God but can never become God.

*Let's be clear about this. From another point of view we are totally infused with God, drenched in the divine.*

We are drenched in God, we can participate in the glory of God's workings, we can have experiences which show the oneness of our consciousness and the divine consciousness but, paradoxically, we can only have those if we are also aware of what we could call our lack, what the Christians call "hamartia," missing the mark, the part in us that is not yet divinized.

Knowing this is precisely what keeps you receptive, humble, and loving enough for innate divinity to come through. Real mystical growth arises from a never-ending dialectic between humility and grace.

I have come to believe, too, that real spiritual guides welcome disagreement and doubt. They are actually delighted when you disagree or have doubt, for two reasons. One is because those who are really awake know that they can learn from anyone, and the other is that doubt is part of the necessary finding out of the secret hiding places of the false self. Someone who is truly realized would have no need to cling to any role or position, so why would they mind being doubted? If they're not interested in power, in money, in control over others, in having an organization, then why not say, "Doubt on! Let's see whether truth is to be found or not in these doubts."

*What you're describing is a relationship of true equality. It bears little resemblance to what mostly passes as a relationship with a master where doubt is the greatest taboo and belief in the master's omniscience is a requirement.*

Indeed. What you feel in the presence of a true spiritual friend is equality, the real equality of soul. That is the priceless gift of somebody who is in that state of humility. It is like a rose opening and sending its fragrance. It isn't involving you in any game, you don't have to believe that it is enlightened. You can just enjoy its perfume.

*We're speaking about a new era of spiritual possibilities. In this tantric, naked, direct relationship with the divine, "How then shall we live?"*

I said at the beginning that I believe we are entering an era of passionate enlightenment. Another way of looking at this era would be to see it as the era of the sacred marriage, the marriage between masculine and feminine, action and prayer, politics and mysticism. We are entering an era in which all of the old distinctions between sacred and profane will be rubbled to inaugurate a new human divine freedom.

For me, one of the main forms of this new human divine freedom is the tantric marriage, a consecrated relationship in which two people devote heart, body, mind, and soul to each other and to God. My own relationship with Eryk has absolutely transformed my spiritual and mystical vision of the world. Through it and through divine grace I have discovered that when deep, passionate, pure love is the architect of the emotional, sexual, mental experience, then what takes place is the alchemical fusion of the entire self. In this alchemical transformation, the heat of love, of consecrated passion, is the shakti, the divine fire that ensouls the body and embodies the soul, and so heals and melts together all division between inner and outer, holy and unholy, heaven and earth.

I have begun to taste that liberation of all the senses into their bliss essence and to know that natural immersion in sacred unity that comes from adoring another human being and being adored by that person in this way. And I have come to realize that there is no separation between human and divine love, because all real love is divine. Keeping a true vision of this great tantric work, however, is hard. Most Eastern and Western philosophical systems have done a tremendous disservice to our vision of sexuality, and we therefore have to steer a reverent and refined balance between denial and shame on the one hand and pornographic license on the other. To create the alchemical vessel in which tantric transformation can take place, both beings have to be dedicated to using their experience of mutual love and abandon as a way of entering more deeply into the divine beauty and glow of the universe. They both have always to be preserving the heartspace of the other by offering total fidelity—and I mean real fidelity—without which the infinite trust which has to be born for merging to take place cannot be engendered. If these laws are observed, ordinary miracles are possible. This kind of sacred marriage,

I am certain, will become more and more the site of the tantric encounter.

*What about a tantric relationship with the divine for people who do not have partners?*

Oh, there are ways other than the relationship with the true soul consort, I think. There is also the deep spiritual friendship in which two or more souls really honor and respect each other in the divine beauty of their spiritual growth and cherish and protect that with every resource available. It's clear that when two or more are gathered together in that spirit, as Christ himself said, "I am present." What I have been discovering in the workshops I have been facilitating is that when thirty or forty people are gathered together with open hearts and sincere passion in the name of the Divine Mother, then not only is astonishing wisdom shared by all, but there are moments in which everyone recognizes a fusion taking place, and everyone realizes that the Mother is speaking through each voice, moving in each hand, laughing in each face, crying in each tear. And that is a tantric experience.

*What about service?*

It can never be said enough that there can be no complete awakening without service. Service is tantric, because it slowly dissolves boundaries between ourselves and others and invites us into the all-healing compassion of the Mother. The highest service is to consider all beings as divine beings and to honor that divinity in them, to see life as a sacred experience from beginning to end. The Mother is offering us union with her, if only we can open ourselves to the essential bliss nature and to live it at every moment, whether putting a flower in a vase, cooking a meal for a friend, listening to someone's pain over the telephone, or giving money and time to a valuable cause.

*Yes, and it means living with a broken heart, because in our ado-*
*ration we develop the eyes and tenderness of a mother ourselves,*
*and we are then open to the sorrow existing all around us.*

And that sorrow is going to become greater and greater. There
is no way out now. We are being brought by the catastrophic
destruction of the planet to the terrifying moment where we
will have to accept the terms of a great alchemical transformation or die out. To save the planet and ourselves we have no
choice but to finally enter our bodies, enter time, enter the world
and to love them with the naked, undefended passion for equality, justice, and creativity of the Mother.

*It is exactly this engaged love that will give us the strength that*
*Is needed to endure, the strength of the mother who lifts a car*
*off of her child.*

Yes, love brings everything—the courage, the intensity, the
peace, the hope. Love brings the capacity to suffer and to go
on suffering in the dark with only the Mother's light for a guide.
Love brings the depths and passion and illumined wisdom necessary to take on this immense burden. This catastrophe that
we face is inviting us into the reign of love.

We haven't been sitting here criticizing the master system
because we want to tear something down. We haven't been trying to define what a real spiritual friendship is and what a real
tantric relationship is simply because we are dissatisfied. We're
doing this because we see an immense evolutionary vista opening up of freedom and love for the human race when each one
of us accepts the gifts and the burdens of the Divine Mother
and realizes our fundamental direct intimacy with her and so
with all beings. Imagine if there were no hierarchical divisions—
political, spiritual, sexual, racial.

Imagine that we understood each of us to be on a unique
path, each of us a unique flower of the Mother, budding in her
wild ramshackle garden as to its own laws. Imagine the diviniza-

tion of life—humble and ordinary life—that the rubbling of all ancient divisions could bring. This vision we are trying to describe does not want to destroy anything, only to strip away the scaffolding that is stopping the light from burning through to the human heart, so that human life can at last be experienced completely as what it is, a continual flow of divinely given, ordinary miracles, the sublime theater of the Mother's love.

*Many people throughout time have imagined glorious possibilities for life on this earth. Do you feel that our imaginings have any chance of catching on?*

This work of massive exposure to love and of ending the old structures is not something we can afford to turn down; it's not a luxury or something we can just discuss in coffee houses. It's not an option; it's an imperative. We must all leave our small prisons of the past and go into this unknown mystery. We would go mad at that moment, which is exactly what we need to do, because if we started to go beautifully and completely mad with love for her, we would become infused with her grace, her confidence, her wisdom, and her power, and nothing could enslave us and nothing could stop us. So let us remember Pythagoras' words, "Take courage, the human race is divine." All of us who know that now have the responsibility to live it totally and passionately, without any barrier. In this lies our hope.

Aurobindo. *Letters on Yoga*. Three Volumes. Pondicherry, India: Sri Aurobindo Ashram, Publication Department, 1971.

_____. *The Life Divine*. Pondicherry, India: Sri Aurobindo Ashram, Publication Department, 1939–40.

_____. *The Mother*. Pondicherry, India: Sri Aurobindo Ashram, Publication Department, 1972.

_____. *Savitri*. Four Volumes. Pondicherry, India: Sri Aurobindo Ashram, Publication Department, 1950–1951.

Baring, Anne, and Jules Cashford. *The Myth of the Goddess: Evolution of an Image*. New York: Viking Press, 1991.

Boff, O.F.M., Leonardo. *The Maternal Face of God: The Feminine and its Religious Expressions*. Translated by Robert Bar and John W. Diercksmeier. New York: Harper & Row, 1987.

*Buddha Mind: An Anthology of Longchen Rabjam's Writings on Dzogpa Chenpo*. Edited by Harold Talbott. Ithaca, New York: Snow Lion Publications, 1989.

*Buddhist Scriptures*. Selected and translated by Edward Conze. New York: Penguin Books, 1959.

Ching-yuen, Loy. *The Book of the Heart: Embracing the Tao*. Translated by Trevor Carolan and Bella Chen. Boston: Shambhala Publications, 1990.

*Chuang Tzu: Basic Writings*. Translated by Burton Watson. New York: Columbia University Press, 1964.

Cleary, Thomas, translator and editor. *Vitality, Energy, Spirit: A Taoist Sourcebook*. Boston: Shambhala Publications, 1991.

Harvey, Andrew. *A Journey in Ladakh*. Boston: Houghton Mifflin Company, 1983.

_____. *Hidden Journey: A Spiritual Awakening*. New York: Arkana Books, 1991.

_____. *The Way of Passion: A Celebration of Rumi*. Berkeley, California: Frog, Ltd., 1994.

Harvey, Andrew, and Mark Matousek. *Dialogues with a Modern Mystic*. Wheaton, Illinois: Quest Books, 1994.

Hixon, Lex. *Mother of the Buddhas: Meditations on the Prajnaparamita Sutra*. Wheaton, Illinois: Quest Books, 1993.

_____. *Mother of the Universe: Visions of the Goddess and Tantric Hymns of Enlightenment*. Wheaton, Illinois: Quest Books, 1994.

I-Ming, Liu. *Awakening to the Tao*. Translated by Thomas Cleary. Boston: Shambhala Publications, 1988.

Ingram, Catherine. *In The Footsteps of Gandhi: Conversations with Spiritual Social Activists*. Berkeley, California: Parallax Press, 1990.

Lawlor, Robert. *Voices of the First Day: Awakening in the Aboriginal Dreamtime*. Rochester, Vermont: Inner Traditions International, Ltd., 1991.

Nhat Hanh, Thich. *Call Me By My True Names: The Collected Poems of Thich Nhat Hanh*. Berkeley, California: Parallax Press, 1993.

Ramakrishna. *The Gospel of Sri Ramakrishna*. Translated into English with an Introduction by Swami Nikhilananda. Mylapore, Madras, India: Sri Ramakrishna Math, n.d.

Schipper, Kristofer. *The Taoist Body*. Translated by Karen C. Duval. Berkeley, California: University of California Press, 1993.

Shaw, Miranda. *Passionate Enlightenment: Women in Tantric Buddhism*. Princeton, New Jersey: Princeton University Press, 1994.

Sogyal Rinpoche. *The Tibetan Book of Living and Dying*. Edited by Patrick Gaffney and Andrew Harvey. San Francisco: HarperSanFrancisco, 1991.

Star, Jonathan, editor. *Two Suns Rising: A Collection of Sacred Writings*. New York: Bantam Books, 1991.

Star, Jonathan, and Shahram Shiva, translators. *A Garden*

*Beyond Paradise: The Mystical Poetry of Rumi.* New York: Bantam Books, 1992.

Tarnas, Richard. *The Passion of the Western Mind: Understanding the Ideas That Have Shaped Our World View.* New York: Harmony Books, 1991.

Thera Piyadassi. *The Buddha's Ancient Path.* Kandy, Sri Lanka: Buddhist Publication Society, 1974.

Underhill, Evelyn. *Ruysbroeck.* London: G. Bell & Sons. Ltd., 1914.

*The Upanishads.* Translations from the Sanskrit with an Introduction by Juan Mascaró. New York, Penguin Books, 1965.

Watts, Alan. *Tao: The Watercourse Way.* New York: Pantheon Books, 1975.

Wilber, Ken. *Eye to Eye: The Quest for the New Paradigm.* New York: Anchor Books, 1983.

# Journals Cited

*Common Boundary.* Published bimonthly by Common Boundary, Inc., 5272 River Road, Suite 560, Bethesda, Maryland 20816.

*Tricycle: The Buddhist Review.* Published quarterly by The Buddhist Ray, Inc., 163 West 22nd Street, New York, New York 10011.

*Yoga Journal.* Published bimonthly by the California Yoga Teachers Association, 2054 University Avenue, Berkeley, California 94704.